Learn Microservices with Spring Boot 3

A Practical Approach Using Event-Driven Architecture, Cloud-Native Patterns, and Containerization

Third Edition

Moisés Macero García
Tarun Telang

Apress®

Learn Microservices with Spring Boot 3: A Practical Approach Using Event-Driven Architecture, Cloud-Native Patterns, and Containerization, Third Edition

Moisés Macero García
New York, NY, USA

Tarun Telang
Hyderabad, Telangana, India

ISBN-13 (pbk): 978-1-4842-9756-8
https://doi.org/10.1007/978-1-4842-9757-5

ISBN-13 (electronic): 978-1-4842-9757-5

Managing Director, Apress Media LLC: Welmoed Spahr
Acquisitions Editor: Melissa Duffy
Development Editor: Laura Berendson
Coordinating Editor: Gryffin Winkler
Copy Editor: Kezia Endsley

Cover designed by eStudioCalamar

Cover image by Image by James DeMers on Pixabay (www.pixabay.com)

Distributed to the book trade worldwide by Apress Media, LLC, 1 New York Plaza, New York, NY 10004, U.S.A. Phone 1-800-SPRINGER, fax (201) 348-4505, e-mail orders-ny@springer-sbm.com, or visit www.springeronline.com. Apress Media, LLC is a California LLC and the sole member (owner) is Springer Science + Business Media Finance Inc (SSBM Finance Inc). SSBM Finance Inc is a **Delaware** corporation.

For information on translations, please e-mail booktranslations@springernature.com; for reprint, paperback, or audio rights, please e-mail bookpermissions@springernature.com.

Apress titles may be purchased in bulk for academic, corporate, or promotional use. eBook versions and licenses are also available for most titles. For more information, reference our Print and eBook Bulk Sales web page at http://www.apress.com/bulk-sales.

Any source code or other supplementary material referenced by the author in this book is available to readers on GitHub (https://github.com/Apress). For more detailed information, please visit https://www.apress.com/gp/services/source-code.

Paper in this product is recyclable

This book is dedicated to my grandparents, parents, wife Nikita, and son Vihan. They have always been a source of inspiration and encouragement to me. It's also for all of the software and technology creators who work hard to make our planet a better place to live.

—Tarun Telang

Table of Contents

About the Authors

Moisés Macero García has been a software developer since he was a kid, when he started playing around with BASIC on his ZX Spectrum. During his career, Moisés has most often worked in development and architecture for small and large projects, and for his own startups as well. He enjoys making software problems simple, and he likes working in teams, where he can coach others as well as learn from them. Moisés is the author of the blog `thepracticaldeveloper.com`, where he shares solutions to technical challenges, guides, and his view on different ways of working in IT companies. He also organizes workshops for companies that need a practical approach to software engineering. In his free time, he enjoys traveling and hiking.

Tarun Telang is a seasoned and hands-on technologist with a wealth of experience in designing and implementing highly scalable software applications. With an impressive career spanning over 18 years, Tarun has been a valuable contributor to renowned companies such as Microsoft, Oracle, Polycom, and SAP. He began his career as an enterprise Java developer at SAP, where he honed his skills in crafting distributed business applications tailored for large enterprises. Through his dedication to continuous learning and professional development, he became an Oracle Certified Java Programmer and SAP Certified Development Consultant for Enterprise Java.

As a prolific author, Tarun frequently writes on Java and related technologies, and he has authored many books and online courses. His earlier books Java EE to Jakarta EE 10 Recipes, and Beginning cloud-native development using MicroProfile, Jakarta EE and Kubernetes have been well-received by the tech community. He has also been a sought-after speaker at developer conferences like SAP TechEd and the Great Indian Developer Summit, sharing his technical expertise with enthusiastic audiences. Tarun regularly shares technological insights at `www.practicaldeveloper.com`.

Tarun's expertise lies in architecting and developing large scale applications, with a particular focus on cloud-native solutions using cutting-edge architectural patterns like microservices and event-driven architecture. He has led the development of numerous end-to-end cloud-based solutions, demonstrating his deep technical understanding to deliver high-performing, reliable, large-scale applications.

An advocate of agile methodologies, Tarun excels at applying domain-driven design and behavioral-driven development principles, ensuring seamless project management and collaboration across cross-functional teams in different geographical locations. His international experience, having worked in India, Canada and Germany, has enriched his global perspective and ability to adapt to diverse environments. Tarun lives in Hyderabad, India, and he enjoys spending time with his wife and child when he's not indulging in his love of technology. You can follow Tarun or contact him on his Twitter account: @taruntelang.

About the Technical Reviewer

Manuel Jordan Elera is an autodidactic developer and researcher who enjoys learning new technologies for his own experiments and creating new integrations. Manuel won the Springy Award 2013 Community Champion and Spring Champion. In his little free time, he reads the Bible and composes music on his guitar. Manuel is known as dr_pompeii. He has tech-reviewed numerous books, including *Pro Spring MVC with WebFlux* (Apress, 2020), *Pro Spring Boot 2* (Apress, 2019), *Rapid Java Persistence and Microservices* (Apress, 2019), *Java Language Features* (Apress, 2018), *Spring Boot 2 Recipes* (Apress, 2018), and *Java APIs, Extensions and Libraries* (Apress, 2018). You can read his detailed tutorials on Spring technologies and contact him through his blog at www.manueljordanelera.blogspot.com. You can follow Manuel on his Twitter account, @dr_pompeii.

Acknowledgments

I would like to thank my wife, Nikita, and son, Vihan, for their patience and love throughout the process of writing this book. I am indebted to all my mentors and friends who always encouraged me to keep growing in every phase of my professional career.

I'd like to thank my parents for pushing me in the right direction with technology and always supporting me every step of the way, even when I decided to do something completely different than they expected. It's also important to note that without them, I probably wouldn't have become a developer and had such a great career. Lastly, thanks again go out to my wife (and soulmate), Nikita. It's an incredible feeling to be with someone who keeps you motivated and challenges you, not only professionally but personally as well.

Thank you for always being there for me!

I'd like to send a special thanks to Manuel Jordan (the technical reviewer), for their impeccable work on this book. I also greatly appreciate Mark Powers, and everyone at Apress Media (`apress.com`) for their support in getting this book published.

Last, but not least, I would like to thank you, the reader, for taking the time to read this book. We have tried our best through this book to offer you a comprehensive, up-to-date, and practical guide that empowers you to build sophisticated and resilient microservices architectures using Spring Boot.

—Tarun Telang

About this Book

Welcome to Learn Microservices with Spring Boot 3: A Practical Approach Using an Event-Driven Architecture, Cloud-Native Patterns, and Containerization.

In today's fast-paced digital landscape, the demand for highly scalable, flexible, and maintainable software solutions has reached new heights. Microservices architecture has emerged as a game-changing paradigm, empowering developers to build complex applications by breaking them down into smaller, decoupled, and independently deployable services. At the heart of this revolution lies Spring Boot, a robust and widely adopted framework that simplifies the development and deployment of Java-based microservices.

This book is your gateway to unlocking the potential of microservices with Spring Boot 3. Whether you are an experienced developer looking to adopt modern software architecture or a newcomer eager to explore the world of microservices, this comprehensive guide will equip you with the knowledge and tools necessary to build cutting-edge applications.

Your Path to Mastering Microservices

In this third edition, we have curated a rich learning journey that starts with the fundamentals and gradually leads you to construct a fully functional microservices ecosystem. We begin by introducing the core concepts of microservices architecture and the advantages it offers over traditional monolithic systems. As you familiarize yourself with the principles, we explore Spring Boot 3, the latest version of the framework, compatible with Java 17 and Jakarta EE 10.

Building Your Microservices Ecosystem

Transitioning from a monolithic architecture to microservices can be a daunting task. However, fear not, as this book provides a smooth and incremental approach to guide you through the transformation process. You learn how to break down your monolithic application into cohesive microservices, each dedicated to specific business functionalities. Along the way, we delve into event-driven architecture, an essential aspect of building scalable and resilient microservices, to enable seamless communication and collaboration between services.

Data Layer, Containerization, and Orchestration

An essential part of microservices development lies in efficiently managing data and ensuring seamless deployment and scalability. We explore Spring Boot's capabilities in accessing the Spring Data project and its APIs to handle data storage and retrieval effectively. Containerization with Docker will become your ally as you learn to package and deploy microservices efficiently.

Security, Monitoring, and Frontend Integration

A successful microservices ecosystem demands robust security measures and diligent monitoring. We cover essential security practices to safeguard your microservices and delve into monitoring their performance for seamless operation. Moreover, we explore integrating frontend development with React.js, enabling you to create user-friendly user interfaces that interact flawlessly with your microservices.

From Expert Insights to Real-World Use Cases

Throughout this book, you will benefit from the expertise of the authors—Tarun Telang and Moisés Macero García—who have a wealth of knowledge in designing and implementing scalable software applications. From their real-world insights to practical examples, you'll receive invaluable guidance to tackle the challenges of modern application development head-on.

Begin Your Microservices Journey

Whether you are an aspiring developer or a seasoned pro, this book offers a comprehensive and up-to-date guide to mastering microservices architecture. Embark on this exciting journey to build scalable, resilient, and cloud-native applications that meet the demands of today's dynamic software landscape. Let's dive in and unlock the potential of microservices with Spring Boot 3!

What You Will Learn

- Gain a thorough understanding of microservices architecture, including its principles and benefits, and how it differs from monolithic architectures.

- Discover the step-by-step process of breaking down a monolithic application into smaller, focused services, each responsible for specific functionalities.

- Learn about TDD techniques and what their benefits are.

- Build microservices with Spring Boot 3, Spring Data, Spring Cloud, Docker, Cucumber, and more.

- Learn to develop Java-based microservices with the latest version of Spring Boot 3, Java 17, and Jakarta EE 10 using a three-tier, three-layer design.

- Use an event-driven architecture. Implement resilience and scalability with RabbitMQ or Apache Kafka.

- Discover architecture patterns for distributed systems such as asynchronous processing, eventual consistency, resilience, scalability, and more.

- Keep flexible configurations per environment with Spring Cloud Consul.

- Gain insights into event-driven communication patterns and learn how to design and build event-driven microservices.

- Master service discovery with Consul and load balancing with Spring Cloud Load Balancer.

- Route requests with Spring Cloud Gateway.

- Trace every request from beginning to end with Sleuth and centralized logging.

- Deploy your microservices anywhere as Docker containers.

- Adopt cloud-native practices to optimize your microservices deployment on modern cloud platforms, enhancing scalability and flexibility.

- Learn the essentials of containerization using Docker, allowing you to package and deploy microservices efficiently.

- Start all the components in the microservice architecture with Docker Compose.

- Learn how to achieve your non-functional requirements with practical case studies for scalability, fault-tolerance, retries, and so on.

- Deploy your microservices anywhere as Docker containers with Buildpacks.

- As a side track, learn how to build simple frontend interfaces with React.

In this book, the authors use a pragmatic approach to explain the benefits of using this type of software architecture, instead of distracting you with theoretical concepts. They cover some of the state-of-the-art techniques in computer programming, from a practical point of view. The emphasis is on what matters most—starting with the minimum viable product but maintaining the ability to adapt and improve over time.

Downloading the Code

The code for the examples shown in this book is available at `https://github.com/Book-Microservices-v3`.

Note The sources for this book may change over time, to provide new implementations that incorporate the most up-to-date features in Spring Boot. That said, if any issues are found in the sources, please submit them via the book's GitHub repo, and the code will be adjusted accordingly.

CHAPTER 1

Setting the Scene

A microservices architecture allows you to design software systems as a collection of independent services that communicate through APIs. Each microservice performs a specific business function and is responsible for its data storage, processing, and delivery.

Microservices have become the de facto standard for building complex and scalable systems. This is not surprising, given the numerous benefits of this software architecture style. Microservices offer increased scalability, flexibility, and resilience, as well as the ability to develop and deploy services independently. Additionally, microservices provide the potential for easier maintenance and updates compared to other architecture styles. Mapping microservices into small teams in an organization also gives you a lot of efficiency in development. However, going on the adventure of microservices while knowing only the benefits is the wrong approach.

The microservices approach also leads to the distribution of the system's functionality across multiple microservices, each running independently and communicating with others through a network. As a result, the overall system becomes distributed, consisting of numerous smaller, independent services that work together to deliver the desired functionality. This architecture style allows for greater flexibility, scalability, and resilience, but it also introduces additional complexity, which you need to manage carefully. You can get a lot of knowledge from many books and articles on the Internet, but when you get hands-on with the code, the story changes.

This book covers some of the essential concepts of microservices practically, but only by explaining those concepts. In this book, you build an application where users can exercise their brains by performing mathematical calculations. Users will be presented with a new problem every time they access the application. They provide their alias (a short name) and submit answers to the problem. After they submit their input, the web page will indicate whether their answer is correct.

© Moisés Macero García and Tarun Telang 2023
M. Macero García and T. Telang, *Learn Microservices with Spring Boot 3*,
https://doi.org/10.1007/978-1-4842-9757-5_1

First, you define a use case: an application to build. Then you start with a small monolith based on some sound reasoning. Once you have the minimal application in place, you evaluate whether it's worth moving to microservices and learn how to do that well, including building RESTful APIs, adding security features, and scaling services. The book also introduces essential microservices design principles, such as the single responsibility principle, loose coupling, service autonomy, and bounded contexts from domain-driven design. With the introduction of the second microservice, we analyze the options you have for their communication. Then, you can describe and implement the event-driven architecture pattern to reach loose coupling by informing other parts of the system about what happened, instead of explicitly calling others to action. Event-driven architecture is a powerful pattern for designing reactive and resilient microservices.

You will also explore commonly used communication patterns that facilitate seamless coordination and collaboration between microservices. These patterns can be classified into two categories—synchronous communication and asynchronous communication.

For *synchronous communication,* you will study patterns such as request-response, message broker, API gateway, choreography, and orchestration. These patterns enable real-time interactions between services, ensuring that requests and responses are handled in a coordinated manner.

On the other hand, for *asynchronous communication,* you will delve into event sourcing and publish-subscribe patterns. These patterns allow services to communicate asynchronously by leveraging events and messages, promoting loose coupling and enabling independent processing.

By examining these communication patterns, you'll gain a comprehensive understanding of how microservices can effectively interact and work together, both in synchronous and asynchronous scenarios. This knowledge empowers you to design robust and efficient communication mechanisms within your microservices architecture.

When you reach that point, you'll notice that a poorly designed distributed system has some flaws that you must fix with popular patterns: service discovery, routing, load balancing, traceability, and more.

You will also explore the circuit breaker pattern as another important communication pattern for microservices. The circuit breaker pattern acts as a safeguard against cascading failures and helps manage the resilience of communication between services.

By studying the circuit breaker pattern, you will understand how it detects failures in remote service calls and provides a fail-fast mechanism. It helps prevent further calls to a failing service, thus reducing the impact of failures on the overall system. The circuit breaker pattern also includes mechanisms for monitoring the health of services and adapting to changing conditions.

Incorporating the circuit breaker pattern into your communication strategies ensures that your microservices ecosystem remains stable, resilient, and responsive, even in the face of potential failures or degradation in service performance.

Adding them individually to your codebase instead of presenting all of them together helps you understand these patterns. You can also prepare these microservices for cloud deployment by understanding cloud-native architectures and containerization, learning about cloud-native architectures and containerization, using Docker for containerization and Kubernetes for orchestration, and comparing the different platform alternatives to run the applications. By following these steps, you can gain a practical understanding of microservices and learn how to design, implement, and deploy microservices-based systems.

Throughout this book you will build microservices from scratch using Spring Boot. The advantage of going step-by-step, pausing when needed to nail down the concepts, is that you will understand which problem each tool is trying to solve. That's why the evolving example is an essential part of this book. You can also grasp the concepts without coding a single line since the source code is presented and explained throughout the chapters.

All the code included in this book is available on GitHub in the organization `Book-Microservices-v3`. Multiple repositories are available and divided into chapters and sections, making it easier to see how the application evolves. The book includes notes with the version covered in each part. By following these steps, you can gain a practical understanding of microservices and learn how to design, implement, and deploy microservices-based systems.

Who Are You?

Let's start with this: how interesting will this book be to you? This book is practical, so let's play this game. If you identify with any of these statements, this book might be good for you:

- "I would like to learn how to build microservices with Spring Boot and how to use the related tools."

- "Everybody is talking about microservices, but I have no clue what a microservice is yet. I have read only theoretical explanations or just hype-enforcing articles. I can't understand the advantages, even though I work in IT...."

- "I would like to learn how to design and develop Spring Boot applications, but all I find are either quick-start guides with too simple examples or lengthy books that resemble the official documentation. I would like to learn the concepts following a more realistic, project-guided approach."

- "I got a new job, and they're using a microservices architecture. I've been working mainly in big, monolithic projects, so I'd like to have some knowledge and guidance to learn how everything works there, as well as the pros and cons of this architecture."

- "Every time I go to the cafeteria, developers talk about microservices, gateways, service discovery, containers, resilience patterns, and so on. I can't socialize anymore with my colleagues if I don't get what they're saying." (This one is a joke; don't read this book because of that, especially if you're not interested in programming.)

Regarding the knowledge required to read this book, the following topics should be familiar to you:

- Java (we use Java 17)

- Spring (you don't need strong experience, but you should know at least how dependency injection works)

- Maven (if you know Gradle, you'll be fine as well)

How Is This Book Different from Other Books and Guides?

Software developers and architects read many technical books and guides because they're interested in learning new technologies, or their work requires it. They need to do that anyway since it's a constantly changing world. You can find all kinds of books and guides out there. You can learn quickly from the good ones, which teach you not only how to do stuff but also explain why you should do it that way.

Using the latest techniques just because they're new is the wrong way to go about it; you need to understand the reasoning behind them, so you use them in the best way possible.

This book uses that philosophy: it navigates through the code and design patterns, explaining the reasons to follow one way and not others.

Learning: An Incremental Process

If you look at the guides available on the Internet, you'll quickly notice that they are not real-life examples. Usually, when you apply those cases to more complex scenarios, they don't fit. Guides need to be deeper to help you build something real. Books, on the other hand, are much better at that. Plenty of good books explain concepts around an example; they are good because applying theoretical concepts to code is only sometimes possible if you don't see the code. The problem with some of these books is that they're less practical than guides. It helps when you read them first to understand the concepts and then code (or see) the example, which we have frequently given as a whole piece. It isn't easy to put concepts into practice when you view the final version directly. This book stays practical and starts with code. It evolves through the chapters so that you grasp the ideas one by one. We cover the problem before exposing the solution.

Because of this incremental way of presenting concepts, this book also allows you to code as you learn and to reflect on the challenges by yourself.

Is This a Guide or a Book?

The pages you have in front of you can't be called a guide: it will take you 15 or 30 minutes to finish them. Besides, each chapter introduces all the required topics to lay the foundation for the new code additions. But this is not the typical book either, in which you go through isolated concepts, illustrated with scattered code fragments explicitly made for that situation. Instead, you start with a real-life application that is yet to be optimal, and you learn how to evolve it after learning about the benefits you can extract from that process.

That does not mean you can't just sit down and read it, but it's better if your code simultaneously plays with the options and alternatives presented. That's part of the book that makes it like a guide. To keep it simple, we call this a book from here onward.

From Basics to Advanced Topics

This book focuses on some essential concepts that build on the rest of the topics (Chapter 2)—Spring Boot, testing, logging, and so on. Then, it covers how to design and implement a production-ready Spring Boot application using a well-known layered design. It dives into how to implement a REST API, business logic, and database repositories (Chapters 3 and 5). While doing that, you see how Spring Boot works internally, so it's not magic to you anymore. You also learn how to build a basic frontend application with React (Chapter 4) because that will help you visualize how the backend architecture impacts the frontend. After that, the book enters the microservices world by introducing a second piece of functionality in a different Spring Boot app. The practical example helps you analyze the factors you should examine before deciding to move to microservices (Chapter 6). Then, you learn the differences between communicating microservices synchronously and asynchronously and how an event-driven architecture can help you keep your system components decoupled (Chapter 7). From there, the book takes you through the journey of tools and frameworks applicable to distributed systems to achieve necessary nonfunctional requirements: resilience, scalability, traceability, and deployment to the cloud, among others (Chapter 8).

If you are already familiar with Spring Boot applications and how they work, you can go quickly through the first chapters and focus more on the second part of the book. More advanced topics are covered in the second part, including event-driven design, service discovery, routing, distributed tracing, testing with Cucumber, and so on. However, pay attention to the foundations set up in the first part: test-driven development, the focus on the minimum viable product (MVP), and monolith-first.

Skeleton with Spring Boot, the Professional Way

First, the book guides you through creating an application using Spring Boot. The contents mainly focus on the backend side, but you will create a simple web page with React to demonstrate how to use the exposed functionality as a REST API.

It's important to point out that you don't create "shortcut code" to showcase Spring Boot features: that's not the objective of this book. It uses Spring Boot as a vehicle to teach concepts, but you could use any other framework, and the ideas of this book would still be valid.

You learn how to design and implement the application following the well-known three-tier, three-layer pattern. You do this supported by an incremental example with hands-on code. While writing the applications, you'll pause a few times to get into the details about how Spring Boot works with so little code (autoconfiguration, starters, etc.).

Test-Driven Development

In the first chapters, you use test-driven development (TDD) to map the prerequisites presented to technical features. This book tries to show this technique so you can see the benefits from the beginning: why it's always a good idea to think about the test cases before writing your code. JUnit 5, AssertJ, and Mockito will serve you to build useful tests efficiently.

The plan is the following: you'll learn how to create the tests first, then make them fail, and finally implement the logic to make them work.

Microservices

Once you have your first application ready, we introduce a second one that will interact with the existing functionality. From that moment on, you'll have a microservices architecture. It doesn't make any sense to try to understand the advantages of microservices if you have only one of them. The real-life scenarios are always distributed systems with functionality split into different services. As usual, to keep it practical, you'll analyze the specific situation for your case study, so you'll see if moving to microservices fits your needs.

The book covers not only the reasons to split the system but also the disadvantages that come with that choice. Once you make the decision to move to microservices, you'll learn which patterns you should use to build a good architecture for the distributed system: service discovery, routing, load balancing, distributed tracing, containerization, and some other supporting mechanisms.

Event-Driven Systems

An additional concept that does not always need to come with microservices is the *event-driven architecture*. This book uses it since it's a pattern that fits well into a microservice architecture, and you'll make your choice based on good examples. You learn about the differences between synchronous and asynchronous communication, as well as their main pros and cons.

This asynchronous way of thinking introduces new ways of designing code, with *eventual consistency* as one of the key changes to embrace. You'll look at it while coding your project, using RabbitMQ or Apache Kafka to send and receive messages between microservices. Both of these messaging systems allow for distributed and decoupled processing within your architecture.

Nonfunctional Requirements

When you build an application in the real world, you must take into account some requirements that are not directly related to functionalities, but that prepare your system to be more robust, to keep working in the event of failures, or to ensure data integrity.

Many of these *nonfunctional requirements* are related to things that can go wrong with your software: network failures that make part of your system unreachable, a high traffic volume that collapses your backend capacity, external services that don't respond, and so on.

In this book, you learn how to implement and verify patterns to make the system more resilient and scalable. In addition, it discusses the importance of data integrity and the tools that help you guarantee it.

The good part about learning how to design and solve all these nonfunctional requirements is that it's knowledge applicable to any system, no matter the programming language and frameworks you're using.

Online Content

For this second edition of the book, we decided to create an online space where you can keep learning new topics related to microservice architectures. On this web page, you'll find new guides that extend the practical use case covering other important aspects of distributed systems. Additionally, new versions of the repositories using up-to-date dependencies are published there.

The first guide that you'll find online is about testing a distributed system with Cucumber (`https://cucumber.io/`). This framework helps you build human-readable test scripts to make sure your functionalities work end-to-end.

Visit `https://github.com/Book-Microservices-v3/book-extras` for all the extra content and new updates about the book.

Summary

This chapter introduced the main goals of this book: to teach you the main aspects of a microservice architecture by starting simple and then growing your knowledge through the development of a sample project.

We also briefly covered the main content of the book: from monolith-first to microservices with Spring Boot, test-driven development, event-driven systems, common architecture patterns, nonfunctional requirements, and end-to-end testing with Cucumber (online).

The next chapter starts with the first step of your learning path: a review of some basic concepts.

CHAPTER 2

Basic Concepts

This book follows a practical approach, so most of the tools covered are introduced as you need them. However, we'll go over some core concepts separately because they're either the foundations of the evolving example or used extensively in the code examples, namely, Spring, Spring Boot, testing libraries, Lombok, and logging. These concepts deserve a separate introduction to avoid long interruptions in your learning path, which is why this chapter includes an overview of them.

Remember that these sections intend to provide a sound knowledge base of these frameworks and libraries. The primary objective of this chapter is to refresh the concepts in your mind (if you already learned them) or grasp the basics so that you don't need to consult external references before reading the rest of the chapters.

Spring

The Spring Framework (`https://spring.io/projects/spring-framework`) is a popular open-source application development framework consisting of a collection of libraries and tools that provide a comprehensive programming and configuration model for developing enterprise-level Java applications. It offers a wide range of features and modules—such as dependency injection, aspect-oriented programming, data access, transaction management, validation, internationalization, web development, and more—that can be used individually or in combination to develop robust and scalable applications. It is widely used by developers and organizations worldwide, and it has become a standard for building complex Java-based applications. At the time of writing the book, the latest version of the Spring framework is 6.0.9.

The Spring Framework primarily supports the Java programming language. However, it also provides support for other JVM-based programming languages such as Groovy and Kotlin.

© Moisés Macero García and Tarun Telang 2023
M. Macero García and T. Telang, *Learn Microservices with Spring Boot 3*,
https://doi.org/10.1007/978-1-4842-9757-5_2

Spring Framework is popular for several reasons:

1. **Modular and flexible**: Spring Framework is highly modular and provides a wide range of features that can be used individually or in combination. It allows developers to use only the modules they need, making it flexible and lightweight.

2. **Dependency injection (DI)**: Spring Framework supports powerful and flexible dependency injection, allowing developers to easily manage dependencies between components of an application, thus reducing code coupling and improving maintainability.

3. **Aspect-Oriented Programming (AOP)**: Spring AOP provides a way to add cross-cutting concerns to an application, such as logging, caching, and security, without having to modify the core application logic.

4. **Data access**: Spring provides several modules for database access and object-relational mapping, including Spring Data JDBC (`https://spring.io/projects/spring-data-jdbc`) and Spring Data JPA.

5. **Transaction management**: Spring provides a powerful transaction management framework, which supports both declarative and programmatic transaction management.

6. **Web applications**: Spring provides robust support for building web applications. The Spring framework offers various features and modules that facilitate the development of web-based solutions with ease and efficiency. At the heart of web application development with Spring lies Spring MVC (Model-View-Controller). Spring MVC is a powerful framework that follows the MVC architectural pattern, enabling developers to build scalable and maintainable web applications. It provides a structured approach to handling HTTP requests and mapping them to appropriate controllers, processing business logic, and rendering views for the user.

7. **Security**: Spring Security (`https://spring.io/projects/spring-security`) provides a comprehensive security framework, which supports authentication, authorization, and other security-related features.

8. **Large community and documentation**: Spring Framework has a large and active community of developers and users, who continuously contribute to the development and improvement of the framework, provide support, and share knowledge and resources.

9. **Integration with other frameworks and libraries**: Spring Framework provides seamless integration with other technologies and frameworks, such as Hibernate, JPA, REST, and more, making it easier to develop and deploy applications.

10. **Testability**: Spring Framework makes it easier to write unit and integration tests, which helps ensure the quality and reliability of the application.

Spring provides lots of built-in implementations for many aspects of software development, such as the following:

- Spring Data (`https://spring.io/projects/spring-data`) simplifies data access for relational and NoSQL databases. It provides support for several popular data access technologies, such as JDBC, Hibernate, JPA, and MongoDB. It makes it easy to work with databases and perform CRUD (Create, Read, Update and Delete) operations.

- Spring Batch (`https://spring.io/projects/spring-batch`) is a framework for building batch processing applications. It is a lightweight, comprehensive framework that provides developers with the tools to create batch jobs that can process large amounts of data efficiently and reliably.

- Spring Security (`https://spring.io/projects/spring-security`) is a security framework that abstracts security features to applications.

- Spring Cloud (`https://spring.io/projects/spring-cloud`)
  provides tools for developers to quickly build some of the common
  patterns in distributed systems.

- Spring Integration (`https://spring.io/projects/spring-integration`)is an implementation of enterprise integration patterns.
  It facilitates integration with other enterprise applications using
  lightweight messaging and declarative adapters.

- Spring MVC is a web framework for building Java web applications
  based on the Model-View-Controller design pattern. It provides
  a flexible and powerful platform for developing scalable and
  maintainable web applications.

- Spring Web Flow (`https://spring.io/projects/spring-webflow`)
  provides a powerful and comprehensive solution for managing
  complex flows in web applications. It simplifies the development
  process by abstracting away the low-level details of flow control and
  state management, allowing developers to focus on creating intuitive
  and efficient user experiences.

- Spring WebFlux is a reactive web framework for building non-
  blocking and event-driven applications on the JVM. It provides an
  alternative to Spring MVC and supports asynchronous and non-
  blocking API for handling HTTP requests and responses using
  reactive programming principles.

These built-in implementations make it easier for developers to build robust,
scalable, and maintainable applications, while reducing the amount of boilerplate code
that needs to be written.

As you can see, Spring is divided into different modules. All the modules are built
on top of the core Spring Framework, which establishes a common programming and
configuration model for software applications. This model itself is another important
reason to choose the framework since it facilitates good programming techniques such
as the use of interfaces instead of classes to decouple application layers via dependency
injection.

A key topic in Spring is the Inversion of Control (IoC) container, which is supported by the `ApplicationContext` interface (`https://docs.spring.io/spring-framework/docs/current/javadoc-api/org/springframework/context/ApplicationContext.html`). The ApplicationContext interface is a key component of the Spring Framework that provides a powerful and flexible mechanism for managing object dependencies and resources in an application. The IoC container creates this "space" in your application where you, and the framework itself, can put some object instances such as database connection pools, HTTP clients, and so on. These objects, called *beans*, can be later used in other parts of your application, commonly through their public interface to abstract your code from specific implementations. The mechanism to reference one of these beans from the application context in other classes is called *dependency injection*, and in Spring this is possible via various techniques like XML, YAML, Java-based annotations, and JavaConfig. This provides a high degree of flexibility in how the application is structured.

With XML configuration, you can define the various components of your web application, such as controllers, views, and dependencies, in XML files. These files typically have a suffix like `.xml` and follow a defined structure based on the Spring framework's XML schema.

Spring also supports configuration using YAML (YAML Ain't Markup Language). YAML is a human-readable data serialization format that is often used for configuration files in various applications, including Spring. With YAML configuration, you can define your Spring beans, properties, and other configuration elements in a structured and easy-to-read format. YAML provides a more concise and visually appealing alternative to XML for configuration purposes. To use YAML configuration in Spring, you typically create a YAML file (with a `.yml` or `.yaml` extension) and define your configuration elements using indentation and key-value pairs. For example, you can define beans, their properties, and their dependencies in a hierarchical structure within the YAML file. Spring Boot offers built-in support for YAML-based configuration files. Spring Boot automatically loads and parses YAML files to configure the application at startup.

With YAML configuration, you can define your Spring beans, properties, and other configuration elements in a structured and an easy-to-read format. YAML provides a more concise and visually appealing alternative to XML for configuration purposes.

Spring also offers the option to configure web applications using annotations, leveraging the power and simplicity of Java code. Annotations provide a more concise and intuitive way to define the components and their configurations.

Spring also offers the option to configure web applications using annotations, leveraging the power and simplicity of Java code. Annotations provide a more concise and intuitive way to define the components and their configurations.

By using annotations, you can mark your classes, methods, or fields with specific annotations provided by Spring. For example, you can annotate a class with `@Controller` to indicate it as a Spring MVC controller, use `@RequestMapping` to specify request mappings, and use `@Autowired` to inject dependencies.

Using annotations reduces the need for YAML or XML configuration files, as the configuration can be directly embedded in the source code. This approach promotes better code readability, simplifies configuration management, and reduces the overall configuration overhead.

Yet another Java-based configuration approach, known as "JavaConfig," has also gained significant popularity. It allows developers to define their application's configuration using plain Java classes annotated with Spring annotations. This provides a more programmatic and type-safe way of configuring Spring components.

You see all these configuration options in action as you work through the sample application.

Spring Boot

Spring Boot (`https://spring.io/projects/spring-boot`) is a framework that leverages Spring to quickly create stand-alone applications in Java-based languages. It has become a popular tool for building microservices.

Having so many available modules in Spring and other related third-party libraries that can be combined with the framework is powerful for software development. Yet, despite a lot of efforts to make Spring configuration easier, you still need to spend some time to set up everything you need for your application. And, sometimes, you just require the same configuration over and over again. *Bootstrapping* an application, meaning the process to configure your Spring application to have it up and running, is sometimes tedious. The advantage of Spring Boot is that it eliminates most of that process by providing default configurations and tools that are set up automatically for you. The main disadvantage is that if you rely too much on these defaults, you may lose control and awareness of what's happening. We unveil some of the Spring Boot implementations in the book to demonstrate how it works internally so that you can always be in control.

Spring Boot provides some predefined *starter packages* that are like collections of Spring modules and some third-party libraries and tools together. As an example, `spring-boot-starter-web` helps you build a stand-alone web application. It groups the Spring Core Web libraries with Jackson (JSON handling), validation, logging, autoconfiguration, and even an embedded Tomcat server, among other tools. Other starters include `spring-boot-starter-data-jpa`, which includes dependencies for Spring Data JPA, Hibernate, and a database driver, and `spring-boot-starter-test`, which includes dependencies for testing Spring Boot applications.

In addition to starters, *autoconfiguration* plays a key role in Spring Boot. This feature makes adding functionality to your application extremely easy. It also helps ensure that the application follows best practices and recommended design patterns, as the autoconfiguration logic is based on well-established Spring patterns and practices. Following the same example, just by including the web starter, you get an embedded Tomcat server. There's no need to configure anything. This is because the Spring Boot auto configuration classes scan your classpath, properties, components, and so on, and load some extra beans and behavior based on that.

To be able to manage different configuration options for your Spring Boot application, the framework introduces *profiles*. You can use profiles, for example, to set different values for the host to connect to when using a database in a development environment and a production environment. Additionally, you can use a different profile for tests, where you may need to expose additional functions or mock parts of your application. We cover profiles more in detail in Chapter 8.

You'll use the Spring Boot Web and Data starters to quickly build a web application with persistent storage. The Test starter will help you write tests, given that it includes some useful test libraries such as JUnit 5 (`https://junit.org/junit5/`) and AssertJ (`https://assertj.github.io/doc/`). Then, you'll see how to add messaging capabilities to your applications by adding the AMQP starter, which includes a message broker integration (RabbitMQ) that you'll use to implement an event-driven architecture. Chapter 8 includes a different type of starters, grouped within the Spring Cloud family. You'll use some of these tools to implement common patterns for distributed systems: routing with Spring Cloud Gateway (`https://cloud.spring.io`), service discovery with Consul (`https://www.consul.io/`), and load balancing with Spring Cloud Load Balancer (`https://spring.io/guides/gs/spring-cloud-loadbalancer/`), among others. Don't worry about all these new terms for now; they'll be explained in detail while you make progress on the practical example.

The next chapter covers in detail how these starters and Spring Boot autoconfiguration work, based on a practical example.

Lombok and Java

The code examples in this book use Project Lombok (`https://projectlombok.org/`), a library that generates Java code based on annotations. The current version of Lombok at the time of writing this book was 1.18.28. The main reason to include Lombok in the book is educational: it keeps the code samples concise, reducing the boilerplate so you can focus on what it matters.

Let's use one of the first simple classes as an example. Say you want to create an immutable multiplication challenge class with two factors. See Listing 2-1.

Listing 2-1. The Challenge Class in Plain Java

```java
/**
 * Represents a challenge with two factors.
 */
public final class Challenge {
    // Both factors
    private final int factorA;
    private final int factorB;
    public Challenge(int factorA, int factorB) {
        this.factorA = factorA;
        this.factorB = factorB;
    }
    public int getFactorA() {
        return this.factorA;
    }
    public int getFactorB() {
        return this.factorB;
    }
    @Override
    public boolean equals(final Object o) {
        if (o == this) return true;
        if (!(o instanceof Challenge)) return false;
```

```
        final Challenge other = (Challenge) o;
        if (this.getFactorA() != other.getFactorA()) return false;
        if (this.getFactorB() != other.getFactorB()) return false;
        return true;
    }
    @Override
    public int hashCode() {
        final int PRIME = 59;
        int result = 1;
        result = result * PRIME + factorA;
        result = result * PRIME + factorB;
        return result;
    }
    @Override
    public String toString() {
        return "Challenge [factorA=" + factorA + ", factorB=" +
        factorB + "]";
    }
}
```

As you can see, the full class has some classic boilerplate code: constructors, getters, and the equals, hashCode, and toString methods. They don't add much to this book, yet you need them for the code to work.

The same class can be reduced with Lombok to its minimum expression. See Listing 2-2.

Listing 2-2. The Challenge Class Using Lombok

```
import lombok.Value;
@Value
public class Challenge {
    // Both factors
    int factorA;
    int factorB;
}
```

The `@Value` annotation provided by Lombok groups some other annotations in this library that you can also use separately. Each of the following annotations instructs Lombok to generate code blocks before the Java build phase:

- `@AllArgsConstructor` creates a constructor with all the existing fields.

- `@FieldDefaults` makes your fields `private` and `final`.

- `@Getter` generates getters for `factorA` and `factorB`.

- `@ToString` includes a simple implementation of concatenating fields.

- `@EqualsAndHashCode` generates basic `equals()` and `hashCode()` methods using all fields by default, but you can also customize it.

Not only does Lombok reduce the code to the minimum, but it also helps when you need to modify these classes. Adding a new field to the `Challenge` class in Lombok means adding one line (excluding usages of the class). If you would use the plain Java version, you would need to add the new argument to the constructor, add the `equals` and `hashCode` methods, and add a new getter. Not only does that mean extra work, but it's also error-prone: if you forgot the extra field in the `equals` method, for example, you would introduce a bug into your application.

Like many tools, Lombok also has detractors. The main reason not to like Lombok is that, since it's easy to add code to your classes, you might end up adding code that you don't really need (e.g., setters or extra constructors). Besides, you could argue that having a good IDE with code generation and a refactoring assistant can help more or less at the same level.

The coming chapters mainly use these Lombok features:

- We annotate with `@Value` the immutable classes.

- For the data entities, we use separately some of the annotations described earlier.

- We add the `@Slf4j` annotation for Lombok to create a logger using the standard Simple Logging Facade for Java API (SLF4J). SLF4J (`https://www.slf4j.org/`) is a logging facade or abstraction layer that provides a common logging API for various logging frameworks in the Java ecosystem. It allows developers to write code that uses a single API for logging while being able to use different logging frameworks under the hood. The section entitled "Logging" in this chapter gives more background about these concepts.

In any case, you learn what these annotations do when you look at the code examples, so you don't need to dive into more details on how they work.

If you prefer plain Java code, just use the Lombok's code annotations in this book as a reference to know what extra code you need to include in your classes.

Java Records   Starting with JDK 14, the Java records feature was introduced in preview mode and became a standard feature in JDK 16. If you use this feature, you could write the `Challenge` class in pure Java in a concise way as well.

```
public record Challenge(int factorA, int factorB) {}
```

Testing Basics

In this section, we go through some important testing approaches and libraries. We put them into practice in the next chapters, so it's good to learn (or review) the basic concepts first.

Test-Driven Development

The first practical chapters in this book encourage you to use *test-driven development* (TDD). TDD is a software development practice that involves writing automated tests before writing the actual code. The idea behind TDD is to write small, incremental tests that verify the functionality of the code at each step of development. This technique helps you by putting the focus first on what you need and what your expectations are and later move to the implementation. It makes you, as a developer, think about what the code should do under certain situations or use cases. In real life, TDD also helps you clarify vague requirements and discard invalid ones. TDD has become increasingly popular in recent years, and it is widely used in agile software development.

Given that this book is driven by a practical case, you'll find that TDD fits quite well within the main purpose.

Behavior-Driven Development

As an addition to the idea of writing your tests before your logic, *behavior-driven development* (BDD) brings some better structure and readability to your tests. BDD is a software development methodology that emphasizes collaboration between developers, testers, and business stakeholders. BDD is a way to design, build, and test software based on the behavior of the system being developed. In BDD, the focus is on defining the behavior of the system from the perspective of the end-users or stakeholders. This is done by creating executable specifications, also known as "feature files," which describe the expected behavior of the system in a language that all stakeholders can understand.

In BDD, we write the tests according to a *Given-When-Then* structure. This removes the gap between developers and business analysts when mapping use cases to tests. Analysts can just read the code and identify what is being tested there.

Keep in mind that BDD, like TDD, is a development process by itself and not simply a way of writing tests. Its main goal is to facilitate conversations to improve the definition of requirements and their test cases. In this book, the focus regarding BDD is on the test structure. See Listing 2-3 for an example of how these tests look.

Listing 2-3. An Example of a BDD Test Case Using a Given-When-Then Structure

```
@Test
public void getRandomMultiplicationTest() throws Exception {
    // given
    given(challengeGeneratorService.randomChallenge())
            .willReturn(new Challenge(70, 20));
    // when
    MockHttpServletResponse response = mvc.perform(
            get("/multiplications/random")
                    .accept(MediaType.APPLICATION_JSON))
            .andReturn().getResponse();
    // then
    then(response.getStatus()).isEqualTo(HttpStatus.OK.value());
    then(response.getContentAsString())
            .isEqualTo(json.write(new Challenge(70, 20)).getJson());
}
```

JUnit 5

JUnit 5 (`https://junit.org/junit5/`) is a popular open-source testing framework for Java-based applications. It provides a set of annotations, assertions, and test runners to help developers write and run repeatable automated tests for their code. The code in this book uses JUnit 5 for the unit tests. The Spring Boot Test starter includes these libraries, so you don't need to include it in your dependencies.

In general, the idea behind unit tests is that you can verify the behavior of your classes (units) separately. In this book, you'll write unit tests for every class where you put logic.

Among all the features in JUnit 5, we use mainly the basic ones, listed here:

- `@BeforeEach` and `@AfterEach` for code that should be executed before and after each test, respectively.

- `@Test` for every method that represents a test we want to execute.

- `@ExtendsWith` at the class level to add JUnit 5 extensions. We use this to add the Mockito extension and the Spring extension to our tests.

Mockito

Mockito (`https://site.mockito.org/`) is a mocking framework for unit tests in Java. When you *mock* a class, you are overriding the real behavior of that class with some predefined instructions of what their methods should return or do for their arguments. This is an important requirement to write unit tests since you want to validate the behavior of one class only and simulate all its interactions.

The easiest way to mock a class with Mockito is to use the `@Mock` annotation in a field combined with `MockitoExtension` for JUnit 5. In Mockito, you can annotate a field with `@Mock` to create a mock of the corresponding class or interface. See Listing 2-4.

Listing 2-4. MockitoExtension and Mock Annotation Usage

```
@ExtendWith(MockitoExtension.class)
public class MultiplicationServiceImplTest {
    @Mock
    private ChallengeAttemptRepository attemptRepository;
    // [...] -> tests
}
```

Once the mock is created, you can define its behavior. For example, you might specify that when a certain method is called on the mock object with certain parameters, it should return a specific value or throw an exception. You could use the static method Mockito.when() to define custom behavior. See Listing 2-5.

Listing 2-5. Defining Custom Behavior with the Mockito.when() Function

```
import static org.mockito.Mockito.when;
// ...
when(attemptRepository.methodThatReturnsSomething())
    .thenReturn(predefinedResponse);
```

However, we will use the alternative methods from BDDMockito (https://javadoc. io/doc/org.mockito/mockito-core/latest/org/mockito/BDDMockito.html), also included in the Mockito dependency. This gives you a more readable, BDD-style way of writing unit tests. See Listing 2-6.

Listing 2-6. Using given to Define Custom Behavior

```
import static org.mockito.BDDMockito.given;
// ...
given(attemptRepository.methodThatReturnsSomething())
    .willReturn(predefinedResponse);
```

After executing the code under test, you can verify that the mock objects were called in the correct way, with the correct parameters, and so on. For example, you can check that an expected call to a mocked class was invoked. With Mockito, you use the verify() method for that. See Listing 2-7.

Listing 2-7. Verifying an Expected Call

```
import static org.mockito.Mockito.verify;
// ...
verify(attemptRepository).save(attempt);
```

As some extra background, it's good to know that there is also a BDD variation of verify(), called then(). Unfortunately, this replacement may be confusing when you combine BDDMockito with BDDAssertions (https://bit.ly/assertj-core-bdd-assertions-documentation) from AssertJ (covered in the next section). Since this book uses assertions more extensively than verifications, we will opt for verifications to better distinguish them.

Listing 2-8 shows a full example of a test using JUnit 5 and Mockito based on a class that you'll implement later in the book. For now, you can ignore the assertion; you'll get there soon.

Listing 2-8. A Complete Unit Test with JUnit5 and Mockito

```
package microservices.book.multiplication.challenge;

import java.util.Optional;

import org.junit.jupiter.api.BeforeEach;
import org.junit.jupiter.api.Test;
import org.junit.jupiter.api.extension.ExtendWith;
import org.mockito.Mock;
import org.mockito.junit.jupiter.MockitoExtension;

import microservices.book.multiplication.event.ChallengeSolvedEvent;
import microservices.book.multiplication.event.EventDispatcher;
import microservices.book.multiplication.user.User;
import microservices.book.multiplication.user.UserRepository;

import static org.assertj.core.api.BDDAssertions.then;
import static org.mockito.BDDMockito.*;

@ExtendWith(MockitoExtension.class)
public class ChallengeServiceImplTest {
  private ChallengeServiceImpl challengeServiceImpl;

  @Mock
  private ChallengeAttemptRepository attemptRepository;

  @Mock
  private UserRepository userRepository;
```

```java
@Mock
private EventDispatcher eventDispatcher;

@BeforeEach
public void setUp() {
    challengeServiceImpl = new ChallengeServiceImpl(attemptRepository,
        userRepository, eventDispatcher);
}
@Test
public void checkCorrectAttemptTest() {
    // given
    long userId = 9L, attemptId = 1L;
    User user = new User("john_doe");
    User savedUser = new User(userId, "john_doe");
    ChallengeAttemptDTO attemptDTO =
        new ChallengeAttemptDTO(50, 60, "john_doe", 3000);
    ChallengeAttempt attempt =
        new ChallengeAttempt(null, savedUser, 50, 60, 3000, true);
    ChallengeAttempt storedAttempt =
        new ChallengeAttempt(attemptId, savedUser, 50, 60, 3000, true);
    ChallengeSolvedEvent event = new ChallengeSolvedEvent(attemptId, true,
        attempt.getFactorA(), attempt.getFactorB(), userId,
        attempt.getUser().getAlias());
    // user does not exist, should be created
    given(userRepository.findByAlias("john_doe"))
        .willReturn(Optional.empty());
    given(userRepository.save(user))
        .willReturn(savedUser);
    given(attemptRepository.save(attempt))
        .willReturn(storedAttempt);
    // when
    ChallengeAttempt resultAttempt =
        challengeServiceImpl.checkAttempt(attemptDTO);
    // then
    then(resultAttempt.isCorrect()).isTrue();
    verify(userRepository).save(user);
```

```
    verify(attemptRepository).save(attempt);
    verify(eventDispatcher).send(event);
  }
}
```

The test method `checkCorrectAttemptTest()` is for a scenario where the challenge attempt is correct. The necessary mock objects are initialized and passed to the `ChallengeServiceImpl` instance in the `setup()` method. Next, the `john_doe` username is defined and an instance named `attemptDTO` of `ChallengeAttemptDTO` is defined with specific values from a correct response. When the `checkAttempt()` method of `challengeServiceImpl` is called with the `attemptDTO`, assertions are made that the result of `checkAttempt` is marked as correct. The `verify()` methods are called to ensure that the methods were called as expected, including saving the user, saving the attempt, and sending the event.

AssertJ

The standard way to verify expected results with JUnit 5 is using assertions.

```
assertEquals("Hello, World!", actualGreeting);
```

There are not only assertions for equality of all kinds of objects but also to verify true/false, null, execution before a timeout, throwing an exception, and so on. You can find them all in the Assertions Javadoc (`https://bit.ly/junit5-assertions-documentation`).

Even though JUnit assertions are enough in most cases, they are not as easy to use and as readable as the ones provided by AssertJ (`https://assertj.github.io/doc/`). This library implements a fluent way of writing assertions and provides extra functionality so you can write more concise tests.

In its standard form, the previous example looks like this:

```
assertThat(actualGreeting).isEqualTo("Hello, World!");
```

However, as mentioned in previous sections, we want to use a BDD language approach. Therefore, we use the `BDDAssertions` class included in AssertJ. This class contains method equivalencies for all the `assertThat` cases, renamed as `then`.

```
then(actualGreeting).isEqualTo("Hello, World!");
```

In the book, we mostly have some basic assertions from AssertJ. If you're interested in extending your knowledge about AssertJ, you can start with the official documentation page (`https://assertj.github.io/doc/`).

Testing in Spring Boot

Both JUnit 5 and AssertJ are included in `spring-boot-starter-test`, so you simply need to include this dependency in your Spring Boot application to use them. Then, you can use different testing strategies.

One of the most popular ways to write tests in Spring Boot is to use the `@SpringBootTest` annotation. It will start a Spring context and make all your configured beans available for the test. If you're running integration tests and want to verify how different parts of your application work together, this approach is convenient.

When testing specific slices or individual classes of your application, it's better to use plain unit tests (without Spring at all) or more fine-grained annotations like `@WebMvcTest`, focused on controller-layer tests. This is the approach we use in the book, and we explain it more in detail when you get there.

For now, let's focus only on the integration between the libraries and frameworks described in this chapter.

- The Spring Test libraries (included via Spring Boot Test starter) come with a `SpringExtension` so you can integrate Spring in your JUnit 5 tests via the `@ExtendWith` annotation.

- The Spring Boot Test package introduces the `@MockBean` annotation that you can use to replace or add a bean in the Spring context, in a similar way to how Mockito's `@Mock` annotation can replace the behavior of a given class. This is helpful to test the application layers separately, so you don't need to bring all your real class behaviors in your Spring context together. You'll see a practical example when testing the application controllers.

Logging

In Java, you can log messages to the console just by using the `System.out` and `System.err` print streams.

```
System.out.println("Hello, standard output stream!");
```

This is considered simply good enough for a 12-factor app (https://12factor.net/logs), a popular set of best practices for writing cloud-native applications. The reason is that, eventually, some other tool will collect them from the standard outputs at the system level and aggregate them in an external framework.

Therefore, we'll write our logs to the standard and the error output. But that doesn't mean that you must stick to the plain, ugly `System.out` variants in Java.

Most professional Java apps use a logger implementation such as LogBack. And, given that there are multiple logging frameworks for Java, it's even better to choose a generic abstraction such as SLF4J.

The good news is that Spring Boot comes with all this logging configuration already set up for you. The default implementation is LogBack, and Spring Boot's preconfigured message format is as follows:

```
2020-03-22 10:19:59.556  INFO 93532 --- [main] o.s.b.w.embedded.
tomcat.TomcatWebServer  : Tomcat started on port(s): 8080 (http) with
context path ''
```

SLF4J loggers are also supported. To use a logger, you create it via the `LoggerFactory`. The only argument it needs is a name. By default, it is common to use the factory method that takes the class itself and gets the logger name from it. See Listing 2-9.

Listing 2-9. Creating and Using a Logger with SLF4J

```java
import org.slf4j.Logger;
import org.slf4j.LoggerFactory;
class ChallengeServiceImpl {
  private static final Logger log = LoggerFactory.
getLogger(ChallengeServiceImpl.class);
  public void dummyMethod() {
    var name = "John";
```

```
    log.info("Hello, {}!", name);
  }
}
```

As you see in the example, loggers support parameter replacement via the curly-braces placeholder.

Given that this book uses Lombok, you can replace that line to create a logger in your class with a simple annotation: @Slf4j. This helps keep your code concise. By default, Lombok creates a static variable named log. See Listing 2-10.

Listing 2-10. Using a Logger with Lombok

```java
import lombok.extern.slf4j.Slf4j;
@Slf4j
class ChallengeServiceImpl {
  public void dummyMethod() {
    var name = "John";
    log.info("Hello, {}!", name);
  }
}
```

Summary and Achievements

This chapter reviewed some basic libraries and concepts that we use in the book: Spring Boot, Lombok, tests with JUnit and AssertJ, and logging. These are only a few of what you'll learn during the journey, but they were introduced separately to avoid long pauses in the main learning path. All the other topics, more related to the evolving architecture, are explained in detail as you navigate through the book pages.

Do not worry if you still feel like you have some knowledge gaps. The practical code examples in the next chapters will help you understand these concepts by providing extra context.

Chapter's Achievements:

- You reviewed the core ideas about Spring and Spring Boot.

- You understood how we'll use Lombok in the book to reduce boilerplate code.

- You learned how to use tools like JUnit, Mockito, and AssertJ to implement test-driven development and how these tools are integrated in Spring Boot.

- You reviewed some logging basics and how to use a logger with Lombok.

CHAPTER 3

A Basic Spring Boot Application

You could start writing code directly, but that, even while being pragmatic, would be far from a real case. Instead, you'll see how to define a product you want to build and split it into small chunks. This requirements-oriented approach is used throughout the book to make it more practical. In real life, you'll always have these business requirements.

The web application you build will encourage users to exercise their brains daily. To begin with, it will present users with two-digit multiplications, one every time they access the page. They will type their alias (a short name) and their guess for the result of the operation. The idea is that they should use only mental calculations. After they send the data, the web page will indicate if the guess was correct or not.

To keep user motivation as high as possible, you will use some gamification. For each correct guess, the users get points and they will see their score in a ranking so that they can compete with other people.

This is the main idea of the complete application. But you won't build it all at once. This book emulates an agile way of working in which you split requirements into *user stories,* small chunks of functionality that give value by themselves. You'll follow this methodology to keep this book as close as possible to real life since a vast majority of IT companies use agile.

Let's start simple and focus first on the multiplication solving logic. Consider the first user story here.

USER STORY 1   As a user of the application, I want to be presented with a random multiplication problem so that I can solve it using mental calculation and exercise my brain.

© Moisés Macero García and Tarun Telang 2023
M. Macero García and T. Telang, *Learn Microservices with Spring Boot 3,*
https://doi.org/10.1007/978-1-4842-9757-5_3

To make this work, you need to build a minimal skeleton of the web application. Therefore, split the user story into several subtasks:

1. Create a basic service with business logic.

2. Create a basic API to access this service (REST API).

3. Create a basic web page to ask the users to solve that calculation.

This chapter focuses on Tasks 1 and 2. After creating the skeleton of your first Spring Boot application, you'll use test-driven development to build the main logic of this component: generating multiplication challenges and verifying attempts from the users to solve those challenges. Then, you'll add the controller layer that implements the REST API. You'll learn about the advantages of this layered design.

This learning path includes some reasoning about one of the most important features in Spring Boot: autoconfiguration. You'll use the practical case to see how, for example, the application includes its own embedded web server, only because you'll add a specific dependency to this project.

Setting Up the Development Environment

To set up the development environment, the following essential tools and components must be installed and configured.

Java Development Kit 17

We use Java 17 in this book. Make sure you get at least that version of the JDK from the official downloads page (`https://jdk.java.net/17/`). Install it following the instructions for your OS.

Integrated Development Environment (IDE)

A good IDE is also convenient for developing Java code. If you have a preferred one, just use it. Otherwise, you can download the community version of IntelliJ IDEA (`https://www.jetbrains.com/idea/download/`).

HTTPie

In this book, we also use HTTPie to quickly test the web applications. It's a command-line tool that allows you to interact with an HTTP server. It is a user-friendly alternative to cURL, another popular command-line tool for working with HTTP requests. You can follow the instructions at `https://httpie.io/cli` to download it for Linux, Mac, or Windows. In addition to downloading and installing HTTPie locally, you can also try it online without any installation. By visiting `https://httpie.io/cli`, you can access a web-based interface that allows you to run HTTPie commands directly from your browser. This is excellent for learning and experimentation and to explore the tool's functionality. Let's go over how you can explicitly define the JSON and XML format when fetching and sending data using the HTTP GET and POST methods.

Working with JSON

To request JSON data with HTTPie, you can add the `Accept: application/json` header to your request.

GET Request

The following is an example of using HTTPie to make a GET request to a given URL (`https://api.example.com/resource`) with the intention of receiving a response in JSON.

```
$ http --json GET https://api.example.com/resource Accept:application/json
```

The `--json` option signals that the request should be sent with the `Content-Type: application/json` header and it sets the `Accept: application/json` header.

GET specifies the HTTP method to be used (in this case, a GET request).

The `https://api.example.com/resource` URL is the server address where the request is being sent. The `Accept:application/json` header explicitly asks the server to respond with JSON-formatted data.

POST Request

To send JSON data with HTTPie, you can use the `--json, -j` option, followed by key-value pairs. For example:

```
$ http --json POST https://api.example.com/resource key1=value1 key2=value2
```

This sends the key-value pairs as a JSON object in the body of the request.

cURL

Alternatively, if you are a cURL user, you can easily map this book's HTTP commands to cURL commands.

Using cURL   cURL (short for "Client URL") is a command-line tool used to transfer data with URLs. Here is an example of using cURL to make a simple HTTP GET request:

```
$ curl https://www.example.com
```

To make a POST request with JSON data, use this command:

```
$ curl -X POST -H "Content-Type: application/json" -d '{"key": "value"}' https://www.example.com/api
```

You can visit cURL's official website (`https://curl.se/`) to learn more about this tool.

The Skeleton Web App

It's time to write some code! Spring offers a fantastic way to build the skeleton of an application: the Spring Initializr. This web-based tool allows you to select the components and libraries you want to include in your Spring Boot project, and it generates the structure and dependency configuration into a ZIP file that you can download. With Spring Initializr, developers can generate a new Spring Boot project with just a few clicks, and the resulting project can be easily imported into their preferred

Integrated Development Environment (IDE) for further development. We'll use the Spring Initializr a few times in the book, since it saves time over creating the project from scratch, but you can also create the project yourself if you prefer that option.

Source Code: chapter03   You can find all the source code for this chapter on GitHub, in the `chapter03` repository.

See `https://github.com/Book-Microservices-v3/chapter03`.

Navigate to `https://start.spring.io/` and fill in some data, as shown in Figure 3-1.

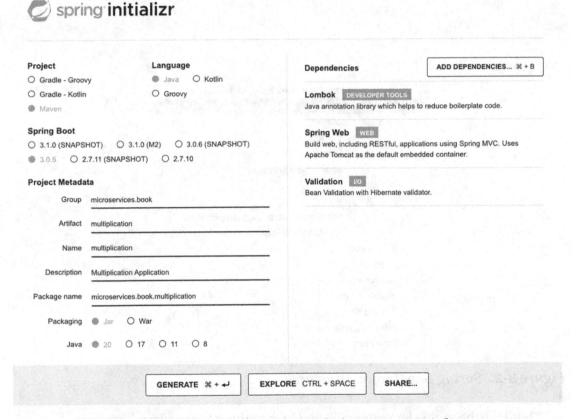

Figure 3-1. *Creating a Spring Boot project with the Spring Initializr*

All the code in this book uses Maven, Java, and the Spring Boot version 3.1.0, so let's stick to them. If that Spring Boot version is not available, you can select a more recent one. In that case, remember to change it later in the generated `pom.xml` file if you want to use the same version as in the book. You may also go ahead with other Java and Spring Boot versions, but then some of the code examples in this book might not work for you.

Give some values to the group (`microservices.book`) and the artifact
(`multiplication`). Select Java 17. Do not forget to add the Spring Web, Validation, and
Lombok dependencies from the list or search tool. You already know what Lombok is
intended for, and you'll see what the other two dependencies do in this chapter. That's all
you need for now.

Generate the project and extract the ZIP contents. The `multiplication` folder
contains everything you need to run the application, you should see the project files
as shown in the Figure 3-2. You can now open this with your favorite IDE, usually by
selecting the `pom.xml` file.

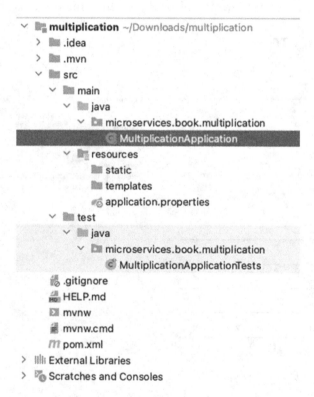

Figure 3-2. *Spring Boot project structure*

These are the main elements you'll find in the auto-generated package:

- There is Maven's `pom.xml` file, an XML file that serves as the Project
  Object Model (POM) for Maven-based Spring Boot applications. It
  defines the project's configuration, dependencies, and build settings.
  This is the main file used by Maven to build the application. When
  a developer adds a new dependency to the `pom.xml` file, Maven

automatically downloads and includes the required libraries in the project's build path. Maven also manages the project's build process, including compiling source code, running tests, and packaging the application. Inside this file, you can also find the configuration to build the application using Spring Boot's Maven plugin, which also knows how to package all its dependencies in a stand-alone `.jar` file and how to run these applications from the command line. You'll separately examine some of the dependencies added by Spring Boot.

- There is the Maven wrapper. This is a stand-alone version of Maven, so you don't need to install it to build your app. There is a `.mvn` folder and the `mvnw` executables for Windows and UNIX-based systems.

- The `HELP.md` file contains links to the Spring Boot's documentation. This file is a helpful resource for developers who are new to Spring Boot, as it provides information on how to get started with a new project and how to configure and customize the project to suit their needs.

- Assuming you'll use Git as a version control system, the included `.gitignore` has some predefined exclusions, so you don't commit the compiled classes or any IDE-generated files to the repository. The file contains a list of patterns that Git uses to match files and directories that should be ignored. When Git tracks changes in a project's source code, it checks the `.gitignore` file to determine which files and directories should be excluded from version control. This can include log files, temporary files, compiled code, and other files that are not essential to the project's source code.

- The `src` folder follows the standard Maven structure that divides the code into the subfolders, `main` and `test`. Both folders contain their respective `java` and `resources` children. In this case, there is a source folder for the main code and tests, and a resource folder for the main code.

  - There is a class created by default in the main sources, called `MultiplicationApplication`. It's already annotated with `@SpringBootApplication` and contains the `main` method that boots up the application. This is the standard way of defining the main class for a

Spring Boot application, as detailed in the reference documentation (`https://docs.spring.io/spring-boot/docs/current/reference/html/using.html#using.using-the-springbootapplication-annotation`). You'll learn about this class later.

– Within the `resources` folder are two empty subfolders: `static` and `templates`. You can safely delete them since they're intended to include static resources and HTML templates, which you won't use in this book.

– The `application.properties` file is where you can configure your Spring Boot application. It can include configuration like server port, database connection information, and logging settings. You'll add some configuration parameters later.

Now that you understand the different pieces of this skeleton, let's try to make it walk. To run this app, you can either use your IDE interface or run this command from the project's root folder:

```
multiplication $ ./mvnw spring-boot:run
```

Running Commands from the Terminal   In this book, we use the $ character to represent the command prompt. Everything after that character is the command itself. Sometimes, it's important to highlight that you must run the command within a given folder in the workspace. In that case, you'll find the folder name before the $ character (e.g., `multiplication $`). Of course, the specific location of your workspace may be different.

Note also that some commands may vary depending on whether you're using a UNIX-based operating system (like Linux or Mac) or Windows. All the commands shown in this book use a UNIX-based system version.

When you run that command, you're using the Maven wrapper included in the project's main folder (`mvnw`) with the goal (what's next to the Maven executable) `spring-boot:run`. This goal is provided by Spring Boot's Maven plugin, included also in the `pom.xml` file generated by the Initializr web page. The Spring Boot application should start successfully. The last line in the logs should look like this:

```
INFO 4139 --- [main] m.b.m.MultiplicationApplication: Started
MultiplicationApplication in 6.599 seconds (JVM running for 6.912)
```

Great! You have your first Spring Boot app running without writing a single line of code! However, there isn't much you can do with it yet. What's this application doing? You'll figure that out soon.

Spring Boot Autoconfiguration

In the logs of the skeleton app, you can also find this log line:

```
INFO 74642 --- [          main] o.s.b.w.embedded.tomcat.TomcatWebServer  :
Tomcat started on port(s): 8080 (http) with context
```

What you get when you add the web dependency is an independently deployable web application that uses Tomcat, thanks to the autoconfiguration feature in Spring.

As introduced in the previous chapter, Spring Boot sets up libraries and the default configuration automatically. This saves you a lot of time when you rely on all these defaults. One of those conventions is to add a ready-to-use Tomcat server when you add the web starter to your project.

To learn more about Spring Boot autoconfiguration, let's go through how this specific case works, step-by-step—Figure 3-3 can some useful visual help.

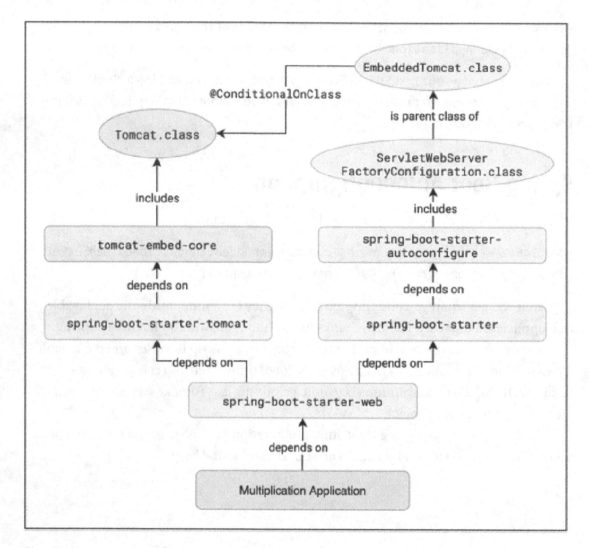

Figure 3-3. *Autoconfiguration example: embedded Tomcat*

The Spring Boot application you generated automatically has a main class annotated with @SpringBootApplication. This is a *shortcut* annotation because it groups several others, among them @EnableAutoConfiguration. As its name suggests, with this one you're enabling the autoconfiguration feature. Therefore, Spring activates this smart mechanism and finds and processes classes annotated with the @Configuration annotation, from your own code but also from your dependencies.

This project includes the spring-boot-starter-web dependency. This is one of the main Spring Boot components, which has all the tooling to build a web application, including the embedded Tomcat server. Inside this artifact's dependencies, the Spring

Boot developers added another starter, called `spring-boot-starter-tomcat`. See Listing 3-1 or the online sources (`https://github.com/spring-projects/spring-boot/blob/main/spring-boot-project/spring-boot-starters/spring-boot-starter-web/build.gradle`).

Listing 3-1. Web Starter Dependencies

```
plugins {
    id "org.springframework.boot.starter"
}
description = "Starter for building web, including RESTful, applications
using Spring MVC. Uses Tomcat as the default embedded container"
dependencies {
    api(project(":spring-boot-project:spring-boot-starters:spring-boot-
    starter"))
    api(project(":spring-boot-project:spring-boot-starters:spring-boot-
    starter-json"))
    api(project(":spring-boot-project:spring-boot-starters:spring-boot-
    starter-tomcat"))
    api("org.springframework:spring-web")
    api("org.springframework:spring-webmvc")
}
```

As you can see, Spring Boot artifacts use Gradle (since version 2.3), but you don't need to know the specific syntax to understand what the dependencies are. If you now check the dependencies of the `spring-boot-starter-tomcat` artifact (in Listing 3-2 or the online sources at `https://github.com/spring-projects/spring-boot/blob/main/spring-boot-project/spring-boot-starters/spring-boot-starter-tomcat/build.gradle`), you can see that it contains a library that doesn't belong to the Spring family, `tomcat-embed-core`. This is an Apache library that you can use to start a Tomcat embedded server. Its main logic is included in a class named `Tomcat`.

Listing 3-2. Tomcat Starter Dependencies

```
plugins {
    id "org.springframework.boot.starter"
}
```

```
description = "Starter for using Tomcat as the embedded servlet container.
Default servlet container starter used by spring-boot-starter-web"
dependencies {
    api("jakarta.annotation:jakarta.annotation-api")
    api("org.apache.tomcat.embed:tomcat-embed-core") {
        exclude group: "org.apache.tomcat", module: "tomcat-
        annotations-api"
    }
    api("org.glassfish:jakarta.el")
    api("org.apache.tomcat.embed:tomcat-embed-websocket") {
        exclude group: "org.apache.tomcat", module: "tomcat-
        annotations-api"
    }
}
```

Coming back to the hierarchy of dependencies, the `spring-boot-starter-web` also depends on `spring-boot-starter` (see Listing 3-1 and Figure 3-3 for some contextual help). That's the *core* Spring Boot starter, which includes the artifact `spring-boot-autoconfigure` (see Listing 3-3 or the online sources, at `https://github.com/spring-projects/spring-boot/blob/main/spring-boot-project/spring-boot-starters/spring-boot-starter/build.gradle`). That Spring Boot artifact has a whole set of classes annotated with `@Configuration`, which are responsible for a big part of the whole Spring Boot magic. There classes are intended to configure web servers, message brokers, error handlers, databases, and many more.

Listing 3-3. Spring Boot's Main Starter

```
plugins {
    id "org.springframework.boot.starter"
}
description = "Core starter, including auto-configuration support, logging
and YAML"
dependencies {
    api(project(":spring-boot-project:spring-boot"))
    api(project(":spring-boot-project:spring-boot-autoconfigure"))
    api(project(":spring-boot-project:spring-boot-starters:spring-boot-
    starter-logging"))
```

```
api("jakarta.annotation:jakarta.annotation-api")
api("org.springframework:spring-core")
api("org.yaml:snakeyaml")
}
```

For this project, the relevant class that takes care of the embedded Tomcat server autoconfiguration is ServletWebServerFactoryConfiguration. Listing 3-4 shows its most relevant code fragment. The complete source code is available online (https://github.com/spring-projects/spring-boot/blob/main/spring-boot-project/spring-boot-autoconfigure/src/main/java/org/springframework/boot/autoconfigure/web/servlet/ServletWebServerFactoryConfiguration.java).

Listing 3-4. ServletWebServerFactoryConfiguration Fragment

```
@Configuration(proxyBeanMethods = false)
class ServletWebServerFactoryConfiguration {
    @Configuration(proxyBeanMethods = false)
    @ConditionalOnClass({ Servlet.class, Tomcat.class, UpgradeProtocol.
    class })
    @ConditionalOnMissingBean(value = ServletWebServerFactory.class,
    search = SearchStrategy.CURRENT)
    static class EmbeddedTomcat {
        @Bean
        TomcatServletWebServerFactory tomcatServletWebServerFactory(
                ObjectProvider<TomcatConnectorCustomizer>
                connectorCustomizers,
                ObjectProvider<TomcatContextCustomizer> contextCustomizers,
                ObjectProvider<TomcatProtocolHandlerCustomizer<?>>
                protocolHandlerCustomizers) {
            TomcatServletWebServerFactory factory = new
            TomcatServletWebServerFactory();
            factory.getTomcatConnectorCustomizers()
                    .addAll(connectorCustomizers.orderedStream().
                     collect(Collectors.toList()));
            factory.getTomcatContextCustomizers()
                    .addAll(contextCustomizers.orderedStream().
                     collect(Collectors.toList()));
```

```
        factory.getTomcatProtocolHandlerCustomizers()
                .addAll(protocolHandlerCustomizers.orderedStream().
                collect(Collectors.toList()));
        return factory;
    }
  }
  // ...
}
```

This class defines some inner classes, one of them being `EmbeddedTomcat`. As you can see, that one is annotated with this annotation:

`@ConditionalOnClass({ Servlet.class, Tomcat.class, UpgradeProtocol.class })`

Spring processes the `@ConditionalOnClass` annotation, which is used to load beans in the context if the linked class can be found in the classpath. In this case, the condition matches, since you already saw how the `Tomcat` class got into the classpath via the starter hierarchy. Therefore, Spring loads the bean declared in `EmbeddedTomcat`, which turns out to be a `TomcatServletWebServerFactory`.

That factory is contained inside Spring Boot's core artifact (`spring-boot`, a dependency included in `spring-boot-starter`). It sets up a Tomcat embedded server with some default configuration. This is where the logic to create an embedded web server finally lives.

Once more, just to recap, the `spring-boot-starter-web` simplifies dependency management and includes everything needed for developing web applications and RESTful web services, including the embedded Tomcat server, validations, and the Jackson library to serialize-deserialize Java objects to JSON and logging. The `spring-boot-starter` is a core starter in Spring Boot and serves as a parent starter for dependencies and autoconfiguration. The `spring-boot-starter-autoconfigure` includes all the autoconfiguration classes responsible for configuring different parts of the Spring application based on certain conditions, such as the presence or absence of certain Java classes in the classpath or beans in the context. The `spring-boot-starter-web` includes the `spring-boot-starter-tomcat` dependency, which provides the embedded Tomcat servlet container. Embedded Tomcat is the trimmed-down version of Tomcat optimized for programmatic use, consisting of the classes to start and manage a Tomcat instance within your application. The `ServletWebServerFactoryConfiguration` class is part of the autoconfiguration that's responsible for setting up the embedded servlet web server, such as Tomcat (`https://tomcat.apache.org/`), Jetty (`https://eclipse.dev/jetty/`), or Undertow (`https://undertow.io/`). This configuration class plays a critical role in defining and customizing the behavior of the embedded web server. They often use conditional annotations like `@ConditionalOnClass`. The `@ConditionalOnClass` annotation is used to define a conditional situation, which allows you to specify that a particular bean should be created only if a specific class is present in the classpath. The `tomcat-embed-core` provides the core functionality required to embed Tomcat within a Java application. The Spring scans all the classes and, given that the condition stated in the `EmbeddedTomcat` is fulfilled (the Tomcat library is an included dependency), it loads a `TomcatServletWebServerFactory` bean in the context. This `factoryclass` starts an embedded Tomcat server with the default configuration, exposing an HTTP interface on the port 8080.

As you can imagine, this same mechanism applies to many other libraries for databases, web servers, message brokers, cloud-native patterns, security, and so on. In Spring Boot, you can find multiple starters that you can add as dependencies. When you do that, the autoconfiguration mechanism comes into play, and you get additional behavior out of the box. Many configuration classes are conditional on the presence of other classes like the ones analyzed here, but there are other condition types, for example, parameter values in the `application.properties` file.

Autoconfiguration is a key concept in Spring Boot. Once you understand it, the features that many developers consider magic are no longer a secret for you. This chapter navigated through the details because it's important that you know this mechanism so you can configure it according to your needs and avoid getting a lot of behavior that you don't want or simply don't need. As a good practice, carefully read the documentation of the Spring Boot modules you're using and familiarize yourself with the configuration options they allow.

Don't worry if you didn't understand this concept fully; we come back to the autoconfiguration mechanism a few times in this book. The reason is that you'll add extra features to your application, and, for that, you need to add extra dependencies to your project and analyze the new behavior they introduce.

Three-Tier, Three-Layer Architecture

The next step in this practical journey is designing how to structure the application and model the business logic in different classes.

A multitier architecture will provide the application with a more production-ready look. Most of the real-world applications follow this architecture pattern. Among web applications, the *three-tier design* is the most popular one and widely extended. These three tiers are as follows:

- *Client tier*: This tier is responsible for the user interface. Typically, this is called the *frontend*.

- *Application tier*: This contains all the business logic together with the interfaces to interact with it and the data interfaces for persistence. This maps to is called the *backend*.

- *Data store tier*: It's the database, file system, and so on, that persists the application's data.

This book mainly focuses on the application tier, although you'll use the other two as well. If you zoom in, the application tier is commonly designed using three layers:

- *Business layer*: This includes the classes that model the domain and the business specifics. It's where the intelligence of the application resides. Sometimes this layer is divided into two parts: domains (entities) and applications (services) providing business logic.

- *Presentation layer*: In this case, it will be represented by the `Controller` classes, which provide the functionality to the web client. The REST API implementation resides here.

- *Data layer*: This layer is responsible for persisting the entities in a data storage, usually a database. It can typically include *data access object* (DAO) classes, which work with objects that map directly to rows in a database, or *repository* classes, which are domain-centric, so they may need to translate from domain representations to the database structure.

The goal is now to apply this pattern to the Multiplication web application, as shown in Figure 3-4.

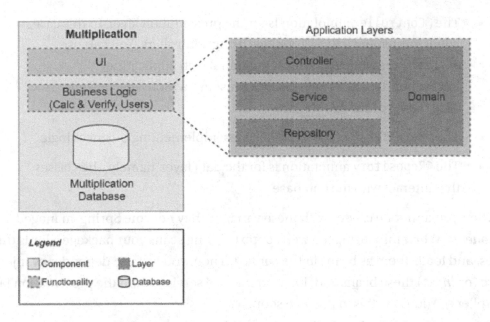

Figure 3-4. *Three-tier, three-layer architecture applied to the Spring Boot project*

The advantages of using this software architecture are all related to achieving loose coupling.

- All layers are interchangeable (such as, for instance, changing the NoSQL database for a SQL database or file storage solution or changing from a REST API to any other interface). This is a key asset because it makes it easier to evolve the codebase. Additionally, you can replace complete layers by test mocks, which keeps your tests simple, as you'll see later in this chapter.

- The domain part is isolated and independent of everything else. It's not mixed with interface or database specifics.

- There is a clear separation of responsibilities: a class to handle database storage of the objects, a separate class for the REST API implementation, and another class for the business logic.

Spring is an excellent option to build this type of architecture, with many out-of-the-box features that will help you easily create a production-ready three-tier application. It provides three *stereotype* annotations for your classes that map to each of this design's layers, so you can use them to implement your architecture.

- The @Controller annotation is for the presentation layer. In this case, you'll implement a REST interface using controllers. You can use @Controller while building a traditional web application, but for building RESTful APIs, you must use a more specialized @RestController annotation.

- The @Service annotation is for classes implementing business logic.

- The @Repository annotation is for the data layer, namely, the classes that interact with the database.

When you annotate classes with these variants, they become Spring-managed *components*. When initializing the web context, Spring scans your packages, finds these classes, and loads them as beans in the context. Then, you can use dependency injection to wire (or *inject*) these beans and, for example, use services from the presentation layer (controllers). You'll see this in practice soon.

Modeling the Domain

Let's start by modeling the business domain because this will help you structure the project.

Domain Definition and Domain-Driven Design

This first web application takes care of generating multiplication challenges and verifying the subsequent attempts from the users. Let's define these three business entities.

- *Challenge*: Contains the two factors of a multiplication challenge.

- *User*: Identifies the person who will try to solve a Challenge.

- *Challenge Attempt*: Represents the attempt from a User to solve the operation from a Challenge.

You can model these domain objects and their relationship as shown in Figure 3-5.

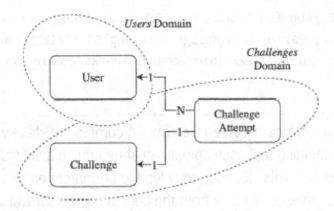

Figure 3-5. *Business model*

The relationships between these objects are as follows:

- Users and Challenges are independent entities. They don't keep any references.

- *Challenge Attempts* are always for a given User and a given Challenge. Conceptually, there could be many attempts for the same Challenge, given that there is a limited number of generated Challenges. Also, the same User may create many attempts since they can use the web application as many times as they want.

In Figure 3-5, you can also see how these three objects are split into two different domains: Users and Challenges. Finding domain boundaries (also known as bounded contexts; see `https://martinfowler.com/bliki/BoundedContext.html`) and defining relationships between your objects are essential tasks of designing software. This design approach based on domains is called *domain-driven design* (DDD). It helps you build an architecture that is modular, scalable, and loosely coupled. In this example, Users and Challenges are completely different concepts. Challenges, and their attempts, are related to Users, but they together have enough relevance to belong to their own domain.

To make DDD clearer, you can think of an evolved version of this small system where other domains relate to Users or Challenges. For instance, you could introduce social network features by creating the domain *Friends* and modeling relationships and interactions between users. If you mixed up the domains Users and Challenges, this evolution would be much harder to accomplish since the new domain has nothing to do with challenges.

For extra reading about DDD, you can get Eric Evans' book (https://www.oreilly.com/library/view/domain-driven-design-tackling/0321125215/) or download the free InfoQ minibook (https://www.infoq.com/minibooks/domain-driven-design-quickly/).

Microservices and Domain-Driven Design   A common mistake when designing microservices is thinking that each domain must be immediately split into a different microservice. This, however, may lead to premature optimization and an exponential complexity increase from the beginning of a software project. Deciding whether a use case should be a microservice requires a careful analysis of the specific context and needs of the system. It involves considering factors like domain boundaries, independence, reusability, complexity, data cohesion, and team organization.

You'll learn more about microservices and the monolith-first approach later. For now, the important takeaway is that modeling domains is a crucial task, but splitting domains doesn't require splitting the code into microservices. In this first application, you include both domains together, but not mixed up. You use a simple strategy for the split: root-level packages.

Domain Classes

It's time to create the Challenge, ChallengeAttempt, and User classes. First, you divide the root package (microservices.book.multiplication) in two—Users and Challenges—following the domains that you identified for the Multiplication application. Then, you create three empty classes with the chosen names in these two packages. See Listing 3-5.

Listing 3-5. Splitting Domains by Creating Different Root Packages

```
+- microservices.book.multiplication.user
|  \- User.java
+- microservices.book.multiplication.challenge
|  \- Challenge.java
|  \- ChallengeAttempt.java
```

Since you added Lombok as a dependency when you created the skeleton app, you can use it to keep the domain classes very small, as described in the previous chapter.

The Challenge class holds both factors of the multiplication. You add getters, a constructor with all fields, and the toString(), equals(), and hashCode() methods. See Listing 3-6.

Listing 3-6. The Challenge Class

```
package microservices.book.multiplication.challenge;

import lombok.*;
/**
 * This class represents a Challenge to solve a Multiplication (a * b).
 */
@Getter
@ToString
@EqualsAndHashCode
@AllArgsConstructor
public class Challenge {
    private int factorA;
    private int factorB;
}
```

The User class has the same Lombok annotations, an identifier for the user, and a friendly alias (e.g., the user's first name). See Listing 3-7.

Listing 3-7. The User Class

```
package microservices.book.multiplication.user;

import lombok.*;
/**
 * Stores information to identify the user.
 */
@Getter
@ToString
@EqualsAndHashCode
@AllArgsConstructor
```

```java
public class User {
    private Long id;
    private String alias;
}
```

Attempts also have an ID, the value input by the user (resultAttempt), and whether it's correct or not. See Listing 3-8. You link it to the user via userId. Note that you also have here both challenge factors. You do this to avoid having a reference to a challenge because you can simply generate new challenges "on the fly" and copy them here to keep your data structures simple. Therefore, as you can see, you have multiple options to implement the business model depicted in Figure 3-5. To model the relationship with users, you use a reference; to model challenges, you embed the data inside the attempt. You will analyze this decision in more detail in Chapter 5, when you learn about data persistence.

Listing 3-8. The ChallengeAttempt Class

```java
package microservices.book.multiplication.challenge;

import lombok.*;
import microservices.book.multiplication.user.User;
/**
 * Identifies the attempt from a {@link User} to solve a challenge.
 */
@Getter
@ToString
@EqualsAndHashCode
@AllArgsConstructor
public class ChallengeAttempt {
    private Long id;
    private Long userId;
    private int factorA;
    private int factorB;
    private int resultAttempt;
    private boolean correct;
}
```

Business Logic

Once you have defined the domain model, it's time to think about the other part of the business logic: the *application services*.

What You Need

Having looked at the requirements, you need the following:

- A way of generating a mid-complexity multiplication problem. Let's make all factors between 11 and 99.

- Some functionality to check whether an attempt is correct or not.

Random Challenges

Let's put test-driven development into practice for the business logic. First, you write a basic interface to generate random challenges. See Listing 3-9.

Listing 3-9. The ChallengeGeneratorService Interface

```
package microservices.book.multiplication.challenge;

public interface ChallengeGeneratorService {
    /**
     * @return a randomly generated challenge with factors between
     11 and 99
     */
    Challenge randomChallenge();
}
```

You place this interface in the Challenge package. Now, you write an empty implementation of this interface that wraps Java's Random class. See Listing 3-10. Besides the no-args constructor, you make the class testable by having a second constructor that accepts the random object.

Listing 3-10. An Empty Implementation of the ChallengeGeneratorService Interface

```java
package microservices.book.multiplication.challenge;

import org.springframework.stereotype.Service;

import java.util.Random;
@Service
public class ChallengeGeneratorServiceImpl implements
ChallengeGeneratorService {
    private final Random random;
    ChallengeGeneratorServiceImpl() {
        this.random = new Random();
    }
    protected ChallengeGeneratorServiceImpl(final Random random) {
        this.random = random;
    }
    @Override
    public Challenge randomChallenge() {
        return null;
    }
}
```

To instruct Spring to load this service implementation in the context, you annotate the class with @Service. You can later inject this service into other layers by using the interface and not the implementation. This way, you keep loose coupling since you could swap the implementation without needing to change anything in other layers. You'll put dependency injection into practice soon. For now, focus on TDD and leave the randomChallenge() implementation non-functional (empty).

The next step is to write a test for this. You create a class in the same package but this time inside the test source folder. See Listing 3-11.

Listing 3-11. Creating the Unit Test Before the Real Implementation

```java
package microservices.book.multiplication.challenge;

import org.junit.jupiter.api.BeforeEach;
import org.junit.jupiter.api.Test;
```

```
import org.junit.jupiter.api.extension.ExtendWith;
import org.mockito.Spy;
import org.mockito.junit.jupiter.MockitoExtension;

import java.util.Random;

import static org.assertj.core.api.BDDAssertions.then;
import static org.mockito.BDDMockito.given;
@ExtendWith(MockitoExtension.class)
public class ChallengeGeneratorServiceTest {
    private ChallengeGeneratorService challengeGeneratorService;
    @Spy
    private Random random;
    @BeforeEach
    public void setUp() {
        challengeGeneratorService = new ChallengeGeneratorServiceImp
        l(random);
    }
    @Test
    public void generateRandomFactorIsBetweenExpectedLimits() {
        // 89 is max - min range
        given(random.nextInt(89)).willReturn(20, 30);
        // when we generate a challenge
        Challenge challenge = challengeGeneratorService.randomChallenge();
        // then the challenge contains factors as expected
        then(challenge).isEqualTo(new Challenge(31, 41));
    }
}
```

In the previous chapter, you learned how you can use Mockito to replace the behavior of a given class with the @Mock annotation and the MockitoExtension class for JUnit 5. In this test, you need to replace the behavior of an object, not a class. You can use @Spy to stub an object. The Mockito extension will help create a Random instance using the empty constructor and stubbing it for you to override the behavior. This is the simplest way to get the test to work, since the basic Java classes implementing random generators do not work on interfaces (which you could then simply *mock* instead of *spy*).

Normally, you initialize what you need for all the tests in a method annotated with @BeforeEach so this happens before each test starts. Here, you construct the service implementation passing this stub object.

The only test method sets up the preconditions with given() following a BDD style. The way to generate random numbers between 11 and 99 is to get a random number between 0 and 89 and add 11 to it. Therefore, you know that the random object should be called with 89 to generate numbers in the range 11, 100, so you override that call to return 20 when it's called the first time and 30 the second time. Then, when you call randomChallenge(), you expect it to get 20 and 30 as random numbers from Random (the stubbed object) and therefore return a Challenge object with some random numbers, say 31 and 41.

So, you made a test that obviously fails when you run it. Let's try it; you can use your IDE or a Maven command from the project's root folder.

```
multiplication$ ./mvnw test
```

As expected, the test will fail. See the result in Listing 3-12.

Listing 3-12. Error Output After Running the Test for the First Time

```
Expecting:
 <null>
to be equal to:
 <Challenge(factorA=20, factorB=30)>
but was not.
Expected :Challenge(factorA=20, factorB=30)
Actual   :null
```

Now, you only need to make the test pass. In this case, the solution is quite simple, and you needed to figure it out while implementing the test. Later, you'll see more valuable cases of TDD, but this one helps to get started with this way of working. See Listing 3-13.

Listing 3-13. Implementing a Valid Logic to Generate Challenges

```
@Service
public class ChallengeGeneratorServiceImpl implements
ChallengeGeneratorService {
```

```
private final static int MINIMUM_FACTOR = 11;
private final static int MAXIMUM_FACTOR = 100;
// ...
private int next() {
    return random.nextInt(MAXIMUM_FACTOR - MINIMUM_FACTOR) +
    MINIMUM_FACTOR;
}
@Override
public Challenge randomChallenge() {
    return new Challenge(next(), next());
}
}
```

Now, run the test again. It passes this time:

```
[INFO] Tests run: 1, Failures: 0, Errors: 0, Skipped: 0
```

Test-driven development is just this simple. First, you design the tests, which will fail in the beginning. Then, you implement your logic to make them pass. In real life, you get the most of it when you get help to build the test cases from the people who define the requirements. You can write better tests and, therefore, a better implementation of what you really want to build.

Attempt Verification

To cover the second part of the business requirements, you implement an interface to verify attempts from users. See Listing 3-14.

Listing 3-14. The ChallengeService Interface

```
package microservices.book.multiplication.challenge;

public interface ChallengeService {
    /**
     * Verifies if an attempt coming from the presentation layer is
     correct or not.
     *
     * @return the resulting ChallengeAttempt object
```

```
    */
   ChallengeAttempt verifyAttempt(ChallengeAttemptDTO resultAttempt);
}
```

As you can see, the code is passing a `ChallengeAttemptDTO` object to the `verifyAttempt` method. This class doesn't exist yet. *Data transfer objects* (DTOs) carry data between different parts of the system. In this case, you use a DTO to model the data needed from the presentation layer to create an attempt. See Listing 3-15. An attempt from the user doesn't have the field `correct` and does not need to know about the user's ID. You can also use DTOs to validate data, as you'll see when you build the controllers.

Listing 3-15. The ChallengeAttemptDTO Class

```
package microservices.book.multiplication.challenge;

import lombok.Value;
/**
 * Attempt coming from the user
 */
@Value
public class ChallengeAttemptDTO {
    int factorA, factorB;
    String userAlias;
    int guess;
}
```

Continuing with a TDD approach, you create do-nothing logic in the `ChallengeServiceImpl` interface implementation. This time you use Lombok's `@Value`, a shortcut annotation to create an immutable class with an `all-args-constructor` and `toString`, `equals`, and `hashCode` methods. It'll also set your fields to be `private final`; that's why you didn't need to add that. See Listing 3-16.

Listing 3-16. An Empty ChallengeService Interface Implementation

```
package microservices.book.multiplication.challenge;

import org.springframework.stereotype.Service;

@Service
```

```
public class ChallengeServiceImpl implements ChallengeService {
    @Override
    public ChallengeAttempt verifyAttempt(ChallengeAttemptDTO attemptDTO) {
        return null;
    }
}
```

And now, you write a unit test for this class, verifying that it works for both correct and wrong attempts. See Listing 3-17.

Listing 3-17. Writing the Test to Verify Challenge Attempts

```
package microservices.book.multiplication.challenge;

import org.junit.jupiter.api.BeforeEach;
import org.junit.jupiter.api.Test;

import static org.assertj.core.api.BDDAssertions.then;

public class ChallengeServiceTest {
    private ChallengeService challengeService;
    @BeforeEach
    public void setUp() {
        challengeService = new ChallengeServiceImpl();
    }
    @Test
    public void checkCorrectAttemptTest() {
        // given
        ChallengeAttemptDTO attemptDTO =
                new ChallengeAttemptDTO(50, 60, "john_doe", 3000);
        // when
        ChallengeAttempt resultAttempt =
                challengeService.verifyAttempt(attemptDTO);
        // then
        then(resultAttempt.isCorrect()).isTrue();
    }
```

```java
    @Test
    public void checkWrongAttemptTest() {
        // given
        ChallengeAttemptDTO attemptDTO =
                new ChallengeAttemptDTO(50, 60, "john_doe", 5000);
        // when
        ChallengeAttempt resultAttempt =
                challengeService.verifyAttempt(attemptDTO);
        // then
        then(resultAttempt.isCorrect()).isFalse();
    }
}
```

The result of multiplying 50 and 60 is 3,000, so the first test case's assertion expects the correct field to be true, whereas the second test expects false for a wrong guess (5,000).

Let's now execute the tests. You can use your IDE or a Maven command and specify the name of the test to run.

```
multiplication$ ./mvnw -Dtest=ChallengeServiceTest test
```

The value after -Dtest= specifies the name of the test class that you want to run. In this case, the test class is ChallengeServiceTest. The test at the end of the command is to actually execute the tests. You'll see output similar to this:

```
[INFO] Results:
[INFO]
[ERROR] Errors:
[ERROR]    ChallengeServiceTest.checkCorrectAttemptTest:28 NullPointer
[ERROR]    ChallengeServiceTest.checkWrongAttemptTest:42 NullPointer
[INFO]
[ERROR] Tests run: 2, Failures: 0, Errors: 2, Skipped: 0
```

As foreseen, both tests will throw a null pointer exception for now because your verifyAttempt method in the ChallengeServiceImpl class is returning null.

Go back to the service implementation and make it work. See Listing 3-18.

Listing 3-18. Implementing the Logic to Verify Attempts

```
@Override
public ChallengeAttempt verifyAttempt(ChallengeAttemptDTO attemptDTO) {
    // Check if the attempt is correct
    boolean isCorrect = attemptDTO.getGuess() ==
            attemptDTO.getFactorA() * attemptDTO.getFactorB();
    // We don't use identifiers for now
    User user = new User(null, attemptDTO.getUserAlias());
    // Builds the domain object. Null id for now.
    ChallengeAttempt checkedAttempt = new ChallengeAttempt(null,
            user,
            attemptDTO.getFactorA(),
            attemptDTO.getFactorB(),
            attemptDTO.getGuess(),
            isCorrect
    );
    return checkedAttempt;
}
```

You need to create a user or find an existing one, connect that user to the new attempt, and store it in a database. We keep it simple for now. Later, this implementation should take care of more tasks.

Run the test again to verify that it's passing:

```
[INFO] Tests run: 2, Failures: 0, Errors: 0, Skipped: 0, Time
elapsed: 0.083 s - in microservices.book.multiplication.challenge.
ChallengeServiceTest
```

Again, you used TDD successfully to build the logic to verify the challenge attempts.

The Users domain doesn't need any business logic within the scope of the first user story, so let's move to the next layer.

Presentation Layer

This section covers the presentation layer.

REST

Instead of building HTML from the server, we decided to approach the presentation layer as it's normally done in real software projects: with an API layer in between. By doing so, not only can you expose your functionality to other backend services, but you can also keep the backend and the frontend completely isolated. This way, you can start, for example, with a simple HTML page and plain JavaScript and later move to a full frontend framework without changing the backend code.

Among all the possible API alternatives, the most popular is REpresentational State Transfer (REST). It's normally built on top of HTTP, so it uses HTTP verbs to perform the API operations: GET, POST, PUT, DELETE, and so on. You'll build RESTful web services in this book, which are simply web services that conform to the REST architectural style. Therefore, you'll follow some conventions for URLs and HTTP verbs that have become the *de facto* standard. See Table 3-1.

***Table 3-1.**   Conventions for the REST APIs*

HTTP Verb	Operation on Collection, e.g., /challenges	Operation on Item, e.g., challenges/3
GET	Gets the full list of items	Gets the item
POST	Creates a new item	Not applicable
PUT	Not applicable	Updates the item
DELETE	Deletes the full collection	Deletes the item

There are a few different styles for writing REST APIs. Table 3-1 shows the most basic operations with some convention choices made for this book. There are also multiple aspects of the contents transferred via the API: pagination, null handling, format (e.g., JSON), security, versioning, and so on. If you are curious about how detailed these conventions can become for a real organization, you can look at Zalando's API Guidelines (https://opensource.zalando.com/restful-api-guidelines/).

REST APIs with Spring Boot

Building a REST API with Spring is a simple task. There is a specialization of the @Controller stereotype intended for building REST controllers called, unsurprisingly, @RestController.

To model resources and mappings for different HTTP verbs, you use the @RequestMapping annotation. It applies to the class and method levels, so you can simply build your API contexts. To simplify it, Spring provides variants like @PostMapping, @GetMapping, and so on, so you don't need to specify the HTTP verb.

Whenever you want to pass the body of a request to the method, you use the @RequestBody annotation. If you use a custom class, Spring Boot will try to deserialize it, using the type passed to the method. Spring Boot uses a JSON serialization format by default, although it also supports other formats when specified via the Accept HTTP header. In the web applications, you'll use all the Spring Boot defaults.

You can also customize the API with request parameters and read values from the request path. Consider this request as an example:

```
GET http://ourhost.com/challenges/5?factorA=40
```

These are its different parts:

- GET is the HTTP verb.
- http://ourhost.com/ is the host where the web server is running. In this example, the application serves from the *root context*, /.
- /challenges/ is an API context created by the application, to provide functionalities around this domain.
- /5 is called a *path variable*. In this case, it represents the Challenge object with identifier 5.
- factorA=40 is a request parameter and its value.

To process this request, you could create a controller with 5 as a path variable called challengeId and 40 as a request parameter called factorA. See Listing 3-19.

Listing 3-19. An Example of Using Annotations to Map REST API URLs

```
@RestController
@RequestMapping("/challenges")
class ChallengeAttemptController {
    @GetMapping("/{challengeId}")
    public Challenge getChallengeWithParam(@PathVariable("challengeId")
    Long challengeId,

                                           @RequestParam("factorA") int
                                           factorA) {...}
}
```

The offered functionality doesn't stop there. You can also validate the requests given that REST controllers integrate with the `jakarta.validation` API. This means you can annotate the classes used during deserialization to avoid empty values or force numbers to be within a given range when you get requests from the client, just as examples.

Don't worry about the number of new concepts introduced. You learn about them, with practical examples, over the following sections.

Designing the APIs

You can use the requirements to design the functionalities you need to expose in the REST API.

- An interface to get a random, medium complexity multiplication

- An endpoint to send a guess for a given multiplication from a given user's alias

These are a read operation for challenges and an action to create attempts. Keeping in mind that multiplication challenges and attempts are different resources, you can split the API in two and assign the corresponding verbs to these actions:

- `GET /challenges/random` will return a randomly generated challenge.

- `POST /attempts/` will be the endpoint to send an attempt to solve a challenge.

Both resources belong to the `Challenges` domain. Eventually, you will also need a `/users` mapping to perform operations with the users, but we're leaving that for later since you don't need it to complete the first requirements (user story).

API-First Approach   It's normally a good practice to define and discuss the API contract in your organization before implementing it. You should include the endpoints, HTTP verbs, allowed parameters, and request and response body examples. This way, other developers and clients can verify if the exposed functionality is what they need and give you feedback before you waste time implementing the wrong solution. This strategy is known as *API First*, and there are industry standards to write the API specifications, like OpenAPI.

If you want to know more about *API First* and *OpenAPI*, see `https://swagger.io/resources/articles/adopting-an-api-first-approach/`, from Swagger, the original creators of the specification.

Your First Controller

Now you'll create a controller that generates a random challenge. You already have that operation in the service layer, so you only need to use that method from the controller. That's what you should do in the presentation layer: keep it isolated from any business logic. You'll use it only to model the API and validate the data. See Listing 3-20.

Listing 3-20. The ChallengeController Class

```
package microservices.book.multiplication.challenge;

import lombok.RequiredArgsConstructor;
import lombok.extern.slf4j.Slf4j;
import org.springframework.web.bind.annotation.*;
/**
 * This class implements a REST API to get random challenges
 */
@Slf4j
@RequiredArgsConstructor
```

```
@RestController
@RequestMapping("/challenges")
class ChallengeController {
    private final ChallengeGeneratorService challengeGeneratorService;
    @GetMapping("/random")
    Challenge getRandomChallenge() {
        Challenge challenge = challengeGeneratorService.randomChallenge();
        log.info("Generating a random challenge: {}", challenge);
        return challenge;
    }
}
```

The `@RestController` annotation tells Spring that this is specialized component modeling a REST controller. It's a combination of `@Controller` and `@ResponseBody`, which instructs Spring to put the result of this method as the HTTP response body. As a default in Spring Boot and if not instructed otherwise, the response will be serialized as JSON and included in the response body.

Note also that a `@RequestMapping("/challenges")` was added at the class level, so all mapping methods will have this added as a prefix.

There are also two Lombok annotations in this controller:

- `@RequiredArgsConstructor` creates a constructor with a `ChallengeGeneratorService` as the argument since the field is private and final, which Lombok understands as required. Spring uses dependency injection, so it'll try to find a bean implementing this interface and wire it to the controller. In this case, it'll take the only candidate, the service `ChallengeGeneratorServiceImpl`.

- `Slf4j` creates a logger named `log`. You use it to print a message to console with the generated challenge.

The `getRandomChallenge()` method has the `@GetMapping("/random")` annotation. It means that this method will handle GET requests to the context `/challenges/random`, the first part coming from the class-level annotation. It simply returns a `Challenge` object.

Let's now run the web application again and do a quick API test. From your IDE, run the `MultiplicationApplication` class or, from the console, use `mvnw spring-boot:run`.

Using HTTPie (see Chapter 2), you can try your new endpoint by doing a simple GET request to `localhost` (your machine) on port 8080 (Spring Boot's default). See Listing 3-21.

Listing 3-21. Making a Request to the Newly Created API

```
$ http localhost:8080/challenges/random
HTTP/1.1 200
Connection: keep-alive
Content-Type: application/json
Date: Fri, 26 May 2023 11:21:40 GMT
Keep-Alive: timeout=60
Transfer-Encoding: chunked
{
    "factorA": 74,
    "factorB": 92
}
```

You got an HTTP response with its header and body, a nicely serialized JSON representation of a challenge object. You did it! The application is finally doing something.

How Automatic Serialization Works

When covering how automatic configuration works in Spring Boot, you had a look at the example of the Tomcat embedded server, and we mentioned that there are many more autoconfiguration classes included as part of the `spring-boot-autoconfigure` dependency. Therefore, this other piece of *magic* involved in taking care of serializing a `Challenge` into a proper JSON HTTP response should no longer be a mystery to you. In any case, let's look at how this works since it's a core concept of the web module in Spring Boot. Also, it's quite common to customize this configuration in real life.

A lot of important logic and defaults for the Spring Boot Web module live in the `WebMvcAutoConfiguration` class (https://github.com/spring-projects/spring-boot/blob/main/spring-boot-project/spring-boot-autoconfigure/src/main/java/org/springframework/boot/autoconfigure/web/servlet/WebMvcAutoConfiguration.java). This class collects all available HTTP message converters in the context together for later use. You can see a fragment of this class in Listing 3-22.

Listing 3-22. A Fragment of WebMvcAutoConfiguration Class Provided by Spring Web

```
@Override
public void configureMessageConverters(List<HttpMessageConverter<?>>
converters) {
    this.messageConvertersProvider
            .ifAvailable((customConverters) -> converters.
addAll(customConverters.getConverters()));
}
```

The `HttpMessageConverter` interface (https://github.com/spring-projects/spring-framework/blob/main/spring-web/src/main/java/org/springframework/http/converter/HttpMessageConverter.java) is included in the core `spring-web` artifact. It defines the media types supported by the converter, which classes can convert to and from, and the `read` and `write` methods to do conversions.

Where are these converters coming from? More autoconfiguration classes. Spring Boot includes a `JacksonHttpMessageConvertersConfiguration` class (https://github.com/spring-projects/spring-boot/blob/main/spring-boot-project/spring-boot-autoconfigure/src/main/java/org/springframework/boot/autoconfigure/http/JacksonHttpMessageConvertersConfiguration.java) that has some logic to load a bean of type `MappingJackson2HttpMessageConverter`. This logic is conditional on the presence of the `ObjectMapper` class in the classpath. That one is a core class of the Jackson libraries, the most popular implementation of JSON serialization for Java. The `ObjectMapper` class is included in the `jackson-databind` dependency. The class is in the classpath because its artifact is a dependency included in `spring-boot-starter-json`, which is itself included in the `spring-boot-starter-web`.

Again, it's easier to understand all this with a diagram. See Figure 3-6.

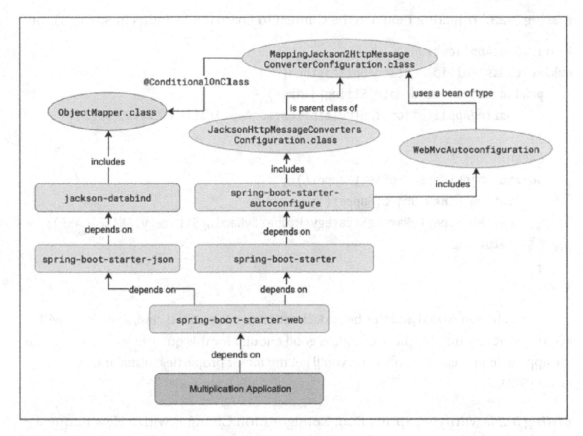

Figure 3-6. *Spring Boot Web JSON autoconfiguration*

The default `ObjectMapper` bean is configured in the `JacksonAutoConfiguration` class (https://github.com/spring-projects/spring-boot/blob/main/spring-boot-project/spring-boot-autoconfigure/src/main/java/org/springframework/boot/autoconfigure/jackson/JacksonAutoConfiguration.java). Everything there is set up in a flexible way. If you want to customize a specific feature, you don't need to consider this whole hierarchy. Normally, it's just a matter of overriding default beans.

For instance, if you wanted to change the JSON property naming to be snake-case instead of camel-case, you could declare a custom `ObjectMapper` in the app configuration that will be loaded instead of the default one. That's what Listing 3-23 does.

Listing 3-23. Injecting Beans in the Context to Override Defaults in Spring Boot

```java
@SpringBootApplication
public class MultiplicationApplication {
    public static void main(String[] args) {
        SpringApplication.run(MultiplicationApplication.class, args);
    }
    @Bean
    public ObjectMapper objectMapper() {
        var om = new ObjectMapper();
        om.setPropertyNamingStrategy(PropertyNamingStrategy.SNAKE_CASE);
        return om;
    }
}
```

Normally, you would add this bean declaration in a separated class annotated with @Configuration, but this piece of code is good enough for this quick example. If you run the app again and call the endpoint, you'll get the factor properties in snake-case. See Listing 3-24.

Listing 3-24. Verifying Spring Boot Configuration Changes with a New Request

```
$ http  localhost:8080/challenges/random
```

As you see, it's really easy to customize Spring Boot configuration by overriding beans. This specific case works because the default ObjectMapper is annotated with @ConditionalOnMissingBean, which makes Spring Boot load the bean only if there is no other bean of the same type defined in the context. Remember to remove this custom ObjectMapper since you use just Spring Boot defaults for now.

You might be missing the TDD approach for these controllers. The reason that we introduced a simple controller implementation is that it's easier for you to grasp the concepts about how controllers work in Spring Boot before diving into the testing strategies.

Testing Controllers with Spring Boot

This second controller will implement the REST API to receive attempts to solve challenges from the frontend. For this one, it's time to go back to a test-driven approach. First, create an empty shell of the new controller. See Listing 3-25.

Listing 3-25. An Empty Implementation of the ChallengeAttemptController

```
package microservices.book.multiplication.challenge;

import lombok.RequiredArgsConstructor;
import lombok.extern.slf4j.Slf4j;
import org.springframework.web.bind.annotation.RequestMapping;
import org.springframework.web.bind.annotation.RestController;
/**
 * This class provides a REST API to POST the attempts from users.
 */
@Slf4j
@RequiredArgsConstructor
@RestController
@RequestMapping("/attempts")
class ChallengeAttemptController {
    private final ChallengeService challengeService;
}
```

Similar to the previous implementation, Lombok adds a constructor with the service interface by annotating it with @RequiredArgsConstructor. Spring will inject the corresponding bean ChallengeServiceImpl. The ChallengeAttemptController class is a Spring @RestController component that handles incoming HTTP requests. Spring's core feature is the ability to manage and wire up beans in a Spring application context. When your Spring Boot application starts, it performs a component scan to find classes annotated with various stereotype annotations, like @Controller, @Service, @Repository, and in this case, @RestController. This phase is known as the *component scan*.

Now let's write a test with the expected logic. Keep in mind that testing a controller requires a slightly different approach since there is a web layer in between. Sometimes you'll want to verify features such as validation, request mapping, or error handling, which are configured by you but provided by Spring Boot. Therefore, you'll normally want a unit test that covers not only the class itself but also all these features around it.

In Spring Boot, there are multiple ways of implementing a controller test:

- *Without running the embedded server*—You can use `@SpringBootTest` without parameters or, even better, `@WebMvcTest` to instruct Spring to selectively load only the required configuration instead of the whole application context. Then, you simulate requests with a dedicated tool included in the Spring Test module, `MockMvc`.

- *Running the embedded server*—In this case, you use `@SpringBootTest` with its `webEnvironment` parameter set to `RANDOM_PORT` or `DEFINED_PORT`. Then, you must make real HTTP calls to the server. Spring Boot includes a `TestRestTemplate` class with some useful features to perform these test requests. This option is good when you want to test some web server configuration you may have customized (e.g., custom Tomcat configuration).

The best option is usually the first one and choosing a fine-grained configuration with `@WebMvcTest`. You get all the configuration surrounding your controller without taking extra time to boot up the server for each test. If you want to learn more about all these different options, check out this blog about how to test a controller in Spring Boot (`https://thepracticaldeveloper.com/guide-spring-boot-controller-tests/`).

You could write a test for a valid request and an invalid one, as shown in Listing 3-26.

Listing 3-26. Testing the Expected ChallengeAttemptController Logic

```
package microservices.book.multiplication.challenge;

import microservices.book.multiplication.user.User;
import org.junit.jupiter.api.Test;
import org.junit.jupiter.api.extension.ExtendWith;
import org.springframework.beans.factory.annotation.Autowired;
import org.springframework.boot.test.autoconfigure.json.
AutoConfigureJsonTesters;
```

```java
import org.springframework.boot.test.autoconfigure.web.servlet.WebMvcTest;
import org.springframework.boot.test.json.JacksonTester;
import org.springframework.boot.test.mock.mockito.MockBean;
import org.springframework.http.HttpStatus;
import org.springframework.http.MediaType;
import org.springframework.mock.web.MockHttpServletResponse;
import org.springframework.test.context.junit.jupiter.SpringExtension;
import org.springframework.test.web.servlet.MockMvc;

import static org.assertj.core.api.BDDAssertions.then;
import static org.mockito.ArgumentMatchers.eq;
import static org.mockito.BDDMockito.given;
import static org.springframework.test.web.servlet.request.
MockMvcRequestBuilders.post;

@ExtendWith(SpringExtension.class)
@AutoConfigureJsonTesters
@WebMvcTest(ChallengeAttemptController.class)
class ChallengeAttemptControllerTest {

    @MockBean
    private ChallengeService challengeService;

    @Autowired
    private MockMvc mvc;

    @Autowired
    private JacksonTester<ChallengeAttemptDTO> jsonRequestAttempt;

    @Autowired
    private JacksonTester<ChallengeAttempt> jsonResultAttempt;

    @Test
    void postValidResult() throws Exception {

        // given
        User user = new User(1L, "john");
        long attemptId = 5L;
```

```java
        ChallengeAttemptDTO attemptDTO = new ChallengeAttemptDTO(50, 70,
        "john", 3500);
        ChallengeAttempt expectedResponse = new ChallengeAttempt(attemptId,
        user, 50, 70, 3500, true);
        given(challengeService
                .verifyAttempt(eq(attemptDTO)))
                .willReturn(expectedResponse);

        // when
        MockHttpServletResponse response = mvc.perform(
                post("/attempts").contentType(MediaType.APPLICATION_JSON)
                        .content(jsonRequestAttempt.write(attemptDTO.
                        getJson())))
                .andReturn().getResponse();

        // then
        then(response.getStatus()).isEqualTo(HttpStatus.OK.value());
        then(response.getContentAsString()).isEqualTo(
                jsonResultAttempt.write(
                        expectedResponse
                ).getJson());
    }

@Test
    void postInvalidResult() throws Exception {
        // given an attempt with invalid input data
        ChallengeAttemptDTO attemptDTO = new ChallengeAttemptDTO(2000, -70,
        "john", 1);

        // when
        MockHttpServletResponse response = mvc.perform(
                post("/attempts").contentType(MediaType.APPLICATION_JSON)
                        .content(jsonRequestAttempt.write(attemptDTO.
                        getJson())))
                .andReturn().getResponse();

        // then
```

```
then(response.getStatus()).isEqualTo(HttpStatus.BAD_REQUEST.
value());
    }
}
```

There are a few new annotations and helper classes in this code. Let's review them one by one:

- `@ExtendWith(SpringExtension.class)` makes sure that the JUnit 5 test loads the extensions for Spring so you can use a test context.

- `JacksonTester` may be used to serialize and deserialize objects using the same configuration (i.e., ObjectMapper) as the app would do at runtime. `@AutoConfigureJsonTesters` tells Spring to configure beans of type `JacksonTester` for some fields you declare in the test. In this case, `@Autowired` injects two `JacksonTester` beans from the test context. Spring Boot, when instructed via this annotation, builds these utility classes.

- `@WebMvcTest`, with the controller class as a parameter, makes Spring treat this as a presentation layer test. Thus, it'll load only the relevant configuration around the controller: validation, serializers, security, error handlers, and so on (see `https://docs.spring.io/spring-boot/docs/current/reference/html/test-auto-configuration.html` for a full list of included autoconfiguration classes).

- `@MockBean` comes with the Spring Boot Test module and helps you develop proper unit tests by allowing you to mock other layers and beans you're not testing. In this case, you replace the service bean in the context by a mock. You set the expected return values within the test methods, using `BDDMockito`'s `given()`.

- `@Autowired` might be familiar to you. It's a basic annotation in Spring to make it inject (or wire) a bean in the context to the field. It used to be common in all classes using Spring, but since version 4.3, it can be omitted from fields if they are initialized in a constructor and the class has only one constructor.

- The MockMvc class is used in Spring to simulate requests to the presentation layer when you make a test that doesn't load a real server. It's provided by the test context so you can just inject it in your test.

Valid Attempt Test

Now you can focus on the test cases and how to make them pass. The first test sets up the scenario for a valid attempt. It creates the DTO that acts as the data sent from the API client with a valid result. It uses BDDMockito's given() to specify that, when the service (a mocked bean) is called with an argument equal to (Mockito's eq) the DTO, it should return the expected ChallengeAttempt response.

You build the POST request with the static method post included in the helper class MockMvcRequestBuilders. The target is the expected path /attempts. The content type is set to application/json, and its body is the serialized DTO in JSON. You use the wired JacksonTester for serialization. Then, mvc does the request via perform(), and you get the response calling to .andReturn(). You could also call the andExpect() method instead if you use MockMvc for assertions, but it's better to do them separately with a dedicated assertions library like AssertJ.

In the last part of the test, you verify that the HTTP status code should be 200 OK and that the result must be a serialized version of the expected response. Again, you use a JacksonTester object for this.

This test fails with a 404 NOT FOUND when you execute it. See Listing 3-27. There is no implementation for that request, so the server can't simply find a logic to map that POST mapping.

Listing 3-27. The ChallengeAttemptControllerTest Fails

```
org.opentest4j.AssertionFailedError:
expected: 200
 but was: 404
Expected :200
Actual   :404
```

Now, go back to the ChallengeAttemptController and implement this mapping. See Listing 3-28.

Listing 3-28. Adding the Working Implementation to ChallengeAttemptController

```
@Slf4j
@RequiredArgsConstructor
@RestController
@RequestMapping("/attempts")
class ChallengeAttemptController {
    private final ChallengeService challengeService;
    @PostMapping
    ResponseEntity<ChallengeAttempt> postResult(@RequestBody
    ChallengeAttemptDTO challengeAttemptDTO) {
        return ResponseEntity.ok(challengeService.verifyAttempt(
        challengeAttemptDTO));
    }
}
```

We're using this new way here to show that there are ways to build different types of responses with the `ResponseEntity` static builder. It's a simple logic that just calls the service layer. The method is annotated with `@PostMapping` without parameters so it will handle a POST request to the context path already set at the class level. Note that here we're using a `ResponseEntity` as the return type instead of using the `ChallengeAttempt` directly. That other option would also work.

That's it! The first test case will pass now.

Validating Data in Controllers

The second test case, `postInvalidResult()`, does not allow the application to accept an attempt with negative or out-of-range numbers. It expects the logic to return a 400 BAD REQUEST, which is a good practice when the error is on the client side, like this one. See Listing 3-29.

Listing 3-29. Verifying That the Client Gets a BAD REQUEST Status Code

```
// then
then(response.getStatus()).isEqualTo(HttpStatus.BAD_REQUEST.value());
```

If you run it before implementing the POST mapping in the controller, it fails with a NOT FOUND status code. With the implementation in place, it also fails. However, in this case, the result is even worse. See Listing 3-30.

Listing 3-30. Posting an Invalid Request Returns a 200 OK Status Code

```
org.opentest4j.AssertionFailedError:
expected: 400
 but was: 200
Expected :400
Actual   :200
```

The application is just accepting the invalid attempt and returning an OK status. This is wrong; you should not pass this attempt to the service layer but reject it in the presentation layer. To accomplish this, you can use the Java Bean Validation API (https://docs.spring.io/spring-framework/docs/current/reference/html/core. html#validation-beanvalidation) integrated with Spring).

In the DTO class, you add some Java Validation annotations to indicate the valid inputs. See Listing 3-31. All these annotations are implemented in the jakarta. validation-api library, available in the classpath via spring-boot-starter-validation. This starter is included as part of the Spring Boot Web starter (spring-boot-starter-web).

Listing 3-31. Adding Validation Constraints to the DTO Class

```
package microservices.book.multiplication.challenge;
import lombok.Value;
import jakarta.validation.constraints.*;
/**
 * Attempt coming from the user
 */
@Value
public class ChallengeAttemptDTO {
    @Min(1) @Max(99)
    int factorA, factorB;
    @NotBlank
```

```
    String userAlias;
    @Positive
    int guess;
}
```

There are a lot of available constraints in that package (https://docs.jboss.org/ hibernate/beanvalidation/spec/2.0/api/javax/validation/constraints/package-summary.html). You use @Min and @Max to define the range of allowed values for the multiplication factors, @NotBlank to make sure you always get an alias, and @Positive for the guess since you know you're handling only positive results (you can also use a predefined range here).

An important step to make these constraints work is to integrate them with Spring via the @Valid annotation in the controller's method argument. See Listing 3-32. If you add this, Spring Boot will analyze the constraints and throw an exception if they don't match.

Listing 3-32. Using the @Valid Annotation to Validate Requests

```
@PostMapping
ResponseEntity<ChallengeAttempt> postResult(
        @RequestBody @Valid ChallengeAttemptDTO challengeAttemptDTO) {
    return ResponseEntity.ok(challengeService.verifyAttempt(challengeAtt
    emptDTO));
}
```

As you might have guessed, there is autoconfiguration to handle the errors and build a predefined response when the object is invalid. By default, the error handler constructs a response with a 400 BAD_REQUEST status code.

Starting with Spring Boot version 2.3, the validation messages are no longer included in the error response by default. This might be confusing for the callers since they don't know exactly what's wrong with the request. The reason to not include them is that these messages could potentially expose information to a malicious API client.

We want to enable validation messages for our educational goal, so we'll add two settings to the application.properties file. See Listing 3-33. These properties are listed in the official Spring Boot docs (https://docs.spring.io/spring-boot/docs/current/reference/htmlsingle/#appendix.application-properties.server), and you'll see what they do soon.

Listing 3-33.   Adding Validation Logging Configuration to the application.
properties File

```
server.error.include-message=always
server.error.include-binding-errors=always
```

To verify all the validation configuration, run the test again. This time it'll pass, and
you'll see some extra logs, as shown in Listing 3-34.

Listing 3-34.   An Invalid Request Causes Now the Expected Result

```
[Field error in object 'challengeAttemptDTO' on field 'factorB': rejected
value [-70];
[...]
[Field error in object 'challengeAttemptDTO' on field 'factorA': rejected
value [2000];
[...]
```

The controller handling REST API calls for users to send attempts is working now.
If you start the application again, you can play with this new endpoint via the HTTPie
command. First, you ask for a random challenge, as before. Then, you post an attempt to
solve it. See Listing 3-35.

Listing 3-35.   Running a Standard Use Case for the Application Using HTTPie
Commands

```
$ http -b :8080/challenges/random
{
    "factorA": 52,
    "factorB": 59
}

$ http POST :8080/attempts factorA=58 factorB=92 userAlias=moises
guess=5400
HTTP/1.1 200
Connection: keep-alive
Content-Type: application/json
Date: Sat, 27 May 2023 09:09:38 GMT
Keep-Alive: timeout=60
```

```
Transfer-Encoding: chunked

{
    "correct": false,
    "factorA": 58,
    "factorB": 92,
    "id": null,
    "resultAttempt": 5400,
    "user": {
        "alias": "moises",
        "id": null
    }
}
```

The first command uses the -b parameter to print only the body of the response. As you see, you can also omit localhost, and HTTPie will use it as default.

As expected, you get a serialized ChallengeAttempt object indicating that the result is incorrect. To send the attempt, you use the POST argument before the URL. JSON is the default content type in HTTPie, so you can simply pass key-value parameters, and this tool will convert it to proper JSON.

You can also try an invalid request to see how Spring Boot handles the validation errors. See Listing 3-36.

Listing 3-36. Error Response Including Validation Messages

```
$ http POST :8080/attempts factorA=58 factorB=92 userAlias=moises
guess=-400
HTTP/1.1 400
Connection: close
Content-Type: application/json
Date: Sat, 27 May 2023 09:09:39 GMT
Transfer-Encoding: chunked
{
    "error": "Bad Request",
    "errors": [
        {
```

```
            "arguments": [
                {
                    "arguments": null,
                    "code": "guess",
                    "codes": [
                        "challengeAttemptDTO.guess",
                        "guess"
                    ],
                    "defaultMessage": "guess"
                }
            ],
            "bindingFailure": false,
            "code": "Positive",
            "codes": [
                "Positive.challengeAttemptDTO.guess",
                "Positive.guess",
                "Positive.int",
                "Positive"
            ],
            "defaultMessage": "must be greater than 0",
            "field": "guess",
            "objectName": "challengeAttemptDTO",
            "rejectedValue": -400
        }
    ],
    "message": "Validation failed for object='challengeAttemptDTO'. Error
count: 1",
    "path": "/attempts",
    "status": 400,
    "timestamp": "2023-05-27T09:09:39.212+00:00"
}
```

It's quite a verbose response. The main reason is that all the *binding errors* (those caused by the validation constraints) are added to the error response. This was switched on with `server.error.include-binding-errors=always`. Besides, the root `message` field also gives the client an overall description of what went wrong. This description is omitted by default, but you enabled it with the `server.error.include-message=always` property.

If this response goes to a user interface, you need to parse that JSON response in the frontend, get the fields that are invalid, and maybe display the `defaultMessage` fields. Changing this default message is simple since you can override it with the constraint annotations. Let's modify this annotation in `ChallengeAttemptDTO` and try this again with the same invalid request. See Listing 3-37.

Listing 3-37. Changing the Validation Message

```
@Positive(message = "How could you possibly get a negative result here? Try
again.")
int guess;
```

What Spring Boot does in this case to handle the errors is to sneakily add a `@Controller` to your context: the `BasicErrorController` (see `https://docs.spring.io/spring-boot/docs/current/api/org/springframework/boot/autoconfigure/web/servlet/error/BasicErrorController.html`). This one uses the `DefaultErrorAttributes` class (`https://docs.spring.io/spring-boot/docs/current/api/org/springframework/boot/web/servlet/error/DefaultErrorAttributes.html`) to compose the error response.

In internationalized applications, it is crucial to provide users with meaningful error messages, especially for validation errors. Different languages and cultures might require different phrasing and wording for error messages to be easily understandable. To include validation messages in error responses for i18n purposes, you can customize the configuration of validation messages in Spring Boot by defining and managing them through message source properties files, which can be easily internationalized.

Summary and Achievements

You started this chapter by learning about the requirements of the application you'll build in this book. Then, we sliced the scope and took the first item for development: the functionality to generate a random challenge and allow users to guess the result.

You learned how to create the skeleton of a Spring Boot application and some best practices regarding software design and architecture: three-tier and three-layer architecture, domain-driven design, test-driven/behavior-driven development, basic unit tests with JUnit 5, and REST API design. In this chapter, you focused on the application tier and implemented the domain objects, the business layer, and the presentation layer as a REST API. See Figure 3-7.

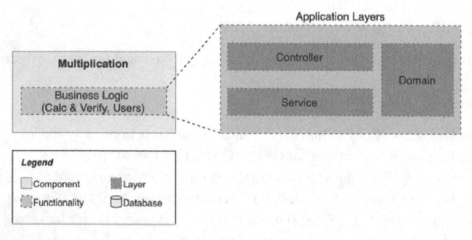

Figure 3-7. *Application status after Chapter 3*

A core concept in Spring Boot was also covered in this chapter: autoconfiguration. Now you know where a big part of the Spring Boot magic lives. In the future, you should be able to find your way through the reference documentation to override other default behaviors in any other configuration class.

The chapter also went through other features in Spring Boot, such as implementing @Service and @Controller components, testing controllers with MockMvc, and validating input via the Java Bean Validation API.

To complete this first web application, you need to build a user interface. Later, you'll also learn about the data layer to make sure you can persist users and attempts.

Chapter's Achievements:

- You learned how to build a properly structured Spring Boot application, following a three-layered design.

- You learned how Spring Boot's autoconfiguration works and the key to unveil its magic, based on two practical examples with supporting diagrams: the Tomcat embedded server and the JSON serialization defaults.

- You modeled an example business case following domain-driven design techniques.

- You developed two of the three layers of the first application (*service, controller*) using a test-driven development approach.

- You used the most important Spring MVC annotations to implement a REST API with Spring Boot.

- You learned how to test the controller layer in Spring using `MockMVC`.

- You added validation constraints to your API to protect it against invalid input.

CHAPTER 4

A Minimal Frontend with React

A book about microservices that claims to be practical must provide a frontend too. In real life, users don't interact with applications via REST APIs.

Since this book focuses on popular technologies used in real life, you'll build a frontend in React. This JavaScript framework allows you to easily develop web pages based on reusable components and services. According to the 2022 StackOverflow's Developer Survey (`https://survey.stackoverflow.co/2022/#section-most-popular-technologies-web-frameworks-and-technologies`), React is the most popular framework when compared to other similar alternatives like Angular or Vue.js. That makes it already a good choice. On top of that, it's a framework that we consider Java-developer-friendly: you can use TypeScript, an extension of JavaScript that adds types to this programming language, which makes everything easier for people used to them. Besides, React's programming style allows you to create classes and build components and services, and this makes the structure of a React project familiar for a Java developer.

You'll also use Node.js, commonly referred to as Node. It's a JavaScript runtime environment built on Chrome's V8 JavaScript engine. It allows developers to run JavaScript code outside of a web browser, enabling server-side and command-line application development. It comes with npm, which stands for "Node Package Manager." npm is a package manager for Node.js. It allows developers to easily manage project dependencies by providing access to a vast ecosystem of open-source packages. These packages contain reusable code and functionality that can be incorporated into Node.js projects. By leveraging existing packages, developers can save time and effort by not having to reinvent the wheel for common tasks and functionality. This way you can get some practical experience with UI technologies and, why not, become a full stack developer if you aren't one yet.

© Moisés Macero García and Tarun Telang 2023
M. Macero García and T. Telang, *Learn Microservices with Spring Boot 3*,
https://doi.org/10.1007/978-1-4842-9757-5_4

In any case, keep in mind this important disclaimer: we won't dive into the details of how to build a web app with React. We want to keep the attention on microservices with Spring Boot. Therefore, don't feel bad if you don't fully grasp all the concepts in this chapter, especially if you've never seen JavaScript code or CSS.

Considering that you have all the source code available in the GitHub repository (`https://github.com/Book-Microservices-v3/chapter04/tree/main/challenges-frontend`), you can approach this chapter in several ways.

- Read it *as is*. You'll get some basic knowledge and will be experimenting with some important concepts in React.

- Pause for a bit to read the Main Concepts Guide (`https://react.dev/blog/2023/03/16/introducing-react-dev`) on the official website and then come back to this chapter. This way you will have more background knowledge about what you're going to build.

- Skip this chapter completely and use the sources from the repository if you're not interested in frontend technologies at all. It's safe to jump to the next chapter and continue with the evolving-application approach.

A Quick Intro to React and Node

React, also known as React.js or ReactJS, is an open-source JavaScript library developed by Facebook. It is widely used for building interactive and dynamic user interfaces (UI) in web applications. It's widely used in many organizations, which also leads to an active job market.

React follows a component-based architecture, where the UI is divided into reusable and self-contained components. Each component encapsulates its own logic, state, and rendering. This is an advantage for backend developers given that the concept of a piece of code that you write once and reuse everywhere sounds familiar.

Instead of writing HTML and JavaScript source code in separate files, in React you can use JSX, which stands for JavaScript XML. It is an extension of the JavaScript syntax that allows developers to combine JavaScript expressions and HTML-like code together. This is useful since you can write components in individual files and isolate them by functionality, keeping all behavior and rendering logic together.

Table 4-1 enumerates all the required JavaScript libraries along with their versions. Additionally, the table provides the reason for the usage of each library.

Table 4-1. *JavaScript Libraries and Their Versions in the Project, Along with Rationale for Usage*

Library	Version	Reason for Use
React	18.2.0	Building dynamic user interfaces efficiently.
Node.js	18.16.0	Server-side JavaScript runtime.
npm	9.6.7	Package manager for managing project dependencies.

Setting Up the Development Environment

First, you need to install Node.js using one of the available installer packages located at the nodejs.org site. This book uses Node v18.16 and npm 9.6.7. After the installation finishes, verify it with the command-line tools, as indicated in Listing 4-1.

Listing 4-1. Getting the Version of Node.js and npm

```
$ node --version
v18.16.0
$ npm --version
9.6.7
```

Now you can use npx, a tool included with npm, to create React's frontend project. Make sure you run this command from your workspace root and not inside the Multiplication service.

```
$ npx create-react-app challenges-frontend
```

Source Code   You can find all the source code for this chapter on GitHub, in the chapter04 repository.

See https://github.com/Book-Microservices-v3/chapter04.

After some time downloading and installing dependencies, you'll get output like the one shown in Listing 4-2.

Listing 4-2. Console Output After Creating the React Project

```
Success! Created challenges-frontend at /Users/ttelang/workspace/learn-
microservices/challenges-frontend
Inside that directory, you can run several commands:
[...]
We suggest that you begin by typing:
  cd challenges-frontend
  npm start
  Happy hacking!
```

If you follow the suggestion and run `npm start`, a node server will start at `http://localhost:3000`, and you may even get a browser window opened showing the default React landing page with a React logo in the center of the page. In case you don't, you can have a quick look at this page if you navigate to `http://localhost:3000` from your browser.

The React Skeleton

The next task is to load the React project into your workspace. For example, in IntelliJ, you can use the option File ➤ New ➤ Module from existing sources to load the frontend folder as a separate module. As you'll see, a lot of files are already created by the `create-react-app` tool. See Figure 4-1.

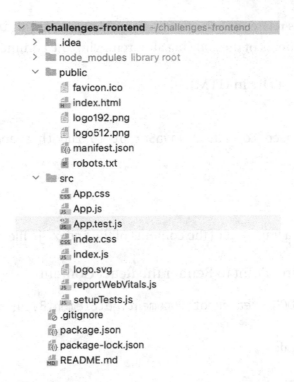

Figure 4-1. React project skeleton

- The package.json and package-lock.json files are npm files.
  They contain basic information about the project, and they also
  list its dependencies. Those dependencies are stored in the
  node_modules folder.

- The public folder is where you can keep all the static files that remain
  untouched after the build. The only exception is index.html, which
  will be processed to include the resulting JavaScript sources.

- All your React sources and their related resources are included in
  the src folder. In this skeleton app, you can find the main entry point
  file index.js and a React component, App. This sample component
  comes with its own stylesheet App.css and a test, App.test.js.
  When you build a React project, all these files end up merged into
  bigger files, but this naming convention and structure are helpful for
  development.

How do these files relate to each other in React? Let's start with index.html. See Listing 4-3 for the contents of the body tag after removing the comment lines.

Listing 4-3. The Root Div in HTML

```
<body>
    <noscript>You need to enable JavaScript to run this app.</noscript>
    <div id="root"></div>
...
</body>
```

Listing 4-4 shows a fragment of the contents of the index.js file.

Listing 4-4. The Entry Point to Render the React Content

```
const root = ReactDOM.createRoot(document.getElementById('root'));
root.render(
    <React.StrictMode>
        <App />
    </React.StrictMode>
);
```

This code shows how to render a React element into the Document Object Model (DOM), a tree representation of the HTML elements. This piece of code renders the React.StrictMode element and its child App component into the HTML. More specifically, they get rendered into the element with the ID root, the div tag inserted in *index.html*. Since App is a component and it may contain other components, it ends up processing and rendering the whole React application.

A JavaScript Client

Before creating your first component, you need to make sure you have a way to retrieve data from the REST API you created in the previous chapter. You're going to use a JavaScript class for this. As you'll see in the rest of the chapter, you'll use a Java-ish programming style to build the frontend, using classes and types.

Classes in JavaScript are like Java classes. For this specific case, you can create a utility class with two static methods. See Listing 4-5.

Listing 4-5. The ApiClient Class

```
class ApiClient {
    static SERVER_URL = 'http://localhost:8080';
    static GET_CHALLENGE = '/challenges/random';
    static POST_RESULT = '/attempts';
    static challenge(): Promise<Response> {
        return fetch(ApiClient.SERVER_URL + ApiClient.GET_CHALLENGE);
    }
    static sendGuess(user: string,
                    a: number,
                    b: number,
                    guess: number): Promise<Response> {
        return fetch(ApiClient.SERVER_URL + ApiClient.POST_RESULT,
            {
                method: 'POST',
                headers: {
                    'Content-Type': 'application/json'
                },
                body: JSON.stringify(
                    {
                        userAlias: user,
                        factorA: a,
                        factorB: b,
                        guess: guess
                    }
                )
            });
    }
}
export default ApiClient;
```

Both methods return promises. A *promise* in JavaScript is comparable to a Java's
Future class: it represents the result of an asynchronous operation. The functions call
fetch (see https://developer.mozilla.org/en-US/docs/Web/API/Fetch_API), a
function in JavaScript that you can use to interact with an HTTP server.

The first method, `challenge()`, uses the `fetch` function in its basic form since it'll default to a GET operation to the passed URL. This method returns a promise of a `Response` object (`https://developer.mozilla.org/en-US/docs/Web/API/Response`).

The `sendGuess` method accepts the parameters you need to build the request to solve a challenge. This time, you use `fetch` with a second argument: an object defining the HTTP method (POST), the content-type of the body in the request (JSON), and the body. To build the JSON request, you use the utility method `JSON.stringify`, which serializes an object.

Last, to make this class publicly accessible, you add `export default ApiClient` at the end of the file. This makes it possible to import the complete class in other components and classes.

The Challenge Component

Let's build your first React component. You will follow modularization in the frontend, and that means this component will take care of the `Challenges` domain. For now, this implies the following:

- Rendering the challenge retrieved from the backend

- Displaying a form for the user to send the guess

See Listing 4-6 for the complete source code of the `ChallengeComponent` class. The following sections dissect this code, and you'll use it to learn how you can structure components in React and some of its basic concepts.

Listing 4-6. The First React Component: ChallengeComponent

```
import * as React from "react";
import ApiClient from "../services/ApiClient";
class ChallengeComponent extends React.Component {
    constructor(props) {
        super(props);
        this.state = {
            a: '', b: '',
            user: '',
            message: '',
```

```
            guess: 0
        };
        this.handleSubmitResult = this.handleSubmitResult.bind(this);
        this.handleChange = this.handleChange.bind(this);
    }
    componentDidMount(): void {
        ApiClient.challenge().then(
            res => {
                if (res.ok) {
                    res.json().then(json => {
                        this.setState({
                            a: json.factorA,
                            b: json.factorB
                        });
                    });
                } else {
                    this.updateMessage("Can't reach the server");
                }
            }
        );
    }
    handleChange(event) {
        const name = event.target.name;
        this.setState({
            [name]: event.target.value
        });
    }
    handleSubmitResult(event) {
        event.preventDefault();
        ApiClient.sendGuess(this.state.user,
            this.state.a, this.state.b,
            this.state.guess)
            .then(res => {
                if (res.ok) {
                    res.json().then(json => {
```

```
                        if (json.correct) {
                            this.updateMessage("Congratulations! Your guess
                            is correct");
                        } else {
                            this.updateMessage("Oops! Your guess " + json.
                            resultAttempt +
                            " is wrong, but keep playing!");
                        }
                    });
                } else {
                    this.updateMessage("Error: server error or not available");
                }
            });
        }
        updateMessage(m: string) {
            this.setState({
                message: m
            });
        }
        render() {
            return (
                <div>
                    <div>
                        <h3>Your new challenge is</h3>
                        <h1>
                            {this.state.a} x {this.state.b}
                        </h1>
                    </div>
                    <form onSubmit={this.handleSubmitResult}>
                        <label>
                            Your alias:
                            <input type="text" maxLength="12"
                                    name="user"
                                    value={this.state.user}
                                    onChange={this.handleChange}/>
```

```
            </label>
            <br/>
            <label>
                Your guess:
                <input type="number" min="0"
                        name="guess"
                        value={this.state.guess}
                        onChange={this.handleChange}/>
            </label>
            <br/>
            <input type="submit" value="Submit"/>
        </form>
        <h4>{this.state.message}</h4>
    </div>
    );
    }
}
export default ChallengeComponent;
```

The Main Structure of a Component

This class extends React.Component, and this is how you create components in React. The only required method you need to implement is render(), which must return DOM elements to display in the browser. In this case, you build these elements using JSX (https://react.dev/learn/writing-markup-with-jsx). See Listing 4-7, which shows the main structure of this component class.

Listing 4-7. Main Structure of a Component in React

```
class ChallengeComponent extends React.Component {
    constructor(props) {
        super(props);
        this.state = {
            a: '', b: '',
            user: '',
            message: '',
```

```
        guess: 0
    };
    this.handleSubmitResult = this.handleSubmitResult.bind(this);
    this.handleChange = this.handleChange.bind(this);
}
componentDidMount(): void {
    // ... Component initialization
}
render() {
    return (
    // ... HTML as JSX ...
    )
}
```

Typically, you also need a constructor to initialize properties, and the component's *state* (in case it's needed). In ChallengeComponent, you create a state to hold the retrieved challenge and the data the user is entering to solve an attempt. The argument props are the input passed to your component as an HTML attribute.

```
<ChallengeComponent prop1="value"/>
```

You don't need props for this component, yet you need to accept it as an argument and pass it to the parent constructor as it's expected if you use a constructor.

Inside the constructor two lines bind the class methods. This is required if you want to use this in the event handlers, which are the functions you need to implement to work with the user's input data. We describe these functions in more detail later in this chapter.

The componentDidMount function is a lifecycle method that you can implement in React to execute logic right after the component is rendered the first time. See Listing 4-8.

Listing 4-8. Running Logic After Rendering the Component

```
componentDidMount(): void {
    ApiClient.challenge().then(
        res => {
            if (res.ok) {
                res.json().then(json => {
```

```
                this.setState({
                    a: json.factorA,
                    b: json.factorB
                });
            });
        } else {
            this.updateMessage("Can't reach the server");
        }
    }
);
}
```

You call the server to retrieve a challenge, using the `ApiClient` utility class you built before. Given that the function returns a promise, you use `then()` to specify what to do when you obtain the response. The inner logic is also simple: If the response is `ok` (meaning a `2xx` status code), you parse the body as `json()`. That's also an asynchronous method, so you resolve the promise again with `then()` and pass the expected `factorA` and `factorB` from the REST API response to `setState()`.

In React, the `setState` function partially reloads the DOM. That means the browser will render the part of the HTML that changed, so you'll see the multiplication factors on the page right after you get the response from the server. In this application, that should be a matter of milliseconds, since you're calling your own local server. In a reallife web page, you could set up a spinner, for example, to improve the user experience if they have a slow connection.

Rendering

JSX allows you to mix HTML and JavaScript. This is powerful since you can benefit from the simplicity of the HTML language, but you can add placeholders and JavaScript logic as well. See the complete source of the `render()` method in Listing 4-9, and its subsequent explanation.

Listing 4-9. Using render() with JSX to Display the Component's Elements

```
render() {
    return (
        <div>
```

```
            <div>
                <h3>Your new challenge is</h3>
                <h1>
                    {this.state.a} x {this.state.b}
                </h1>
            </div>
            <form onSubmit={this.handleSubmitResult}>
                <label>
                    Your alias:
                    <input type="text" maxLength="12"
                            name="user"
                            value={this.state.user}
                            onChange={this.handleChange}/>
                </label>
                <br/>
                <label>
                    Your guess:
                    <input type="number" min="0"
                            name="guess"
                            value={this.state.guess}
                            onChange={this.handleChange}/>
                </label>
                <br/>
                <input type="submit" value="Submit"/>
            </form>
            <h4>{this.state.message}</h4>
        </div>
    );
}
```

The Challenge component has a root div element with three main blocks. The first one displays the challenge by showing both factors included in the state. At rendering time they'll be undefined, but immediately after they'll be reloaded once, you get the response from the server (the logic inside componentDidMount). A similar block is the last one; it displays the message state property, which you set when you get the response for a sent attempt request.

For users to enter their guess, you add a form that calls handleSubmitResult when submitted. This form has two inputs: a field for the user's alias and another field for the guess. Both follow the same approach: their value is a property of the state object, and they call the same function (handleChange) on every keystroke. This function uses the name attribute of your inputs to find the corresponding property in the component state to update. Note that event.target points to the HTML element where the event happened. See Listing 4-10 for the source code of these handler functions.

Listing 4-10. Handling User's Input

```
handleChange(event) {
    const name = event.target.name;
    this.setState({
        [name]: event.target.value
    });
}
handleSubmitResult(event) {
    event.preventDefault();
    ApiClient.sendGuess(this.state.user,
        this.state.a, this.state.b,
        this.state.guess)
        .then(res => {
            if (res.ok) {
                res.json().then(json => {
                    if (json.correct) {
                        this.updateMessage("Congratulations! Your guess is
                        correct");
                    } else {
                        this.updateMessage("Oops! Your guess " + json.
                        resultAttempt +
                        " is wrong, but keep playing!");
                    }
                });
```

```
        } else {
            this.updateMessage("Error: server error or not available");
        }
    });
}
```

On form submission, you call the server's API to send a guess. When you get the response, you check if it's OK, parse the JSON, and then update the message in the state. Then, that part of the HTML DOM is rendered again.

Integration with the App

Now that you have finished the code for the component, you can use it in your application. To do so, modify the App.js file, which is the main (or root) component in the React codebase. See Listing 4-11.

Listing 4-11. Adding the Component as a Child of App.js, the Root Component

```
import React from 'react';
import './App.css';
import ChallengeComponent from './components/ChallengeComponent';
function App() {
    return (
        <div className="App">
            <header className="App-header">
                <ChallengeComponent/>
            </header>
        </div>
    );
}
export default App;
```

As described earlier, the skeleton app uses this App component in the index.js file. When you build the code, the resulting scripts are included in the index.html file.

You should also either adapt the test included in App.test.js or simply delete it. We won't dive into details about React testing, so you can delete it for now.

Running the Frontend the First Time

You modified the skeleton application built with `create-react-app` to include your custom React component. Note that you didn't get rid of other files such as stylesheets, which you could customize too. You are reusing some of those classes, as you can see in the code in `App.js`.

It's time to determine if your frontend and backend work together. Make sure you run the Spring Boot application first and then execute the React frontend using `npm` from the frontend app's root folder.

```
$ npm start
```

After a successful compilation, this command-line tool should open your default browser and display the page located at `http://localhost:3000`. This is where the development server lives. See Figure 4-2 showing the web page rendered when you visit that URL from your browser.

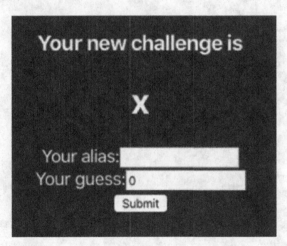

Figure 4-2. *App with blank factors*

Something is wrong there. The factors are blank, but the code retrieves them after the component rendering. Let's debug this problem.

Debugging

Sometimes things don't go as expected and your app simply doesn't work. You're running the app on a browser, so how do you figure out what happens? The good

105

news is that most of the popular browsers come with powerful tools for developers. In Chrome, you can use the Chrome DevTools (see `https://developer.chrome.com/docs/devtools/`). Press Ctrl+May+I (Windows) or Cmd+Opt+I (Mac) to open an area in your browser with several tabs and sections showing network activity, the JavaScript console, and so on.

Open the Development Mode and refresh your browser. One of the functionalities you can check is if your frontend is interacting properly with the server. Click the Network tab and, in the list, you'll see a failing HTTP request to `http://localhost:8080/challenges/random`, as displayed in Figure 4-3.

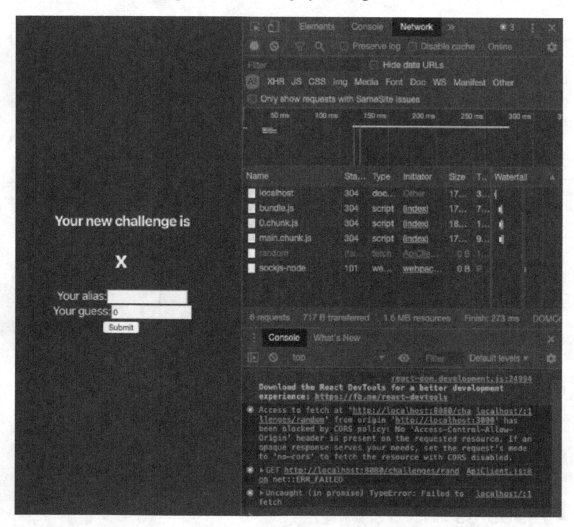

Figure 4-3. *Chrome DevTools*

This console also shows a descriptive message:

"Access to fetch at 'http://localhost:8080/challenges/random' from origin 'http://localhost:3000' has been blocked by CORS policy: No 'Access-Control-Allow-Origin' header is present on the requested resource [...]".

By default, your browser blocks requests that try to access resources in a different domain than the one in which your frontend is located. This is to prevent a malicious page in your browser from accessing data in a different page, and it's called the *same-origin policy*. In this case, you're running the frontend and the backend in localhost, but they run on different ports, so they are considered different *origins*.

There are multiple ways to fix this. In this case, you're going to enable cross-origin resource sharing (CORS), a security policy that can be enabled on the server side to allow the frontend to work with the REST API from a different origin. CORS is a security feature that permits servers to specify which origins can access their resources. It serves to prevent unauthorized access and data leakage. Nevertheless, enabling CORS without appropriate security measures can create vulnerabilities. To implement CORS for real-life situations, a more cautious and secure approach is necessary.

Adding CORS Configuration to the Spring Boot App

Go back to the backend codebase and add a Spring Boot @Configuration class that will override some defaults. According to the reference documentation (https://docs.spring.io/spring-framework/reference/web/webmvc-cors.html), you can implement the WebMvcConfigurer interface and override the addCorsMapping method to add a generic CORS configuration. To keep classes organized, create a new package named configuration for this class. See Listing 4-12.

Listing 4-12. Adding the CORS Configuration to the Backend Application

```
package microservices.book.multiplication.configuration;

import org.springframework.context.annotation.Configuration;
import org.springframework.web.servlet.config.annotation.CorsRegistry;
import org.springframework.web.servlet.config.annotation.WebMvcConfigurer;
```

```
@Configuration
public class WebConfiguration implements WebMvcConfigurer {

    @Override
    public void addCorsMappings(final CorsRegistry registry) {
        registry.addMapping("/**").allowedOrigins("http://localhost:3000");
    }
}
```

This method works with an injected `CorsRegistry` instance that you can customize. You add a mapping allowing the frontend's origin to access *any* path, represented by `/**`. You could also omit the `allowedOrigins` part in this line. Then, all origins would be allowed instead of only `http://localhost:3000`.

Remember that Spring Boot scans your packages looking for configuration classes. This is one of them, so this CORS configuration will be applied automatically the next time you start the application.

An important remark about CORS, in general, is that you probably need it only for development purposes. If you deploy your application's frontend and backend to the same host, you won't experience any issues, and you shouldn't enable CORS to keep the security policies as strict as you can. When you deploy the backend and frontend to different hosts, you should still be very selective in your CORS configuration and avoid adding complete access to all origins.

Playing with the Application

The frontend and backend should now work together. Restart the Spring Boot app if you haven't done it yet and refresh your browser (see Figure 4-4).

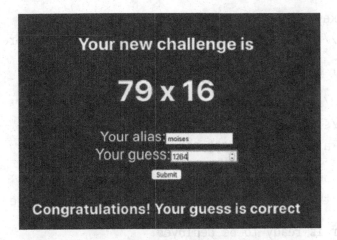

Figure 4-4. *The first version of the application*

Exciting times! Now you can enter your alias and make a few attempts. Remember to respect the rules and use only your brain to guess the result.

Deploying the React App

So far, you've been using the development mode for your frontend. You started the web server with `npm start`. This is not how it would work in a production environment, of course.

To prepare your React application for deployment, you need to build it first. See Listing 4-13.

Listing 4-13. Building the React App for a Production Deployment

```
$ npm run build

> challenges-frontend@0.1.0 build
> react-scripts build

Creating an optimized production build...
Compiled with warnings.

[eslint]
src/index.js
  Line 6:13:  'serviceWorker' is defined but never used  no-unused-vars
```

```
Search for the keywords to learn more about each warning.
To ignore, add // eslint-disable-next-line to the line before.

File sizes after gzip:

  47.98 kB build/static/js/main.b7e6fc16.js
  1.79 kB  build/static/js/787.342bd2a4.chunk.js
  541 B    build/static/css/main.073c9b0a.css

The project was built assuming it is hosted at /.
You can control this with the homepage field in your package.json.

The build folder is ready to be deployed.
You may serve it with a static server:

  npm install -g serve
  serve -s build

Find out more about deployment here:

  https://create-react-app.dev/docs/deployment/
```

As you can see, this command generated all the scripts and files under the build folder. A copy of the files you placed in the public folder is also found there. These logs also tell you how to install a static web server using npm. But you already have a web server, Tomcat, embedded in the Spring Boot application. Couldn't you just use that one? Sure, you can.

For this deployment example, you'll follow the easiest path and pack the entire app, including the backend and the frontend, in the same deployable unit: the *fat JAR* file generated by Spring Boot.

What you need to do is copy all the files inside the frontend's build folder to a folder named static inside the src/main/resources folder in the Multiplication codebase. See Figure 4-5. The default server configuration in Spring Boot adds some predefined locations for static web files, and this static folder in the classpath is one of them. These files are mapped to the root context of the application, located at /.

Figure 4-5. *Static resources in the project structure*

As usual, you could configure these resource locations and their mappings if you want. One of the places where you can fine-tune this is the same `WebMvcConfigurer` interface implementation that you used for the CORS registry configuration. Check the section called "Static Content" in the Spring Boot reference documentation if you want to know more about configuring the web server to serve static pages (`https://docs.spring.io/spring-boot/docs/current/reference/htmlsingle/#web.servlet.spring-mvc.static-content`).

Now, restart the multiplication application. This time it is important you run it via the command line (not through your IDE), using `./mvnw spring-boot:run`. The reason is that IDEs might use the classpath differently while running the app, and you could get errors in that case (e.g., the page isn't found).

If you navigate to `http://localhost:8080`, the embedded Tomcat server in your Spring Boot application will try to find a default `index.html` page, which exists because you copied it from the React build. The React application is now loaded from the same embedded server you use for the backend side. See Figure 4-6.

111

Figure 4-6. *React app served from embedded Tomcat*

You might be wondering what happens with the CORS configuration you added in a previous section, given that the frontend and backend now share the same origin. The CORS addition is no longer needed when you deploy the React application inside the same server. You could remove it since the static frontend files and the backend API are both located in the origin `http://localhost:8080`. Anyway, let's keep that configuration there since you'll be using the development server while you evolve your React app. You can now remove the contents inside the `static` folder in the Spring Boot application.

Summary and Achievements

It's time to look back at what you achieved in this chapter. When you started, you had a REST API you interacted with through command-line tools. In this chapter, you added a user interface that interacts with the backend to retrieve challenges and send attempts. You now have a real web application for your users. See Figure 4-7.

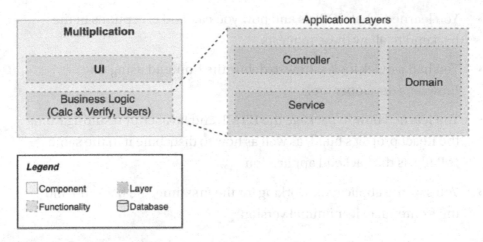

Figure 4-7. *Logical view of the application at the end of Chapter 4*

You created the foundations of the React application using the `create-react-app` tool, and you looked at how it is structured. Then, you developed a service in JavaScript to connect with the APIs, as well as a React component that uses this service and renders a simple HTML code block.

To be able to interconnect the backend and frontend living in different origins, you added CORS configuration to the backend.

Finally, you saw how to build your React application for production. You also took the resulting static files and moved them to the backend project codebase to illustrate how to serve this static content from the embedded Tomcat server.

Ideally, this chapter helped you understand the basics of a frontend application and see a practical example of interaction with your APIs. Even being only the basics, that knowledge might be helpful in your career.

You'll use this frontend application in the next chapters to see how a microservice architecture can impact the REST API clients.

Chapter's Achievements:

- You learned the basics of React, one of the most popular JavaScript frameworks in the market.

- You built the skeleton of a React application using the `create-react-app` tool.

- You developed a React component with a basic user interface for the user to send attempts.

- You learned what CORS is and how you can add exceptions in the backend to allow these requests.

- You had a quick look at how to debug the frontend using the browser's developer tools.

- You learned how to package the HTML and JavaScript resulting from the React project's build, as well as how to distribute it in the same JAR file as the backend application.

- You saw the application working for the first time, the backend and the frontend, in its minimal version.

CHAPTER 5

The Data Layer

It took two chapters to complete your first user story. Now, you have an MVP that you can use for experimentation. MVP stands for Minimum Viable Product. It is a concept widely used in product development and startups. An MVP is a version of a product or service that you develop with the minimum set of features and functionalities required to meet the needs of early adopters or customers. The primary purpose of an MVP is to gather feedback and validate assumptions about the product with real users in the market.

Requirement slicing, also known as feature slicing or backlog slicing, is a technique used in Agile development to break down hefty requirements or user stories into smaller, manageable pieces. It allows for incremental development and delivery of value to the users. In agile, slicing requirements in this way is a powerful technique. You can start collecting feedback from some test users and decide which feature to build next. Also, it's early enough to change something if your product ideas are wrong.

Learning how to slice product requirements vertically instead of horizontally may save you a lot of time while building software. That means you don't wait until you complete the whole set of layers to move to the next one. Instead, you develop pieces in multiple layers to have something that works. It also helps you build a better product or service since you get feedback when you can quickly react to it. If you want to know more about strategies for story splitting, check out `https://techbeacon.com/app-dev-testing/practical-guide-user-story-splitting-agile-teams`.

Imagine that your test users gave this application a try. Most of them came back to you saying that it would be great if they could access their statistics to know how they're performing over time. Your team sits together and comes back with a new user story.

User Story 2   As a user of the application, I want to be able to access my previous attempts so that I can track my progress and determine if my brain skills are improving over time.

© Moisés Macero García and Tarun Telang 2023
M. Macero García and T. Telang, *Learn Microservices with Spring Boot 3*,
https://doi.org/10.1007/978-1-4842-9757-5_5

When mapping this story to a technical solution, you quickly notice that you need to store the attempts. This chapter introduces the missing layer in the three-layer application architecture: the data layer. That also means you'll work with a different tier of the three-tier architecture: the database. See Figure 5-1.

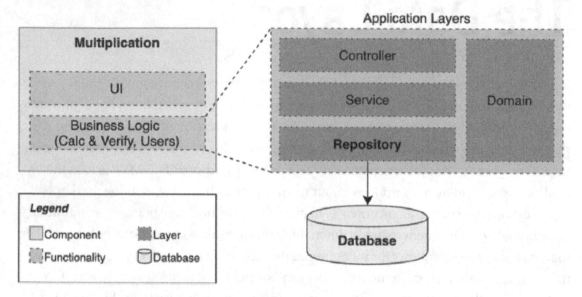

Figure 5-1. *The target application design*

You'll need to integrate these new requirements into the rest of the layers too. To sum up, you can work with this list of tasks:

- Store all the user attempts and have a way to query them per user.

- Expose a new REST endpoint to get the latest attempts for a given user.

- Create a new service (business logic) to retrieve those attempts.

- Show the attempts' history to the users on the web page after they send a new one.

The Data Model

In the conceptual model created in Chapter 3, there were three domain objects: Users, Challenges, and Attempts. Then, we made the decision to break the link between a challenge and an attempt. Instead, to keep the domain simple, we copied both factors inside attempts. That leaves only one relationship to model between the objects: attempts belonging to a particular user.

Note that you could have gone one step further in this simplification and included the user's data (for now, the alias) in the attempts as well. In that case, the only objects you would have needed to store would be the attempts. You could then use the user alias in the same table to query the data. But that comes with a price, higher than the one you assumed by copying the factors: You considered Users a different domain that may evolve over time and have interactions with other domains. Mixing up domains so tightly in the data layer is not a good idea.

There was also another design alternative. You could have created your domain classes by exactly mapping the conceptual domain with three separate objects and have a link between ChallengeAttempt and Challenge. See Figure 5-2.

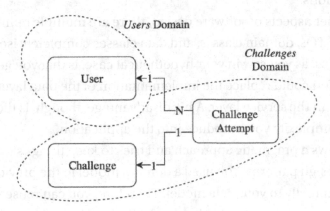

Figure 5-2. *A reminder of the conceptual model*

This could have been accomplished the same way you did with User. See Listing 5-1.

Listing 5-1. An Alternative Implementation of ChallengeAttempt

```
public record ChallengeAttempt(
        Long id,
        User user,
```

```
        // We decided to include factors
        //        int factorA,
        //        int factorB,
        // This is an alternate
        Challenge challenge,
        int resultAttempt,
        boolean correct) {
}
```

Then, you could have opted for a simplification only now, while designing the data model. In that approach, you would have the new version of the domain class `ChallengeAttempt`, as shown in the previous code snippet, and a different class in the data layer. You could name that class `ChallengeAttemptDataObject`, for example. That one would include the factors inside, so you would need to implement mappers between layers to combine and split challenges and attempts. As you have already identified, this approach is like what you did with the DTO pattern. Back then, you created a new version of the `Attempt` object in the presentation layer, where you also added some validation annotations.

As in many other aspects of software design, there are multiple opinions in favor and against of having DTOs, domain classes, and data classes completely isolated. One of the main advantages, as you saw in your hypothetical case, is that you get an even higher level of isolation. You could replace the implementation of the data layer without having to modify the code in the service layer. A big disadvantage, though, is the amount of code duplication and complexity you introduce into the application.

This book follows a pragmatic approach and tries to keep things simple while applying proper design patterns. You used a domain model in the previous chapter that you can now map directly to your data model. Therefore, you can reuse the same classes for domain and data representations. It's a good compromise solution since you still keep the domains isolated. Figure 5-3 shows the objects and the relationship you have to persist in your database.

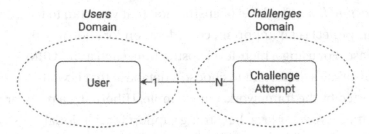

Figure 5-3. *Data model of the Multiplication application*

Choosing a Database

When choosing a database for your project, it is important to consider the project's requirements and the abstraction level you'll use. The choice of the database should be based on the specific requirements of your project, such as the availability, volume of data, expected traffic, data model complexity, and desired performance. Additionally, you need to think about the scalability requirements and consider whether the chosen database can handle future growth.

It's also important to carefully analyze your data requirements. How are you planning to query the data? Do you need high availability? How complex is your data model? Are you writing millions of records? Do you need very fast readings? Also, keep in mind the nonfunctional requirements of your system, such as scalability and performance. For example, in the example in this book, you could accept that the system is not available for a few hours per year (or even days). However, it would be a different situation if you're developing a web application for the healthcare sector, where lives might be at risk. We'll come back to nonfunctional requirements in the coming chapters to analyze some of them in more detail.

The project may require a relational database (SQL database), or a NoSQL database, or a combination of both. Let's discuss in detail some of the key factors to consider:

1. *Data model:* The choice of the database depends on the data model that best suits your project. If your project requires a structured and predefined schema, a relational database management system (RDBMS) like MySQL or PostgreSQL might be appropriate. On the other hand, if your project deals with unstructured or semi-structured data and requires flexibility, a NoSQL database like MongoDB or Cassandra could be a better fit.

2. *Abstraction level:* The level of abstraction that you plan to use in your project is an important consideration for choosing the database. For using a high-level abstraction, such as an ORM framework, it's important to choose a database that is well-supported by the framework. For example, Hibernate, a popular ORM framework for Java, has strong support for relational databases like MySQL, PostgreSQL, and Oracle. On the other hand, if you plan to work with a lower-level abstraction, such as database-specific APIs or direct SQL queries, you may have more flexibility in your database selection.

3. *Performance and scalability:* You need to also consider factors like read and write speed, caching mechanisms, replication capabilities, and clustering options. The chosen database should be able to handle the expected workload and can scale horizontally or vertically as your project grows.

4. *Integration and compatibility:* Consider the compatibility of the database with your chosen programming language and framework. Ensure that there are suitable drivers, libraries, or connectors available for seamless integration. Compatibility with your deployment environment, such as cloud platforms or containerization technologies, should also be considered.

5. *Cost and licensing:* Evaluate the cost implications and licensing terms associated with the database. Some databases are open-source and free, while others require licensing fees based on factors like usage, deployment, and enterprise-level features.

6. *Community and ecosystem:* You should also check about the community support and ecosystem surrounding the database. A strong and active community can provide helpful resources, documentation, and a pool of experienced developers. It also ensures that the database receives regular updates, bug fixes, and security patches.

SQL vs. NoSQL

There are plenty of database engines available in the market. Each of them has its own particularities, but most of the time, everybody groups them in two: SQL and NoSQL.

SQL databases are relational, with a fixed schema, and they allow you to make complex queries. NoSQL databases are intended for unstructured data and can be oriented for example to key-value pairs, documents, graphs, or column-based data.

In short, you could also say that NoSQL databases are better for big volumes of records since these databases are distributed. You can deploy multiple nodes (or instances), so they allow for good performance at writing data, reading it, or both. The price you pay is that these databases follow the CAP theorem (`https://en.wikipedia.org/wiki/CAP_theorem`). When you store data in a distributed way, you have to choose only two of the availability, consistency, and partition tolerance guarantees. You normally want partition tolerance since network errors will simply happen, so you should be able to cope with them. Therefore, most of the time you must choose between making the data available as much as possible or making it consistent.

On the other hand, relational databases (SQL) follow the ACID guarantees: *atomicity* (transactions either succeed or fail as a whole unit), *consistency* (data always transitions between valid states), *isolation* (ensures that concurrency doesn't cause side effects), and *durability* (after a transaction the state is persisted even in the event of a system failure). Those are great features, but to ensure them, these databases can't deal properly with horizontal scalability (multiple distributed nodes), meaning they don't scale that well. Table 5-1 summarizes the difference between SQL and NoSQL databases.

Table 5-1. *SQL vs NoSQL Databases*

Characteristics	Relational (or SQL) Database	NoSQL Database
Data model	Fixed schema. Altering schemas can be more complex	Flexible schema. Schema changes are easier
Use cases	Applications with structured and related data	Applications with unstructured data such as key-value pairs, documents, graphs, or column-based data
Transactional consistency	ACID-compliant (Atomicity, Consistency, Isolation, Durability)	Eventual consistency
Data integrity	Strong data integrity and validation by defining complex relationships and constraints	Less strict data integrity checks, as it usually provides minimal support for defining complex relationships
Query support	SQL-based queries and multi-table joins	Query capabilities differ among different NoSQL database
Performance	Well-suited for complex queries	Excellent performance for read-heavy workloads
Horizontal scaling	Limited options	Flexible scaling options
Cost	Higher cost due to hardware upgrades	Lower cost due to distributed architecture

The model in this book is *relational*. Besides, you don't plan to deal with millions of concurrent reads and writes. This example uses a SQL database for the web application to benefit from the ACID guarantees.

In any case, one of the advantages of keeping your application (a future microservice) small enough is that you can change the database engine later in case you need it, without a big impact on the overall software architecture.

H2, Hibernate, and JPA

The next step is to decide what relational database to use from all the possibilities: MySQL, MariaDB, PostgreSQL, H2, Oracle, MS SQL Server, and so on. In this book, we choose the H2 Database Engine since it's small and easy to install. It's so easy that it can be embedded within your application.

On top of the relational database, we'll go for an object/relational mapping (ORM) framework: Hibernate ORM. Instead of dealing with tabular data and plain queries, we'll use Hibernate to map the Java objects to SQL records. If you want to know more about ORM technologies, check out `https://hibernate.org/orm/what-is-an-orm/`.

Instead of using the native API in Hibernate to map the objects to database records, we'll use an abstraction: the Java Persistence API (JPA).

This is how these technology choices relate to each other:

- From the Java code, we'll use the Spring Boot JPA annotations and integrations, so we keep the code decoupled from Hibernate specifics.

- On the implementation side, Hibernate takes care of all the logic to map the objects to database entities.

- Hibernate supports multiple SQL dialects for different databases, and the H2 dialect is one of them.

- Spring Boot autoconfiguration sets up H2 and Hibernate for us, but we can also customize behaviors.

This loose coupling between specifications and implementations provides a big advantage: changing to a different database engine would be seamless since it's abstracted by Hibernate and Spring Boot configuration.

Spring Boot Data JPA

Let's analyze what the Spring Boot Data JPA module offers.

Dependencies and Autoconfiguration

The Spring Framework has multiple modules available to work with databases, grouped into the Spring Data family: JDBC, Cassandra, Hadoop, Elasticsearch, and so on. One of them is Spring Data JPA, which abstracts access to databases using the Java Persistence API in a Spring-based programming style.

Spring Boot takes the extra step with a dedicated starter that uses autoconfiguration and some extra tooling to quickly bootstrap database access: the `spring-boot-starter-data-jpa` module. It can also autoconfigure embedded databases such as H2, which is used for this application.

You didn't add these dependencies when you created the application to respect the step-by-step approach. Now it's time to do that. In the `pom.xml` file, add the Spring Boot starter and the H2 embedded database implementation. See Listing 5-2. You only need the H2 artifact in runtime since you'll be using the JPA and Hibernate abstractions in your code.

Listing 5-2. Adding the Data Layer Dependencies to Your Application

```
<dependencies>
[...]
    <dependency>
        <groupId>org.springframework.boot</groupId>
        <artifactId>spring-boot-starter-data-jpa</artifactId>
    </dependency>
    <dependency>
        <groupId>com.h2database</groupId>
        <artifactId>h2</artifactId>
        <scope>runtime</scope>
    </dependency>
[...]
</dependencies>
```

Source Code   You can find all the source code for this chapter on GitHub, in the `chapter05` repository.

See `https://github.com/Book-Microservices-v3/chapter05`.

Hibernate is the reference implementation for JPA in Spring Boot. That means that the starter brings the Hibernate dependencies inside. It also includes the core JPA artifacts and the dependency with its parent module, Spring Data JPA.

We already mentioned that H2 can behave as an embedded database. Therefore, you don't need to install, start, or shut down the database. The Spring Boot application will control its lifecycle. Nevertheless, we'd also like to access the database from outside for educational purposes, so add the following property to the `application.properties` file to enable the H2 database console.

```
# Gives us access to the H2 database web console
spring.h2.console.enabled=true

# H2 Database Configuration

# JDBC URL for connecting to the H2 in-memory database
spring.datasource.url=jdbc:h2:mem:testdb

# Driver class for H2 Database
spring.datasource.driverClassName=org.h2.Driver

# Username for connecting to the H2 Database
spring.datasource.username=sa

# Password for connecting to the H2 Database
spring.datasource.password=

# Hibernate dialect for H2 Database
spring.jpa.database-platform=org.hibernate.dialect.H2Dialect
```

The H2 console is a simple web interface that you can use to manage and query data. Let's verify that this new configuration works by starting the application again. You'll see some new log lines coming from the Spring Boot Data JPA autoconfiguration logic. See Figure 5-4.

```
o.a.c.c.C.[Tomcat].[localhost].[/]          : Initializing Spring embedded WebApplicationContext
w.s.c.ServletWebServerApplicationContext : Root WebApplicationContext: initialization completed in 1000 ms
com.zaxxer.hikari.HikariDataSource          : HikariPool-1 - Starting...
com.zaxxer.hikari.pool.HikariPool           : HikariPool-1 - Added connection conn0:

com.zaxxer.hikari.HikariDataSource          : HikariPool-1 - Start completed.
o.s.b.a.h2.H2ConsoleAutoConfiguration       : H2 console available at '/h2-console'. Database available at

o.hibernate.jpa.internal.util.LogHelper   : HHH000204: Processing PersistenceUnitInfo [name: default]
org.hibernate.Version                       : HHH000412: Hibernate ORM core version 6.2.2.Final
org.hibernate.cfg.Environment               : HHH000406: Using bytecode reflection optimizer
o.h.b.i.BytecodeProviderInitiator           : HHH000021: Bytecode provider name : bytebuddy
o.s.o.j.p.SpringPersistenceUnitInfo         : No LoadTimeWeaver setup: ignoring JPA class transformer
org.hibernate.orm.dialect                   : HHH035001: Using dialect: org.hibernate.dialect.H2Dialect, version:

o.h.b.i.BytecodeProviderInitiator           : HHH000021: Bytecode provider name : bytebuddy
o.h.e.t.j.p.i.JtaPlatformInitiator          : HHH000490: Using JtaPlatform implementation: [org.hibernate.engine

j.LocalContainerEntityManagerFactoryBean : Initialized JPA EntityManagerFactory for persistence unit 'default'
```

Figure 5-4. *Application Logs Showing Database Autoconfiguration*

Spring Boot detects Hibernate in the classpath and configures a data source. Since H2 is also available, Hibernate connects to H2 and selects the H2Dialect. It also initialized an `EntityManagerFactory` for you; you'll see soon what that means. There is also a log line claiming that the H2 console is available at `/h2-console` and that there is a database, available at `jdbc:h2:mem:testdb`. If there is no other configuration specified. Spring Boot autoconfiguration creates a ready-to-use, in-memory database named `testdb`.

Navigate to `http://localhost:8080/h2-console` to look at the console UI. See Figure 5-5.

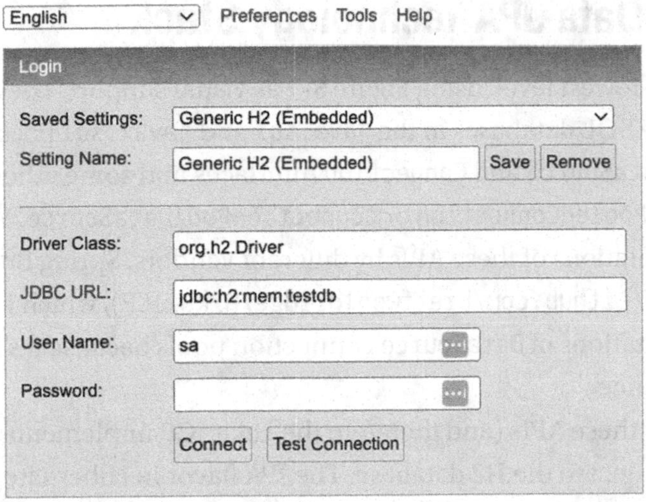

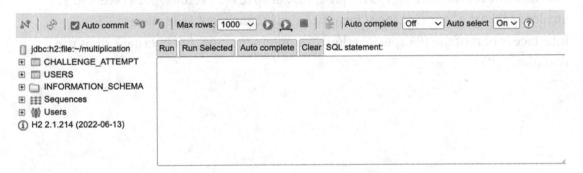

Figure 5-5. *H2 Console, login*

You can copy and paste jdbc:h2:mem:testdb as the JDBC URL and leave the other values as they are. Then, click Connect to access the main console view. See Figure 5-6.

Figure 5-6. *H2 console, connected*

It seems that you have indeed an in-memory database named testdb and that you can connect to it using the H2 default administrator credentials. Where is this database coming from? That's something you'll analyze soon.

You'll use the H2 console interface later in this chapter to query your data. For now, continue your learning path by exploring the technology stack that comes with Spring Boot and the Data JPA starter.

Spring Boot Data JPA Technology Stack

Let's start from the lowest level, using Figure 5-7 as visual support. There are some core Java APIs to handle SQL databases in the `java.sql` and `javax.sql` packages. There, you can find the `DataSource` and `Connection` interfaces and some others for pooled resources, such as `PooledConnection` or `ConnectionPoolDataSource`. You can find multiple implementations of these APIs by different vendors. Spring Boot comes with HikariCP (`https://github.com/brettwooldridge/HikariCP`), which is one of the most popular implementations of `DataSource` connection pools because it's lightweight and has good performance.

Hibernate uses these APIs (and therefore the HikariCP implementation in your application) to connect to the H2 database. The JPA flavor in Hibernate for managing the database is the `SessionImpl` class (`https://github.com/hibernate/hibernate-orm/blob/main/hibernate-core/src/main/java/org/hibernate/internal/SessionImpl.java`), which includes *a lot* of code to perform statements, execute queries, handle the session's connections, and so on. This class, via its hierarchy tree, implements the JPA interface `EntityManager` (`https://jakarta.ee/specifications/persistence/3.1/apidocs/jakarta.persistence/jakarta/persistence/entitymanager`). This interface is part of the JPA specification. Its implementation, in Hibernate, does the complete ORM.

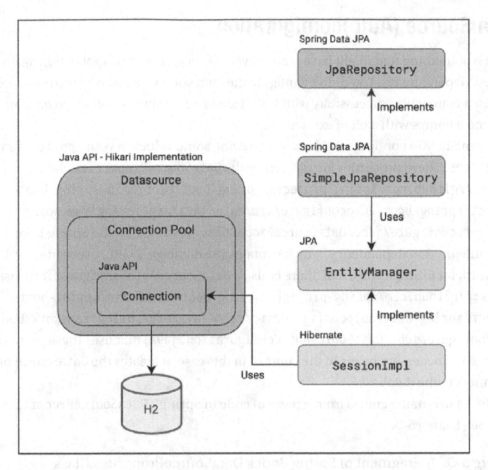

Figure 5-7. *Spring Data JPA technology stack*

On top of JPA's EntityManager, Spring Data JPA defines a JpaRepository interface (https://github.com/spring-projects/spring-data-jpa/blob/main/spring-data-jpa/src/main/java/org/springframework/data/jpa/repository/JpaRepository.java) with the most common methods you need to use normally: find, get, delete, update, and so on. The SimpleJpaRepository<T,ID> class (https://github.com/spring-projects/spring-data-jpa/blob/main/spring-data-jpa/src/main/java/org/springframework/data/jpa/repository/support/SimpleJpaRepository.java) is the default implementation in Spring and uses the EntityManager under the hood. This means you don't need to use the pure JPA standard nor Hibernate to perform database operations in your code since you can use these Spring abstractions.

You'll explore some of the cool features that Spring offers with the JPA Repository classes later in this chapter.

Data Source (Auto)configuration

There is something that might have amazed you when you ran the application again with the new dependencies. You didn't configure the data source yet, so why were you able to open a connection successfully with H2? The answer is always *autoconfiguration*, but this time it comes with a bit of extra magic.

Normally, you configure the data source using some values in your `application.properties`. These properties are defined by the `DataSourceProperties` class (`https://github.com/spring-projects/spring-boot/blob/main/spring-boot-project/spring-boot-autoconfigure/src/main/java/org/springframework/boot/autoconfigure/jdbc/DataSourceProperties.java`) within the Spring Boot autoconfiguration dependency, which contains the database's URL, username, and password, for example. As usual, there is also a `DataSourceAutoConfiguration` class (`https://github.com/spring-projects/spring-boot/blob/main/spring-boot-project/spring-boot-autoconfigure/src/main/java/org/springframework/boot/autoconfigure/jdbc/DataSourceAutoConfiguration.java`) that uses these properties to create the necessary beans in the context. In this case, it creates the `DataSource` bean to connect to the database.

The `sa` username comes from a piece of code in Spring's `DataSourceProperties` class. See Listing 5-3.

Listing 5-3. A Fragment of Spring Boot's DataSourceProperties Class

```
/**
 * Determines the username to use based on this configuration and the
 environment.
 *
 * @return the username to use
 * @since 1.4.0
 */
public String determineUsername() {
    if (StringUtils.hasText(this.username)) {
        return this.username;
    }
    if (EmbeddedDatabaseConnection.isEmbedded(determineDriverClassName(),
    determineUrl())) {
```

```
    return "sa";
    }
    return null;
}
```

Since the Spring Boot developers know these conventions, they can prepare Spring Boot so you can work with a database out-of-the-box. There is no need to pass any configuration because they hard-coded the username, and the password is an empty String by default. There are other conventions such as the database name; that's how you also got the testdb database.

You won't use the default database created by Spring Boot. Instead, you set the name after the application's name and change the URL to create a database stored in a file. If you would go ahead with the in-memory database, all the attempts would be lost when you shut down the application. Besides, you must add the DB_CLOSE_ON_EXIT=false parameter, as described in the reference documentation (see https://docs.spring. io/spring-boot/docs/current/reference/htmlsingle/#data.sql.datasource. embedded), so you disable automatic shutdown and let Spring Boot decide when to close the database. See Listing 5-4 for the resulting URL, as well as the rest of the changes in the application.properties file. There is some extra explanation afterward.

Listing 5-4. application.properties File with New Parameters for Database Configuration

```
# Gives us access to the H2 database web console
spring.h2.console.enabled=true
# Creates the database in a file
spring.datasource.url=jdbc:h2:file:~/multiplication;DB_CLOSE_ON_EXIT=FALSE
# Creates or updates the schema if needed
spring.jpa.hibernate.ddl-auto=update
# For educational purposes we will show the SQL in console
spring.jpa.show-sql=true
```

- As described, you change the data source to use a file named multiplication in the user's home directory, ~. You do that by specifying :file: in the URL. To learn all about the configuration possibilities you have in H2's URLs, see http://www.h2database. com/html/features.html#database_url.

- For simplicity, you can let Hibernate create your database schema for you. That feature is called an automatic data definition language (DDL). It's set it to `update` so the schema is created and updated when you create or modify the entities (as you'll do in the next section). Using `spring.jpa.hibernate.ddl-auto=update` might seem convenient for development, but it is recommended for production due to potential risks of data loss or unintended changes and lack of control over database schema.

- Last, enable the `spring.jpa.show-sql` property so you can see the queries in the logs. This is useful for learning purposes.

Entities

From a data perspective, JPA calls entities to the Java objects. Therefore, given that you intend to store users and attempts, you have to make the `Users` and `ChallengeAttempt` classes become entities. As discussed, you could create new classes for the data layer and use mappers, but we want to keep the codebase simple, so we reuse the domain definitions.

First, add some JPA annotations to the `Users` class. See Listing 5-5.

Listing 5-5. The User Class After Adding JPA Annotations

```
package microservices.book.multiplication.user;

import lombok.*;

import jakarta.persistence.*;
/**
 * Stores information to identify the user.
 */
@Entity
@Data
@AllArgsConstructor
@NoArgsConstructor
```

```
public class Users {
    @Id
    @GeneratedValue
    private Long id;
    private String alias;
    public Users(final String userAlias) {
        this(null, userAlias);
    }
}
}
```

Let's go through the characteristics of this updated Users class, one by one:

- The @Entity annotation was added to mark this class as an object to be mapped to a database record. You could add a value to the annotation if you want to name your table differently from the default user. Also by default, all fields exposed via getters in the class will be persisted in the mapped table with default column names. You could exclude fields by tagging them with the JPA's @Transient annotation.

- Hibernate's User Guide (https://docs.jboss.org/hibernate/orm/current/userguide/html_single/Hibernate_User_Guide.html#entity-pojo-accessors) states that you should provide setters or make your fields modifiable by Hibernate. Luckily, Lombok has a shortcut annotation, @Data, which is perfect for classes that are used as data entities. This annotation groups equals and hashCode methods, toString, getters, and setters. Another section in Hibernate's User Guide instructs you not to use final classes. This way, you allow Hibernate to create runtime proxies, which improve performance. You'll see an example of how a runtime proxy works later in this chapter.

- JPA and Hibernate also require your entities to have a default, empty constructor (see https://docs.jboss.org/hibernate/orm/current/userguide/html_single/Hibernate_User_Guide.html#entity-pojo-constructor). You can quickly add it with Lombok's @NoArgsConstructor annotation.

- The id field is annotated with @Id and @GeneratedValue. This will be the column that uniquely identifies each row. You use a generated value so Hibernate will fill in that field for you, getting the next value of the sequence from the database.

For the ChallengeAttempt class, you're using some additional features. See Listing 5-6.

Listing 5-6. The ChallengeAttempt Class with JPA Annotations

```
package microservices.book.multiplication.challenge;
import lombok.*;
import microservices.book.multiplication.user.User;
import jakarta.persistence.*;
@Entity
@Data
@AllArgsConstructor
@NoArgsConstructor
public class ChallengeAttempt {
    @Id
    @GeneratedValue
    private Long id;
    @ManyToOne(fetch = FetchType.LAZY)
    @JoinColumn(name = "USER_ID")
    private Users users;
    private int factorA;
    private int factorB;
    private int guess;
    private boolean correct;
}
```

Different from the previous class, this challenge attempt model has not only basic types but also an embedded entity type, called Users. Hibernate knows how to map it because you added the JPA annotations, but it doesn't know the relationship between these two entities. In databases, you can model these relationships as *one-to-one*, *one-to-many*, *many-to-one*, and *many-to-many*.

This example defines a many-to-one relationship since you already had a preference to avoid coupling users to attempts and to link attempts to users instead. To make these decisions in your data layer, you should also consider how to plan to query the data. In this case, you don't need the link from users to attempts. If you want to know more about entity relationships in Hibernate, check out the Associations section of the Hibernate User's Guide (`https://docs.jboss.org/hibernate/orm/current/userguide/html_single/Hibernate_User_Guide.html#associations`).

As you can see in the code, you're passing a parameter to the `@ManyToOne` annotation: the `fetch` type. When collecting the attempts from the data store, you have to tell Hibernate *when* to collect the values for the nested user too, which are stored in a different table. If you set it to `EAGER`, the user data gets collected with the attempt. With `LAZY`, the query to retrieve those fields will be executed only when you try to access them. This works because Hibernate configured proxy classes for your entity classes. See Figure 5-8. These proxy classes extend yours; that's why you shouldn't declare them `final` if you want this mechanism to work. For this case, Hibernate will pass a proxy object that triggers the query to fetch the user only when the accessor (getter) is used the first time. That's where the *laziness* term comes from—it doesn't do that until the very last moment.

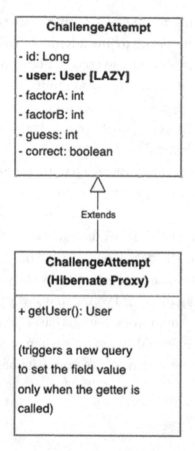

Figure 5-8. *Hibernate, intercepting classes*

In general, you should prefer lazy associations to avoid triggering extra queries for data you may not need. In this example, you don't need the user's data when you collect the attempts.

The @JoinColumn annotation makes Hibernate link both tables with a join column. For consistency, you're passing it the same name of the column that represents the index for users. This will translate to a new column added to the CHALLENGE_ATTEMPT table, called USER_ID, which will store the reference to the ID record of the corresponding user in the USER table.

This is a basic yet representative example of ORM with JPA and Hibernate. If you want to extend your knowledge about all the possibilities you have with JPA and Hibernate, the User Guide (https://docs.jboss.org/hibernate/orm/current/userguide/html_single/Hibernate_User_Guide.html) is a good place to start.

Consequences of Reusing Domain Objects as Entities   Because of JPA and Hibernate's requirements, you need to add setters to your classes and an ugly empty constructor (Lombok hid it, but it's still there). This is inconvenient since it prevents you from creating classes following good practices such as immutability. You could argue that your domain classes became corrupted by the data requirements.

This is not a big problem when you are building small applications and you know the reasons behind these decisions. You simply avoid using the setters or the empty constructor in your code. However, when working with a big team or in a mid- or big-size project, this may become an issue since a new developer might be tempted to break good practices just because the class allows them to do so. In that scenario, you may consider splitting the domain and the entity classes, as mentioned earlier. That'll bring some code duplication, but you can then better enforce good practices.

Repositories

When we described the three-layer architecture, we briefly explained that the data layer may contain data access objects (DAOs) and repositories. DAOs are typically classes that are coupled to the database structure, whereas repositories, on the other hand, are domain-centric, so these classes can work with aggregates.

Given that you're following domain-driven design, you'll use repositories to connect to the database. More specifically, you'll use JPA repositories and the features included in Spring Data JPA.

The previous section about the technology stack introduced the Spring's `SimpleJpaRepository<T,ID>` class (see `https://docs.spring.io/spring-data/jpa/docs/current/api/org/springframework/data/jpa/repository/support/SimpleJpaRepository.html`), which uses JPA's `EntityManager` (see `https://jakarta.ee/specifications/persistence/3.1/apidocs/jakarta.persistence/jakarta/persistence/entitymanager`) to manage your database objects. The Spring abstraction adds some features such as pagination and sorting, and some methods that make it more convenient to use than the plain JPA interface (e.g., `saveAll`, `existsById`, `count`, etc.).

Spring Data JPA also comes with a superpower not offered by plain JPA: the query methods (see `https://docs.spring.io/spring-data/jpa/docs/current/reference/html/#jpa.query-methods`).

Let's use the codebase to demonstrate this functionality. Say you need a query to get the last attempts of a given user so you can display the stats on the web page. Apart from that, you need some basic entity management to create, read, and delete attempts. The interface shown in Listing 5-7 provides that functionality.

Listing 5-7. The ChallengeAttemptRepository Interface

```java
package microservices.book.multiplication.challenge;

import org.springframework.data.repository.CrudRepository;

import java.util.List;

public interface ChallengeAttemptRepository extends CrudRepository
<ChallengeAttempt, Long> {
    /**
     * @return the last 10 attempts for a given user, identified by
     * their alias.
     */
    List<ChallengeAttempt> findTop10ByUserAliasOrderByIdDesc(String
    userAlias);
}
```

You create the interface by extending the `CrudRepository<T,ID>` interface (`https://github.com/spring-projects/spring-data-commons/blob/main/src/main/java/org/springframework/data/repository/CrudRepository.java`) in Spring Data Commons. `CrudRepository<T,ID>` defines a list of basic methods to create, read, update, and delete (CRUD) objects. The `SimpleJpaRepository<T,ID>` class in Spring Data JPA implements this interface too (`https://github.com/spring-projects/spring-data-jpa/blob/main/spring-data-jpa/src/main/java/org/springframework/data/jpa/repository/support/SimpleJpaRepository.java`). Apart from `CrudRepository<T,ID>`, there are two other alternatives you can use.

- If you choose to extend the plain `repository`, you don't get CRUD functionality. However, that interface works as a marker when you want to fine-tune the methods you want to expose from `CrudRepository<T,ID>`, instead of getting them all by default. See `https://docs.spring.io/spring-data/jpa/docs/current/reference/html/#repositories.definition-tuning` to learn more about this technique.

- If you also need pagination and sorting, you can extend `PagingAndSortingRepository<T,ID>`. This is helpful when you have to deal with big collections that are better queried in chunks, or *pages*.

When you extend any of these three interfaces, you have to use Java generics, as in this line:

```
... extends CrudRepository<ChallengeAttempt, Long> {
```

The first type specifies the class of the returned entity, `ChallengeAttempt` in this case. The second class must match the type of the index, which is a `Long` in this repository (the `id` field).

The most striking part of this code is the method name added to the interface. In Spring Data, you can create methods that define queries by using naming conventions in the method name. In this particular case, you want to query attempts by user alias, order them by id descending (the newest first), and pick the top ten of the list. Following the method structure, you could describe the query as follows: find Top 10 (any matching `ChallengeAttempt`) by (field `userAlias` equal to passed argument) order by (field `id`) descending.

Spring Data will process the methods you define in your interface, looking for those that don't have an explicit query defined and match the naming convention for creating query methods. That's exactly the case here. Then, it parses the method name, decomposes it in chunks, and builds a JPA query that corresponds with that definition (keep reading for an example query).

You can build many other queries using the JPA query method definition; see `https://docs.spring.io/spring-data/jpa/docs/current/reference/html/#jpa.query-methods.query-creation` for details.

Sometimes you might want to perform some queries that can't be achieved with a query method. Or maybe you just don't feel comfortable using this feature because the method names start getting a bit weird. No worries, it's also possible to define your own queries. In this case, you can still keep the implementation abstracted from the database engine by writing the queries in Jakarta Persistence Query Language (JPQL; formerly Java Persistence Query Language), a SQL language that is also part of the JPA standard. See Listing 5-8.

Listing 5-8. A Defined Query as an Alternative to a Query Method

```
/**
 * @return the last attempts for a given user, identified by their alias.
 */
@Query("SELECT a FROM ChallengeAttempt a WHERE a.user.alias = :userAlias
ORDER BY a.id DESC")
List<ChallengeAttempt> lastAttempts(@Param("userAlias") String userAlias);
```

As you can see, it looks like standard SQL. The following are the differences:

- You don't use a table name, but the class name instead
  (ChallengeAttempt).

- You refer to fields not as columns but as object fields, using dots to
  traverse the object structure (a.user.alias).

- You can use named parameters, like :userAlias in this example, to
  refer to the passed argument.

We'll stick to the query method since it's shorter and descriptive enough, but you'll need to write JPQL queries soon for other requirements.

That was all you needed to manage attempt entities in the database. Now, you're missing the repository to manage the User entities. This one is straightforward to implement, as shown in Listing 5-9.

Listing 5-9. The UserRepository Interface

```
package microservices.book.multiplication.user;

import org.springframework.data.repository.CrudRepository;
```

```
import java.util.Optional;

public interface UserRepository extends CrudRepository<User, Long> {

    Optional<User> findByAlias(final String alias);
}
```

The `findByAlias` query method will return a user wrapped in a Java `Optional<T>` if there is a match, or an empty `Optional<T>` object if no user matches the passed alias. This is another feature provided by Spring Data's JPA query methods.

With these two repositories, you have everything you need to manage your database entities. You don't need to implement these interfaces. You don't even need to add the Spring's `@Repository` annotation. Spring, using the Data module, will find interfaces extending the base ones and will inject beans that implement the desired behavior. That also involves processing the method names and creating the corresponding JPA queries.

Storing Users and Attempts

After finishing the data layer, you can start using the repositories from the service layer.

First, let's extend the test cases with the new expected logic:

- The attempt should be stored, no matter if it was correct or not.

- If it's the first attempt for a given user, identified by their alias, you should create the user. If the alias exists, the attempt should be linked to the existing user.

You have to update the `ChallengeServiceTest` class. To start with, you need to add two mocks for both repositories. This way, you keep the unit test focused on the service layer, without including any real behavior from other layers. As introduced in Chapter 2, this is one of the advantages of Mockito.

To use mocks with Mockito, you can annotate the fields with the `@Mock` annotation and add the `MockitoExtension` to the test class to have them initialized automatically. With this extension, you also get other Mockito features, like the detection of unused stubs, which makes the tests fail if you specify a mock behavior that you don't use during the test case. See Listing 5-10.

Listing 5-10. Using Mockito in the ChallengeServiceTest Class

```
@ExtendWith(MockitoExtension.class)
public class ChallengeServiceTest {

    private ChallengeService challengeService;

    @Mock
    private UserRepository userRepository;
    @Mock
    private ChallengeAttemptRepository attemptRepository;

    @BeforeEach
    public void setUp() {
        challengeService = new ChallengeServiceImpl(
                userRepository,
                attemptRepository
        );
        given(attemptRepository.save(any()))
                .will(returnsFirstArg());
    }
    //...
}
```

Besides, you can use the method annotated with JUnit's @BeforeEach to add some common behavior to all your tests. In this case, you use the service's constructor to include the repositories (note that this constructor doesn't exist yet). You need to add this line too:

```
given(attemptRepository.save(any()))
        .will(returnsFirstArg());
```

This instruction uses BDDMockito's given method to define what the mock class should do when you call specific methods during the test. Remember that you don't want to use the real class's functionality, so you have to define, for example, what to return when invoking functions on this fake object (or *stub*). The method you want to override is passed as an argument: attemptRepository.save(any()). You could match a specific argument passed to save(), but you can also define this predefined behavior for any argument by using any() from Mockito's *argument matchers* (check

out https://javadoc.io/doc/org.mockito/mockito-core/latest/org/mockito/
ArgumentMatchers.html for the complete list of matchers). The second part of the
instruction, using will(), specifies what Mockito should do when the previously defined
condition matches. The returnsFirstArg() utility method is defined in Mockito's
AdditionalAnswers class, which includes some convenient predefined answers you can
use (see https://javadoc.io/doc/org.mockito/mockito-core/latest/org/mockito/
AdditionalAnswers.html). You can also declare your own functions to provide custom
answers if you need to implement more complex scenarios. In this case, you want the
save method to do nothing but return the first (and only) argument passed. That's good
enough for you to test this layer without calling the real repository.

Add the extra verifications to your existing test cases. See Listing 5-11, which
includes the correct attempt's test case as an example.

Listing 5-11. Verifying Stub Calls in ChallengeServiceTest

```
@Test
public void checkCorrectAttemptTest() {
    // given
    ChallengeAttemptDTO attemptDTO =
            new ChallengeAttemptDTO(50, 60, "john_doe", 3000);
    // when
    ChallengeAttempt resultAttempt =
            challengeService.verifyAttempt(attemptDTO);
    // then
    then(resultAttempt.isCorrect()).isTrue();
    // newly added lines
    verify(userRepository).save(new User("john_doe"));
    verify(attemptRepository).save(resultAttempt);
}
```

Mockito's verify checks that we store a new user with a null ID and the expected
alias. The identifier will be set at the database level. We also verify that the attempt
should be saved. The test case that verifies a wrong attempt should contain those two
new lines as well.

To make these tests more complete, you can add a new case that verifies that extra
attempts from the same user won't create new user entities, but will reuse the existing
one. See Listing 5-12.

Listing 5-12. Verifying That Only the First Attempt Creates the User Entity

```java
@Test
public void checkExistingUserTest() {
    // given
    User existingUser = new User(1L, "john_doe");
    given(userRepository.findByAlias("john_doe"))
            .willReturn(Optional.of(existingUser));
    ChallengeAttemptDTO attemptDTO =
            new ChallengeAttemptDTO(50, 60, "john_doe", 5000);
    // when
    ChallengeAttempt resultAttempt =
            challengeService.verifyAttempt(attemptDTO);
    // then
    then(resultAttempt.isCorrect()).isFalse();
    then(resultAttempt.getUser()).isEqualTo(existingUser);
    verify(userRepository, never()).save(any());
    verify(attemptRepository).save(resultAttempt);
}
```

This example defines the behavior of the userRepository mock to return an existing user. Since the challenge DTO contains the same alias, the logic should find your predefined user, and the returned attempt must include it, with the same alias and ID. To make the test more exhaustive, check that the save() method in UserRepository is never called.

At this point, you have a test that doesn't compile. The service should provide a constructor with both repositories. When you start the application, Spring will use dependency injection via the constructor to initialize the repositories. This is how Spring helps you keep your layers loosely coupled.

Then, you also need the main logic to store both the attempt and the user (if it doesn't exist yet). See Listing 5-13 for the new implementation of ChallengeServiceImpl.

Listing 5-13. The Updated ChallengeServiceImpl Class Using the Repository Layer

```
package microservices.book.multiplication.challenge;

import lombok.RequiredArgsConstructor;
import lombok.extern.slf4j.Slf4j;
import microservices.book.multiplication.user.User;
import microservices.book.multiplication.user.UserRepository;
import org.springframework.stereotype.Service;

@Slf4j
@RequiredArgsConstructor
@Service
public class ChallengeServiceImpl implements ChallengeService {

    private final UserRepository userRepository;
    private final ChallengeAttemptRepository attemptRepository;

    @Override
    public ChallengeAttempt verifyAttempt(ChallengeAttemptDTO attemptDTO) {
        // Check if the user already exists for that alias, otherwise
        create it
        User user = userRepository.findByAlias(attemptDTO.getUserAlias())
                .orElseGet(() -> {
                    log.info("Creating new user with alias {}",
                            attemptDTO.getUserAlias());
                    return userRepository.save(
                            new User(attemptDTO.getUserAlias())
                    );
                });
        // Check if the attempt is correct
        boolean isCorrect = attemptDTO.getGuess() ==
                attemptDTO.getFactorA() * attemptDTO.getFactorB();
        // Builds the domain object. Null id since it'll be generated
        by the DB.
```

```
        ChallengeAttempt checkedAttempt = new ChallengeAttempt(null,
                user,
                attemptDTO.getFactorA(),
                attemptDTO.getFactorB(),
                attemptDTO.getGuess(),
                isCorrect
        );
        // Stores the attempt
        ChallengeAttempt storedAttempt = attemptRepository.
        save(checkedAttempt);
        return storedAttempt;
    }
}
```

The first block inside `verifyAttempt` uses the `Optional<T>`, returned by the repository, to decide whether the user should be created. The `orElseGet` method in an `Optional<T>` invokes the passed function only if it's empty. Therefore, you create a new user only if it's not there yet.

You pass the returned `User` object from the repository when you construct an attempt. Hibernate will take care of linking them properly in the database when you call `save()` to store the attempt entity. Then it returns the result, so it includes all the identifiers from the database.

All the test cases should pass now. Again, you used TDD to create this logic based on your expectations. It's clear now how a unit test helps you verify the specific layer's behavior without depending on the other layers. For the service class, you replaced both repositories by stubs for which you defined preset values.

There is an alternative implementation of these tests. You could use the `@SpringBootTest` flavor and `@MockBean` for the repository classes. However, that doesn't bring any added value and requires the Spring context, so the tests take more time to finish. As mentioned in a previous chapter, it's better to keep your unit tests as simple as possible.

Repository Tests   We're not creating tests for the application's data layer. These tests don't make much sense since we're not writing any implementation anyway. We would end up verifying the Spring Data implementation itself.

Displaying Last Attempts

You learned how to modify the existing service logic to store users and attempts, but you're still missing the other half of the functionality: retrieving the last attempts and displaying them on the page.

The service layer can simply use the query method from the repository. On the controller layer, you'll expose a new REST endpoint to get the list of attempts by user alias.

Exercise   Keep following TDD and complete some tasks before moving forward with the implementation. You'll find the solution in this chapter's code repository (`https://github.com/Book-Microservices-v3/chapter05`).

- Extend the `ChallengeServiceTest` and create a test case to verify that you can retrieve the last attempts. The logic behind the test is a one-liner, but it's good to have the test in case the service layer grows. Note that you may get complaints from Mockito about the unnecessary stub of the `save` method in this test case. That's one of the features of the `MockitoExtension`. You can then move that stub inside the test cases that use it.

- Update the `ChallengeAttemptController` class to include a test for the new endpoint: GET `/attempts?alias=john_doe`.

Service Layer

In this section, you add a method to the `ChallengeService` interface called `getStatsForUser`. See Listing 5-14.

Listing 5-14. Adding the getStatsForUser Method to the ChallengeService Interface

```
package microservices.book.multiplication.challenge;
import java.util.List;
public interface ChallengeService {
    /**
```

```
 * Verifies if an attempt coming from the presentation layer is
 correct or not.
 *
 * @return the resulting ChallengeAttempt object
 */
ChallengeAttempt verifyAttempt(ChallengeAttemptDTO attemptDTO);
/**
 * Gets the statistics for a given user.
 *
 * @param userAlias the user's alias
 * @return a list of the last 10 {@link ChallengeAttempt}
 * objects created by the user.
 */
List<ChallengeAttempt> getStatsForUser(String userAlias);
}
```

The code block in Listing 5-15 shows the implementation. As predicted, it's just a single line of code.

Listing 5-15. Implementing the getStatsForUser Method

```
@Slf4j
@RequiredArgsConstructor
@Service
public class ChallengeServiceImpl implements ChallengeService {
    // ...
    @Override
    public List<ChallengeAttempt> getStatsForUser(final String userAlias) {
        return attemptRepository.findTop10ByUserAliasOrderByIdDesc(u
        serAlias);
    }
}
```

Controller Layer

Let's move one layer up and see how to connect the service layer from the controller. This time, you use a query parameter, but that doesn't add much complexity to the API definitions. Similar to how you got the request body injected as a parameter in the first method, you can now use @RequestParam to tell Spring to pass you an URL parameter. Check the reference docs (https://docs.spring.io/spring-framework/reference/web/webmvc/mvc-controller/ann-methods/arguments.html) for other method arguments you can define (e.g., session attributes or cookie values). See Listing 5-16.

Listing 5-16. Adding a New Endpoint to the Controller to Retrieve Statistics

```
@Slf4j
@RequiredArgsConstructor
@RestController
@RequestMapping("/attempts")
class ChallengeAttemptController {
    private final ChallengeService challengeService;
    @PostMapping
    ResponseEntity<ChallengeAttempt> postResult(
            @RequestBody @Valid ChallengeAttemptDTO challengeAttemptDTO) {
        return ResponseEntity.ok(challengeService.verifyAttempt(challenge
        AttemptDTO));
    }
    @GetMapping
    ResponseEntity<List<ChallengeAttempt>> getStatistics(
    @RequestParam("alias") String alias) {
        return ResponseEntity.ok(
                challengeService.getStatsForUser(alias)
        );
    }
}
```

If you implemented the tests, they should pass now. Listing 5-17 shows the command to run the Spring Boot application.

Listing 5-17. Commands to Start the Backend

```
/multiplication $ mvnw spring-boot:run
```

However, if you run a quick test using HTTPie, you find an unexpected result. See Listing 5-18. Sending one attempt and then trying to retrieve the list gives you an error.

Listing 5-18. Error During Serialization of the Attempt List

```
$ http POST :8080/attempts factorA=58 factorB=92 userAlias=ttelang
guess=5303
Connection: keep-alive
Content-Type: application/json
Date: Thu, 29 Jun 2023 16:29:01 GMT
Keep-Alive: timeout=60
Transfer-Encoding: chunked
Vary: Origin
Vary: Access-Control-Request-Method
Vary: Access-Control-Request-Headers

{
    "correct": false,
    "factorA": 58,
    "factorB": 92,
    "guess": 5303,
    "id": 1002,
    "user": {
        "alias": null,
        "id": 302
    }
}

$ http ":8080/attempts?alias=moises"
HTTP/1.1 500
Connection: close
Content-Type: application/json
Date: Thu, 29 Jun 2023 16:31:12 GMT
Transfer-Encoding: chunked
```

```
Vary: Origin
Vary: Access-Control-Request-Method
Vary: Access-Control-Request-Headers
```

```
{
  "error": "Internal Server Error",
  "message": "Type definition error: [simple type, class org.hibernate.
  proxy.pojo.bytebuddy.ByteBuddyInterceptor]",
 "path": "/attempts",
 "status": 500,
 "timestamp": "2023-06-29T16:31:12.518+00:00"
}
```

That's an ugly server error. You can also find the counterpart exception in the backend logs. What is a ByteBuddyInterceptor, and why is your ObjectMapper trying to serialize it? There should be only ChallengeAttempt objects in the result, with nested User instances, right? Well, not really.

You configured the nested User entities to be fetched in LAZY mode, so they're not being queried from the database. We also said that Hibernate creates proxies for your classes in runtime. That's the reason behind the ByteBuddyInterceptor class. You can try switching the fetch mode to EAGER, and you will no longer get this error. But that's not the proper solution to this problem, since then you'll be triggering many queries for data you don't need.

Let's keep the LAZY fetch mode and fix this accordingly. The first option is to customize the JSON serialization so it can handle Hibernate objects. Luckily, FasterXML, the provider of Jackson libraries, has a specific module for Hibernate that you can use in your ObjectMapper objects: jackson-datatype-hibernate (https://github.com/FasterXML/jackson-datatype-hibernate/wiki). To use it, you have to add this dependency to your project since it's not included by Spring Boot starters. See Listing 519.

Listing 5-19. Adding the Dependency for Jackson Module for Hibernate that Is Compatible with the Jakarta Persistence (JPA) API

```
<dependencies>
<!-- ... -->
    <dependency>
```

```
        <groupId>com.fasterxml.jackson.datatype</groupId>
        <artifactId>jackson-datatype-hibernate5-jakarta</artifactId>
    </dependency>
<!-- ... -->
</dependencies>
```

Then you follow the documented way in Spring Boot (see https://docs.spring.io/spring-boot/docs/current/reference/htmlsingle/#howto.spring-mvc.customize-jackson-objectmapper) to customize ObjectMappers:

"Any beans of type com.fasterxml.jackson.databind.Module are automatically registered with the autoconfigured Jackson2ObjectMapperBuilder and are applied to any ObjectMapper instances that it creates. This provides a global mechanism for contributing custom modules when you add new features to your application."

You create a bean for your new Hibernate module for Jackson. Spring Boot's Jackson2ObjectMapperBuilder will use it via autoconfiguration, and all your ObjectMapper instances will use the Spring Boot defaults plus your own customization. Listing 5-20 shows this new JsonConfiguration class.

Listing 5-20. Loading the Jackson's Hibernate Module to Be Picked Up by Autoconfiguration

```
package microservices.book.multiplication.configuration;

import com.fasterxml.jackson.databind.Module;
import com.fasterxml.jackson.datatype.hibernate5.jakarta.
Hibernate5JakartaModule;
import org.springframework.context.annotation.Bean;
import org.springframework.context.annotation.Configuration;

@Configuration
public class JsonConfiguration {
    @Bean
```

```
    public Module hibernateModule() {
        return new Hibernate5JakartaModule();
    }
}
```

Now you start your application using the same `mvnw spring-boot:run` command, and you verify that you can retrieve the attempts successfully. The nested `user` object is `null`, which is perfect since you don't need it for the list of attempts. See Listing 5-21. We avoided the extra queries.

Listing 5-21. Correct Serialization of the Attempts After Adding the Hibernate Module

```
$ http ":8080/attempts?alias=moises"
HTTP/1.1 200
Connection: keep-alive
Content-Type: application/json
Date: Thu, 29 Jun 2023 16:45:18 GMT
Keep-Alive: timeout=60
Transfer-Encoding: chunked
Vary: Origin
Vary: Access-Control-Request-Method
Vary: Access-Control-Request-Headers...
[
{
        "correct": false,
        "factorA": 63,
        "factorB": 87,
        "guess": 5421,
        "id": 952,
        "user": null
    },
...
]
```

An alternative to adding this new dependency and the new configuration is to follow the recommendation that was printed in the message of the exception that you got:

```
...(to avoid exception, disable SerializationFeature.FAIL_ON_EMPTY_
BEANS)[...]
```

Let's try it. You can add features to Jackson serializers directly in the `application.properties` file (see `https://docs.spring.io/spring-boot/docs/current/reference/htmlsingle/#howto-customize-the-jackson-objectmapper`). This is achieved with a naming convention, prefixing the Jackson properties with `spring.jackson.serialization`. See Listing 5-22.

Listing 5-22. Adding a Property to Avoid Serialization Errors on Empty Beans

```
[...]
spring.jpa.show-sql=true
spring.jackson.serialization.fail_on_empty_beans=false
```

If you try this (after removing the code from the previous solution) and then collect the attempts, you'll find a funny result. See Listing 5-23.

Listing 5-23. Retrieving Attempts with fail_on_empty_beans=false

```
$ http ":8080/attempts?alias=moises"
HTTP/1.1 200
...
[
    {
        "correct": false,
        "factorA": 63,
        "factorB": 87,
        "guess": 5421,
        "id": 952,
        "user": {
            "alias": "ttelang",
            "hibernateLazyInitializer": {},
```

```
        "id": 202
    }
  },
...
]
```

There are two unexpected outcomes. First, the `hibernateLazyInitializer` property from the proxy object is being serialized to JSON, and it's empty. That's the empty bean, and it's actually the source of the error you got earlier. You can avoid that with some Jackson configuration to ignore that field. But the real issue is that the user's data is there too. The serializer traversed the proxy to get the user's data, and that triggered the extra query from Hibernate to fetch it, which makes the LAZY parameter configuration useless. You can also verify that in the logs, because you got an extra query compared to the previous solution. See Listing 5-24.

Listing 5-24. Unwanted Query When Fetching Attempts with Suboptimal Configuration

```
Hibernate: select c1_0.id,c1_0.correct,c1_0.factora,c1_0.factorb,c1_0.
guess,c1_0.user_id from challenge_attempt c1_0 left join users u1_0 on
u1_0.id=c1_0.user_id where u1_0.alias=? order by c1_0.id desc fetch first ?
rows only
Hibernate: select u1_0.id,u1_0.alias from users u1_0 where u1_0.id=?
```

Let's hold to the first option with the Hibernate module for Jackson, since it's the proper way to handle lazy fetching with JSON serialization.

The takeaway from the analysis we did of both alternatives is that, with so much behavior hidden behind the scenes in Spring Boot, you should avoid going for quick solutions without really understanding what the implications are. Get to know the tools and read the reference documentation.

User Interface

The last part in the stack where you need to integrate the new functionality to display the last attempts is in the React frontend. Like in the previous chapter, you can skip this section if you don't want to dive into details about the UI.

See Listing 5-25 to view the project file structure.

Listing 5-25. Project File Structure

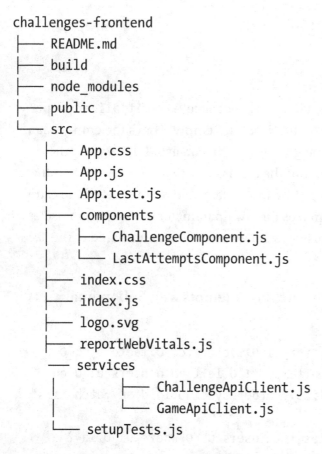

```
challenges-frontend
├── README.md
├── build
├── node_modules
├── public
└── src
    ├── App.css
    ├── App.js
    ├── App.test.js
    ├── components
    │   ├── ChallengeComponent.js
    │   └── LastAttemptsComponent.js
    ├── index.css
    ├── index.js
    ├── logo.svg
    ├── reportWebVitals.js
    ── services
    │           ├── ChallengeApiClient.js
    │           └── GameApiClient.js
    └── setupTests.js
```

Let's stick to a basic user interface for now and add a table to the page that will show the last tries of the user. You can make this request after a new attempt is sent since you'll get the user's alias.

But, before that, replace the predefined CSS to make sure all the contents fit on the page.

First, move the ChallengeComponent to be rendered directly, without any wrapper. See the resulting App.js file in Listing 5-26.

Listing 5-26. /challenges-frontend/src/App.js File After Moving the Component Up

```
import './App.css';
import ChallengeComponent from "./components/ChallengeComponent";
```

```
function App() {
    return <ChallengeComponent/>;
}
```

```
export default App;
```

App component renders the ChallengeComponent, it will display the relevant content on your application's interface.

Next, you remove all the predefined CSS and adapt it to your needs. You can add these basic styles to the index.css and App.css files, respectively. See Listings 5-27 and 5-28.

Listing 5-27. The Modified /challenges-frontend/src/index.css File

```
body {
    font-family: 'Segoe UI', Roboto, Arial, sans-serif;
}
```

Listing 5-28. The Modified /challenges-frontend/src/App.css File

```
.display-column {
    display: flex;
    flex-direction: column;
    align-items: center;
}

.challenge {
    font-size: 4em;
}

.form-container {
    display: flex;
    padding: 5px;
    justify-content: space-between;
}
```

```
th {
  padding-right: 0.5em;
  border-bottom: solid 1px;
}
```

Apply the `display-column` to the main HTML container to stack the components vertically and align them to the center. The `challenge` style is for the multiplication, and you can also customize the table header style to have some padding and use a bottom line.

Once you've made some room for the new table, you have to extend `ChallengeApiClient` in JavaScript to retrieve the attempts. Like before, use `fetch` with its default GET verb and build the URL to include the user's alias as a query parameter. See Listing 5-29.

Listing 5-29. ChallengeApiClient Class Update with the Method to Fetch Attempts in /challenges-frontend/src/services/ApiClient.js

```
class ChallengeApiClient {
    static SERVER_URL = 'http://localhost:8080';
    static GET_CHALLENGE = '/challenges/random';
    static POST_RESULT = '/attempts';
    static GET_ATTEMPTS_BY_ALIAS = '/attempts?alias=';
    static challenge(): Promise<Response> {
        return fetch(ChallengeApiClient.SERVER_URL + ChallengeApiClient.
        GET_CHALLENGE);
    }
    static sendGuess(user: string,
                     a: number,
                     b: number,
                     guess: number): Promise<Response> {
        // ...
    }
    static getAttempts(userAlias: string): Promise<Response> {
        return fetch(ChallengeApiClient.SERVER_URL +
            ChallengeApiClient.GET_ATTEMPTS_BY_ALIAS + userAlias);
    }
}
export default ChallengeApiClient;
```

The next task is to create a new React component for this list of attempts. This way, you keep your frontend modularized. This new component doesn't need a state since you will use the parent's state to hold the last attempts.

You use a simple HTML table to render the objects passed through the props object. As a nice addition on the UI level, you can show the correct result of the challenge if it was incorrect. Also, you'll have a conditional style attribute that will make the text color green or red depending on whether the attempt was correct. See Listing 5-30.

Listing 5-30. The New LastAttemptsComponent in React in the /challenges-frontend/src/components/LastAttemptsComponent.js file

```
import * as React from 'react';
class LastAttemptsComponent extends React.Component {
    render() {
        return (
            <table>
                <thead>
                <tr>
                    <th>Challenge</th>
                    <th>Your guess</th>
                    <th>Correct</th>
                </tr>
                </thead>
                <tbody>
                {this.props.lastAttempts.map(a =>
                    <tr key={a.id}
                        style={{ color: a.correct ? 'green' : 'red' }}>
                        <td>{a.factorA} x {a.factorB}</td>
                        <td>{a.resultAttempt}</td>
                        <td>{a.correct ? "Correct" :
                            ("Incorrect (" + a.factorA * a.factorB +
                            ")")}</td>
                    </tr>
                )}
                </tbody>
            </table>
```

```
        );
    }
}
export default LastAttemptsComponent;
```

As shown in the code, you can use `map` when rendering React components to easily iterate over arrays. Each element of the array should use a key attribute to help the framework identify changing elements. See `https://react.dev/learn/rendering-lists` for more details about rendering lists with unique keys.

Now you need to put everything to work together in the existing `ChallengeComponent` class. See Listing 5-31 for the code after adding some modifications.

- A new function that uses `ChallengeApiClient` to retrieve the last attempts, check if the HTTP response was `OK`, and store the array in the state.

- A call to this new function right after you get a response to the request that sends a new attempt.

- The component's HTML tag inside the `render()` function of this parent component.

- As an improvement, you also extract the logic to refresh the challenge (included before in `componentDidMount`) to a new function, `refreshChallenge`. You can create a new challenge for the users after they send an attempt.

Listing 5-31. The Updated ChallengeComponent to Include the LastAttemptsComponent in the /challenges-frontend/src/components/ LastAttemptsComponent file

```
import * as React from "react";
import ApiClient from "../services/ChallengeApiClient";
import LastAttemptsComponent from './LastAttemptsComponent';

class ChallengeComponent extends React.Component {

    constructor(props) {
        super(props);
        this.state = {
```

```
        a: '', b: '',
        user: '',
        message: '',
        guess: 0,
        lastAttempts: [],
    };
    this.handleSubmitResult = this.handleSubmitResult.bind(this);
    this.handleChange = this.handleChange.bind(this);
}
// ...
handleSubmitResult(event) {
    event.preventDefault();
    ApiClient.sendGuess(this.state.user,
        this.state.a, this.state.b,
        this.state.guess)
        .then(res => {
            if (res.ok) {
                res.json().then(json => {
                    if (json.correct) {
                        this.updateMessage("Congratulations! Your guess
                        is correct");
                    } else {
                        this.updateMessage("Oops! Your guess " + json.
                        resultAttempt +
                        " is wrong, but keep playing!");
                    }
                    this.updateLastAttempts(this.state.user); // NEW!
                    this.refreshChallenge(); // NEW!
                });
            } else {
                this.updateMessage("Error: server error or not
                available");
            }
        });
}
```

```
    // ...
    updateLastAttempts(userAlias: string) {
        ChallengeApiClient.getAttempts(userAlias).then(res => {
            if (res.ok) {
                let attempts: Attempt[] = [];
                res.json().then(data => {
                    data.forEach(item => {
                        attempts.push(item);
                    });
                    this.setState({
                        lastAttempts: attempts
                    });
                })
            }
        })
    }
    render() {
        return (
            <div className="display-column">
                <div>
                    <h3>Your new challenge is</h3>
                    <div className="challenge">
                        {this.state.a} x {this.state.b}
                    </div>
                </div>
                <form onSubmit={this.handleSubmitResult}>
                {/* ... */}
                </form>
                <h4>{this.state.message}</h4>
                {this.state.lastAttempts.length > 0 &&
                    <LastAttemptsComponent lastAttempts={this.state.
                    lastAttempts}/>
                }
            </div>
        );
```

```
    }
}
export default ChallengeComponent;
```

In React, you can update parts of the state if you pass only that property to the setState method, which will then merge the contents. You add the new property called lastAttempts to the state and update it with the contents of the array returned by the backend. Given that the items of the array are JSON objects, you can access its attributes in plain JavaScript using the property names.

You also used something new in this code: a conditional rendering with the && operator. The content on the right will be rendered by React only if the condition on the left is true. See https://react.dev/learn/conditional-rendering#logical-and-operator- for different ways of doing this. The lastAttempts HTML property added to the component tag is passed to the child component's code via the props object.

Note that this example also used the new styles display-column and challenge. In React, you use the className attribute, which will be mapped to the standard HTML class.

Playing with the New Feature

After adding the new data layer and the logic to all other layers up to the UI, you're ready to play with the full application. Either using the IDE or using two different terminal windows, you can run the backend and frontend with the commands shown in Listing 5-32.

Listing 5-32. Commands to Start the Backend and Frontend, Respectively

```
/multiplication $ mvnw spring-boot:run
...
/challenges-frontend $ npm start
...
```

Then, navigate to `http://localhost:3000` to access the React frontend running in development mode. The default port for running a React application created with Create React App is 3000. Since rendering this new component is conditional, you don't see the new table, so play a few challenges to see how the table is populated with your attempts. You should see something similar to Figure 5-9.

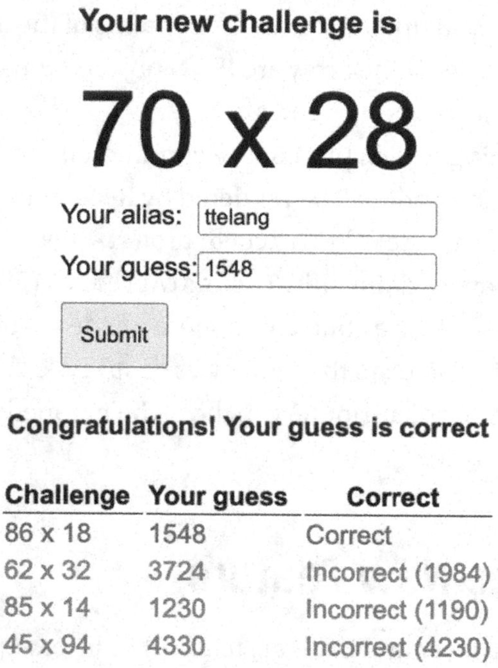

Your new challenge is

70 x 28

Your alias: | ttelang |

Your guess: | 1548 |

| Submit |

Congratulations! Your guess is correct

Challenge	Your guess	Correct
86 x 18	1548	Correct
62 x 32	3724	Incorrect (1984)
85 x 14	1230	Incorrect (1190)
45 x 94	4330	Incorrect (4230)

Figure 5-9. *The app after adding the LastAttempts feature*

Great, you made it! It's not the most beautiful frontend, but it's nice to see this new functionality up and running. The `Challenge` component performs the requests to the backend and renders the child component, the `LastAttempts` table.

If you're curious about how the data looks, you can also navigate to the backend's H2 console to get access to the data in these tables. Remember that the console is located at `http://localhost:8080/h2-console`. You should see both tables for users and attempts and some content in them. This basic console allows you to perform queries and even edit the data. For example, you can click the name of the `CHALLENGE_ATTEMPT` table, and a SQL query will be generated in the panel to the right. Then, you can click the Run button to query the data. See Figure 5-10.

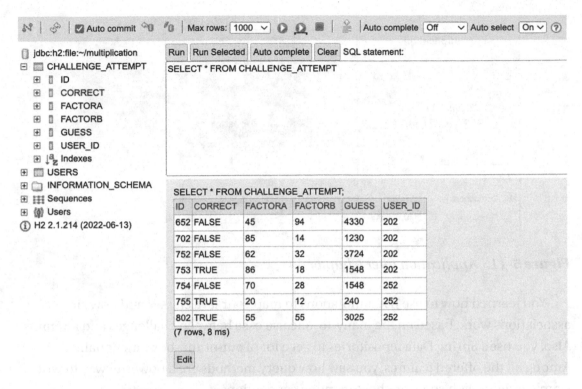

Figure 5-10. *Attempts data in the H2 console*

Summary and Achievements

In this chapter, you saw how to model your data for persistence, and you used object-relational mapping to convert your domain object to database records. During the journey, the chapter covered some Hibernate and JPA fundamentals. Figure 5-11 shows the current status of the application.

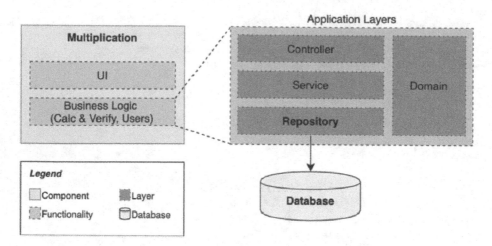

Figure 5-11. *Application after Chapter 5*

You learned how to use JPA annotations to map your Java classes and how simple associations work, based on the many-to-one use case between challenges and attempts. Also, you used Spring Data repositories to get a lot of out-of-the-box functionality. Among all the offered features, you saw how query methods are a powerful way to write simple queries with some method's naming conventions.

The second user story is done. You went through the service and the controller layers and added your new functionality there. You also included a new component in the UI to visualize the last attempts on your web application.

You have finished the first part of the book. Until now, you have seen in detail how a small web application works. The book dedicated time to explain Spring Boot's core concepts and some specific modules for the different layers, like Spring Data and Spring Web. You even learned how to build a small React frontend.

Now it's time to start the microservices adventure.

Chapter's Achievements:

- You got the complete picture of how a three-layer, three-tier architecture works, with the introduction of the repository classes and the database.

- You learned how to model your data, taking into account your requirements for querying it and the proper domain isolation.

- You went through the main differences between SQL and NoSQL and the criteria you can use to make future choices.

- You learned about JPA and its integration with Hibernate, Spring Data, and Spring Boot.

- You developed a real persistence layer for an application using JPA annotations and Spring Data repositories, using query methods and defined queries.

- You integrated the new attempts history feature all the way up to the frontend, improving your practical case study.

## CHAPTER 6

Starting with Microservices

This chapter pauses your practical journey to analyze how you've built the application and consider the impact of moving to microservices architecture.

First, you learn about the advantages of starting with a single codebase. Then, we describe the new requirements, which include an overview of gamification techniques. Essentially, *gamification* involves incorporating game-design principles into applications, encouraging engagement, and motivating users. You can achieve this by adding features like enabling competition, rewards, achievements, and progress tracking into various activities. The main objective here is to leverage the user's natural inclination toward play to drive desired behaviors, increase motivation, and improve overall engagement. By implementing game-like elements, such as points, leaderboards, levels, badges, quests, or challenges, gamification aims to make activities more enjoyable, stimulating, and interactive.

Next, you explore the factors you must consider while transitioning to microservices. Additionally, you will learn about the advantages and disadvantages of making that decision.

The second part of this chapter is all practical again. You build your new microservice using the design patterns you learned in previous chapters and connect it to your existing application, the first microservice. Then, you analyze some unique challenges of this new *distributed system*.

Distributed systems refer to a network of interconnected autonomous computers or nodes (which can even be located remotely) that work together to achieve a common goal. They allow for efficient resource utilization, improved performance, fault tolerance, and the ability to handle large-scale computations. However, building and managing distributed systems involves additional challenges like network communication, data consistency, synchronization, and load balancing.

© Moisés Macero García and Tarun Telang 2023
M. Macero García and T. Telang, *Learn Microservices with Spring Boot 3*,
https://doi.org/10.1007/978-1-4842-9757-5_6

The Small Monolith Approach

In the previous chapter, you had a single deployment unit containing all the required functionalities (including the frontend). You identified two domains—Challenges and Users—which were loosely coupled. But still we decided not to split them into multiple microservices from the beginning.

You can consider the Multiplication application a small monolith.

Why a Small Monolith?

Compared to microservices, starting with a single codebase simplifies the development process, allowing you to deploy the first version of your product quickly. Besides, it makes changing the architecture and software designs much easier at the beginning of the project's lifecycle, when it's critical to make adaptations after you validate your ideas.

If your organization lacks experience working with microservices, it will likely underestimate the technical complexity they bring to a software project. After finishing this book, you should have a comprehensive understanding of microservices. In the following chapters, we cover a range of design patterns and technical requirements you should adopt for implementing microservices, as they can be challenging.

The Problems with Microservices from Day Zero

As an alternative to the approach you have followed so far, you could have chosen a microservices architecture from the beginning. It would have involved splitting Users and Challenges into two separate Spring Boot applications.

One advantage of starting with a split is that it allows multiple teams in the organization to work simultaneously without interfering with each other. You could achieve this by assigning different microservices to separate teams right from the start of the project. In the book example, there are only two domains, but even if there were ten different bounded contexts, a large organization can utilize its resources effectively to expedite project completion.

You could also use the split into microservices to accomplish your target architecture. Usually, this is referred to in the software industry as the reverse *Conway*. Conway's law (see `https://en.wikipedia.org/wiki/Conway's_law`) states that a system design tends to resemble the structure of the organization that is building it. Therefore, you should try to use this prediction and adapt your organization to be like the software architecture you want to materialize. You draft your complete software architecture, identify the domains, and divide them between the teams.

Being able to work in parallel and achieving the target architecture are considerable advantages. However, there are two problems with a too-early split into microservices. The first is that when you develop software the agile way, you usually can't spend weeks designing the complete system in advance. You will make mistakes when trying to identify loosely coupled domains. And, when you realize that there were flaws, it'll be too late. It's hard to fight against the inertia of multiple teams working simultaneously based on a wrong split of domains, especially if the organization is not flexible enough to cope with those changes. Under these circumstances, the reverse Conway and an early split will play against your goals. You'll create a software system that reflects your initial architecture, but that might no longer be what you want. You may check out this video lecture, "The Six Pitfalls of building a Microservices Architecture" by Moisés Macero (see https://youtu.be/6xOBPHGOdRY?t=545) to get more insights about this topic.

The second big issue of starting directly with microservices is that it usually means that you're not splitting the system into vertical slices. We started the previous chapter describing why it's a good idea to deliver software as soon as possible so you can get feedback. Then, we explained how you can build small portions of the application layers to deliver value, instead of designing and implementing the complete layers individually. If you start from scratch with multiple microservices, you're going horizontal. A microservice architecture always introduces technical complexity. They're harder to set up, deploy, orchestrate, and test. It will cost you more time to have a minimum viable product, and which may also have a technical impact. In the worst case, you could have made software designs based on wrong assumptions, making them obsolete after you get user feedback.

Small Monoliths Are for Small Teams

A small monolith is a good plan if you can keep the team small initially. You can focus on domain definition and experimentation. When you have your product ideas validated and a clearer software architecture, more people can gradually join the team, and you can think of splitting the codebase and conforming new teams. You could then move to microservices or choose another approach, such as a modular system, depending on your requirements (we elaborate more on these two options at the end of this chapter).

However, sometimes you can't avoid starting a project with a big team. It's just a given in your organization. You can't convince the right people that this is not a good idea. If that's the case, the small monolith could become a giant monolith quickly, with a spaghetti codebase that might be difficult to modularize later. Besides, it's hard to focus on one vertical slice at a time since there would be many team members doing nothing. The small monolith for a small team idea doesn't work well under this organizational constraint. You need to do some splitting. In that scenario, you must put extra effort into defining the bounded contexts and the communication interfaces between those future modules. Whenever you design features spanning multiple modules or microservices, you must involve the corresponding teams to define what kind of inputs/outputs these modules will produce and consume. The better you define these contracts, the more independent the teams will be. In an Agile environment, this means that the delivery of features can go slower than expected at the beginning, since the teams need to define not only these contracts but a lot of common technical foundations.

Embracing Refactoring

Another situation where a small monolith seems problematic is when your organization doesn't embrace code changes. As described before, you start with a small monolith to validate product ideas and get feedback. Then, there will be a time when you see the need to start splitting the monolith into microservices. As we describe later, that split comes with organizational and technical advantages. Both technical people and project managers should have a conversation at the beginning of the project to decide when it is appropriate to do this split based on functional and technical requirements.

Nevertheless, sometimes developers think that this moment will never arrive: if they start with a monolith, they'll be chained to it forever. They fear there'll never be a pause in the project's roadmap to plan and accomplish the needed refactor into microservices. With that in mind, technical people may push the organization and force microservices from the beginning. This is usually a bad idea because it might frustrate stakeholders who may think such technical complexity is delaying the project unnecessarily. Instead of selling a microservices architecture as the only option, improving communication with business stakeholders and project managers is better for preparing a good plan.

Planning the Small Monolith for a Future Split

When you choose to go for a small monolith, you can follow some good practices for it to be split later with little effort.

- *Compartmentalize the code in root packages defining the domain contexts*: This is what you did in the application with the challenge and user root packages. Then, you could create sub-packages for the layering (e.g., controller, repository, domain, and service) if you start dealing with many classes to ensure layer isolation. Make sure you follow good practices for class visibility (e.g., interfaces are public, but their implementations are package-private). The main advantages of this structure are that you can keep business logic inaccessible across domain contexts and that, later, you should be able to extract one complete root package as a microservice if you need it, with less refactoring.

- *Take advantage of dependency injection*: Base your code on interfaces, and let Spring do its job injecting the implementations. Refactoring using this pattern is much easier. For example, you may change an implementation to call a different microservice later instead of using local classes, without impacting the rest of the logic.

- *Once you have identified the contexts (e.g., Challenges and Users), give them a consistent name across your application*: Properly naming the concepts is critical at the beginning of the design phase to ensure everybody understands the different domain boundaries.

- Don't be afraid of moving classes around (more straightforward with a small monolith) during the design phase until boundaries are clear: After that, respect the boundaries. Never take shortcuts tangling business logic across contexts just because you can. Always keep in mind that the monolith needs to be constantly evolving. In a microservices architecture, it's not uncommon to have repeated classes or shared objects across multiple microservices. It's essential to evaluate the trade-offs and benefits specific to your use case and requirements. It's important to ensure that it aligns with your design goals, maintains service independence, and is well-managed to avoid excessive duplication and complexity.

- Find common patterns and identify what you can later extract as shared libraries; for example: Move them to a different root package.

- *Use peer reviews to ensure the architecture designs are sound and facilitate knowledge transfer*: It's better to do this as a small group instead of following a top-bottom approach where all designs come from a single person.

- *Communicate clearly to the project manager and business representatives to plan time later to split the monolith*: Explain the strategy and create the culture. Refactoring is going to be necessary, and there is nothing wrong with it.

Try to keep a small monolith, at least until your first release. Don't be afraid of it; a small monolith will bring you some advantages.

- Faster development in early phases is better to get quick product feedback.

- You can easily change the domain boundaries.

- People get used to the same technical guidelines. That helps achieve future consistency.

- Common cross-domain functionality can be identified and shared as libraries (or guidelines).

- The team will get a complete view of the system instead of only parts of it. Then, these people can move to other teams and bring that helpful knowledge with them.

New Requirements and Gamification

Imagine that you release your application and connect it to an analytics engine. You get new users daily and recurrent users who come back regularly thanks to your last feature showing the attempts' history. However, you see in the metrics that, after a week, users tend to abandon the routine of training their brains with new challenges.

Therefore, you decide based on your data to try to improve these figures. This simple process is called *data-driven decision-making* (DDDM), and it's important for all kinds of projects. You use data to choose your next move instead of basing it on intuition or only observation. If you're interested in DDDM, multiple articles and courses are available on the Internet. The article at `https://www.datapine.com/blog/data-driven-decision-making-in-businesses/` is a good one to start with.

In this case, you'll introduce some *gamification* to improve engagement in the application. Remember that we reduce gamification to points, badges, and leaderboards to keep the book focused on the technical topics. If you're interested in this field, the books *Reality Is Broken* and *For the Win* are good places to start. Before introducing gamification and how it applies to this application, let's present the new user story.

User Story 3   As a user of the application, I want to feel motivated to engage in challenges daily, ensuring I don't abandon the application after a while. This will enable me to exercise my brain consistently and experience continual improvement.

Gamification: Points, Badges, and Leaderboards

Gamification is the design process in which you apply techniques that are used in games to another field that is not a game. You do that because you want to get some well-known benefits from games, such as getting players motivated and interacting with your process, application, or whatever you're *gamifying*.

One basic idea about making a game out of something else is introducing *points*: every time you perform an action and do well, you get some points. You can even get points if you didn't perform so well, but it should be a fair mechanism: you get more if you do better. Winning points makes the player feel like they're progressing and gives them feedback.

Leaderboards make the points visible to everybody, so they motivate players by activating feelings of competition. We want to get more points than the person above us and rank higher. It is even more fun if you play with friends.

Last but not least, *badges* are virtual symbols of achieving status. We like badges because they say more than points. Also, they can represent different things: you can have the same points as another player (e.g., five correct answers), but you could have won them in a different way (e.g., five in a minute!).

Some software applications that are not games use these elements very well. Take StackOverflow, for example. It's full of game elements to encourage people to keep participating.

You'll assign points to every correct answer that users submit. To keep it simple, you'll give points only if they send a correct attempt—ten points each time.

A leaderboard with the top scores will be shown on the page, so players can find themselves in the ranking and compete with others.

You'll also create some basic badges: Bronze (10 correct attempts), Silver (25 correct attempts), and Gold (50 correct attempts). Because the first correct attempt deserves a nice feedback message, you'll also introduce a First Correct! badge. Also, to introduce a surprise element, you'll have a badge that users can win only if they solve a multiplication where the number 42 is one of the factors.

With these basics, you can motivate your users to return and keep playing, competing with their peers.

Moving to Microservices

There is nothing in these new requirements that you couldn't achieve with your small monolith. If this were a project with one developer and the objective wasn't educational, the best option would be to create a new root package called `gamification` and start coding the classes within the same deployable unit.

Let's situate ourselves in a different scenario. Imagine that you identify other new features that could help you achieve your business goals. Some of these improvements could be the following:

- Adapt the complexity of the challenge based on the user's statistics.

- Add hints.

- Allow the user to log in instead of using an alias.

- Ask the users for some personal information to collect better metrics.

Those improvements would impact the existing Challenges and Users domains. Besides, since the first release went really well, imagine you also got some capital investment. Your team can grow. The development of your application doesn't need to be sequential anymore. You could work on the Gamification domain at the same time you're improving the existing domains with extra features.

Say also that the investors brought some conditions, and now you want to scale up to 100,000 monthly active users. You need to design the architecture to cope with that. And you could soon realize that the new gamification component you're planning to build is not as critical as the main feature: solving a challenge. If the gamification features are not available for a short period of time, as long as the users can still solve challenges, you're fine.

From this analysis, you can conclude the following:

1. The Users and Challenges domains are critical in your application. You should aim to keep them highly available. Horizontal scalability would fit very well in this case: you deploy multiple instances of the first application, and use load balancing and divert the traffic if one of the instances goes down. Besides, replicating the service would also give you more capacity to cope with many concurrent users.

2. The new Gamification domain has different requirements in terms of availability. You don't need to scale up this logic at the same pace. You can accept that it performs slower than other domains and allow it to stop working for some time.

3. You could benefit from having independently deployable units since your team is growing. If you keep the Gamification module loosely coupled and release it independently, you can work in your organization with multiple teams and minimal interference.

Taking those nonfunctional requirements (e.g., scalability, availability, and extensibility) into account, it seems like a good idea to move to microservices. Let's cover these advantages in more detail.

Independent Workflows

You already saw in previous chapters how to accomplish a modular architecture following DDD principles. You could split the resulting bounded contexts into different code repositories so multiple teams can work on them more independently.

However, if these modules are part of the same deployable unit, you still have some dependencies between teams. You need to integrate all these modules, make sure they work with each other, and deploy the whole thing to your production environment. If other infrastructure elements are shared across modules, like databases, these dependencies become even bigger.

Microservices take modularity to the next level because you can deploy them independently. Teams can have not only different repositories but also different workflows.

In this system, you can develop a few Spring Boot applications in separate repositories. Each will have its own embedded web server, so that you can deploy them separately. This removes all the friction generated during the release of a big monolith: tests, packaging, interdependent database updates, and so on.

Let's also look at the maintenance and support aspects. Microservices help build a DevOps culture because each application may own its corresponding infrastructure elements: web server, database, metrics, logs, and so on. When you use a framework like Spring Boot, the system can be seen as a group of mini-applications interacting with each other. If there is a problem with one of these pieces, the team that owns that microservice can be the one fixing it. With a monolith, it's usually harder to draw these lines.

Horizontal vs. Vertical Scalability

When you want to scale up a monolithic application, you have the option of doing it *vertically*, with a bigger server/container, or *horizontally*, with more instances and a load balancer. Vertical scalability involves increasing resources (CPU, memory, storage) to individual instances of a microservice. Instead of deploying multiple instances of a microservice, you upgrade the existing instance's hardware specifications to handle increased load. The decision between horizontal and vertical scalability depends on factors such as the nature of the workload, budget, and the application's architecture. Horizontal scalability is usually the preferred choice since multiple small-size machines are cheaper than a big powerful one. Besides, you can better react to different workload patterns by switching instances on and off. Vertical scalability is often preferred for stateful microservices that can't be easily replicated or partitioned.

With microservices, you can choose more flexible strategies for scalability. In this practical example, the Multiplication application is a critical part of the system, having to cope with many concurrent requests. Therefore, you could deploy two instances of the multiplication microservice but only one instance of the (not yet developed) gamification microservice. If you kept all the logic in one place, you would also replicate the gamification logic, even though you probably don't need those resources. Figure 6-1 shows an example of this.

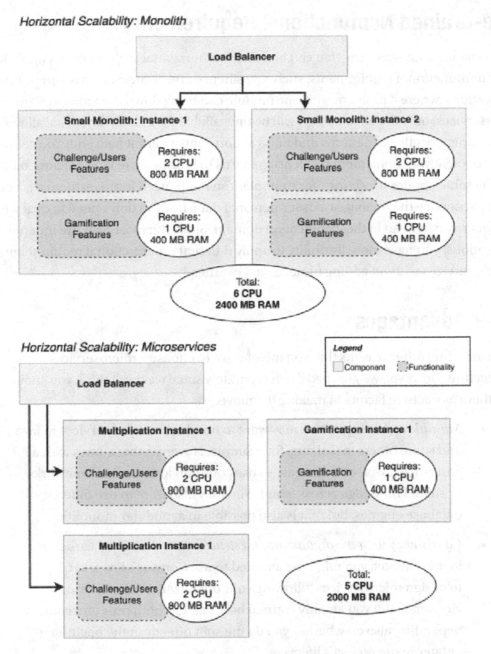

Figure 6-1. *Horizontal scalability in a monolith versus microservices*

Fine-Grained Nonfunctional Requirements

When you use microservices, you can benefit from horizontal scalability and apply it to other nonfunctional requirements, such as resilience and security. Unlike monolithic applications, where a problem with one module can bring down the entire system, with microservices, only the affected part will be unavailable for a short time. This allows you to implement resilience patterns and build a more fault-tolerant backend. You see later in this book how to implement resilience patterns to build a more fault-tolerant backend.

The same applies to security, for example. You might need more restrictive access to a microservice that manages a user's personal data, but you don't need to deal with that security overhead in the gamification domain. Since microservices are independent applications, you have more flexibility to apply different nonfunctional requirements to specific services without adding unnecessary overhead.

Other Advantages

There are some other reasons that you might want to choose a microservices architecture. However, we grouped them separately since we don't think you should treat them as decisive factors in making the move.

- *Multiple technologies*: You may want to build some microservices in Java and some others in GoLang, for example. However, that comes with a cost since it won't be that easy to use common artifacts or frameworks or share knowledge across teams. You may also want to use different database engines, but that is also possible in a modular monolith.

- *Consistency with the organizational structure*: As described earlier in this chapter, you might be tempted to use Conway's law and try to design microservices following your organization structure, or vice versa. But you already learned how that has both pros and cons, depending also on whether you do the split directly at the beginning or later in the project's lifecycle.

- *Ability to replace parts of your system*: If microservices bring more isolation to your software architecture, it's logical to think that it should be easier to replace them without causing much impact on other services. But, in real life, microservices could also become strongly coupled to each other when some basic rules are not respected. And, on the other hand, you can achieve replaceability with a good modular system. Therefore, we don't see this as a decisive driver for change either.

Disadvantages

As covered in the previous sections, microservice architectures have many disadvantages too, so they're not the panacea to solve all the issues that may arise with a monolithic architecture. We covered some of these disadvantages while analyzing why it's a good idea to start with a small monolith.

- *You need more time to deliver a first working version*: Due to its complexity, a microservice architecture requires much more time to set up correctly when compared to a single service.

- *Moving functionality across domains becomes harder*: Once you've done the first split, it requires extra work to merge code or move functionalities across microservices when compared to a single codebase or deployment unit.

- *There is an implicit introduction of new paradigms*: Given that a microservice architecture makes your system distributed, you'll face new challenges like asynchronous processing, distributed transactions, and eventual consistency. We analyze these new paradigms in detail in this chapter and the next one.

- *It requires learning new patterns*: When you have a distributed system, you know better how to implement routing, service discovery, distributed tracing, logging, and so on. These patterns are not easy to implement and maintain. We cover them in Chapter 8.

- *You may require adopting new tools*: There are some frameworks and tools that can help you implement a microservice architecture: Spring Cloud, Docker, Message Brokers, Kubernetes, and so on. You may not need them in a monolithic architecture, and that means extra maintenance, setup, potential costs, and time to learn all these new concepts. Again, this book will help you understand these tools over the next chapters.

- *More resources are needed to run your system*: At the beginning of a project, when the system traffic is not high yet, maintaining a microservice-based system can be much more expensive than a monolithic one. Having multiple idle services is less efficient than having a single one. Besides, the surrounding tools and patterns (that we cover in this book) introduce an extra overload. The impact only starts being positive when you benefit from scalability, fault tolerance, and other characteristics we describe later in this book.

- *There might be a diversion from standards and common practices*: One of the reasons to move to microservices could be to achieve more independence across teams. However, that may also have a negative impact if everybody starts creating their own solutions to solve the same problems, instead of reusing common patterns. That could cause a waste of time and makes it harder for people to understand other parts of the system.

- *The architecture is much more complex*: Explaining how your system works might become harder with a microservice architecture. That means new joiners will require extra time to understand how the complete system works. One might argue that this is not needed as long as people understand the domain they work on, but it's always better to get to know how all the pieces interact together.

- *Managing transactions is complex*: In a microservices environment, transaction management can become complex due to the distributed nature of services and databases. Coordinating transactions across multiple microservices can be challenging, as you need to ensure data consistency, deal with distributed locks, and manage rollbacks in case of failures.

- *You could be distracted with new techniques you don't need*: Once you board the train of microservices with their fancy tools around them, some people could be attracted by new products and patterns that are *cool* to implement. However, you might not need them, so they become just a distraction. Even though this can happen with any architecture, it happens more often when you work with microservices.

- *End-to-end testing can be challenging*: Testing across multiple microservices can be time-consuming and more complex. As services evolve independently, ensuring compatibility and proper behavior of the entire system becomes more complicated.

Some of these points might still be unclear to you. Don't worry, you'll understand exactly what they mean by the end of your journey. This book follows a pragmatic and realistic approach to these subjects to help you understand both the advantages and the disadvantages of microservice architecture so you can make the best decision in the future.

Architecture Overview

In this scenario, after comparing the alternatives you have and analyzing the pros and cons of microservices, let's say you have decided to make a move and create a new Spring Boot application for your gamification requirements. The scalability of both the system and the organization plays a major role in this decision, given the hypothetical scenario.

Now you can refer to these two applications as the Multiplication microservice and the Gamification microservice. It didn't make sense until now to call the first application a microservice since it wasn't part of a microservices architecture yet.

Figure 6-2 represents the different components in this system and how they'll be connected by the end of this chapter.

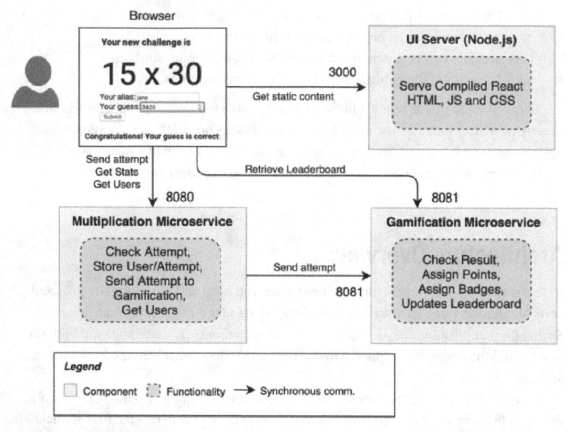

Figure 6-2. *Logical view*

Let's review the new additions to this design.

- There will be a new microservice, called Gamification. To prevent local port conflicts, you'll deploy it on port 8081.

- The Multiplication microservice will send each attempt to the Gamification microservice to process new scores and badges and update the leaderboard.

- There will be a new component in the React UI to render the leaderboard with the score and badges. As you can see in the drawing in Figure 6-2, the UI will call both microservices.

Some notes about this design:

- You could also deploy the UI from one of the embedded web servers. However, treating the UI server as a different deployment unit is better. The same advantages apply here: independent workflow, flexible scalability, and so on.

- It might look weird that the UI needs to call two services. You could consider that it's better to put a reverse proxy in front of the other two to do the routing and keep the API client unaware of the backend's software architecture (see `https://en.wikipedia.org/wiki/Reverse_proxy`). That's actually the Gateway pattern, and we cover it in detail later in this book. Let's keep it simple for now.

- If you paid attention to this book's summary, the synchronous call from Multiplication to Gamification surely caught your attention. That's not the best design indeed, but let's keep the evolving approach example and learn first why it isn't the best idea.

Designing and Implementing the New Service

In this section, you'll design and implement the Gamification microservice following a similar approach to what you did with your first Spring Boot service, Multiplication.

Interfaces

When working with a modular system, you must pay attention to the *contract* between the modules. With microservices, this is even more relevant since, as a team, you want to clarify as soon as possible all the expected dependencies.

In this case, the Gamification microservice is required to expose an interface to accept new attempts. It needs that data to compute the statistics for users. For now, this interface will be a REST API. The exchanged JSON object can simply contain the same fields as the attempt you store on the Multiplication microservice: the attempt's data and the user's data. On the Gamification side, you'll use only the data you need.

On the other hand, the UI needs to collect the leaderboard details. You'll also create new REST endpoints in the Gamification microservice to access this data.

Info   Starting here, this chapter's section goes through the source code of the new Gamification microservice. It's good to take a look at it since you'll use some new, small features across the different layers. However, you saw the main concepts already in previous chapters, so you may decide to take a shortcut. That's also possible. If you don't want to dive into the development of the Gamification microservice, you can jump directly to the section titled "Playing with the System" and use the code for this chapter, available at `https://github.com/Book-Microservices-v3/chapter06`.

The Spring Boot Skeleton for Gamification

You can use the Spring Initializr at `https://start.spring.io/` again to create the basic skeleton for your new application. This time, you know in advance that you'll need some extra dependencies, so you can add them directly from here: Lombok, Spring Web, Validation, Spring Data JPA, and the H2 Database. Fill in the details as shown in Figure 6-3.

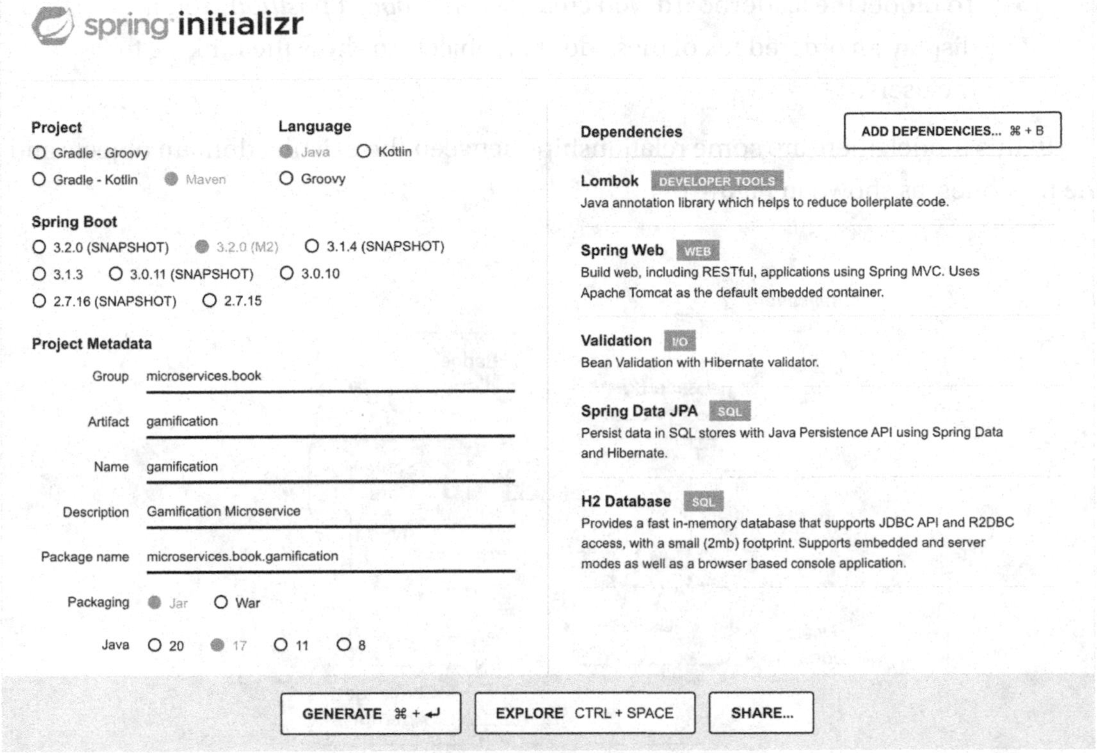

Figure 6-3. *Creating the Gamification application*

Download the ZIP file and extract it as a `gamification` folder next to the existing `multiplication` one. You can add this new project as a separate module in the same workspace, to keep everything organized within the same IDE instance.

Domain

Let's model the gamification domain by trying to respect the context boundaries and minimizing the coupling with the existing functionality.

- You create a scorecard object, which holds the amount of score that a user obtains for a given challenge attempt.

- Similarly, you have a badge card object, representing a specific type of badge that has been won at a given time by a user. It doesn't need to be tied to a score card since you may win a badge when you surpass a given score threshold.

- To model the leaderboard, you create a *leaderboard position*. You'll display an ordered list of these domain objects to show the ranking to the users.

In this model, there are some relationships between the existing domain objects and the new ones, as shown in Figure 6-4.

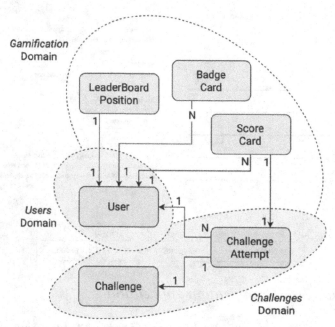

Figure 6-4. *The new Gamification domain*

As you see, you still keep these domains loosely coupled:

- The Users domain remains completely isolated. It doesn't keep any reference to any other object.

- The Challenges domain only needs to know about Users. You don't need to link their objects to the gamification concepts.

- The Gamification domain needs to reference Users and Challenge Attempts. You planned to get this data after an attempt is sent, so you'll store some references locally (the identifiers of the user and the attempt).

The domain objects can be mapped to Java classes easily. You'll use JPA/Hibernate also for this service so you can already add the JPA annotations. First, Listing 6-1 shows the ScoreCard class, with an extra constructor that will set some default values.

Source Code   You can find all the source code for this chapter on GitHub, in the chapter06 repository.

See `https://github.com/Book-Microservices-v3/chapter06`.

Listing 6-1. The ScoreCard Domain/Data Class

```java
package microservices.book.gamification.game.domain;

import lombok.*;
import jakarata.persistence.*;

/**
 * This class represents the Score linked to an attempt in the game,
 * with an associated user and the timestamp in which the score
 * is registered.
 */
@Entity
@Data
@AllArgsConstructor
@NoArgsConstructor
public class ScoreCard {
    // The default score assigned to this card, if not specified.
    public static final int DEFAULT_SCORE = 10;
    @Id
    @GeneratedValue
    private Long cardId;
    private Long userId;
    private Long attemptId;
    @EqualsAndHashCode.Exclude
    private long scoreTimestamp;
    private int score;
```

```java
    public ScoreCard(final Long userId, final Long attemptId) {
        this(null, userId, attemptId, System.currentTimeMillis(),
        DEFAULT_SCORE);
    }
}
```

It used a new Lombok annotation this time, @EqualsAndHashCode.Exclude. As the name suggests, this will make Lombok omit that field in the generated equals and hashCode methods. The reason is that this will make your tests easier when you compare objects, and in fact, you don't need the timestamp to determine whether two cards are equal.

The different badges are defined in an enum, BadgeType. You add a `description` field to have a friendly name for each one. See Listing 6-2.

Listing 6-2. The BadgeType Enum

```java
package microservices.book.gamification.game.domain;

import lombok.Getter;
import lombok.RequiredArgsConstructor;
/**
 * Enumeration with the different types of Badges that a user can win.
 */
@RequiredArgsConstructor
@Getter
public enum BadgeType {
    // Badges depending on score
    BRONZE("Bronze"),
    SILVER("Silver"),
    GOLD("Gold"),
    // Other badges won for different conditions
    FIRST_WON("First time"),
    LUCKY_NUMBER("Lucky number");
    private final String description;
}
```

As you can see in the previous code, you also benefit from some Lombok annotations in enums. In this case, you use them to generate a constructor and the getter for the description field.

The BadgeCard class uses BadgeType, and it's also a JPA entity. See Listing 6-3.

Listing 6-3. The BadgeCard Domain/Data Class

```
package microservices.book.gamification.game.domain;

import lombok.*;
import jakarta.persistence.*;

@Entity
@Data
@AllArgsConstructor
@NoArgsConstructor
public class BadgeCard {
    @Id
    @GeneratedValue
    private Long badgeId;
    private Long userId;
    @EqualsAndHashCode.Exclude
    private long badgeTimestamp;
    private BadgeType badgeType;
    public BadgeCard(final Long userId, final BadgeType badgeType) {
        this(null, userId, System.currentTimeMillis(), badgeType);
    }
}
```

A constructor was also added to set some default values. Note that you don't need to add any specific JPA annotation to the enum type. Hibernate will map the values to the enum's ordinal value (an integer) by default. This works just fine if you keep in mind that you should only append new enum values at the end, but you could also configure the mapper to use the string values.

To model the leaderboard position, you create the LeaderBoardRow class. See Listing 6-4. You don't need to persist this object in the database since it's going to be created on the fly by aggregating scores and badges from your users.

Listing 6-4. The LeaderBoardRow Class

```java
package microservices.book.gamification.game.domain;

import lombok.*;
import java.util.List;

@Value
@AllArgsConstructor
public class LeaderBoardRow {
    Long userId;
    Long totalScore;
    @With
    List<String> badges;
    public LeaderBoardRow(final Long userId, final Long totalScore) {
        this.userId = userId;
        this.totalScore = totalScore;
        this.badges = List.of();
    }
}
```

The @Value annotation from Lombok generates an immutable class. Immutable objects are objects whose state cannot be modified after creation. The annotation automatically generates a constructor that initializes all final fields, getter methods for all the fields, the equals(), and the hashCode() method. The @With annotation added to the badges field is provided by Lombok and generates a method for you to clone an object and add a new field value to the copy (in this case, withBadges). This is a good practice when you work with immutable classes since they don't have setters. You'll use this method when you create the business logic to merge the score and the badges for each leaderboard row.

Service

You can divide the business logic in this new Gamification microservice into two.

- The game logic, responsible for processing the attempt and generating the resulting score and badges

- The leaderboard logic, which aggregates data and builds the ranking based on score

The game logic will reside in the GameServiceImpl class, which implements the GameService interface. The specification is simple: based on an attempt, it computes the score and badges and stores them. This business logic is accessible to the Multiplication microservice via a controller named GameController, which will expose a POST endpoint to send the attempt to. On the persistence layer, the business logic will require a ScoreRepository to save scorecards and a BadgeRepository to do the same thing with badge cards. Figure 6-5 shows a UML diagram with all the classes needed to build the game logic functionality.

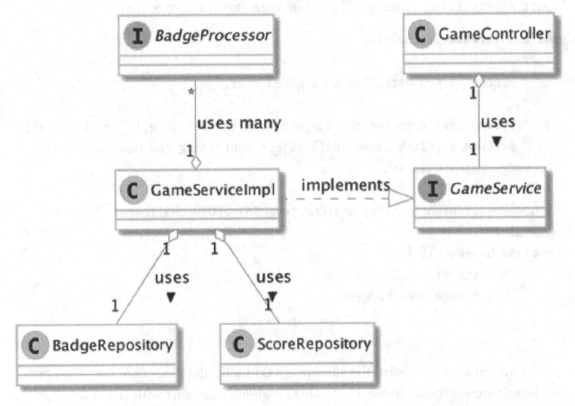

Figure 6-5. *UML: game logic*

You can define the GameService interface as shown in Listing 6-5.

Listing 6-5. The GameService Interface

```java
package microservices.book.gamification.game;

import java.util.List;
import lombok.Value;
import microservices.book.gamification.challenge.ChallengeSolvedDTO;
import microservices.book.gamification.game.domain.BadgeCard;
import microservices.book.gamification.game.domain.BadgeType;
import microservices.book.gamification.game.domain.ScoreCard;

public interface GameService {
    /**
     * Process a new attempt from a given user.
     *
     * @param challenge the challenge data with user details, factors, etc.
     * @return a {@link GameResult} object containing the new score and
     * badge cards obtained
     */
    GameResult newAttemptForUser(ChallengeSolvedDTO challenge);
    @Value
    class GameResult {
        int score;
        List<BadgeType> badges;
    }
}
```

The output after processing the attempt is a GameResult object, defined within the interface. It groups the score obtained from that attempt together with any new badge that the user may get. You could also consider not returning anything since it'll be the leaderboard logic showing the results. However, it's better to have a response from your method so you can test it.

The ChallengeSolvedDTO class defines the contract between the Multiplication and Gamification microservices, and we'll create it in both projects to keep them independent. For now, focus on the Gamification codebase. See Listing 6-6.

Listing 6-6. The ChallengeSolvedDTO Class

```
package microservices.book.gamification.challenge;

import lombok.Value;
@Value
public class ChallengeSolvedDTO {
    long attemptId;
    boolean correct;
    int factorA;
    int factorB;
    long userId;
    String userAlias;
}
```

Now that you have defined the domain classes and the skeleton of your service layer, you can use TDD and create some test cases for your business logic, using an empty interface implementation and the DTO class.

Exercise   Create the GameServiceTest with two test cases: a correct attempt and a wrong one. You'll find the solution in this chapter's code sources.

For now, focus only on the score calculation and not on the badges. You'll create a separate interface and the tests for that part.

A valid implementation of the GameService interface would be the one shown in Listing 6-7. It creates a ScoreCard object only if the challenge is correctly solved and stores it. The badges are processed in a separate method for better readability. You also need some repository methods to save the score and badges and to retrieve the previously created records. For now, you can just assume these methods work; we explain them in detail later in the "Data" section.

Listing 6-7. Implementing the GameService Interface in the
GameServiceImpl Class

```
package microservices.book.gamification.game;

import java.util.*;
import java.util.stream.Collectors;
import org.springframework.stereotype.Service;
import lombok.RequiredArgsConstructor;
import lombok.extern.slf4j.Slf4j;
import microservices.book.gamification.challenge.ChallengeSolvedDTO;
import microservices.book.gamification.game.badgeprocessors.BadgeProcessor;
import microservices.book.gamification.game.domain.BadgeCard;
import microservices.book.gamification.game.domain.BadgeType;
import microservices.book.gamification.game.domain.ScoreCard;

@Service
@Slf4j
@RequiredArgsConstructor
class GameServiceImpl implements GameService {
    private final ScoreRepository scoreRepository;
    private final BadgeRepository badgeRepository;
    // Spring injects all the @Component beans in this list
    private final List<BadgeProcessor> badgeProcessors;
    @Override
    public GameResult newAttemptForUser(final ChallengeSolvedDTO
    challenge) {
        // We give points only if it's correct
        if (challenge.isCorrect()) {
            ScoreCard scoreCard = new ScoreCard(challenge.getUserId(),
                    challenge.getAttemptId());
            scoreRepository.save(scoreCard);
            log.info("User {} scored {} points for attempt id {}",
                    challenge.getUserAlias(), scoreCard.getScore(),
                    challenge.getAttemptId());
            List<BadgeCard> badgeCards = processForBadges(challenge);
            return new GameResult(scoreCard.getScore(),
```

```
                badgeCards.stream().map(BadgeCard::getBadgeType)
                    .collect(Collectors.toList())));
    } else {
        log.info("Attempt id {} is not correct. " +
                    "User {} does not get score.",
                challenge.getAttemptId(),
                challenge.getUserAlias());
        return new GameResult(0, List.of());
    }
}
/**
 * Checks the total score and the different score cards obtained
 * to give new badges in case their conditions are met.
 */
private List<BadgeCard> processForBadges(
        final ChallengeSolvedDTO solvedChallenge) {
    Optional<Integer> optTotalScore = scoreRepository.
            getTotalScoreForUser(solvedChallenge.getUserId());
    if (optTotalScore.isEmpty()) return Collections.emptyList();
    int totalScore = optTotalScore.get();
    // Gets the total score and existing badges for that user
    List<ScoreCard> scoreCardList = scoreRepository
            .findByUserIdOrderByScoreTimestampDesc(solvedChallenge.
            getUserId());
    Set<BadgeType> alreadyGotBadges = badgeRepository
            .findByUserIdOrderByBadgeTimestampDesc(solvedChallenge.
             getUserId())
            .stream()
            .map(BadgeCard::getBadgeType)
            .collect(Collectors.toSet());
    // Calls the badge processors for badges that the user doesn't
    have yet
    List<BadgeCard> newBadgeCards = badgeProcessors.stream()
            .filter(bp -> !alreadyGotBadges.contains(bp.badgeType()))
            .map(bp -> bp.processForOptionalBadge(totalScore,
```

197

```
                              scoreCardList, solvedChallenge)
                ).flatMap(Optional::stream) // returns an empty stream
                if empty
                // maps the optionals if present to new BadgeCards
                .map(badgeType ->
                        new BadgeCard(solvedChallenge.getUserId(),
                        badgeType)
                )
                .collect(Collectors.toList());
        badgeRepository.saveAll(newBadgeCards);
        return newBadgeCards;
    }
}
```

As you can conclude from this implementation, the BadgeProcessor interface is accepting some contextual data and the solved attempt, and it's deciding whether to assign a given type of badge. Listing 6-8 shows the source code of that interface.

Listing 6-8. The BadgeProcessor Interface

```
package microservices.book.gamification.game.badgeprocessors;

import java.util.List;
import java.util.Optional;
import microservices.book.gamification.challenge.ChallengeSolvedDTO;
import microservices.book.gamification.game.domain.BadgeType;
import microservices.book.gamification.game.domain.ScoreCard;

public interface BadgeProcessor {
    /**
     * Processes some or all of the passed parameters and decides if
       the user
     * is entitled to a badge.
     *
     * @return a BadgeType if the user is entitled to this badge,
       otherwise empty
     */
```

```
Optional<BadgeType> processForOptionalBadge(
        int currentScore,
        List<ScoreCard> scoreCardList,
        ChallengeSolvedDTO solved);
/**
 * @return the BadgeType object that this processor is handling.
 You can use
 * it to filter processors according to your needs.
 */
BadgeType badgeType();
}
```

Since you use constructor injection in GameServiceImpl with a list of
BadgeProcessor objects, Spring will find all the beans that implement this interface and
pass them to you. This is a flexible way of extending your game without interfering with
other existing logic. You just need to add new BadgeProcessor implementations and
annotate them with @Component so they are loaded in the Spring context.

Listings 6-9 and 6-10 are two of the five badge implementations that you need to
fulfill the functional requirements, BronzeBadgeProcessor and FirstWonBadgeProcessor.

Listing 6-9. BronzeBadgeProcessor Implementation

```
package microservices.book.gamification.game.badgeprocessors;

import microservices.book.gamification.challenge.ChallengeSolvedDTO;
import microservices.book.gamification.game.domain.BadgeType;
import microservices.book.gamification.game.domain.ScoreCard;
import org.springframework.stereotype.Component;
import java.util.List;
import java.util.Optional;
@Component
class BronzeBadgeProcessor implements BadgeProcessor {
    @Override
    public Optional<BadgeType> processForOptionalBadge(
                int currentScore,
                List<ScoreCard> scoreCardList,
                ChallengeSolvedDTO solved) {
```

```
        return currentScore > 50 ?
                Optional.of(BadgeType.BRONZE) :
                Optional.empty();
    }
    @Override
    public BadgeType badgeType() {
        return BadgeType.BRONZE;
    }
}
```

Listing 6-10. FirstWonBadgeProcessor Implementation

```
package microservices.book.gamification.game.badgeprocessors;

import microservices.book.gamification.challenge.ChallengeSolvedDTO;
import microservices.book.gamification.game.domain.BadgeType;
import microservices.book.gamification.game.domain.ScoreCard;
import org.springframework.stereotype.Component;
import java.util.List;
import java.util.Optional;

@Component
class FirstWonBadgeProcessor implements BadgeProcessor {
    @Override
    public Optional<BadgeType> processForOptionalBadge(
                int currentScore,
                List<ScoreCard> scoreCardList,
                ChallengeSolvedDTO solved) {
        return scoreCardList.size() == 1 ?
                Optional.of(BadgeType.FIRST_WON) : Optional.empty();
    }
    @Override
    public BadgeType badgeType() {
        return BadgeType.FIRST_WON;
    }
}
```

Exercise   Implement the other three badge processors and all the unit tests to verify they work as expected. If you need help, you may consult this chapter's source code.

1.   The Silver badge. Won if the score exceeds 150.

2.   The Gold badge. Won if the score exceeds 400.

3.   The Lucky Number badge. Won if any of the factors of the attempt is 42.

Once you finish the first block of the business logic, you can move to the second one: the leaderboard functionality. Figure 6-6 shows the UML diagram of the three layers you'll implement in this chapter to build the leaderboard.

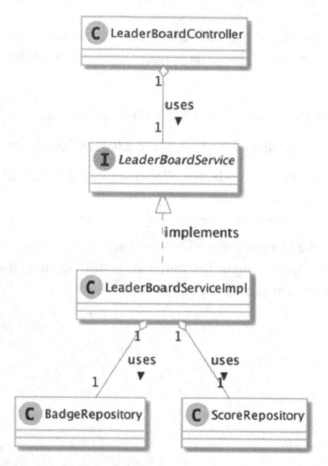

Figure 6-6. *Leaderboard, UML diagram*

The LeaderBoardService interface has a single method to return a sorted list of LeaderBoardRow objects. See Listing 6-11.

Listing 6-11. The LeaderBoardService Interface

```
package microservices.book.gamification.game;

import java.util.List;
import microservices.book.gamification.game.domain.LeaderBoardRow;

public interface LeaderBoardService {
    /**
```

```
 * @return the current leader board ranked from high to low score
 */
List<LeaderBoardRow> getCurrentLeaderBoard();
}
```

Exercise   Create LeaderBoardServiceImplTest to verify that the implementation should query ScoreCardRepository to find the users with the top score and should query BadgeCardRepository to merge the score with their badges. As before, the repository classes are not there yet, but you can create some dummy methods and mock them for the tests.

The implementation of the leaderboard service can remain simple if you have the ability to aggregate the score and sort the resulting rows in the database. You'll see how in the next section. For now, assume that you can get the score ranking from ScoreRepository (the findFirst10 method). Then, you query the database to retrieve the badges for the users included in the ranking. See Listing 6-12.

Listing 6-12. The LeaderBoardService Implementation

```
package microservices.book.gamification.game;

import java.util.List;
import java.util.stream.Collectors;
import org.springframework.stereotype.Service;
import lombok.RequiredArgsConstructor;
import microservices.book.gamification.game.domain.LeaderBoardRow;

@Service
@RequiredArgsConstructor
class LeaderBoardServiceImpl implements LeaderBoardService {
    private final ScoreRepository scoreRepository;
    private final BadgeRepository badgeRepository;
    @Override
    public List<LeaderBoardRow> getCurrentLeaderBoard() {
        // Get score only
        List<LeaderBoardRow> scoreOnly = scoreRepository.findFirst10();
```

```
        // Combine with badges
        return scoreOnly.stream().map(row -> {
            List<String> badges =
                        badgeRepository.findByUserIdOrderByBadgeTimestampDesc(
                                row.getUserId()).stream()
                                .map(b -> b.getBadgeType().getDescription())
                                .collect(Collectors.toList());
                return row.withBadges(badges);
        }).collect(Collectors.toList());
    }
}
```

Note that this code used the withBadges method to copy an immutable object with a new value. The first time you generate the leaderboard, all rows have an empty list of badges. When you collect the badges, you can replace (using stream's map) each object with a copy with the corresponding badge list.

Data

In the business logic layer, you made some assumptions about the ScoreRepository and BadgeRepository methods. It's time to build these repositories.

Remember that you get basic CRUD functionality just by extending Spring Data's CrudRepository<T,ID>, so you can save badges and score cards easily. For the rest of the queries, you'll use both query methods and JPQL.

The BadgeRepository interface defines a query method to find badges for a given user, ordered by date with most recent ones on top. See Listing 6-13.

Listing 6-13. The BadgeRepository Interface with a Query Method

```
package microservices.book.gamification.game;

import microservices.book.gamification.game.domain.BadgeCard;
import microservices.book.gamification.game.domain.BadgeType;
import org.springframework.data.repository.CrudRepository;
import java.util.List;
/**
 * Handles data operations with BadgeCards
 */
```

```java
public interface BadgeRepository extends CrudRepository<BadgeCard, Long> {
    /**
     * Retrieves all BadgeCards for a given user.
     *
     * @param userId the id of the user to look for BadgeCards
     * @return the list of BadgeCards, ordered by most recent first.
     */
    List<BadgeCard> findByUserIdOrderByBadgeTimestampDesc(Long userId);
}
```

For scorecards, you need other query types. There are three requirements thus far.

1. Calculate the total score of a user.

2. Get a list of users with the highest score, ordered, as LeaderBoardRow objects.

3. Read all ScoreCard records by user ID.

Listing 6-14 shows the complete source code for ScoreRepository.

Listing 6-14. The ScoreRepository Interface, Using Query Methods and JPQL Queries

```java
package microservices.book.gamification.game;

import java.util.List;
import java.util.Optional;
import org.springframework.data.jpa.repository.Query;
import org.springframework.data.repository.CrudRepository;
import org.springframework.data.repository.query.Param;
import microservices.book.gamification.game.domain.LeaderBoardRow;
import microservices.book.gamification.game.domain.ScoreCard;
/**
 * Handles CRUD operations with ScoreCards and other related score queries
 */
public interface ScoreRepository extends CrudRepository<ScoreCard, Long> {
    /**
     * Gets the total score for a given user: the sum of the scores of all
     * their ScoreCards.
```

```
 *
 * @param userId the id of the user
 * @return the total score for the user, empty if the user doesn't exist
 */
@Query("SELECT SUM(s.score) FROM ScoreCard s WHERE s.userId = :userId
GROUP BY s.userId")
Optional<Integer> getTotalScoreForUser(@Param("userId") Long userId);
/**
 * Retrieves a list of {@link LeaderBoardRow}s representing the
 Leader Board
 * of users and their total score.
 *
 * @return the leader board, sorted by highest score first.
 */
@Query("SELECT NEW microservices.book.gamification.game.domain.
LeaderBoardRow(s.userId, SUM(s.score)) " +
        "FROM ScoreCard s " +
        "GROUP BY s.userId ORDER BY SUM(s.score) DESC")
List<LeaderBoardRow> findFirst10();
/**
 * Retrieves all the ScoreCards for a given user, identified by his
 user id.
 *
 * @param userId the id of the user
 * @return a list containing all the ScoreCards for the given user,
 * sorted by most recent.
 */
List<ScoreCard> findByUserIdOrderByScoreTimestampDesc(final Long userId);
}
```

Unfortunately, Spring Data JPA's query methods don't support aggregations. The good news is that JPQL, the JPA Query Language, does support them, so you can use standard syntax to keep your code as database-agnostic as possible. You can get the total score for a given user with this query:

```
SELECT SUM(s.score) FROM ScoreCard s WHERE s.userId = :userId GROUP BY
s.userId
```

Like in standard SQL, the GROUP BY clause indicates how to sum up the values. You can define parameters with the :param notation. Then, you annotate the corresponding method arguments with @Param. You could also use the approach followed in the previous chapter, with argument position's placeholders like ?1.

The second query is a bit special. In JPQL, you can use the constructors available in your Java classes. What you do in this example is an aggregation based on the total score, and you construct LeaderBoardRow objects using the two-argument constructor you defined (which sets an empty list of badges). Keep in mind that you have to use the fully qualified name of the class in JPQL, as shown in the source code.

Controller

While designing the Gamification domain, you agreed on a *contract* with the Multiplication service. It'll send each attempt to a REST endpoint on the gamification side. It's time to build that controller. See Listing 6-15.

Listing 6-15. The GameController Class

```
package microservices.book.gamification.game;

import org.springframework.http.HttpStatus;
import org.springframework.web.bind.annotation.*;
import lombok.RequiredArgsConstructor;
import microservices.book.gamification.challenge.ChallengeSolvedDTO;

@RestController
@RequestMapping("/attempts")
@RequiredArgsConstructor
public class GameController {
    private final GameService gameService;
    @PostMapping
    @ResponseStatus(HttpStatus.OK)
    void postResult(@RequestBody ChallengeSolvedDTO dto) {
        gameService.newAttemptForUser(dto);
    }
}
```

There is a REST API available on POST /attempts that accepts a JSON object containing data about the user and the challenge. In this case, you don't need to return any content, so you can use the ResponseStatus annotation to configure Spring to return a 200 OK status code. Actually, this is the default behavior when a controller's method returns void and has been processed without errors. In any case, it's good to add it explicitly for better readability. Remember that if there is an error like a thrown exception, for example, Spring Boot's default error handling logic will intercept it and return an error response with a different status code.

You could also add validation to the DTO class to make sure other services don't send invalid data to the Gamification microservice, but, for now, let's keep it simple. You'll change this API in the next chapter anyway.

Exercise   Don't forget to add the tests for this first controller and the next one. You can find these tests in this chapter's source code.

The second controller is for the leaderboard functionality and exposes a GET /leaders method that returns a JSON array of serialized LeaderBoardRow objects. This data is coming from the service layer, which uses the badge and score repositories to merge users' scores and badges. Therefore, the presentation layer remains simple. See the code in Listing 6-16.

Listing 6-16. The LeaderBoardController Class

```
package microservices.book.gamification.game;

import lombok.RequiredArgsConstructor;
import microservices.book.gamification.game.domain.LeaderBoardRow;
import org.springframework.web.bind.annotation.*;
import java.util.List;
/**
 * This class implements a REST API for the Gamification LeaderBoard
service.
 */
@RestController
@RequestMapping("/leaders")
@RequiredArgsConstructor
```

```
class LeaderBoardController {
    private final LeaderBoardService leaderBoardService;
    @GetMapping
    public List<LeaderBoardRow> getLeaderBoard() {
        return leaderBoardService.getCurrentLeaderBoard();
    }
}
```

Configuration

You went through the three layers of the application: business logic, data, and presentation. You're still missing some Spring Boot configuration that you defined in the Multiplication microservice as well.

First, you need to add some values to the application.properties file in the Gamification microservice. See Listing 6-17.

Listing 6-17. The application.properties File for the Gamification App

```
server.port=8081
# Gives us access to the H2 database web console
spring.h2.console.enabled=true
# Creates the database in a file
spring.datasource.url=jdbc:h2:file:~/gamification;DB_CLOSE_ON_EXIT=FALSE
# Creates or updates the schema if needed
spring.jpa.hibernate.ddl-auto=update
# For educational purposes we will show the SQL in console
spring.jpa.show-sql=true
```

The only new addition is the server.port property. You must change it since you can't use the same default 8080 in the second application when you run them locally. You also need to set a different H2 filename in the data source URL to create a separate database for this microservice, named gamification.

Besides, you'll need to enable CORS for this microservice too since the UI needs to be able to access the leaderboard API. Take a look at the section "Running the Frontend the First Time" in Chapter 4 if you don't remember what CORS does. This file's contents are identical to the one you added in Multiplication. See Listing 6-18.

Listing 6-18. Adding CORS Configuration to the Gamification App

```
package microservices.book.gamification.configuration;

import org.springframework.context.annotation.Configuration;
import org.springframework.web.servlet.config.annotation.CorsRegistry;
import org.springframework.web.servlet.config.annotation.WebMvcConfigurer;

@Configuration
public class WebConfiguration implements WebMvcConfigurer {
    @Override
    public void addCorsMappings(final CorsRegistry registry) {
        registry.addMapping("/**").allowedOrigins("http://localhost:3000");
    }
}
```

Given that you also want to use the Hibernate's Jackson module, you have to add this dependency in Maven. By adding this dependency to your project, Jackson can handle Hibernate-specific features when converting objects to JSON and vice versa. Remember that you also need to inject the module in the context to be picked up by autoconfiguration. See Listings 6-19 and 6-20.

Listing 6-19. Adding the Jackson's Hibernate Module to Gamification's pom. xml File

```
<dependencies>
<!-- ... -->
    <dependency>
        <groupId>com.fasterxml.jackson.datatype</groupId>
        <artifactId>jackson-datatype-hibernate5</artifactId>
    </dependency>
</dependencies>
```

Listing 6-20. Defining the Bean for JSON's Hibernate Module to Be Used for Serialization

```
package microservices.book.gamification.configuration;
import com.fasterxml.jackson.databind.Module;
import com.fasterxml.jackson.datatype.hibernate5.Hibernate5Module;
```

```
import org.springframework.context.annotation.Bean;
import org.springframework.context.annotation.Configuration;
@Configuration
public class JsonConfiguration {
    @Bean
    public Module hibernateModule() {
        return new Hibernate5Module();
    }
}
```

Changes in Multiplication Microservice

You have finished the first version of the Gamification microservice. Now you have
to integrate both microservices together by communicating Multiplication with the
new one.

Previously, you created a few REST APIs on the server's side. This time, you have
to build a REST API Client instead. The Spring Web module offers a tool for that
purpose: the RestTemplate class. Spring Boot provides an extra layer on top: the
RestTemplateBuilder. This builder is injected by default when you use the Spring Boot
Web starter, and you can use its methods to create RestTemplate objects in a fluent
way with multiple configuration options. You can add specific message converters,
security credentials if you need them to access the server, HTTP interceptors, and
so on. In this case, you can use the default settings since both applications are using
Spring Boot's predefined configuration. That means that the serialized JSON object
sent by the RestTemplate can be deserialized without problems on the server's side (the
Gamification microservice).

To keep this implementation modular, you need to create the Gamification's REST
client in a separate class: GamificationServiceClient. See Listing 6-21.

Listing 6-21. The GamificationServiceClient Class, in the Multiplication App

```
package microservices.book.multiplication.serviceclients;

import org.springframework.beans.factory.annotation.Value;
```

```java
import org.springframework.boot.web.client.RestTemplateBuilder;
import org.springframework.http.ResponseEntity;
import org.springframework.stereotype.Service;
import org.springframework.web.client.RestTemplate;
import lombok.extern.slf4j.Slf4j;
import microservices.book.multiplication.challenge.ChallengeAttempt;
import microservices.book.multiplication.challenge.ChallengeSolvedDTO;
@Slf4j
@Service
public class GamificationServiceClient {
    private final RestTemplate restTemplate;
    private final String gamificationHostUrl;
    public GamificationServiceClient(final RestTemplateBuilder builder,
                                     @Value("${service.gamification.host}")
                                     final String gamificationHostUrl) {
        restTemplate = builder.build();
        this.gamificationHostUrl = gamificationHostUrl;
    }
    public boolean sendAttempt(final ChallengeAttempt attempt) {
        try {
            ChallengeSolvedDTO dto = new ChallengeSolvedDTO(attempt.getId(),
                    attempt.isCorrect(), attempt.getFactorA(),
                    attempt.getFactorB(), attempt.getUser().getId(),
                    attempt.getUser().getAlias());
            ResponseEntity<String> r = restTemplate.postForEntity(
                    gamificationHostUrl + "/attempts", dto,
                    String.class);
            log.info("Gamification service response: {}",
            r.getStatusCode());
            return r.getStatusCode().is2xxSuccessful();
        } catch (Exception e) {
            log.error("There was a problem sending the attempt.", e);
            return false;
        }
    }
}
```

This new Spring @Service can be injected into your existing ones. It uses the builder to initialize the RestTemplate with defaults (just calling build()). It also accepts in the constructor the host URL of the gamification service, which you want to extract as a configuration parameter.

In Spring Boot, you can create your own configuration options in the application. properties file and inject their values in components with the @Value annotation. The gamificationHostUrl argument will be set to the value of this new property, which you have to add to the Multiplication's properties file. See Listing 6-22.

Listing 6-22. Adding the URL of the Gamification Microservice as a Property in Multiplication

```
# ... existing properties

# Gamification service URL
service.gamification.host=http://localhost:8081
```

The rest of the implementation of the service client is simple. It constructs a (new) ChallengeSolvedDTO based on data from the domain object, the ChallengeAttempt. Then, it uses the postForEntity method in RestTemplate to send the data to the /attempts endpoint in Gamification. You don't expect a response body, but the method's signature requires it, so you can set it to String, for example.

The complete logic is wrapped inside a try/catch block. The reason for this is that you don't want an error trying to reach the Gamification microservice to end up breaking the main business logic in the Multiplication microservice. This decision is further explained at the end of this chapter.

The ChallengeSolvedDTO class is a copy of the one you created on the Gamification side. See Listing 6-23.

Listing 6-23. The ChallengeSolvedDTO Class Needs to Be Included in the Multiplication Microservice Too

```
package microservices.book.multiplication.challenge;
import lombok.Value;
@Value
public class ChallengeSolvedDTO {
    long attemptId;
    boolean correct;
```

```
    int factorA;
    int factorB;
    long userId;
    String userAlias;
}
```

Now you can inject this service in the existing ChallengeServiceImpl class and use it to send the attempt after it has been processed. Listing 6-24 shows the modifications required in this class.

Listing 6-24. Adding Logic to ChallengeServiceImpl to Send an Attempt to the Gamification Microservice

```
@Slf4j
@RequiredArgsConstructor
@Service
public class ChallengeServiceImpl implements ChallengeService {
    private final UserRepository userRepository;
    private final ChallengeAttemptRepository attemptRepository;
    private final GamificationServiceClient gameClient;
    @Override
    public ChallengeAttempt verifyAttempt(ChallengeAttemptDTO attemptDTO) {
        // ... existing logic
        // Stores the attempt
        ChallengeAttempt storedAttempt = attemptRepository.save
        (checkedAttempt);
        // Sends the attempt to gamification and prints the response
        boolean status = gameClient.sendAttempt(storedAttempt);
        log.info("Gamification service response: {}", status);
        return storedAttempt;
    }
    // ...
}
```

The test should be also updated to check that the call happens for each attempt. You can add a new mocked class to ChallengeServiceTest.

```
@Mock private GamificationServiceClient gameClient;
```

214

Then, you use Mockito's `verify()` method in your test cases to make sure this call is performed with the same data as stored in the database.

```
verify(gameClient).sendAttempt(resultAttempt);
```

Besides the REST API client, you need to add a second change to the Multiplication microservice: a controller to retrieve a collection of user aliases based on their identifiers. You need this because the leaderboard API you implemented in the `LeaderBoardController` class returns the score, badges, and position based on user IDs. The UI needs a way to map each ID to a user alias, to render the table in a friendlier manner. See the new `UserController` class in Listing 6-25.

Listing 6-25. The New UserController Class

```
package microservices.book.multiplication.user;

import java.util.List;
import org.springframework.web.bind.annotation.*;
import lombok.RequiredArgsConstructor;
import lombok.extern.slf4j.Slf4j;

@Slf4j
@RequiredArgsConstructor
@RestController
@RequestMapping("/users")
public class UserController {
    private final UserRepository userRepository;
    @GetMapping("/{idList}")
    public List<User> getUsersByIdList(@PathVariable final List<Long>
    idList) {
        return userRepository.findAllByIdIn(idList);
    }
}
```

This time you use a list of identifiers as a path variable, which Spring splits and passes to you as a standard `List`. In practice, this means that the API call can include one or more numbers separated by commas, such as `/users/1,2,3`.

As you see, you're injecting a repository in the controller, so you're not following the three-layer architecture principle here. The reason is that you don't need business logic for this specific use case, so, in these situations, it's better to keep the code simple. If you need business logic any time in the future, you could benefit from the loose coupling between layers and create the service layer in between these two.

The repository interface uses a new query method to perform a select in the users table, filtering those users whose identifiers are in the passed list. See the source code in Listing 6-26.

Listing 6-26. The New Query Methods in the UserRepository Interface

```
package microservices.book.multiplication.user;
import java.util.List;
import java.util.Optional;
import org.springframework.data.repository.CrudRepository;

public interface UserRepository extends CrudRepository<User, Long> {

    Optional<User> findByAlias(final String alias);
    List<User> findAllByIdIn(final List<Long> ids);
}
```

Exercise   Update the tests in the Multiplication microservice to cover the new calls to the REST client and create a new one for UserController. You can find the solutions in this chapter's source code.

UI

The backend logic is ready, so you can move to the frontend part. You need two new JavaScript classes:

- A new API client to retrieve the leaderboard data from the Gamification microservice

- An additional React component to render the leaderboard

You'll also add a new method to the existing API client to retrieve a list of users based on their IDs.

The GameApiClient class in Listing 6-27 defines a different host and uses the fetch API to retrieve the JSON array of objects. For clarity, you also rename the existing ApiClient to ChallengesApiClient. Then, you include in this one a new method to retrieve the users. See Listing 6-28.

Listing 6-27. The GameApiClient Class in the /challenges-frontend/src/ services/GameApiClient.js File

```
class GameApiClient {
    static SERVER_URL = 'http://localhost:8081';
    static GET_LEADERBOARD = '/leaders';
    static leaderBoard(): Promise<Response> {
        return fetch(GameApiClient.SERVER_URL +
            GameApiClient.GET_LEADERBOARD);
    }
}
export default GameApiClient;
```

Listing 6-28. Renaming the Former ApiClient Class and Including the New Call

```
class ChallengesApiClient {
    static SERVER_URL = 'http://localhost:8080';
    // ...
    static GET_USERS_BY_IDS = '/users';
    // existing methods...
    static getUsers(userIds: number[]): Promise<Response> {
        return fetch(ChallengesApiClient.SERVER_URL +
            ChallengesApiClient.GET_USERS_BY_IDS +
            '/' + userIds.join(','));
    }
}
export default ChallengesApiClient;
```

The returned promises will be used in the new LeaderBoardComponent, which retrieves the data and updates its state's leaderboard attribute. Its render() method should map the array of objects to an HTML table with a row per position. You'll use JavaScript's Timing Events (see https://www.w3schools.com/js/js_timing.asp) to refresh the leaderboard every five seconds with the setInterval function.

See the complete source code of LeaderBoardComponent in Listing 6-29. Then, we dive a bit more into its logic.

Listing 6-29. The New LeaderBoardComponent in the /challenges-frontend/ src/components/LeaderBoardComponent.js File

```
import * as React from 'react';
import GameApiClient from '../services/GameApiClient';
import ChallengesApiClient from '../services/ChallengesApiClient';
class LeaderBoardComponent extends React.Component {
    constructor(props) {
        super(props);
        this.state = {
            leaderboard: [],
            serverError: false
        }
    }
    componentDidMount() {
        this.refreshLeaderBoard();
        // sets a timer to refresh the leaderboard every 5 seconds
        setInterval(this.refreshLeaderBoard.bind(this), 5000);
    }
    getLeaderBoardData(): Promise {
        return GameApiClient.leaderBoard().then(
            lbRes => {
                if (lbRes.ok) {
                    return lbRes.json();
                } else {
                    return Promise.reject("Gamification: error response");
                }
            }
```

```
        );
    }
    getUserAliasData(userIds: number[]): Promise {
        return ChallengesApiClient.getUsers(userIds).then(
            usRes => {
                if(usRes.ok) {
                    return usRes.json();
                } else {
                    return Promise.reject("Multiplication: error
                    response");
                }
            }
        )
    }
    updateLeaderBoard(lb) {
        this.setState({
            leaderboard: lb,
            // reset the flag
            serverError: false
        });
    }
    refreshLeaderBoard() {
        this.getLeaderBoardData().then(
            lbData => {
                let userIds = lbData.map(row => row.userId);
                this.getUserAliasData(userIds).then(data => {
                    // build a map of id -> alias
                    let userMap = new Map();
                    data.forEach(idAlias => {
                        userMap.set(idAlias.id, idAlias.alias);
                    });
                    // add a property to existing lb data
                    lbData.forEach(row =>
                        row['alias'] = userMap.get(row.userId)
                    );
```

```
                    this.updateLeaderBoard(lbData);
            }).catch(reason => {
                console.log('Error mapping user ids', reason);
                this.updateLeaderBoard(lbData);
            });
        }
    ).catch(reason => {
        this.setState({ serverError: true });
        console.log('Gamification server error', reason);
    });
}
render() {
    if (this.state.serverError) {
        return (
            <div>We're sorry, but we can't display game
            statistics at this
                moment.</div>
        );
    }
    return (
        <div>
            <h3>Leaderboard</h3>
            <table>
                <thead>
                <tr>
                    <th>User</th>
                    <th>Score</th>
                    <th>Badges</th>
                </tr>
                </thead>
                <tbody>
                {this.state.leaderboard.map(row => <tr key={row.userId}>
                    <td>{row.alias ? row.alias : row.userId}</td>
                    <td>{row.totalScore}</td>
                    <td>{row.badges.map(
```

```
                    b => <span className="badge" key={b}>{b}</span>)}
                </td>
            </tr>)}
            </tbody>
        </table>
    </div>
);
    }
}
export default LeaderBoardComponent;
```

The main logic is included in the refreshLeaderBoard function. First, it tries to fetch the leaderboard rows from the Gamification server. If it can't (the catch clause), it sets the serverError flag to true, so it'll render a message instead of the table. When the data is retrieved normally, the logic performs a second call, this time to the Multiplication microservice. If you get a proper response, you map the user identifiers included in the data to their corresponding aliases and add a new field alias to each position in the leaderboard. If there is a failure in this second call, it still uses the original data without the extra field.

The render() function differentiates between the error case and the standard case. If there is an error, it shows a message instead of the table. This way, you make the application resilient because the main functionality (solving challenges) is working even when the Gamification microservice fails. The leaderboard data is displayed in rows with the user alias (or the ID if it couldn't be fetched), the total score, and the badge list.

The badge CSS class is used in the rendering logic. Let's create this custom style in the App.css stylesheet. See Listing 6-30.

Listing 6-30. Adding the Badge Style to App.css

```
/* ... existing styles ... */
.badge {
  font-size: x-small;
  border: 2px solid dodgerblue;
  border-radius: 4px;
  padding: 0.2em;
  margin: 0.1em;
}
```

Now, you should include the leaderboard component in the root container, the ChallengeComponent class. See the modifications made to the source code in Listing 6-31.

Listing 6-31. Adding the LeaderBoardComponent Inside the ChallengeComponent

```
import LeaderBoardComponent from './LeaderBoardComponent';
class ChallengeComponent extends React.Component {
    // ...existing methods...
    render() {
        return (
            <div className="display-column">
                {/* we add this just before closing the main div */}
                <LeaderBoardComponent />
            </div>
        );
    }
}
export default ChallengeComponent;
```

Playing with the System

You implemented the new Gamification microservice, connected the Multiplication application to it via a REST API client service, and built the UI to fetch the leaderboard and render it every five seconds.

It's time to play with the complete system. Use your IDE or the command line to start both backend applications and the Node.js server. If you use the terminal, open three separate instances and run one of the commands in Listing 6-32 in each of them so you have access to all the logs separately.

Listing 6-32. Starting the Apps from the Console

```
/multiplication $ mvnw spring-boot:run
...
/gamification $ mvnw spring-boot:run
```

```
...
/challenges-frontend $ npm start
...
```

If everything goes well, you'll see the UI running in your browser at http://
localhost:3000. There will be an empty leaderboard (unless you experimented a
bit while coding). If you send a correct attempt, you should see something similar to
Figure 6-7.

Your new challenge is

92 x 53

Your alias: nikita

Your guess: 4080

Submit

Congratulations! Your guess is correct

Challenge	Your guess	Correct
80 x 51	4080	Correct

Leaderboard

User	Score	Badges
nikita	10	First time

Figure 6-7. *UI connected to both microservices*

You can play the game by entering your alias and your guess in the corresponding
input boxes and clicking the Submit button. The moment you send a first correct
attempt, you'll get ten points and the "First Time" badge. The game works! You can keep

playing to see whether you score any metal badges or the Lucky Number one. Thanks to the automatic rendering every five seconds, you can even play in multiple browser tabs and the leaderboard will be refreshed in each tab.

Now let's take a look at the logs. On the Multiplication side, you'll see this line in the logs when you send a new attempt:

```
INFO 36283 --- [nio-8080-exec-4] m.b.m.challenge.ChallengeServiceImpl    :
Gamification service response: 200 OK
```

The Gamification app will output either a line saying that the attempt was not correct and therefore there is no new score, or this line if you were right:

```
INFO 36280 --- [nio-8081-exec-9] m.b.gamification.game.GameServiceImpl    :
User nikita scored 10 points for attempt id 2
```

You'll also see many repeated log lines showing queries since you configured the app to show all JPA statements, and the UI is making periodic calls to retrieve the leaderboard and the user aliases.

Fault Tolerance

While refining these requirements, you established that the Gamification features are not critical and therefore you could accept some downtime in that part of the system. Let's bring this new microservice down and see what happens. If you still have the applications running, stop the Gamification application. Otherwise, start the UI server and Multiplication only.

You'll see the fallback message of the leaderboard component displayed on the screen, as shown in Figure 6-8. As you can verify using the Network tab in the developer tools, the HTTP calls to the gamification service (on port 8081) are failing.

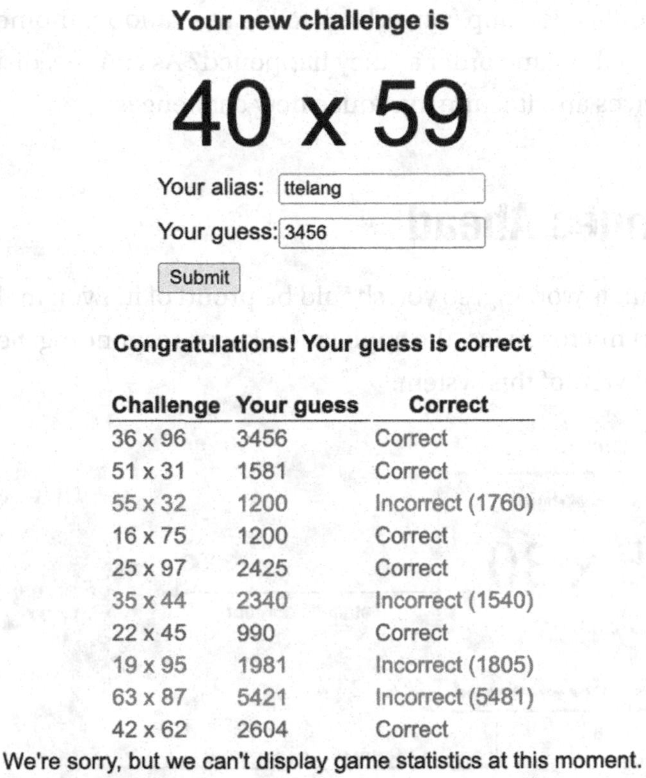

Your new challenge is

40 x 59

Your alias: [ttelang]

Your guess: [3456]

[Submit]

Congratulations! Your guess is correct

Challenge	Your guess	Correct
36 x 96	3456	Correct
51 x 31	1581	Correct
55 x 32	1200	Incorrect (1760)
16 x 75	1200	Correct
25 x 97	2425	Correct
35 x 44	2340	Incorrect (1540)
22 x 45	990	Correct
19 x 95	1981	Incorrect (1805)
63 x 87	5421	Incorrect (5481)
42 x 62	2604	Correct

We're sorry, but we can't display game statistics at this moment.

Figure 6-8. *Gamification microservice is down*

Besides, if you try to send an attempt, it'll still work. The error causes an exception that is captured within the GamificationServiceClient class.

```
ERROR 36666 --- [nio-8080-exec-2] m.b.m.s.GamificationServiceClient : There
was a problem sending the attempt.
```

The core functionality is still working even with half of the backend being down. But keep in mind that, in that case, you would miss data, so users will not get a score for successful attempts.

As an alternative implementation, you could have used retry logic. You could implement a loop to keep trying to post the attempt until you get an OK response from the gamification microservice or until a certain amount of time passes. But, even though there are libraries that you can use to implement this pattern, the complexity of the system increases. What if the Multiplication microservice also goes down while retrying? Should you keep track of the attempts that you didn't send yet in the database? In that case, when the Gamification app comes back to life at a random moment, should you send the attempts in the same order as they happened? As you see, distributed systems like this microservices architecture introduce new challenges.

The Challenges Ahead

The system you built is working, so you should be proud of it. Even in the case of a failure in the Gamification microservice, the application keeps responding. See Figure 6-9 for the updated logical view of this system.

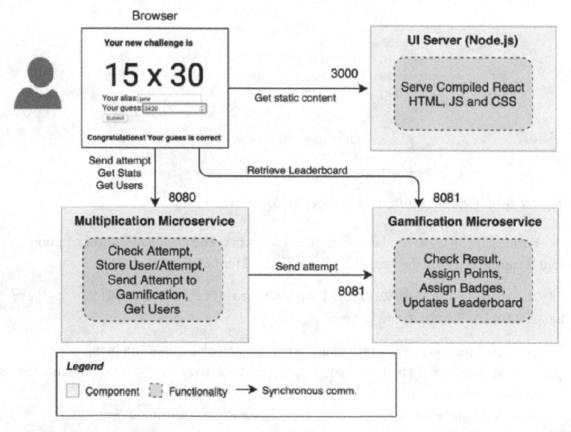

Figure 6-9. Logical view

The backend logic is now distributed across these two Spring Boot applications. Let's review the implications of building distributed systems, focusing on the microservice architecture and the new challenges you're facing.

Tight Coupling

When you model the domains, we argued that they're loosely coupled because you used only minimal references between the domain objects. However, we introduced awareness of the Gamification logic in the Multiplication microservice. The latter is explicitly calling the Gamification API to send an attempt and is responsible for delivering the message. We're using an imperative style that isn't that bad in a monolith, but it might become a big issue in a microservices architecture because it introduces tight coupling between microservices.

In the current design, the Gamification microservice becomes orchestrated by the Multiplication microservice, which actively triggers the action. Instead of using this Orchestration pattern, you could use a Choreography pattern and let the Gamification microservice decide when to trigger its logic. The next chapter explains the differences between Orchestration and Choreography when covering event-driven architectures.

Synchronous Interfaces vs. Eventual Consistency

The Multiplication microservice expects the Gamification server to be available when an attempt is sent, as detailed earlier. If it isn't, that part of the process remains incomplete. All of this happens within the request's lifecycle. By the time the Multiplication server sends the response to the UI, the score and badges are either updated or something went wrong. You built synchronous interfaces: the requests remain blocked until they're fully done, or they fail.

When you have many microservices, you'll unavoidably have flows that span across them, like in this example, even when they have nicely designed context boundaries. To depict this, let's create a more sophisticated scenario as a hypothetical evolution of your backend. As a first update, you want to email the users when they reach 1,000 points. Without being judgmental about domain boundaries, let's say you have a dedicated microservice for that, which needs to be updated after assigning a new score. You also need to add a microservice that collects data for reporting and needs to be connected to both Multiplication and Gamification. See Figure 6-10 for a complete view of this hypothetical system.

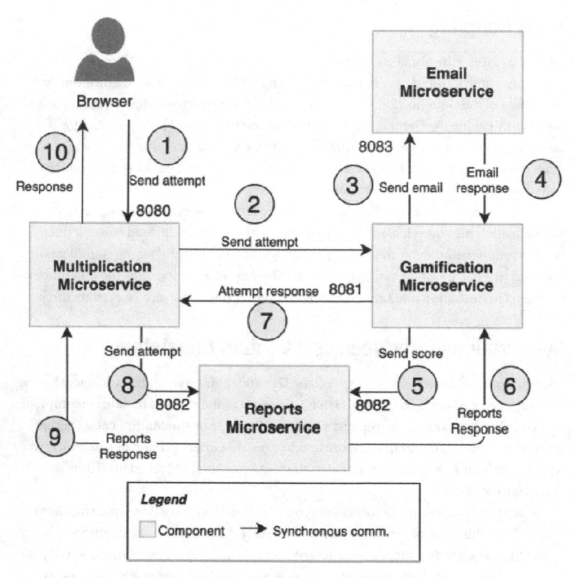

Figure 6-10. *Hypothetical evolution of the system*

You could keep building synchronous interfaces with REST API calls. Then, you would have a chain of calls, as shown in Figure 6-10's sequence of numbers. The request from the browser would need to wait until all of them are completed. The more services you have in the chain, the longer the request will be blocked. If one microservice is slow, the whole chain becomes slow. The overall performance of the system is at least as bad as the worst microservice in the chain.

Synchronous dependencies are even worse when you don't build the microservices with fault tolerance in mind. In this example, a simple failing update operation from the Gamification microservice to the Reports microservice could crash the entire flow. If you implement a retry mechanism within the same blocking thread, the performance degrades even more. If you let them fail too easily, you may end up with a lot of partially completed operations.

There is a clear conclusion thus far: synchronous interfaces introduce a strong dependency between microservices.

As an advantage, you know that the reports are updated in the backend by the time the user gets a response. So, it's the score. You even know if you could send an email or not, so you can give immediate feedback.

In a monolith, you wouldn't face this challenge because all these modules would live within the same deployable unit. You don't have issues due to network latency or errors if you're just calling other methods. Besides, if something goes down, it will be the whole system, so you don't need to design it while taking into account fine-grained fault tolerance.

So, if synchronous interfaces are bad, the important question is: do you need to block the complete request in the first place? Do you need to know that everything was completed before returning a response? To answer that question, let's modify the hypothetical case to detach the subsequent interactions between microservices. See Figure 6-11.

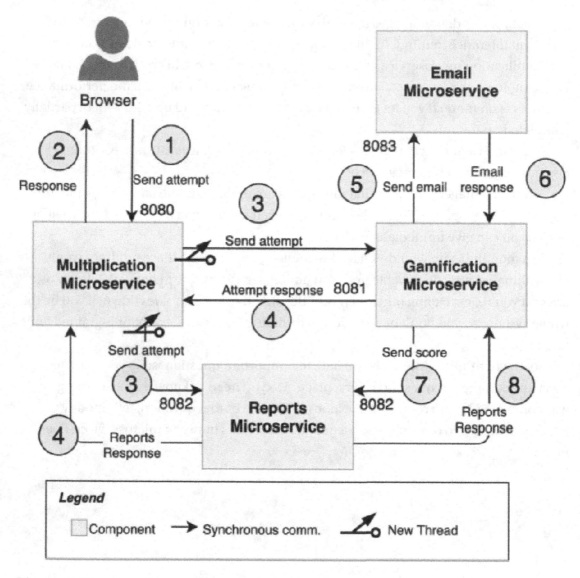

Figure 6-11. *Asynchronous processing*

This new design initiates some requests in new threads, unblocking the main one. You could use, for example, Java Futures. That would cause the response to be delivered to the client much earlier, so you solve all the problems described before. But, as a consequence, you would introduce eventual consistency. Imagine that, on the API client's side, there is a single sequential thread waiting for the response of sending the attempt. Then, this client's process will try to collect the score and the report. In the blocking-thread scenario, the API clients (e.g., the UI) know for sure that, after getting the response from Multiplication, the score in Gamification is consistent with the attempt. In this new asynchronous landscape, you can't guarantee that. If your network latency is good, the client might get the updated score. It may take one second to complete, or you have services down for a longer period, and it's updated only after some retries. You can't predict it.

Therefore, one of the hardest challenges you'll face when building microservice architectures is embracing eventual consistency. You should accept that the Gamification microservice's data might not be consistent with the Multiplication microservice's data at a given moment in time. It'll only be eventually consistent. In the end, with a proper design that makes your system robust, the Gamification microservice will be up to date. In the meantime, your API clients can't assume consistency between different API calls. And that's the key: it's not only your backend system; it's also about your API calls. If you're the only ones consuming your APIs, that might not be a big issue: you can develop your REST clients with eventual consistency in mind. However, if you offer your APIs as a service, you must educate your clients too. They have to know what to expect.

Thus, the original question about whether you need to block the request or not can be replaced by a more important question: can your system be eventually consistent? Of course, the answer depends on the functional and technical requirements.

For example, in some cases, the functional description of a system might imply strong consistency, but you can adapt it without a big impact. As a practical case, if you detach the email sub-flow as an asynchronous step, you could change the message prompted to the user from "You should have received an email with instructions" to "You will receive an email with instructions in a few moments. If you don't, please contact customer support." But being able to make changes like this always depends on the requirements and the appetite of the organization to embrace eventual consistency.

Microservices Are Not Always the Best Solution (Part I)   If your project's requirements are not compatible with eventual consistency across domains, a modular monolithic application might suit you better.

On the other hand, you don't need to go fully asynchronous everywhere. In some cases, it makes sense to have synchronous calls between microservices. That's not a problem nor a reason to make a drama about your software architecture. You just need to keep an eye on those interfaces since sometimes it's a symptom of tight coupling between domains. In that case, you could consider merging them into the same microservice.

Looking back at the current system status, you can conclude that it's ready for eventual consistency. Since you don't rely on the response to refresh the leaderboard, you could switch to an asynchronous call between your microservices without any impact.

As you can imagine, there is a better way to implement asynchronous communication between microservices than having REST API calls with a retry pattern. We cover it in the next chapter.

Transactions

In a monolith, you could store users, attempts, scores, and badges in the same relational database. Then, you could benefit from database transactions. You would get the ACID guarantees covered briefly in the previous chapter: atomicity, consistency, isolation, and durability. In the case of an error saving scorecard, you could revert all previous commands in the transaction so the attempt wouldn't be stored either. That operation is known as a *rollback*. You could always ensure data integrity since you could avoid partial updates.

You can't have ACID guarantees across microservices because you can't achieve real transactions in a microservices architecture. They are deployed independently, so they live in different processes, and their databases should also be decoupled. Besides, to avoid interdependencies, we also concluded that you should accept eventual consistency.

Atomicity, or ensuring that either all related data is stored or nothing is, is hard to achieve across microservices. In this system, the first request stores the attempt, and then the Multiplication microservice calls the Gamification microservice to do its part. Even if you keep that request synchronous, you never know if the score and badges were stored if you don't receive a response. What do you do then? Do you roll back the transaction? Do you always store the attempt no matter what happens in Gamification (as you did)?

In fact, there are imaginative—and complex—ways to achieve transaction rollbacks in a distributed system.

- *Two-phased commits (2PC)*: In this approach, you could send the attempt from Multiplication to Gamification, but you wouldn't store the data yet on either side. Then, once you get the response indicating that data is ready to be stored, you send a second request as a signal to store the score and badges on Gamification, and you store the attempt on Multiplication. With these two phases (prepare and commit), you minimize the time when something can go wrong. Yet you didn't eliminate the possibility since the second phase might fail anyway. In our opinion, this is a horrible idea since you have to stick to synchronous interfaces, and the complexity grows exponentially.

- *Sagas*: This design pattern involves two-way communication. You could build an asynchronous interface between both microservices, and if something goes wrong on the Gamification side, this microservice should be able to reach the Multiplication microservice to let it know. In this example, Multiplication would then delete the attempt that was just saved. That way, you *compensate* for a transaction. This comes with a high price in terms of complexity as well.

Undoubtedly, the best solution is to try to keep the functional flows that must use database transactions within the same microservice. If you can't split a transaction because it's critical to your system, the process should belong to the same domain anyway. For other flows, you can try to split the transaction boundaries and embrace eventual consistency.

You can also apply patterns to make your system more robust, so you minimize the risk of having partially executed operations. Any design pattern that can ensure the delivery of data between microservices will help with that goal. That is covered in the next chapter as well.

This system doesn't use distributed transactions. It doesn't require them either, since you don't need immediate consistency between the attempts and the score. But there is still a design flaw: the Multiplication microservice ignores errors from Gamification so you might get successfully solved attempts without their corresponding score and badges. You'll learn how to improve that soon without needing to implement a retry mechanism.

Microservices Are Not Always the Best Solution (Part II)   If you find yourself implementing distributed transactions with 2PC or sagas all over the place, you should take some time to reflect on your requirements and your microservice boundaries. You might want to merge some of them or make a better distribution of functionalities. If you can't fix it in a simpler way, consider a modular monolithic application with a single relational database.

API Exposure

You created a REST endpoint in the Gamification microservice that you intended for the Multiplication microservice. But the UI also needs access to the Gamification microservice so anybody can access it. Smart users could send fake data to the Gamification microservice if they use an HTTP client (like HTTPie). You would be in a bad situation since that would break your data integrity. Users could score points and get badges without the corresponding attempts stored on the Multiplication side.

There are multiple ways to solve this problem. You could add a security layer to your endpoints and ensure that internal APIs are available only for other backend services. A more straightforward option is to use a reverse proxy (with the Gateway pattern) to ensure you expose only the public endpoints. Chapter 8 covers this option in more detail.

Summary and Achievements

This chapter discussed the reasons to move to a microservices architecture. It started detailing the approach you have followed so far, a small-monolith architecture. It analyzed the pros and cons of continuing your journey toward a modular, monolithic application compared to transitioning to microservices.

The chapter also examined how a small monolith can help you define your domains better and complete the first version of your product faster to get early feedback from your users. The list of good practices to structure your code in modules should help if you need to make a split. But you also saw how sometimes a small monolith is not the best idea, especially if the development team is large from the beginning.

Deciding to move to microservices (or start with them) requires a deep analysis of your system's functional and nonfunctional characteristics to figure out requirements in terms of scalability, fault tolerance, transactionality, eventual consistency, and so on. That decision can be crucial to the success or the failure of a software project. We hope that all the considerations included in this chapter, and supported by the practical case, help you scrutinize all factors that are present in your project and make a sound decision and a good plan if you make the move.

As expected from this book, we decided to go for microservices architecture. On the practical side, you navigated through the layers of the new Gamification application: services, repositories, controllers, and the new React component. You connected Multiplication to Gamification using a simple, *imperative* approach, and you used this interface between your microservices to discover some of the unique challenges faced with a microservices architecture.

By the end of this chapter, you also learned why the synchronous interface we chose for communicating both microservices was the wrong decision. It introduces tight coupling and makes your architecture fragile against errors. This is a perfect baseline for the next chapter, where we introduce the advantages of an event-driven architecture.

Chapter's Achievements:

- You saw how a small monolith approach can help you when starting new projects.

- You were introduced to the pros and cons of microservice architectures (you'll keep learning them over the upcoming chapters).

- You learned about the differences between synchronous and asynchronous processing in distributed systems and how they relate to eventual consistency.

- You learned why it's important to embrace those new paradigms— asynchronous processes and eventual consistency—in microservice architectures to avoid tight coupling and domain pollution.

- You saw why microservices are not the best solution for all cases (e.g., if you need transactionality and immediate data consistency).

- You identified the first challenges you're facing in the practical case and saw how the current implementation is not the right way of implementing microservices.

## CHAPTER 7

Event-Driven Architectures

The last chapter analyzed how the interface between your microservices plays a key role concerning tight coupling. The Multiplication microservice acts as the orchestrator of the process by calling the Gamification microservice. If there were additional services that were also required to retrieve the data for each attempt, you would need to add extra calls from the Multiplication application to these services. This could result in a distributed monolith with a central brain. We discussed this problem in detail while examining a hypothetical extension of the backend.

This chapter explores a new approach of designing these interfaces known as the Publish-Subscribe pattern. This method, called an event-driven architecture, involves *publishers* sending events to *subscribers* without knowledge of their specific destinations. As a result, subscribers do not need to understand the publishers' logic. While this paradigm makes the system loosely coupled and scalable, it also presents new challenges.

One such challenge of the event-driven architecture is ensuring that events are handled in the correct order. Additionally, ensuring that events are not lost or duplicated can be another challenge. Without proper planning, designing the system to handle a large number of events can be difficult to manage. Event-driven architecture can be more complex to design and implement than traditional architectures, as they might require additional resources and expertise.

The goal of this chapter is to understand the core concepts of event-driven architectures, their advantages, and the consequences of working with them. As usual, you'll apply this knowledge to the system following a hands-on approach.

© Moisés Macero García and Tarun Telang 2023
M. Macero García and T. Telang, *Learn Microservices with Spring Boot 3*,
https://doi.org/10.1007/978-1-4842-9757-5_7

Core Concepts

As discussed earlier, event-driven architecture is an approach to software architecture that focuses on responding to events that either occur within a system or in the external environment. This section highlights the core concepts of event-driven architectures.

The Message Broker

A *message broker* is a software component that enables communication and message exchange between different system components. In an event-driven architecture, the *message broker* plays a vital role. The system components communicate with the broker instead of connecting directly to each other. This helps maintain the loose coupling between the components.

Message brokers typically include routing functionalities. They allow the creation of multiple *channels,* so you can separate messages based on your requirements. One or more publishers may generate messages in each of these channels, which one or more subscribers (or even none) may consume. In this chapter, you'll see in more detail what a message is and the different messaging topologies you might want to use. See Figure 7-1 for a conceptual view of common scenarios using a message broker.

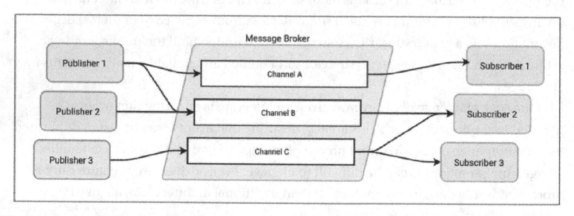

Figure 7-1. *Message brokers: high-level view*

These concepts are not new. Developers who have been active for a while surely identify similar patterns in enterprise service bus (ESB) architectures. An enterprise service bus (ESB) is a software architecture model used for designing and implementing the interaction and communication between software components in a service-oriented architecture (SOA). It represents a middleware solution that controls communication among various services, ensuring everything works together seamlessly. The bus pattern facilitates the communication between the different system components, providing data transformation and mapping, message queuing and sorting, routing, orchestration, error handling, load balancing, protocol conversion, and so on.

There is still a bit of controversy about the exact differences between ESB architectures and those based on message brokers. A broadly accepted distinction is that, in ESB, the channel itself has much more relevance in the system. The service bus sets the protocol standards for communication, and it transforms and routes the data to the specific target. Some implementations can take care of distributed transactions. In some cases, they even have a sophisticated UI to model business processes and transform these rules into configuration and code. Typically, ESB architectures tend to concentrate a big part of the system's business logic inside the bus, so they become the system's orchestration layer. See Figure 7-2.

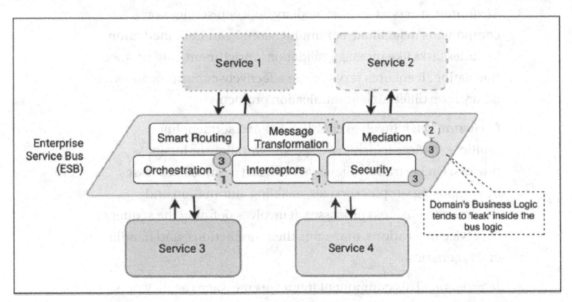

Figure 7-2. _ESB architectures concentrate business logic inside the bus_

Enterprise service bus (ESB) is an architecture that provides a way to integrate different services and applications by facilitating communication between them. The key concepts of ESB are as follows:

1. *Smart routing*: It dynamically determines the best message path based on various factors like message content, metadata, system state, and predefined rules. This ensures that messages are directed efficiently and optimally to the appropriate services, enabling effective communication.

2. *Message transformation*: It involves converting a message from one format to another. In ESB architecture, messages have varying formats like XML, JSON, CSV, and so on. Message transformation enables seamless communication and integration between different services.

3. *Mediation*: It acts as an intermediary between services or components to facilitate communication. In an ESB, mediation includes tasks like message validation, enrichment, and protocol translation. It ensures services can effectively communicate even if they have different communication protocols.

4. *Orchestration*: It involves coordinating and sequencing multiple services to achieve a specific workflow or business process. Orchestration allows you to build complex processes by composing simpler services, enabling automation and streamlined business processes. It involves defining the sequence of service invocations, managing their interactions, and handling error scenarios.

5. *Interceptors*: This component intercepts messages as they pass through the system. They can perform various tasks such as logging, monitoring, security checks, and more. You can use Interceptors to add functionality to the message-processing pipeline without modifying the core services.

6. *Security*: It involves ensuring the confidentiality, integrity, and authenticity of messages and data between different services. It includes implementing encryption, authentication, authorization,

and other security mechanisms to protect sensitive information. These security measures are crucial for preventing unauthorized access, data breaches, and other cyber threats.

Moving all the business logic inside the same component and having a central orchestrator in the system are software architecture patterns that tend to fail. Systems that follow that route have a single point of failure, and their core part (the bus in this case) becomes harder to maintain and evolve over time since the whole organization depends on it. The logic embedded in the bus tends to become a big mess. That's one of the reasons why the ESB architectures got such a bad reputation over the last few years.

Based on these bad experiences, many people now tend to move away from this centrally orchestrating, too-smart messaging channel and implement a simpler approach with a message broker, using it just for the communication between different components.

At this point, you might be picturing a clear line between ESB as complex channels and message brokers as simple channels. However, we mentioned earlier that there is a bit of controversy, so it's not easy to draw that line. On the one hand, you could use an ESB platform but keep the business logic adequately isolated. On the other hand, some modern messaging platforms, such as Kafka, offer tools that allow you to embed some business logic in the channel. If required, you can transform messages with functions that may include the business logic. You can also query data in the channel as you would with a database, and you can process the output as needed. For example, based on some data in a message, you could decide to take it out of a specific channel and move it to another one, with a different format. Therefore, you can switch between tools that are normally associated with different architecture patterns (ESB/message brokers) but still use them similarly. This idea already gives you an early introduction of a core takeaway of the coming chapters: first, you need to understand the patterns, and then you can choose the tool that best suits your needs.

We recommend you avoid including business logic in the communication channel as much as possible. Keep that logic where it belongs—in your distributed system, respecting a domain-driven design approach. That's what you'll do in the system in this example: you'll use a message broker to keep the services loosely coupled and scalable, keeping the business processes inside each microservice.

Events and Messages

In event-driven architectures, an *event* indicates that something happened in the system. Events get published to a messaging channel (e.g., a message broker) by the business logic that owns the domain where those events happened. Other components in the architecture that are interested in a given event type subscribe to the channel to consume all the subsequent event instances. As you can see, events relate to the publish-subscribe pattern, so they are linked to message brokers or buses too. You'll implement an event-driven architecture using a message broker, so let's focus on that specific case.

A *message*, on the other hand, is a more generic term. Many people distinguish between the two in this manner—messages are elements that you can directly address to a system component, and events are pieces of information that reflect facts that happened at a given domain and don't have a specific addressee. However, an event is actually a message from a technical perspective when you send it via a message broker (because there is no such thing as an event broker). To keep it simple, we'll use in the book the term *message* to refer to a generic piece of information that goes through a message broker, and the term *event* when we refer to a message that follows an event-driven design.

Note that there is nothing that prevents you from modeling events and sending them using REST APIs (similar to what you did in the book's application). However, that doesn't help reduce tight coupling: the producers need to be aware of the consumers to target the events to them.

When you use events with a message broker, you can better isolate all the components in your software architecture. Publishers and subscribers can function independently without needing to be aware of each other. This approach is ideal for microservice architecture since you aim to keep microservices as independent as possible. By following this strategy, you can introduce new microservices that consume events from the channels without having to modify the microservice that publishes those events, or any other subscribers.

Thinking in Events

Bear in mind that the introduction of a message broker and some classes with the suffix *Event* don't make your architecture "event driven" automatically. You have to design your software thinking in events, which requires effort if you're not used to it. Let's use the Multiplication application to analyze this a bit deeper.

In the first scenario, imagine that you created a Gamification API to assign scores and badges to a given user. See the top part of Figure 7-3. In a microservice architecture, the Multiplication microservice should use the `updateScore` API to assign a score for a solved attempt. It's important to note that this microservice will become aware of the existence of the `updateScore` API and will also become the owner of part of its business logic. Many people who are new to microservice architectures and come from an imperative programming style make the mistake of not realizing this. They tend to change method calls by API calls between microservices, implementing a remote procedure call (RPC) pattern, sometimes without even noticing it. To improve the coupling between microservices, you could introduce a message broker. Then, you replace the REST API call with a message directed to the Gamification microservice, the `UpdateScore` message. But, would you actually improve the system with this change? Very little. The message still has a specific destination, so any new microservices can't reuse it. Besides, both parts of the system remain tightly coupled, and, as a side effect, you replaced the synchronous interface with an asynchronous one, introducing extra complexity (as you saw in the previous chapter and will also see further in this one).

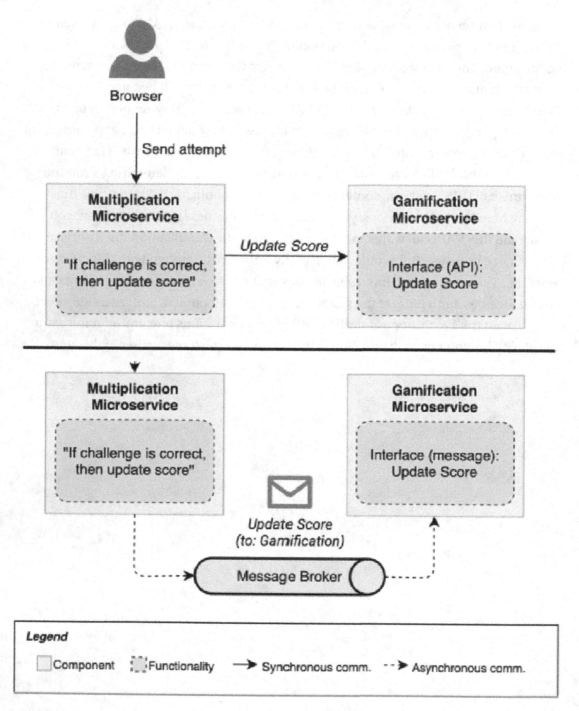

Figure 7-3. *Imperative approach: REST vs. message*

The second scenario is based on the current implementation. See Figure 7-4. You pass a `ChallengeSolvedDTO` object from Multiplication to Gamification so that you respect the domain boundaries. You don't include gamification logic in the first service. However, you still need to address Gamification directly, so the tight coupling remains. With the introduction of a message broker, you could solve this problem. The Multiplication microservice could send a `ChallengeSolvedDTO` to a generic channel and continue doing its logic. The second microservice could subscribe to this channel and process the message (which is already an event conceptually) to calculate the new score and badges. New microservices added to the system could transparently subscribe to the channel if they are also interested in the `ChallengeSolvedDTO` message to, for example, generate reports or send messages to the users.

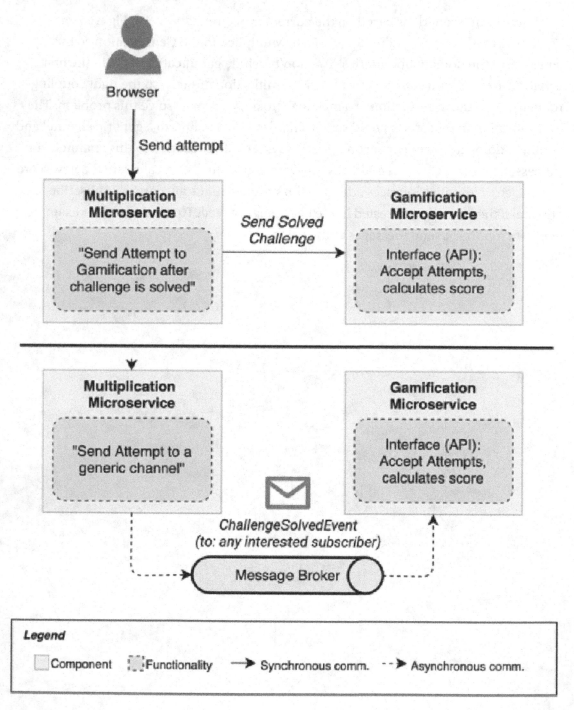

Figure 7-4. *Events: REST vs. message*

This first scenario implements a command pattern, where the Multiplication microservice instructs what to do to the Gamification microservice (aka, orchestration). The second scenario implements the event pattern by sending a notification about something that has already happened, together with contextual data. The consumers will process this data, which may trigger their business logic and possibly other events as a result. This approach is sometimes called *choreography*, as opposed to orchestration. When you base your software architecture on these event-driven designs, it's referred to as an *event-driven architecture*.

As you see, to achieve a pure event-driven architecture, you have to rethink business processes that you may express in an imperative style and define them instead as (re) actions and events. Not only should you define domains using DDD, but you should also model interactions between them as events. If you want to know more about a technique to help you conduct these design sessions, check out `http://ziobrando.blogspot.com/2013/11/introducing-event-storming.html`.

Before moving forward, let us insist again on an important remark: you don't need to change every single communication interface in your system to follow an event-driven style. You need to implement the command and the request/response patterns when events don't fit. Don't try to force a business requirement that only serves as a command to behave as an event artificially. On the technical side, feel free to use REST APIs for use cases where they make more sense, like commands that need a synchronous response.

Microservices Are Not Always the Best Solution (III)   When you build a microservice architecture that uses mostly imperative, targeted interfaces, you have a lot of hard dependencies between all these system components. Many people refer to this scenario as a *distributed monolith* since you still have the disadvantages of a monolithic application: tight coupling and therefore less flexibility to modify microservices.

If you need some time to build an event-driven mindset in your organization, you could instead set up a modular system and start implementing event patterns across the modules. Then, you benefit from learning one thing at a time and keeping a manageable complexity. Once you achieve loose coupling, you can split the modules into microservices.

Asynchronous Messaging

The previous chapter dedicated a section to analyzing the impact of changing synchronous interfaces into asynchronous ones. With the introduction of a message broker as a tool to build an event-driven architecture, the adoption of asynchronous messaging is implicit. Publishers send events and don't wait for a response from any event consumer. That will keep the architecture loosely coupled and scalable. See Figure 7-5.

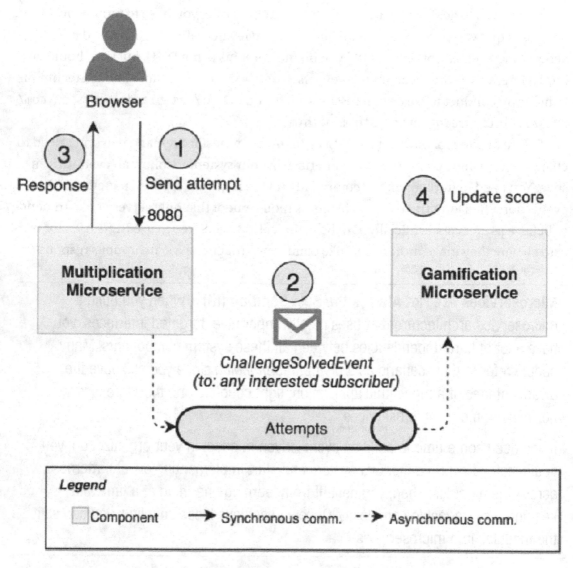

Figure 7-5. *Asynchronous process with a message broker*

However, you could also use a message broker and keep the processes synchronous. Let's use the current system as an example again. Say you plan to replace the REST API interface with a message broker. Yet, instead of creating a single channel to send your events, you could create two channels and use the second one to receive a response from the Gamification microservice. See Figure 7-6. In the code, you could then block the request's thread and wait for that acknowledgment before continuing the process.

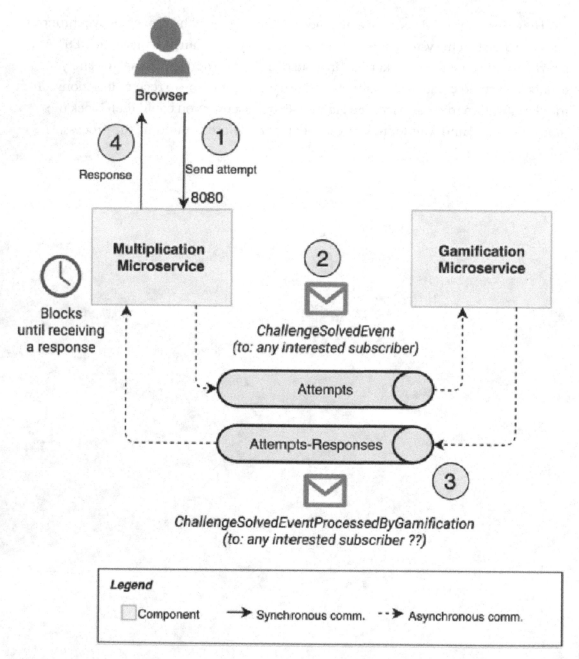

Figure 7-6. Synchronous processing with a message broker

That's actually a request/response pattern on top of a message broker. This combination can be useful in some use cases, but it's not recommended in an event-driven approach. The main reason is that you get the tight coupling again: the

Multiplication microservice needs to know about the subscribers and how many there are to make sure it receives all the responses. You would still get some advantages like scalability (as we'll detail later), but there are other patterns you can apply to improve the scalability with synchronous interfaces like a load balancer (as you'll see in the next chapter). Therefore, you could consider using a simpler synchronous interface like a REST API, in situations where your process needs to be synchronous anyway. See Table 7-1 for a summary of how you can combine patterns and tools. Keep in mind that this is just a recommendation. As you have learned, you might have your own preferences to implement these patterns using different tooling.

Table 7-1. *Combining Patterns and Tools*

Pattern	Type	Implementation
Request/response	Synchronous	REST API
Commands that require blocking	Synchronous	REST API
Commands that don't require blocking	Asynchronous	Message broker
Events	Asynchronous	Message broker

It's worth noting that, even though the end-to-end communication can be asynchronous, you'll get a synchronous interface with the message broker from your applications. That's an important characteristic. When you publish a message, you want to be sure the broker received it before continuing with something else. The same applies to subscribers, where the broker requires acknowledgment after consuming messages to mark them as processed and move to the next ones. These two steps are critical to keep your data safe and make your system reliable. We'll explain these concepts using a practical case later in this chapter.

Reactive Systems

The word *reactive* can be used in multiple contexts, having a different meaning depending on the technical layer that refers to. The most accepted definition of a *reactive system* describes it as a set of design principles to apply in software architecture to make the system responsive (responds on time), resilient (stays responsive if there are failures), elastic (adapts to be responsive under different workloads), and message-driven (ensures loose coupling and boundary isolation). These design principles are listed in the Reactive Manifesto (`https://www.reactivemanifesto.org/`). You'll follow these patterns while building your system, so you can claim you're building a reactive system.

On the other hand, *reactive programming* refers to a set of techniques used in programming languages around patterns such as futures (or promises), reactive streams, backpressure, and so on. There are popular libraries that help you implement these patterns in Java, like Reactor (`https://projectreactor.io/`) and RxJava (`https://github.com/ReactiveX/RxJava`). With reactive programming, you can split your logic into a set of smaller blocks that can run asynchronously and later compose or transform the result. That brings a concurrency improvement since you can go faster when you do tasks in parallel.

Switching to reactive programming doesn't make your architecture reactive. They work at different levels: reactive programming helps achieve improvements inside components and in terms of concurrency. Reactive systems are changes at a higher level, between components, and they help build loosely coupled, resilient, and scalable systems. See `https://www.oreilly.com/radar/reactive-programming-vs-reactive-systems/` for more details on the differences between these techniques.

Pros and Cons of Going Event-Driven

The previous chapter covered through the pros and cons of moving to microservices. You gain in flexibility and scalability, but you face new challenges such as eventual consistency, fault tolerance, and partial updates.

Going event-driven with a message broker pattern helps with these challenges. This section briefly describes how, using the practical example.

- *Loose coupling between microservices*: You already learned how you can make the Multiplication service unaware of the Gamification service. The first sends an event to the broker, and Gamification subscribes and reacts to the event, updating score and badges for a user.

- *Scalability*: As you'll see in this chapter, it's easy to add new instances of a given application to scale up your system horizontally. Moreover, it would be easy to introduce new microservices in your architecture. They could subscribe to events and work independently. For example, in the hypothetical situation , you could generate reports or send emails based on events triggered by existing services.

- *Fault tolerance and eventual consistency*: If you make the message broker reliable enough, you can use it to guarantee eventual consistency even when system components fail. If the Gamification microservice goes down for some time, it could catch up with the events later when it comes back, since the broker can persist the messages. That gives you some flexibility. You'll see this in practice at the end of this chapter.

On the other hand, adopting event-based design patterns confirms the choice for eventual consistency. You avoid creating blocking, imperative flows. Instead, you use asynchronous processes that simply notify other components. This, as you saw, requires a different mindset, so you (and possibly your API clients) accept that the state of the data might not be consistent across microservices all the time.

Additionally, with the introduction of the message broker, you're adding a new component to your system. You can't simply say that the message broker doesn't fail, so you have to prepare the system for new potential errors.

- *Dropped messages*: It might be the case that the ChallengeSolvedEvent never reaches Gamification. If you're building a system where you shouldn't miss an event, you should configure the broker to fulfill the *at-least-once* guarantee. This policy ensures the messages are delivered at least once by the broker, although they could be duplicated.

- *Duplicated messages*: The message broker, under certain situations, may send some messages more than once that were published only once. In your system, if you get the event twice, you'll increment the score incorrectly. Therefore, you have to think about making the event consumption *idempotent*. In computing, an operation is idempotent if it can be called more than once without different outcomes. A possible solution in this case would be marking the events that you already processed on the Gamification side (e.g., in the database) and ignoring any repeated ones. Some brokers like RabbitMQ and Kafka also offer a good *at-most-once* guarantee if you configure them properly, and that helps prevent duplicates.

- *Unordered messages*: Even though the broker can try its best to avoid unordered messages, this can still happen if something fails or if there's a bug in the software. You have to prepare your code to cope with that. When possible, try to avoid the assumption that the events will be consumed in the same order in which they were published.

- *Broker's downtime*: In the worst case, the broker can also become unavailable. Both publishers and subscribers should try to deal with that situation (e.g., with a retry strategy or a cache). You could also flag the services as *unhealthy* and stop accepting new operations (as we'll cover in the next chapter). That could imply downtime for the complete system, but might be a better option than accepting partial updates and inconsistent data.

These example solutions proposed in each of the previous bullets are *resilience patterns*. Some of them could be translated into coding tasks that you should do to make your system work even in case of failures, such as idempotency, retries, or health checks. As mentioned, a good resilience is important in distributed systems such as a microservice architecture, so it's always handy to know these patterns to have solutions for the unhappy flows during your design sessions.

Another liability of an event-driven system is that *traceability* becomes harder. You call a REST API, and that might trigger events; then, there could be components reacting to those events, subsequently publishing some other events, and the chain continues. Knowing what event caused what action in a different microservice might not be a problem when you only have a few distributed processes. However, when the system grows, having an overall view of these chains of events and actions is a big challenge in an event-driven microservice architecture. You need this view because you want to be able to debug operations that go wrong and find out why you trigger a given process. Fortunately, there are tools to implement *distributed tracing*: a way for you to link events and actions and visualize them as a chain of actions/reactions. For example, the Spring family has Spring Cloud Sleuth, a tool that automatically injects some identifiers (span IDs) in the logs and propagates those identifiers when you make/receive HTTP calls, publish/consume messages via RabbitMQ, and so on. Then, if you use centralized logging, you can link all these processes using the identifiers. The next chapter covers some of these strategies.

Messaging Patterns

You can identify several patterns in messaging platforms that you can apply, depending on what you want to accomplish. This section details them from a high-level perspective, without going into implementation details for any specific platform. You can use Figure 7-7 as a guide to understanding these concepts, detailed in the next pages.

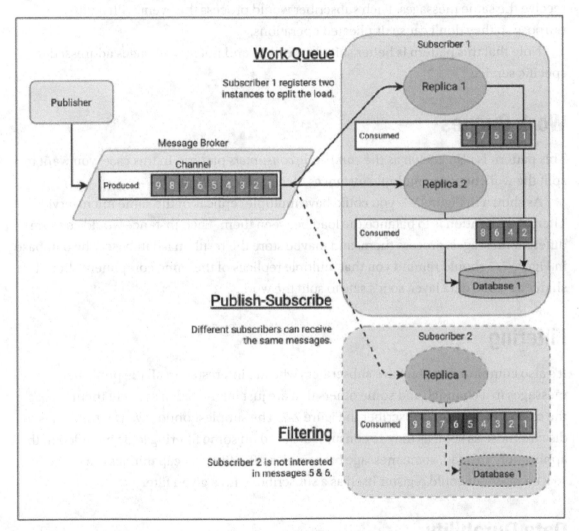

Figure 7-7. *Messaging patterns*

Publish-Subscribe

In this pattern, different subscribers receive copies of the same messages. For example, you could have multiple components in your system that are interested in `ChallengeSolvedEvent`, like the Gamification microservice and a hypothetical Reporting microservice. In this case, it's important to configure these subscribers so they both receive the same messages. Each subscriber would process the event with a different purpose so they don't cause duplicated operations.

Note that this pattern is better suited for events and not for messages addressed to a specific service.

Work Queues

This pattern is also known as the *competing consumers* pattern. In this case, you want to split the work between multiple instances of the same application.

As shown in Figure 7-7, you could have multiple replicas of the same microservice. Then, the intention is to balance the load between them. Each instance would consume different messages, process them, and maybe store the result in a database. The database in Figure 7-7 should remind you that multiple replicas of the same component should share the same data layer, so it's safe to split the work.

Filtering

It's also common that you have subscribers who are interested in all the published messages in a channel, and some others that are just interested in some of them. That's the case of the second subscriber in Figure 7-7. The simplest option we can think of is to discard those as soon as they're consumed, based on some filtering logic included in the application. Instead, some message brokers also offer filtering capabilities out of the box, so a component could register itself as a subscriber with a given filter.

Data Durability

If the broker persists the messages, the subscribers don't need to be running all the time to consume all the data. Each subscriber has an associated *marker* in the broker to identify the last message they consumed. If they can't get messages at a given time, the data flow can continue later from where they left it.

Even after all subscribers retrieved a specific message, you may want to keep it stored in the broker for some time. This is useful if you want new subscribers to get messages that were sent prior to their existence. Also, persisting all messages for a given period can be helpful if you want to "reset the marker" for a subscriber, causing all messages to be reprocessed. This can be used, for example, to repair corrupted data, but it might also be a risky operation when subscribers are not idempotent.

In a system that models all operations as events, you could benefit from event persistence even more. Imagine that you wipe all the data from any existing database. Theoretically, you could replay all events from the beginning and re-create the same state. Therefore, you don't need to keep the last state of a given entity in the database at all, since you can see it as an "aggregate" of multiple events. This, in a nutshell, is the core concept of *event sourcing*. We won't dive into the details of this technique since it adds an extra layer of complexity, but check out `https://martinfowler.com/eaaDev/EventSourcing.html` if you want to know more about it.

Message Broker Protocols, Standards, and Tools

Over the years, a few messaging protocols and standards related to message brokers have arisen. This is a reduced list with some popular examples:

- *Advanced Message Queuing Protocol (AMQP)*: This is an open standard application layer protocol that defines both the network layer protocol and high-level architecture for message brokers. It supports sending and receiving messages, queueing, routing (including point-to-point and publish-and-subscribe), reliability and security.

- *Message Queuing Telemetry Transport (MQTT)*: This is also a protocol, and it has become popular for Internet of Things (IoT) devices since it can be implemented with little code, and it can work with constrained devices and under low-bandwidth, high-latency, or unreliable network conditions.

- *Streaming Text Oriented Messaging Protocol (STOMP)*: This is a text-based protocol like HTTP but oriented to messaging middleware.

- *Jakarta Messaging (formerly Java Message Service or JMS API)*: Unlike the previous ones, Jakarta Messaging is an API standard. It focuses on the behavior that a messaging system should implement. Therefore, you can find different Jakarta Messaging client implementations that connect to message brokers using different underlying protocols.

The following are popular software tools that implement some of these protocols and standards, or have their own:

- RabbitMQ (`https://www.rabbitmq.com/`) is an open-source message broker implementation that supports the AMQP, MQTT, and STOMP protocols, among others. It also offers a Jakarta Messaging API client and has a powerful routing configuration.

- Eclipse Mosquitto (`https://mosquitto.org/`) is a message broker that implements the MQTT protocol, so it's a popular choice for IoT systems.

- PubSub+ Platform (`https://solace.com/products/platform/`) is a complete suite of the event streaming and management platform that provides support for a wide range of open standard protocols, including AMQP, MQTT, Jakarta Messaging, REST, Web Sockets, and more.

- Apache Kafka (`https://kafka.apache.org/`) was designed originally by LinkedIn, and it uses its own binary protocol over TCP. Even though the Kafka core features don't offer the same functionalities as a traditional message broker (e.g., routing), it's a powerful messaging platform when the requirements for the messaging middleware are simple. It's commonly used in applications that handle a big volume of data in streams.

As in any case where you need to choose between different tools, you should familiarize yourself with the documentation and analyze how your requirements can benefit from its functionalities—the data volumes you're planning to handle, the delivery guarantees (at-least-once, at-most-once), the error handling strategies, the distributed setup possibilities, and so on. RabbitMQ and Kafka are popular tools when building event-driven architectures with Java and Spring Boot. Besides, the Spring framework has integrations for these tools, so it's easy to work with them from a coding perspective.

In this book, we use RabbitMQ and the AMQP protocol. The main reason is that this combination offers a wide variety of configuration possibilities, so you can learn most of these options and later reuse this knowledge in any other messaging platform you choose.

AMQP and RabbitMQ

RabbitMQ (`https://www.rabbitmq.com/`) has native support for the AMQP protocol version 0.9.1 (`https://www.amqp.org/`) and supports the AMQP 1.0 version via a plugin. For the most accurate and up-to-date information on supported versions of AMQP, refer to the official RabbitMQ documentation at `https://www.rabbitmq.com/specification.html`. We use the included 0.9.1 version since it's simpler and has better support; see `https://www.rabbitmq.com/protocols.html#amqp-10`.

This section looks at the main AMQP 0.9.1 concepts. If you want to dive into these concepts in more detail, we recommend you refer to `https://www.rabbitmq.com/tutorials/amqp-concepts.html` in the RabbitMQ documentation.

Overall Description

As described earlier in this chapter, publishers are components or applications in a system that publish messages to the broker. Consumers, also known as *subscribers*, receive and process these messages.

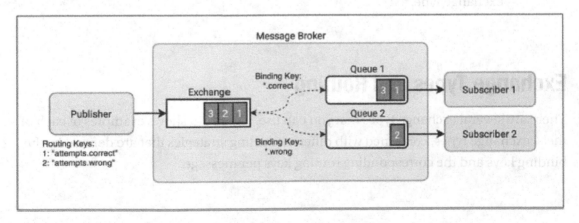

Figure 7-8. *RabbitMQ: concepts*

AMQP also defines exchanges, queues, and bindings. See Figure 7-8 to better understand these concepts.

- *Exchanges* are the entities where the messages are sent. They do the routing to the queues following a logic defined by the exchange type and rules, known as *bindings*. The exchanges can be durable if they persist after a broker restart, or transient if they don't.

- *Queues* are the objects in AMQP that store the messages to be consumed. Queues may have zero, one, or multiple consumers. A queue can also be durable or transient, but keep in mind that a durable queue doesn't mean that all its messages are persisted. To make messages survive a broker restart, they also have to be published as persistent messages.

- *Bindings* are rules to route messages published to the exchanges to certain queues. Therefore, a queue is bound to a given exchange. Some exchange types support an optional *binding key* to determine which messages published to an exchange should end up in a given queue. In that sense, you can see a binding key as a filter. On the other hand, publishers can specify *routing keys* when sending messages, so they can be filtered properly based on binding keys if these configurations are in use. Routing keys are composed of words delimited by dots, like `attempt.correct`. Binding keys have a similar format, but they may include pattern matchers, depending on the exchange type.

Exchange Types and Routing

There are several exchange types that you can use. Figure 7-9 shows examples of each of these exchange types, combined with different routing strategies that are defined by the binding keys and the corresponding routing keys per message.

- The *default exchange* is predeclared by the broker. All created queues are bound to this exchange with a binding key equal to the queue name. From a conceptual perspective, it means that messages can be published with a destination queue in mind if you use that name as a routing key. Technically, these messages still go through the exchange. This setup is not commonly used since it defeats the whole routing purpose.

- The *direct exchange* is commonly used for unicast routing. The difference with the default exchange is that you can use your own binding keys, and you can also create multiple queues with the same binding key. Then, these queues will all get messages whose routing key matches the binding key. Conceptually, you use it when you publish messages knowing the destination (unicast), but you don't need to know how many queues will get the message.

- The *fanout exchange* doesn't use routing keys. It routes all the messages to all the queues that are bound to the exchange, so it's perfect for a broadcast scenario.

- The *topic exchange* is the most flexible. Instead of binding queues to this exchange using a given value, you can use a pattern. That allows subscribers to register queues to consume a filtered set of messages. Patterns can use # to match any set of words or * to match only one word.

- The *headers exchange* uses the message headers as routing keys for better flexibility since you can set up the match condition to one or many headers and for an all-match or any-match configuration. Standard routing keys are therefore ignored.

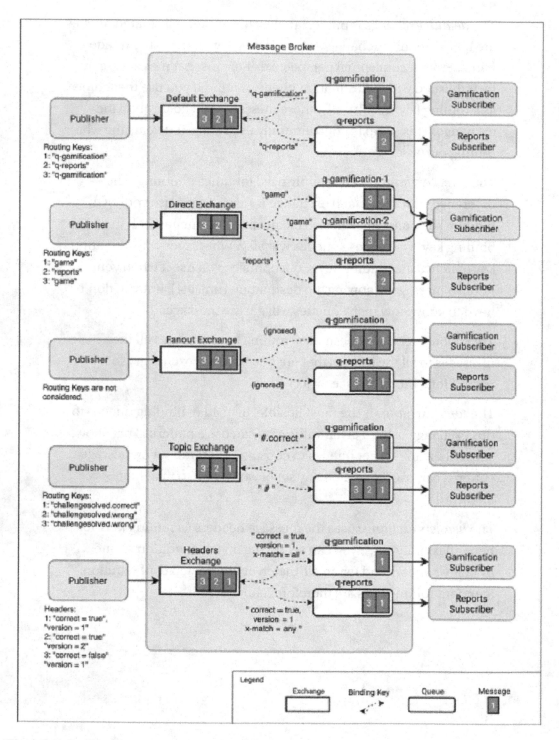

Figure 7-9. *Exchange types: examples*

As you can see, the publish-subscribe and filtering patterns described earlier in this chapter are applied in these scenarios. The direct exchange example in Figure 7-9 might look like a work queue pattern, but it's not. This example is there on purpose to demonstrate that, in AMQP 0.9.1, load balancing happens between consumers of the same queue, not between queues. To implement the work queue pattern, you normally subscribe more than once to the same queue. See Figure 7-10.

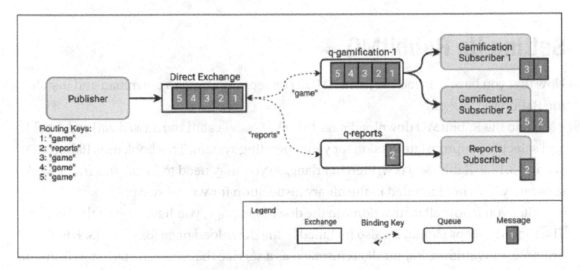

Figure 7-10. *Work queue in AMQP*

Message Acknowledgments and Rejection

AMQP defines two different acknowledgment modes for consumer applications. Understanding them is important since, after a consumer sends an acknowledgment, the message is removed from the queue.

The first alternative is to use *automatic acknowledgment*. With this strategy, messages are considered delivered when they're sent to the application. The second option is called *explicit acknowledgment*, and it consists of waiting until the application sends an ACK signal. This second option is much better to guarantee that all messages are processed. The consumer can read the message, run some business logic, persist related data, and even trigger a subsequent event before sending the acknowledgment signal to the broker. In this case, the message is removed from the queue only if it has been fully processed. If the consumer dies before sending the signal (or there is an error), the broker will try to deliver the message to another consumer or, if there is none, it'll wait until there is one available.

Consumers can also *reject* messages. For example, imagine that one of the consumer instances can't access the database due to network errors. In this case, the consumer can reject the message, specifying if it should be requeued or discarded. Note that, if the error that caused the message rejection remains for some time and there are no other consumers that can handle it successfully, you could end up in an infinite loop of requeuerejection.

Setting Up RabbitMQ

Now that you have learned the main AMQP concepts, it's time to download and install the RabbitMQ broker.

Go to the RabbitMQ download page (`https://www.rabbitmq.com/download.html`) and select the appropriate version for your operating system. This book uses RabbitMQ version 3.12.2. RabbitMQ is written in Erlang, so you may need to install this framework separately if it's not included in the binary installation for your system.

After you follow all instructions on the download page, you have to start the broker. The required steps should be also included in the download page for your OS. For example, in Windows, RabbitMQ is installed as a service that you can start/stop from the Start menu. In macOS, you have to run a command from the command line.

RabbitMQ includes some standard plugins, but not all of them are enabled by default. As an extra step, you will enable the management plugin, which gives you access to a Web UI and an API to monitor and manage the broker. From the `sbin` folder inside the broker's installation folder, execute the following:

```
$ rabbitmq-plugins enable rabbitmq_management
```

Then, when you restart the broker, you should be able to navigate to `http://localhost:15672` and see a login page. Since you're running locally, you can use the default username and password values: `guest/guest`. RabbitMQ supports customization of the access control to the broker; check out `https://www.rabbitmq.com/access-control.html` if you want to know more about user authorization. Figure 7-11 shows the RabbitMQ management plugin UI after you log in.

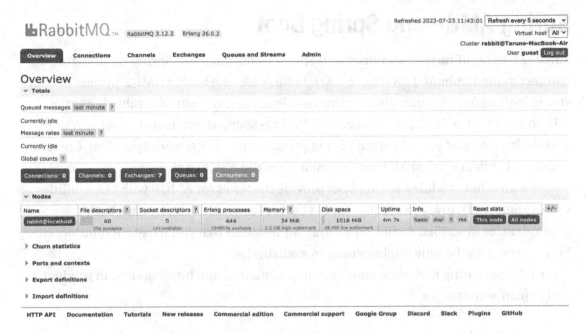

Figure 7-11. *RabbitMQ management plugin UI*

From this UI, you can monitor queued messages, processing rates, statistics about the different registered nodes, and so on. The toolbar gives you access to many other features such as monitoring and management of queues and exchanges. You can even create or delete these entities from this interface. You'll create exchanges and queues programmatically instead, but this tool is useful to understand how your application works with RabbitMQ.

In the main section, Overview, you can see a list of nodes. You just installed it locally, so as you can see there is only one node named `rabbit@<host name>` in the `Nodes table`. You could add more RabbitMQ broker instances over a network and then set up a distributed cluster over different machines. That would give you better availability and fault tolerance since the broker can replicate data, so you can still operate if nodes go down or in case of network partitions. The Clustering Guide (`https://www.rabbitmq.com/clustering.html`) in the official RabbitMQ documentation describes the possible configuration options.

Spring AMQP and Spring Boot

Since you're building microservices with Spring Boot, you'll use Spring modules to connect to the RabbitMQ message broker. In this case, the Spring AMQP project is what you're looking for. This module contains two dependencies: `spring-rabbit`, a set of utils to work with a RabbitMQ broker, and `spring-amqp`, which includes all the AMQP abstractions, so that you can make your implementation vendor-independent. Currently, Spring only offers a RabbitMQ implementation of the AMQP protocol.

As with other modules, Spring Boot provides a starter for AMQP with extra utilities such as autoconfiguration: `spring-boot-starter-amqp`. This starter uses both dependencies described earlier, so it implicitly assumes that you'll use a RabbitMQ broker (since it's the only implementation available).

You'll use Spring to declare your exchanges, queues, and bindings and to produce and consume messages.

Solution Design

While reading about the concepts in this chapter, you already had a quick preview of what you're going to build. See Figure 7-12. This diagram still includes the sequence numbers to make it clear that the response from the Multiplication microservice to the client may happen before the Gamification microservice processes the message. It's an asynchronous, eventually consistent flow.

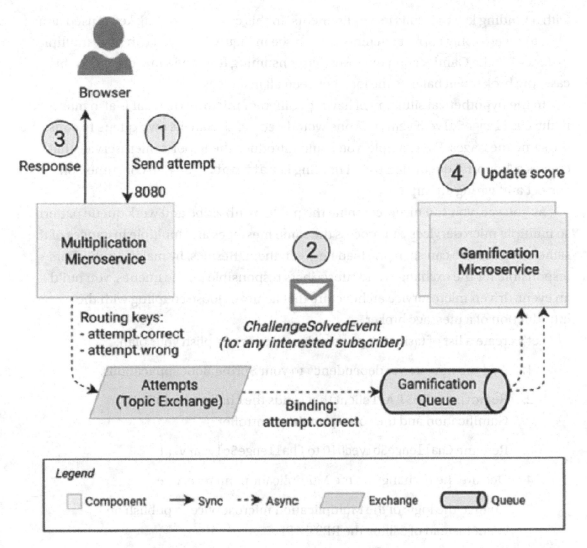

Figure 7-12. *Asynchronous process with a message broker*

As shown in the diagram, you'll create an attempted exchange, of type Topic. In an event-driven architecture like this one, this gives you the flexibility to send the events with certain routing keys and allow consumers to subscribe to all of them or set up their own filters in their queues.

Conceptually, the Multiplication microservice owns the attempted exchange. It'll use it to publish events that are related to attempts coming from the users. In principle, it'll publish both correct and wrong items, since it doesn't know anything about the consumers' logic. On the other hand, the Gamification microservice declares a queue with a binding key that suits its requirements. In this case, this routing key is used as a filter to receive only correct attempts. As you see in Figure 7-12, you can have multiple instances of the Gamification microservice consuming from the same queue. In this case, the broker will balance the load between all instances.

In the hypothetical situation of having a different microservice that is also interested in the `ChallengeSolvedEvent`, this one would need to declare its own queue to consume the same messages. For example, you could introduce the Reports microservice that creates a "reports" queue and uses a binding key `attempt.*` (or #) to consume both correct and wrong attempts.

As you see, you can nicely combine the publish-subscribe and work queue patterns so multiple microservices can process the same messages and multiple instances of the same microservice can share the load between them. Besides, by making publishers responsible for the exchanges and subscribers responsible for the queues, you build an event-driven microservice architecture that achieves loose coupling with the introduction of a message broker.

Let's create a list of tasks that you need to do to accomplish your plan:

1. Add the new starter dependency to your Spring Boot applications.

2. Remove the REST API client that sends the challenge explicitly to Gamification and the corresponding controller.

3. Rename `ChallengeSolvedDTO` to `ChallengeSolvedEvent`.

4. Declare the exchange on the Multiplication microservice.

5. Change the logic of the Multiplication microservice to publish an event instead of calling the REST API.

6. Declare the queue on the Gamification microservice.

7. Include the consumer logic to get the events from the queue and connect it to the existing service layer to process the correct attempts for score and badges.

8. Refactor the tests accordingly.

At the end of this chapter, you'll also play with the new setup and experiment with the load-balancing and fault-tolerance benefits that RabbitMQ introduces.

Adding the AMQP Starter

To use the AMQP and RabbitMQ features in Spring Boot applications, you'll add the corresponding starter to your pom.xml files. Listing 7-1 shows this new dependency.

Listing 7-1. Adding the AMQP Starter to Both Spring Boot Projects

```
<dependencies>
    <!-- ... existing dependencies -->
    <dependency>
        <groupId>org.springframework.boot</groupId>
        <artifactId>spring-boot-starter-amqp</artifactId>
    </dependency>
</dependencies>
```

Source Code   You can find all the source code for this chapter on GitHub, in the chapter07 repository.

See https://github.com/Book-Microservices-v3/chapter07.

This starter includes the aforementioned spring-rabbit and spring-amqp dependencies. The transitive dependency spring-boot-autoconfigure, which you know from previous chapters, includes some classes that take care of the connection to RabbitMQ and the setup of some convenient defaults.

In this case, one of the most interesting classes is RabbitAutoConfiguration (see https://github.com/spring-projects/spring-boot/blob/main/spring-boot-project/spring-boot-autoconfigure/src/main/java/org/springframework/boot/autoconfigure/amqp/RabbitAutoConfiguration.java). It uses a group of properties defined in the RabbitProperties class (see https://github.com/spring-projects/spring-boot/blob/main/spring-boot-project/spring-boot-autoconfigure/src/main/java/org/springframework/boot/autoconfigure/amqp/RabbitProperties.java) that you can override in your application.properties file. There, you can find for example the predefined port (15672), username (guest), and password (guest). The autoconfiguration class builds the connection factory and the *configurer* for RabbitTemplate objects, which you can use to send (and even receive) messages to RabbitMQ. You'll use the abstraction interface, AmqpTemplate (see https://docs.spring.io/spring-amqp/api/org/springframework/amqp/core/AmqpTemplate.html).

The autoconfiguration package also includes some default configuration for receiving messages using an alternative mechanism: the RabbitListener annotation. You'll learn about this in more detail while coding the RabbitMQ subscriber.

Event Publishing from Multiplication

This section focuses on the publisher, the Multiplication microservice. After you add the new dependency, you can include some extra configuration.

- *The name of the exchange*: It's useful to have it in the configuration in case you need to modify it later depending on the environment you're running your application, or share it across applications, as you'll see in the next chapter.

- *Logging settings*: You add them to see extra logs when the app interacts with RabbitMQ. To do this, you'll change the log level of the RabbitAdmin class to DEBUG. This class interacts with the RabbitMQ broker to declare the exchanges, queues, and bindings.

Besides, you can remove the property that points to the Gamification service; you don't need to call it directly anymore. Listing 7-2 shows all the property changes.

Listing 7-2. Adjusting application.properties in the Multiplication Microservice

```
# ... all properties above remain untouched

# For educational purposes we will show the SQL in console
# spring.jpa.show-sql=true <- it's time to remove this

# Gamification service URL <-- We remove this block
# service.gamification.host=http://localhost:8081

amqp.exchange.attempts=attempts.topic

# Shows declaration of exchanges, queues, bindings, etc.
logging.level.org.springframework.amqp.rabbit.core.RabbitAdmin=DEBUG
```

amqp.exchange.attempts=attempts.topic is a custom property defined to manage exchanges. Custom properties are not recognized by Spring Boot unless you implemented code to handle them. Now you add the Exchange declaration to a separate configuration file for AMQP. The Spring module has a convenient builder for this, called

ExchangeBuilder. You add a bean of the topic type you want to declare in the broker. Besides, you'll use this configuration class to switch the predefined serialization format to JSON. See Listing 7-3 before you move to the explanation.

Listing 7-3. Adding AMQP Configuration Beans

```
package microservices.book.multiplication.configuration;

import org.springframework.amqp.core.ExchangeBuilder;
import org.springframework.amqp.core.TopicExchange;
import org.springframework.amqp.support.converter.
        Jackson2JsonMessageConverter;
import org.springframework.beans.factory.annotation.Value;
import org.springframework.context.annotation.Bean;
import org.springframework.context.annotation.Configuration;
/**
 * Configures RabbitMQ via AMQP abstraction to use events in our
 application.
 */
@Configuration
public class AMQPConfiguration {
    @Bean
    public TopicExchange challengesTopicExchange(
            @Value("${amqp.exchange.attempts}") final String exchangeName) {
        return ExchangeBuilder.topicExchange(exchangeName).durable(true).
        build();
    }
    @Bean
    public Jackson2JsonMessageConverter producerJackson2MessageConverter() {
        return new Jackson2JsonMessageConverter();
    }
}
```

The topic is *durable*, so it'll remain in the broker after RabbitMQ restarts. Also, you declare it a topic exchange since that's the solution that was envisioned in this event-driven system. The name is picked up from configuration thanks to the already known @ Value annotation.

By injecting a bean of type `Jackson2JsonMessageConverter`, you're overriding the default Java object serializer by a JSON object serializer. You do this to avoid various pitfalls of Java object serialization.

- It's not a proper standard that you can use between programming languages. If you introduced a consumer that's not written in Java, you would have to look for a specific library to perform cross-language deserialization.

- It uses a hard-coded, fully qualified type name in the header of the message. The deserializer expects the Java bean to be located in the same package and to have the same name and fields. This is not flexible at all, since you may want to deserialize only some properties and keep your own version of the event data, following good domain-driven design practices.

The `Jackson2JsonMessageConverter` uses a Jackson's `ObjectMapper` preconfigured in Spring AMQP. This bean will be used then by the `RabbitTemplate` implementation, the class that serializes and sends objects as AMQP messages to the broker. On the subscriber side, you can benefit from the popularity of the JSON format to deserialize the contents using any programming language. You could also use your own object representation and ignore properties you don't need on the consumer side, thereby reducing the coupling between microservices. If the publisher includes new fields in the payload, the subscribers don't need to change anything.

JSON is not the only standard supported by Spring AMQP message converters. You can also use XML or Google's Protocol Buffers (aka, *protobuf*). You'll stick to JSON in this system since it's an extended standard, and it's also good for educational purposes because the payload is readable. In real systems where performance is critical, you should consider an efficient binary format (e.g., protobuf). See `https://en.wikipedia.org/wiki/Comparison_of_data-serialization_formats` for a comparison of data serialization formats.

The next step is to remove the `GamificationServiceClient` class. Then, you also need to rename the existing `ChallengeSolvedDTO` to make it an event. You don't need to modify any of the fields, just the name. See Listing 7-4.

Listing 7-4. Renaming ChallengeSolvedDTO to ChallengeSolvedEvent

```java
package microservices.book.multiplication.challenge;

import lombok.Value;

@Value
public class ChallengeSolvedEvent {
    long attemptId;
    boolean correct;
    int factorA;
    int factorB;
    long userId;
    String userAlias;
}
```

The naming convention shown here is a good practice for events. They represent a fact that already happened, so the name should use the past tense. Also, by adding the Event suffix, it's really clear that you're using an event-driven approach.

Next, you create a new component to publish the event. This is the equivalent to the REST client you already removed, but this time you communicate with the message broker. You annotate this new class, ChallengeEventPub, with the @Componnt annotation, and use constructor injection to wire an AmqpTemplate object and the name of the exchange. See Listing 7-5 for the complete source code.

Listing 7-5. The ChallengeSolvedEvent's Publisher

```java
package microservices.book.multiplication.challenge;
import org.springframework.amqp.core.AmqpTemplate;
import org.springframework.beans.factory.annotation.Value;
import org.springframework.stereotype.Service;

@Component
public class ChallengeEventPub {
    private final AmqpTemplate amqpTemplate;
    private final String challengesTopicExchange;
    public ChallengeEventPub(final AmqpTemplate amqpTemplate,
                             @Value("${amqp.exchange.attempts}")
                             final String challengesTopicExchange) {
```

```java
        this.amqpTemplate = amqpTemplate;
        this.challengesTopicExchange = challengesTopicExchange;
    }
    public void challengeSolved(final ChallengeAttempt challengeAttempt) {
        ChallengeSolvedEvent event = buildEvent(challengeAttempt);
        // Routing Key is 'attempt.correct' or 'attempt.wrong'
        String routingKey = "attempt." + (event.isCorrect() ?
                "correct" : "wrong");
        amqpTemplate.convertAndSend(challengesTopicExchange,
                routingKey,
                event);
    }
    private ChallengeSolvedEvent buildEvent(final ChallengeAttempt attempt) {
        return new ChallengeSolvedEvent(attempt.getId(),
                attempt.isCorrect(), attempt.getFactorA(),
                attempt.getFactorB(), attempt.getUser().getId(),
                attempt.getUser().getAlias());
    }
}
```

AmqpTemplate is just an interface that defines the AMQP standards. The underlying implementation is RabbitTemplate, and it uses the JSON converter you configured earlier. We plan to call the challengeSolved method from the main Challenge service logic, within the ChallengeServiceImpl class. This method translates the domain object to the event object using the auxiliary method buildEvent, and it uses the amqpTemplate to convert (to JSON) and send the event with a given routing key. This one is either attempt.correct or attempt.wrong, depending on whether the user was right or not.

As you can see, publishing a message to the broker with Spring and Spring Boot is simple thanks to the provided AmqpTemplate/RabbitTemplate and the default configuration, which abstracts the connection to the broker, message conversion, exchange declaration, and so on.

The only part you're missing in this code is connecting the challenge logic with this publisher's class. You just need to replace the injected GamificationServiceClient service you use in ChallengeServiceImpl with the new ChallengeEventPub and use the new method call. You can also rewrite the comment to clarify that you're not calling the Gamification service but sending an event for any component in your system that might be interested. See Listing 7-6.

Listing 7-6. Modifying the ChallengeServiceImpl Class to Send the New Event

```
@Slf4j
@RequiredArgsConstructor
@Service
public class ChallengeServiceImpl implements ChallengeService {
    private final UserRepository userRepository;
    private final ChallengeAttemptRepository attemptRepository;
    private final ChallengeEventPub challengeEventPub; // replaced
    @Override
    public ChallengeAttempt verifyAttempt(ChallengeAttemptDTO attemptDTO) {
        // ...
        // Stores the attempt
        ChallengeAttempt storedAttempt = attemptRepository.
        save(checkedAttempt);
        // Publishes an event to notify potentially interested subscribers
        challengeEventPub.challengeSolved(storedAttempt);
        return storedAttempt;
    }
    // ...
}
```

Exercise   Modify the existing ChallengeServiceTest to verify that it uses the new service instead of the removed REST client.

Instead of leaving aside the ChallengeEventPubTest as an exercise, let's cover it in the book since it poses a new challenge. You want to check that the AmqpTemplate, which you'll mock, is called with the desired routing key and event object, but you can't access that data from outside the method. Making the method return an object with these values seems like adapting the code too much to your tests. What you can do in this case is use Mockito's ArgumentCaptor<T> class (see https://www.javadoc.io/doc/org.mockito/mockito-core/latest/org/mockito/ArgumentCaptor.html) to *capture* the arguments passed to a mock, so you can assert these values later.

Besides, since you made a quick break in this journey to visit a test again, we introduce another JUnit feature: *parameterized tests* (see https://junit.org/junit5/ docs/current/user-guide/#writing-tests-parameterized-tests). The test cases to verify correct and wrong attempts are similar, so you can write a generic test for both cases and use a parameter for the assertion. See the ChallengeEventPubTest source code in Listing 7-7.

Listing 7-7. A Parameterized Test to Check Behavior for Correct and Wrong Attempts

```
package microservices.book.multiplication.challenge;

import org.junit.jupiter.api.BeforeEach;
import org.junit.jupiter.api.extension.ExtendWith;
import org.junit.jupiter.params.ParameterizedTest;
import org.junit.jupiter.params.provider.ValueSource;
import org.mockito.ArgumentCaptor;
import org.mockito.Mock;
import org.mockito.junit.jupiter.MockitoExtension;
import org.springframework.amqp.core.AmqpTemplate;

import microservices.book.multiplication.user.User;

import static org.assertj.core.api.BDDAssertions.*;
import static org.mockito.Mockito.*;
@ExtendWith(MockitoExtension.class)
class ChallengeEventPubTest {
    private ChallengeEventPub challengeEventPub;
    @Mock
    private AmqpTemplate amqpTemplate;
    @BeforeEach
    public void setUp() {
        challengeEventPub = new ChallengeEventPub(amqpTemplate,
                "test.topic");
    }
    @ParameterizedTest
    @ValueSource(booleans = {true, false})
    public void sendsAttempt(boolean correct) {
```

```
    // given
    ChallengeAttempt attempt = createTestAttempt(correct);
    // when
    challengeEventPub.challengeSolved(attempt);
    // then
    var exchangeCaptor = ArgumentCaptor.forClass(String.class);
    var routingKeyCaptor = ArgumentCaptor.forClass(String.class);
    var eventCaptor = ArgumentCaptor.
    forClass(ChallengeSolvedEvent.class);
    verify(amqpTemplate).convertAndSend(exchangeCaptor.capture(),
            routingKeyCaptor.capture(), eventCaptor.capture());
    then(exchangeCaptor.getValue()).isEqualTo("test.topic");
    then(routingKeyCaptor.getValue()).isEqualTo("attempt." +
            (correct ? "correct" : "wrong"));
    then(eventCaptor.getValue()).isEqualTo(solvedEvent(correct));
}
private ChallengeAttempt createTestAttempt(boolean correct) {
    return new ChallengeAttempt(1L, new User(10L, "john"), 30, 40,
            correct ? 1200 : 1300, correct);
}
private ChallengeSolvedEvent solvedEvent(boolean correct) {
    return new ChallengeSolvedEvent(1L, correct, 30, 40, 10L, "john");
}
}
```

Gamification as a Subscriber

Now that you finished the publisher's code, it's time to move to the subscriber's: the Gamification microservice. In a nutshell, you need to replace the existing controller that accepts attempts by an event subscriber. That implies creating an AMQP queue and binding it to the topic exchange that you declared earlier in the Multiplication microservice.

First, you fill in the configuration settings. You also remove the property to show the queries and add extra logging for RabbitMQ. Then, you set up the names of the new queue and the exchange, which match the values you added to the previous service. See Listing 7-8.

Listing 7-8. Defining Queue and Exchange Names in Gamification

```
# ... all properties above remain untouched

amqp.exchange.attempts=attempts.topic
amqp.queue.gamification=gamification.queue

# Shows declaration of exchanges, queues, bindings, etc.
logging.level.org.springframework.amqp.rabbit.core.RabbitAdmin=DEBUG
```

To declare the new queue and the binding, you'll also use a configuration class named `AMQPConfiguration`. Bear in mind that you should also declare the exchange on the consumer's side. Even though the subscriber doesn't own the exchange conceptually, you want your microservices to be able to start in any given order. If you don't declare the exchange on the Gamification microservice and the broker's entities have not been initialized yet, you're forced to start the Multiplication microservice before. The exchange has to be there when you declare the queue. This applies only the first time since you make the exchange durable, yet it's a good practice to declare all exchanges and queues that a microservice requires in its code, so it doesn't rely on any other. Note that the declaration of RabbitMQ entities is an idempotent operation; if the entity is there, the operation doesn't have any effect.

You also need some configuration on the consumer side to deserialize the messages using JSON, instead of the format provided by the default's message converter. Take a look at the full source code of the configuration class in Listing 7-9, and you'll learn more about some parts later.

Listing 7-9. The AMQP Configuration for the Gamification Microservice

```
package microservices.book.gamification.configuration;

import com.fasterxml.jackson.annotation.JsonCreator;
import com.fasterxml.jackson.module.paramnames.ParameterNamesModule;

import org.springframework.amqp.core.*;
```

```java
import org.springframework.amqp.rabbit.annotation.RabbitListenerConfigurer;
import org.springframework.beans.factory.annotation.Value;
import org.springframework.context.annotation.Bean;
import org.springframework.context.annotation.Configuration;
import org.springframework.messaging.converter.
MappingJackson2MessageConverter;
import org.springframework.messaging.handler.annotation.support.
DefaultMessageHandlerMethodFactory;
import org.springframework.messaging.handler.annotation.support.
MessageHandlerMethodFactory;
@Configuration
public class AMQPConfiguration {
    @Bean
    public TopicExchange challengesTopicExchange(
            @Value("${amqp.exchange.attempts}") final String
            exchangeName) {
        return ExchangeBuilder.topicExchange(exchangeName).durable(true).
        build();
    }
    @Bean
    public Queue gamificationQueue(
            @Value("${amqp.queue.gamification}") final String queueName) {
        return QueueBuilder.durable(queueName).build();
    }
    @Bean
    public Binding correctAttemptsBinding(final Queue gamificationQueue,
                                        final TopicExchange
                                        attemptsExchange) {
        return BindingBuilder.bind(gamificationQueue)
                .to(attemptsExchange)
                .with("attempt.correct");
    }
    @Bean
    public MessageHandlerMethodFactory messageHandlerMethodFactory() {
```

```
    DefaultMessageHandlerMethodFactory factory = new
    DefaultMessageHandlerMethodFactory();
    final MappingJackson2MessageConverter jsonConverter =
            new MappingJackson2MessageConverter();
    jsonConverter.getObjectMapper().registerModule(
            new ParameterNamesModule(JsonCreator.Mode.PROPERTIES));
    factory.setMessageConverter(jsonConverter);
    return factory;
}
@Bean
public RabbitListenerConfigurer rabbitListenerConfigurer(
        final MessageHandlerMethodFactory messageHandler
        MethodFactory) {
    return (c) -> c.setMessageHandlerMethodFactory(messageHandler
    MethodFactory);
}
}
```

The declaration of the exchange, queue, and binding are straightforward with the provided builders. You declare a durable queue to make it survive broker restarts, with a name coming from the configuration value. The Bean's declaration method for the `Binding` uses the two other beans, injected by Spring, and links them with the value `attempt.correct`. As mentioned, you're interested only in the correct attempts to process scores and badges.

Next to that, you set up a `MessageHandlerMethodFactory` bean to replace the default one. You actually use the default factory as a baseline but then replace its message converter with a `MappingJackson2MessageConverter` instance, which handles the message deserialization from JSON to Java classes. You fine-tune its included `ObjectMapper` and add the `ParameterNamesModule` to avoid having to use empty constructors for your event classes. Note that you didn't need to do this when passing DTOs via REST APIs (the previous implementation) because Spring Boot configures this module in the web layer autoconfiguration. However, it doesn't do this for RabbitMQ because JSON is not the default option; therefore, you need to configure it explicitly.

This time, you won't use the AmqpTemplate to receive messages since that's based on polling, which consumes network resources unnecessarily. Instead, you want the broker to notify subscribers when there are messages, so you'll use an asynchronous option. The AMQP abstraction doesn't support this, but the spring-rabbit component offers two mechanisms for consuming messages asynchronously. The simplest, most popular one is the @RabbitListener annotation, which you'll use to get the events from the queue. To configure the listeners to use a JSON deserialization, you have to override the RabbitListenerConfigurer bean with an implementation that uses the custom MessageHandlerMethodFactory.

The next task is to rename ChallengeSolvedDTO to ChallengeSolvedEvent. See Listing 7-10. Technically, there is no need to use the same class name since the JSON format only specifies the field names and values. However, this is a good practice because then you can easily find related event classes across your projects.

Listing 7-10. Renaming ChallengeSolvedDTO to ChallengeSolvedEvent in Gamification

```
package microservices.book.gamification.challenge;
import lombok.Value;
@Value
public class ChallengeSolvedEvent {
    long attemptId;
    boolean correct;
    int factorA;
    int factorB;
    long userId;
    String userAlias;
}
```

Following domain-driven design practices, you could adjust this event's deserialized fields. For instance, you don't need the userAlias for the Gamification's business logic, so you could remove it from the consumed event. Since Spring Boot configures the ObjectMapper to ignore unknown properties by default, that strategy would work without needing to configure anything else. Not sharing the code of this class across microservices is a good practice because it also allows for loose coupling, backward compatibility, and independent deployments. Imagine that the Multiplication microservice would evolve and store extra data, for example, a third factor for harder challenges. This extra factor would then be added to the published event's code. The good news is that, by using different representations of the event per domain and configuring the mapper to ignore unknown properties, the Gamification microservice would still work after such change without needing to update its event representation.

Let's code the event consumer now. As introduced earlier, you'll use the @ RabbitListener annotation for this. You can add this annotation to a method to make it act as the processing logic of a message when it arrives. In this case, you only need to specify the queue name to subscribe to, since you already declared all RabbitMQ entities in a separate configuration file. There are options to embed these declarations in this annotation, but the code doesn't look that clean anymore (see https://docs.spring. io/spring-amqp/docs/current/reference/html/#async-annotation-driven if you're curious).

Check the source of the consumer in Listing 7-11, and then you'll read about the most relevant parts.

Listing 7-11. The RabbitMQ Consumer's Logic

```
package microservices.book.gamification.game;

import org.springframework.amqp.AmqpRejectAndDontRequeueException;
import org.springframework.amqp.rabbit.annotation.RabbitListener;
import org.springframework.stereotype.Service;

import lombok.RequiredArgsConstructor;
import lombok.extern.slf4j.Slf4j;
import microservices.book.gamification.challenge.ChallengeSolvedEvent;

@RequiredArgsConstructor
@Slf4j
@Service
public class GameEventHandler {
    private final GameService gameService;
    @RabbitListener(queues = "${amqp.queue.gamification}")
    void handleMultiplicationSolved(final ChallengeSolvedEvent event) {
        log.info("Challenge Solved Event received: {}", event.
        getAttemptId());
        try {
            gameService.newAttemptForUser(event);
```

```
    } catch (final Exception e) {
        log.error("Error when trying to process Challenge
        SolvedEvent", e);
        // Avoids the event to be re-queued and reprocessed.
        throw new AmqpRejectAndDontRequeueException(e);
    }
  }
}
```

As you see, the amount of code needed to implement a RabbitMQ subscriber is minimal. You can pass the queue name using the configuration property to the RabbitListener annotation. Spring processes this method and analyzes the arguments. Given that you specified a ChallengeSolvedEvent class as the expected input, Spring automatically configures a deserializer to transform the message from the broker into this object type. It'll use JSON since you override the default RabbitListenerConfigurer in the AMQPConfiguration class.

From the consumer's code, you can also infer what the error-handling strategy is. By default, the logic that Spring builds based on the RabbitListener annotations will send the acknowledgment to the broker when the method finalizes without exceptions. In Spring Rabbit, this is called the AUTO acknowledgment mode. You could change it to NONE if ou want the ACK signal to be sent even before processing it, or to MANUAL if you want to be fully in control (then you have to inject an extra parameter to send this signal). You can set up this parameter and other configuration values at the factory level (global configuration) or at the listener level (via passing extra parameters to the RabbitListener annotation).

The error strategy here is to use the default value AUTO but catch any possible exception, log the error, and then rethrow an AmqpRejectAndDontRequeueException. This is a shortcut provided by Spring AMQP to reject the message and tell the broker not to requeue it. That means that if there is an unexpected error in the Gamification's consumer logic, we'll lose the message. That is acceptable in this case. If you want to avoid this situation, you could also set up the code to retry a few times by rethrowing an exception with the opposite meaning, ImmediateRequeueAmqpException, or use some tools available in Spring AMQP like an error handler or *message recoverer* to process these failed messages. See the Exception Handling section (https://docs.spring.io/ spring-amqp/docs/current/reference/html/#exception-handling) in the Spring AMQP docs for more detailed information.

You can do a lot with the RabbitListener annotation. These are a few of the included functionalities:

- Declare exchanges, queues, and bindings.

- Receive messages from multiple queues with the same method.

- Process the message headers by annotating extra arguments with @Header (for a single value) or @Headers (for a map).

- Inject a Channel argument, so you can control acknowledgments, for example.

- Implement a Request-Response pattern, by returning a value from the listener.

- Move the annotation to the class level and use @RabbitHandler for methods. This approach allows you to configure multiple methods to process different message types that are coming through the same queue.

For details about these use cases, check out the Spring AMQP documentation (https://docs.spring.io/spring-amqp/docs/current/reference/html/).

Exercise   Create a test for the new GameEventHandler class. Verify that the service is called and that an exception in its logic causes the re-throwing of the expected AMQP exception. The solution is included in the provided source code for this chapter.

Now that you have the subscriber's logic, you can safely remove the GameController class. Then, you refactor the existing GameService interface and its implementation, GameServiceImpl, to accept the renamed ChallengeSolvedEvent. The rest of the logic can remain the same. See Listing 7-12 with the resulting newAttemptForUser method.

Listing 7-12. The Updated newAttemptForUser Method Using the Event Class

```
@Override
public GameResult newAttemptForUser(final ChallengeSolvedEvent challenge) {
    // We give points only if it's correct
    if (challenge.isCorrect()) {
```

```java
        ScoreCard scoreCard = new ScoreCard(challenge.getUserId(),
                challenge.getAttemptId());
        scoreRepository.save(scoreCard);
        log.info("User {} scored {} points for attempt id {}",
                challenge.getUserAlias(), scoreCard.getScore(),
                challenge.getAttemptId());
        List<BadgeCard> badgeCards = processForBadges(challenge);
        return new GameResult(scoreCard.getScore(),
                badgeCards.stream().map(BadgeCard::getBadgeType)
                        .collect(Collectors.toList()));
    } else {
        log.info("Attempt id {} is not correct. " +
                    "User {} does not get score.",
                challenge.getAttemptId(),
                challenge.getUserAlias());
        return new GameResult(0, List.of());
    }
}
```

You could remove the check for the correct attempt, but then you would depend too much on proper routing on the Multiplication microservice. If you keep it, it's easier for everyone to read the code and know what it does without having to figure out that there is a filter logic based on routing keys. You can benefit from the broker's routing, but remember that you don't want to embed too much behavior inside the channel.

With these changes, you have finalized the required modifications to switch to an event-driven architecture in your microservices. Keep in mind that there are more classes affected by the renamed DTO as ChallengeSolvedEvent. We omitted them since your IDE should take care of these changes automatically. Once more, let's review the list of changes made to this system:

1. You added the new AMQP starter dependency to your Spring Boot applications to use AMQP and RabbitMQ.

2. You removed the REST API client (in Multiplication) and the controller (in Gamification) because you switched to an event-driven architecture using RabbitMQ.

3. You renamed `ChallengeSolvedDTO` to `ChallengeSolvedEvent`. The renaming caused the modification of other classes and tests, but those changes are not relevant.

4. You declared the new topic exchange in both microservices.

5. You changed the logic of the Multiplication microservice to publish an event instead of calling the REST API.

6. You defined the new queue on the Gamification microservice.

7. You implemented the RabbitMQ consumer logic in the Gamification microservice.

8. You refactored the tests accordingly to adapt them to the new interface.

Remember that all the code shown in this chapter is available in the book's online repository.

Analysis of Scenarios

Let's try a few different scenarios with this new event-driven system. The goal is to prove that the introduction of the new architecture design with the message broker brings real advantages.

To recap, Figure 7-13 shows the current state of this system.

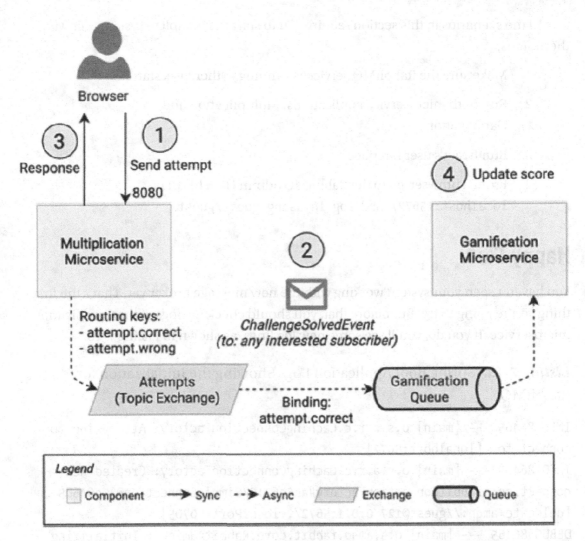

Figure 7-13. Logical view

287

All the scenarios in this section require you to start the complete system following these steps:

1. Make sure the RabbitMQ service is running. Otherwise, start it.

2. Run both microservice applications: Multiplication and Gamification.

3. Run React's user interface.

4. From a browser, go to the RabbitMQ admin UI at `http://localhost:15672/` and log in using `guest/guest`.

Happy Flow

You haven't seen your system working with the new message broker yet. That's the first thing you're going to try. But before that, you should check the logs of the Gamification microservice. If you do, you'll see some new log lines, as shown in Listing 7-13.

Listing 7-13. Spring Boot Application Logs Showing the Initialization for RabbitMQ

```
INFO 86465 --- [main] o.s.a.r.c.CachingConnectionFactory: Attempting to
connect to: [localhost:5672]
INFO 86465 --- [main] o.s.a.r.c.CachingConnectionFactory: Created new
connection: rabbitConnectionFactory#ab5e63:0/SimpleConnection@35c646b5
[delegate=amqp://guest@127.0.0.1:5672/, localPort=50705]
DEBUG 86465 --- [main] o.s.amqp.rabbit.core.RabbitAdmin  : Initializing
declarations
DEBUG 86465 --- [main] o.s.amqp.rabbit.core.RabbitAdmin  : declaring
Exchange 'attempts.topic'
DEBUG 86465 --- [main] o.s.amqp.rabbit.core.RabbitAdmin  : declaring Queue
'gamification.queue'
DEBUG 86465 --- [main] o.s.amqp.rabbit.core.RabbitAdmin  : Binding
destination [gamification.queue (QUEUE)] to exchange [attempts.topic] with
routing key [attempt.correct]
DEBUG 86465 --- [main] o.s.amqp.rabbit.core.RabbitAdmin  : Declarations
finished
```

The first two lines are usually logged when you use Spring AMQP. They indicate that the connection to the broker was successful. As mentioned, you didn't need to add any connection properties such as the host or the credentials since you're using the defaults. The rest of the log lines are there because you changed the logging level of the `RabbitAdmin` class to `DEBUG`. These are self-explanatory, including the values of the exchange, queue, and binding you created.

On the Multiplication side, there are no RabbitMQ logs yet. The reason is that the connection and the declaration of the exchange happen only when you publish your first message. This means that the topic exchange is declared first by the Gamification microservice. It's good you prepared your code not to mind the booting sequence.

You can now look at the RabbitMQ UI to see the current status. On the Connections tab, you'll see one created by the Gamification microservice. See Figure 7-14.

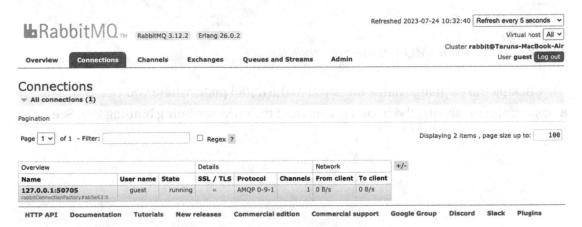

Figure 7-14. *RabbitMQ UI: a single connection*

If you switch to the Exchanges tab, you'll see the `attempts.topic` exchange, of type `topic`, and declared as *durable* (D). See Figure 7-15.

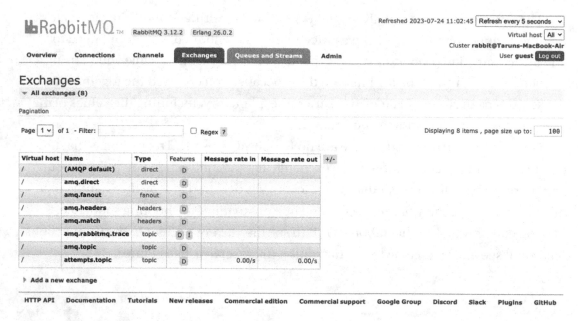

Figure 7-15. *RabbitMQ UI: the exchange list*

Clicking the exchange name takes you to the detail page, where you can even see a basic graph displaying the bound queues and the corresponding binding key. See Figure 7-16.

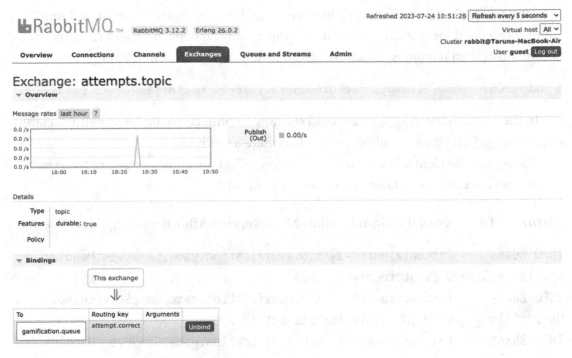

Figure 7-16. *RabbitMQ UI: exchange detail*

The Queues and Streams tab shows the recently created queue with its name, also configured as durable. See Figure 7-17.

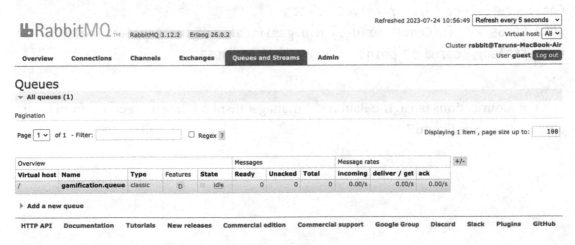

Figure 7-17. *RabbitMQ UI: queue list*

After you look at how everything has been initialized, navigate to the UI and send some correct and incorrect attempts. If you prefer, you can cheat a bit and run this command at least ten times, which will generate ten correct attempts.

```
$ http POST :8080/attempts factorA=15 factorB=20 userAlias=test1 guess=300
```

In the Multiplication logs, you should see how it connects to the broker and declares the exchange (which has no effect since it was there already).

The logs of the Gamification app should then reflect the consumption of the events and the corresponding updated score. See Listing 7-14.

Listing 7-14. Logs of the Gamification Microservice After Receiving New Events

```
INFO 86465 --- [ntContainer#0-1] m.b.gamification.game.GameEventHandler    :
Challenge Solved Event received: 2903
INFO 86465 --- [ntContainer#0-1] m.b.gamification.game.GameServiceImpl    :
User ttelang scored 10 points for attempt id 2903
INFO 86465 --- [ntContainer#0-1] m.b.gamification.game.GameEventHandler    :
Challenge Solved Event received: 2904
INFO 86465 --- [ntContainer#0-1] m.b.gamification.game.GameServiceImpl    :
User ttelang scored 10 points for attempt id 2904
INFO 86465 --- [ntContainer#0-1] m.b.gamification.game.GameEventHandler    :
Challenge Solved Event received: 2905
INFO 86465 --- [ntContainer#0-1] m.b.gamification.game.GameServiceImpl    :
User ttelang scored 10 points for attempt id 29053
...
```

The Connections tab in the RabbitMQ manager displays the connections from both applications. See Figure 7-18.

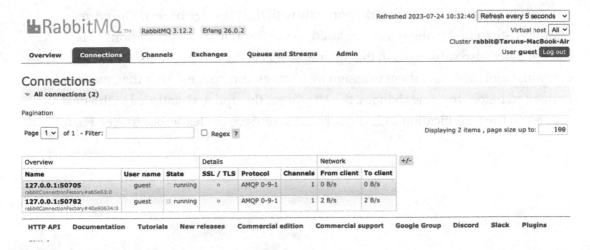

Figure 7-18. *RabbitMQ UI: both connections*

Besides, you can see some activity happening in the broker if you go to the Queues and Streams tab and click the queue name. You can change the filter to the last ten minutes on the Overview panel to make sure you capture all the events. See Figure 7-19.

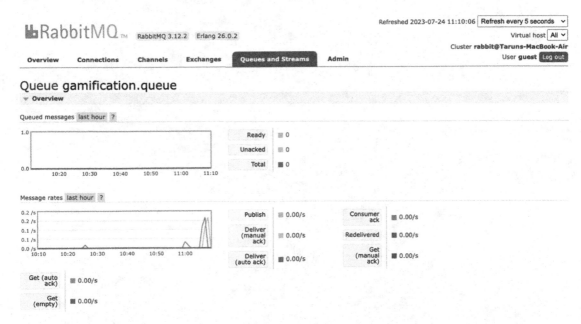

Figure 7-19. *RabbitMQ UI: queue detail*

This is great. The system works perfectly with the message broker. The correct attempts are routed to the queue declared by the Gamification application. This microservice also subscribes to that queue, so it gets the events published to the exchange and processes them to assign new scores and badges. After that, as already happened before the new changes, the UI will get the updated statistics in the next request to the Gamification's REST endpoint to retrieve the leaderboard. See Figure 7-20.

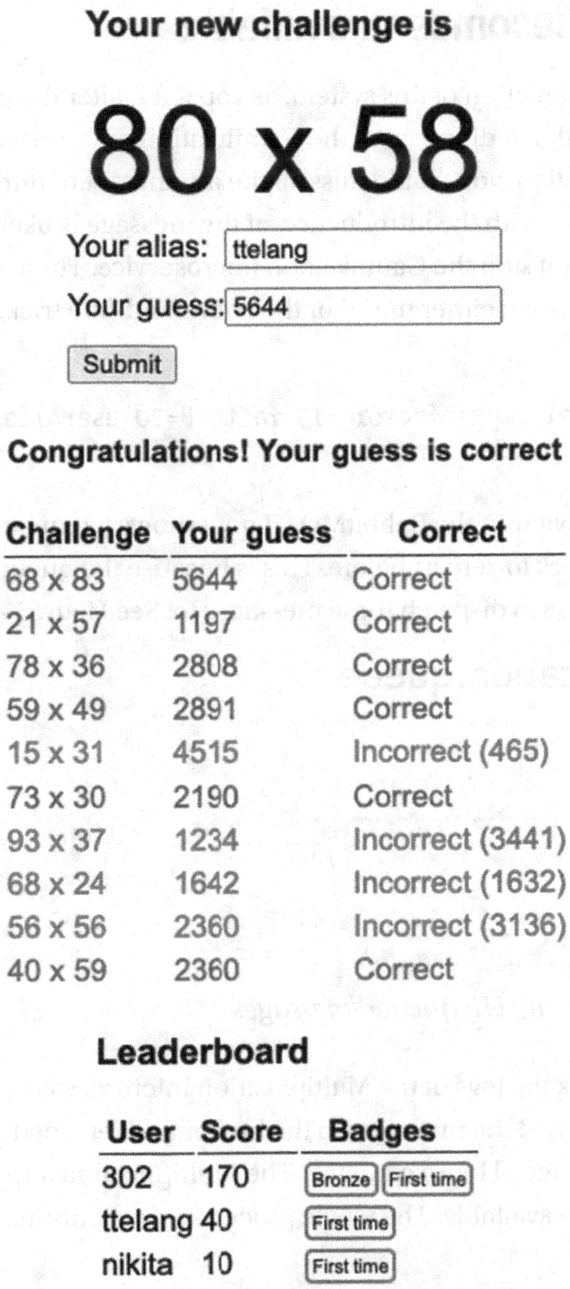

Your new challenge is

80 x 58

Your alias: [ttelang]

Your guess: [5644]

[Submit]

Congratulations! Your guess is correct

Challenge	Your guess	Correct
68 x 83	5644	Correct
21 x 57	1197	Correct
78 x 36	2808	Correct
59 x 49	2891	Correct
15 x 31	4515	Incorrect (465)
73 x 30	2190	Correct
93 x 37	1234	Incorrect (3441)
68 x 24	1642	Incorrect (1632)
56 x 56	2360	Incorrect (3136)
40 x 59	2360	Correct

Leaderboard

User	Score	Badges
302	170	[Bronze] [First time]
ttelang	40	[First time]
nikita	10	[First time]

Figure 7-20. *UI: app working with the message broker*

Gamification Becomes Unavailable

The previous implementation of this system, as you left it after the previous chapter, was resilient in the sense that it didn't fail if the Gamification microservice was unavailable. However, in that situation, you would miss all the attempts sent during the incident. Let's see what happens now, with the introduction of the message broker.

First, make sure you stop the Gamification microservice. Then, you can send another ten attempts using either the UI or the command-line trick. Let's use the alias `test-g-down`:

```
$ http POST :8080/attempts factorA=15 factorB=20 userAlias=test-g-down
guess=300
```

The Queue detail view in the RabbitMQ UI now shows ten queued messages. This number doesn't go back to zero as before. This is because the queue is still there, but there are no consumers to dispatch these messages to. See Figure 7-21.

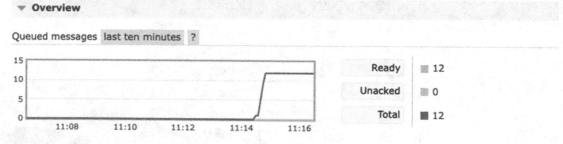

Figure 7-21. RabbitMQ UI: queued messages

You can also check the logs of the Multiplication microservice and verify that there are no errors. It published the messages to the broker and returned an OK response to the API client. You achieved loose coupling. The Multiplication app doesn't need to know if consumers are available. The whole process is asynchronous and event-driven now.

When you bring the Gamification service back again, you'll see in the logs how immediately after booting up it receives all the event messages from the broker. Then, this service just triggers its logic, and the score is updated accordingly. You didn't miss any data this time. Listing 7-15 shows an extract of the Gamification logs after you start it again.

Listing 7-15. The Application Consumes the Pending Events After Becoming
Available Again

```
INFO 24808 --- [             main] m.b.g.GamificationApplication      :
Started GamificationApplication in 3.446 seconds (JVM running for 3.989)
INFO 24808 --- [ntContainer#0-1] m.b.gamification.game.GameServiceImpl    :
User test-g-down scored 10 points for attempt id 61
INFO 24808 --- [ntContainer#0-1] m.b.gamification.game.GameEventHandler   :
Challenge Solved Event received: 62
INFO 24808 --- [ntContainer#0-1] m.b.gamification.game.GameServiceImpl    :
User test-g-down scored 10 points for attempt id 62
INFO 24808 --- [ntContainer#0-1] m.b.gamification.game.GameEventHandler   :
Challenge Solved Event received: 63
INFO 24808 --- [ntContainer#0-1] m.b.gamification.game.GameServiceImpl    :
User test-g-down scored 10 points for attempt id 63
INFO 24808 --- [ntContainer#0-1] m.b.gamification.game.GameEventHandler   :
Challenge Solved Event received: 64
...
```

You can also verify how the leaderboard shows up again with the updated score for
the user test-g-down. You made the system not only resilient but also able to recover
after a failure. The queue detail in the RabbitMQ interface also shows a zero counter for
queued messages, since they all have been consumed already.

As you can imagine, RabbitMQ allows you to configure how long the messages can
be kept in a queue before discarding them (time-to-live, TTL). You can also configure
a maximum length for the queue if you prefer so. By default, these parameters are not
set, but you can enable them per message (at publishing time) or when you declare the
queue. See Listing 7-16 for an example of how you could have configured your queue
to have a custom TTL of six hours and a max length of 25000 messages. This is just an
example of how important it is that you get familiar with the configuration of the broker,
so you can adjust it to your needs.

Listing 7-16. An Example Queue Configuration Showing Some Extra
Parameter Options

```
@Bean
public Queue gamificationQueue(
        @Value("${amqp.queue.gamification}") final String queueName) {
    return QueueBuilder.durable(queueName)
            .ttl((int) Duration.ofHours(6).toMillis())
            .maxLength(25000)
            .build();
}
```

The Message Broker Becomes Unavailable

Let's go one step further and bring the broker down while the queue has pending
messages to be delivered. To test this scenario, follow these steps:

1. Stop the Gamification microservice.

2. Send a few correct attempts with the user alias `test-rmq-down`
   and verify in the RabbitMQ UI that the queue is keeping those
   messages.

3. Stop the RabbitMQ broker.

4. Send one extra correct attempt.

5. Start the Gamification microservice.

6. After about ten seconds, start the RabbitMQ broker again.

The outcome of this manual test is that only the attempt you sent while the broker
was down fails to be processed. Actually, you'll get an HTTP error response from the
server since you didn't catch any potential exception within the publisher, nor in the
main service logic located at `ChallengeServiceImpl`. You could add a `try/catch` clause,
so you are still able to respond. The strategy would be to suppress the error silently.
A possibly better approach is to implement a custom HTTP error handler to return a
specific error response such as `503 SERVICE UNAVAILABLE` to indicate that the system is
not operational when you lose connection with the broker. As you see, you have multiple
options. In a real organization, the best approach is to discuss these alternatives and

choose the one that best suits your nonfunctional requirements, like *availability* (you want to have the challenge features available as much as possible) or *data integrity* (you want to always have a score for every sent attempt).

A second observation from this test is that none of the two microservices crashes when the broker goes unavailable. Instead, the Gamification microservice keeps retrying to connect every few seconds, and the Multiplication microservice does the same when a new attempt request comes. When you bring the broker up again, both microservices recover their connections. This is a nice feature included in the Spring AMQP project, to try to recover the connection when it's unavailable.

If you perform these steps, you also see how the consumer gets the messages even after the broker restarted while there were pending ones to be sent. The Gamification microservice reconnects to RabbitMQ, and this one sends the queued events. This is not only because you declared a durable exchange and queue, but because the Spring implementation uses the *persistent delivery mode* while publishing all messages. This is one of the message properties that you could also set yourself if you use `RabbitTemplate` (instead of `AmqpTemplate`) to publish messages. Listing 7-17 shows how you could change the delivery mode to make your messages not survive a broker restart.

Listing 7-17. Example of How to Change the Delivery Mode to Nonpersistent

```
MessageProperties properties = MessagePropertiesBuilder.newInstance()
        .setDeliveryMode(MessageDeliveryMode.NON_PERSISTENT)
        .build();
rabbitTemplate.getMessageConverter().toMessage(challengeAttempt,
properties);
rabbitTemplate.convertAndSend(challengesTopicExchange,routingKey,event);
```

This example also demonstrates why it is important to know the configuration options of the tool you use. Sending all messages as persistent brings a nice advantage, but it has an extra cost in performance. If you configured a cluster of RabbitMQ instances that it's properly distributed, chances of the whole cluster going down would be minimal, so you might prefer to accept a potential loss of messages to improve performance. Again, this depends on your requirements; missing some score is not the same as missing a purchase order in an online store, for example.

Transactionality

The previous test exposed an undesired situation, but it was difficult to spot it. When you send the attempt while the broker is down, you get a server error with a 500 error code. That gives the API client the impression that the attempt wasn't processed correctly. However, it was partially processed.

Let's test that part again, but, this time, check the database entries. You only need the Multiplication microservice running and the broker stopped. Then, you send an attempt with a user alias `test-tx` to get the error response again. See Listing 7-18.

Listing 7-18. Error Response When the Broker Is Unreachable

```
$ http POST :8080/attempts factorA=15 factorB=20 userAlias=test-tx
guess=300
HTTP/1.1 500
[...]
{
    "error": "Internal Server Error",
    "message": "",
    "path": "/attempts",
    "status": 500,
    "timestamp": "2023-07-24T05:55:08.944+00:00"
}
```

Now, navigate to the H2 console for the Multiplication database at `http://localhost:8080/h2-console`. Make sure you connect using the URL `jdbc:h2:file:~/multiplication`. Then, run this query to get all data from both tables where the user's alias is `test-tx`:

```
SELECT * FROM USERS u, CHALLENGE_ATTEMPT a WHERE u.ALIAS = 'test-tx' AND
u.ID = a.USER_ID
```

The query gives one result, as shown in Figure 7-22. That means the attempt was stored even though you got an error response. This is a bad practice because the API client doesn't know the result of the challenge, so it can't display a proper message. Yet the challenge has been saved. However, it's the expected outcome provided that your code persists with the object before trying to send the message to the broker.

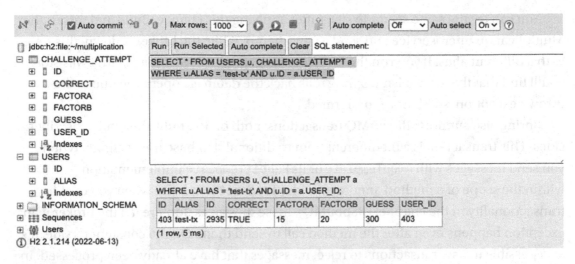

Figure 7-22. *H2 console: record is stored despite the failure*

Instead, you could treat the whole logic included in the `verifyAttempt` service method as a *transaction*. A database transaction can be rolled back (not executed). That's what you want if you get an error even after calling the `save` method in the repository. Doing this is easy with the Spring framework since you just need to add a Jakarta Transactions annotation to your code, `jakarta.transaction.Transactional`. See Listing 7-19.

Listing 7-19. Adding the @Transactional Annotation to the Service Logic in Multiplication

```
@Transactional
@Override
public ChallengeAttempt verifyAttempt(ChallengeAttemptDTO attemptDTO) {
    // ...
}
```

If there is an exception in a method annotated with `@Transactional`, the transaction will be rolled back. If you need all your methods within a given service to be transactional, you can add this annotation at the class level instead.

You can try the same scenario steps after applying this change. Build and restart the Multiplication microservice and send a new attempt while the broker is down, this time with a different alias. If you run the corresponding query to see if the attempt was stored, you'll find that this time it isn't. Spring rolls back the database operation due to the thrown exception, so it's never performed.

Spring also supports RabbitMQ transactions, both on the publisher and subscriber sides. This transaction is a bit different from traditional database transactions. When you send messages with `AmqpTemplate` or its `RabbitTemplate` implementation within the scope of a method annotated with `@Transactional` and when you enable transactionality in the channel (RabbitMQ), these messages don't reach the broker if an exception happens even after the method call to send them. On the consumer's side, it's also possible to use transactions to reject messages that have already been processed. In this case, the queue would need to be set up to requeue the rejected messages (which is the default behavior). The Transactions section in the Spring AMQP documentation explains how they work in detail; see `https://docs.spring.io/spring-amqp/reference/html/#transactions`.

There are two kinds of transactions—local and global (distributed). Local transactions are confined to a single data source or resource within a single microservice or component. Global transactions span multiple data sources or resources often involving multiple microservices or components. Global transactions involve a distributed transaction manager (e.g., Jakarta Transactions (`https://jakarta.ee/specifications/transactions/`)/eXtended Architecture(XA) - `https://jakarta.ee/specifications/transactions/2.0/jakarta-transactions-spec-2.0#xaresource-interface`) that coordinates the transactional behavior across multiple resources. The transaction manager ensures that all participating resources commit or roll back changes together, ensuring data integrity.

In many cases, you can simplify the strategy for transactions and limit it only to the database.

- While publishing, if you have only one broker operation, you can publish the message at the end of the process. Any error that happens before or while sending the message will cause the rollback of the database operation.

- On the subscriber's side, the message will be rejected by default if there is an exception, and you can requeue it if that's what you want. Then, you could also use the `Transactional` annotation in the `newAttemptForUser`'s service method, so database operations will be rolled back too in case of a failure.

Local transactionality within a microservice is critical to keep data consistent and avoid partially completed processes inside a domain. Therefore, you should think of things that can go wrong in your business logic when it entails multiple steps and possible interactions with external components such as a database or a message broker.

Exercise   Add the @`Transactional` annotation to the `GameServiceImpl` service so either both scorecards and badges are stored or none of them if something goes wrong. You already decided to discard messages if you can't process them, so you don't need transactionality over the message broker's operation.

Scaling Up Microservices

Until now, you have been running a single instance of each microservice. As we described previously in the book, one of the main advantages of a microservice architecture is that you can scale up parts of your system independently. We also listed this feature as a benefit of introducing the event-driven approach with a message broker: you can add more instances of publishers and subscribers transparently. However, you can't claim that this architecture supports adding more copies of each microservice yet.

Let's focus on the first reason that these applications can't work with multiple instances: the database. When you scale up microservices horizontally, all the replicas should share the data tier and store the data in a common place, not isolated per instance. We say microservices must be stateless. The reason is that different requests or messages may end up in different microservice instances. For example, you should not assume that two attempts sent from the same user are going to be processed by the same Multiplication instance, so you can't keep any in-memory state across attempts. See Figure 7-23.

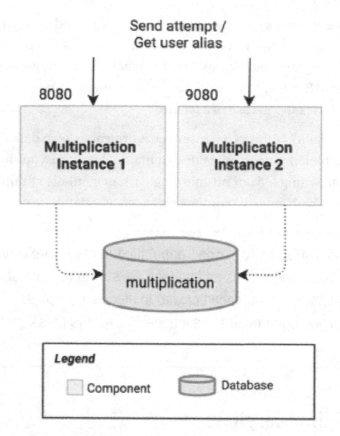

Figure 7-23. *Scaling up: interface questions*

The good news is that your microservices are already stateless; you process each request or message independently, and the result ends up in the database. However, there is a technical issue. If you boot up a second Multiplication instance on port 9080, it'll fail to start because it tries to create a new database instance. That's not what you want, since it should connect to a common database server shared across replicas. Let's reproduce this error. First, run the Multiplication microservice as usual (the first instance).

To start a second instance of a given service locally, you just need to override the server.port parameter so you avoid port conflicts. You can do this from your IDE or using the command line from the multiplication microservice directory.

```
$ ./mvnw spring-boot:run -Dspring-boot.run.arguments="--server.port=9080"
```

When you start this second replica, the logs prompt the following error:

```
[...]  Database may be already in use: null. Possible solutions: close all
other connection(s); use the server mode [90020-200]
```

This error happened because you're using the H2 database engine, which is designed to behave as an embedded process by default, not as a server. Anyway, H2 supports the *server mode* as the error message suggests. The only thing you need to do is add a parameter to both URLs that you used to connect to the database from your microservices. Then, the first time the engine starts, it'll allow other instances to use the same file and therefore the same database. Remember to apply this change to both the Multiplication and Gamification microservices. See Listing 7-20.

Listing 7-20. Enabling the Server Mode in H2 to Connect from Multiple Instances

```
# ... other properties
# Creates the database in a file (adding the server mode)
spring.datasource.url=jdbc:h2:file:~/multiplication;DB_CLOSE_ON_
EXIT=FALSE;AUTO_SERVER=true;
```

Now, you can start multiple instances of each microservice, and they'll share the same data tier across replicas. First problem solved.

The second challenge is about load balancing. If you start two instances of each application, how do you connect to them from the user interface? This same question also applied to the REST API call you had at the end of the previous chapter between both microservices: which Gamification instance would you call to send the attempt? If you want to balance the system's HTTP traffic across copies, you need something else. The next chapter covers HTTP load balancing in detail.

For now, this section focuses on how the message broker helps you achieve load balancing between RabbitMQ message subscribers. See Figure 7-24.

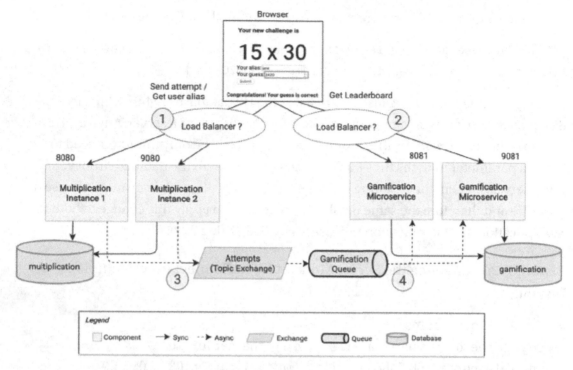

Figure 7-24. *Scaling up: interface questions*

There are four numbered interfaces in Figure 7-24. As mentioned, you'll see how to implement an HTTP load balancer pattern in the next chapter, so let's examine how interfaces 3 and 4 work with multiple copies.

Message brokers like RabbitMQ support message publication from multiple sources. That means you can have more than one copy of the Multiplication microservice publishing events to the same topic exchange. This works transparently: these instances open different connections, declare the exchange (it'll be created only the first time), and publish data without needing to know that there are other publishers. On the subscriber's side, you already learned how a RabbitMQ queue can be shared by multiple consumers. When you start more than one instance of the Gamification microservice, they all declare the same queue and binding, and the broker is smart enough to do the load balancing between them.

So, you solved load balancing at the message level. It turns out you don't need to do anything. Let's see this in practice.

Follow the same steps as in previous scenarios to boot up one instance of each microservice, the UI, and the RabbitMQ service. Then, run the commands in Listing 7-21 in two separate terminals to have the same setup as shown in the previous Figure 7-23, with two replicas of each microservice. Keep in mind that you need to execute them from each corresponding microservice's home folder.

Listing 7-21. Starting a Second Instance of Each Microservice

```
multiplication $ ./mvnw spring-boot:run -Dspring-boot.run.arguments="--
server.port=9080"
[... logs ...]
gamification $ ./mvnw spring-boot:run -Dspring-boot.run.arguments="--
server.port=9081"
[... logs ...]
```

Once you get all instances up and running, enter four correct attempts with the same new alias from the UI. Note that the attempts will hit only the first instance of the Multiplication microservice, but the event consumption is balanced across both Gamification copies. Check the logs to verify how each application should have processed two events. Besides, since the database is shared across instances, it doesn't matter that the UI is requesting the leaderboard from the instance running at port 8081. This instance will aggregate all the scorecards and badges stored by all replicas. See Figure 7-25.

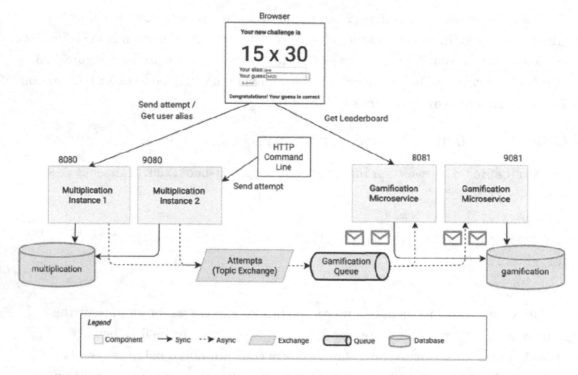

Figure 7-25. *Scaling up: first test*

As shown in Figure 7-25, you can also verify that multiple publishers work together using the command line to send correct attempts to the second instance of the Multiplication microservice. Let's send a few calls to the instance located at port 9080 and check how they're also processed. As expected, in this case, the messages are also balanced across subscribers. See Listing 7-22 for an example call to the second instance.

Listing 7-22. Sending a Correct Attempt to the Second Instance of Multiplication

```
$ http POST :9080/attempts factorA=15 factorB=20 userAlias=test-multi-pub
guess=300
```

That's a great achievement. You saw how the message broker helps reach a good system scalability, and you implemented a worker queue pattern with multiple subscriber instances sharing the load between them.

As a consequence, you also improved resilience. In the previous section "Gamification Becomes Unavailable," you stopped the Gamification instance and saw how it'll catch up with the pending events when it becomes alive again. With the introduction of multiple instances, if one of them becomes unavailable, the broker will automatically direct all messages to the other ones. You can try this by stopping the first instance of Gamification (running on port 8081). Then, send two correct attempts and check the logs to see how they're both processed successfully by the second instance. With this test, you can also verify that this resilience's improvement is limited—for now—to the event consumer interface. The UI can't balance the load or detect that one replica is down. Consequently, the UI doesn't display the leaderboard because the browser is trying to access the first Gamification instance. You'll see how to fix these problems in the next chapter.

Summary and Achievements

This chapter introduced an important concept that is usually tied to microservice architectures: the event-driven software patterns. To give you a complete background, you focused first on one of the most popular tools you can use to implement it: the message broker.

You learned how a message broker can help you achieve loose coupling between your microservices, the same as similar patterns have helped other service-oriented architectures in the past years. The event pattern goes an extra step toward loose coupling by modeling a type of message that is not directed to any specific target since it just represents a fact that happened in a particular domain. Different consumers can then subscribe to these event streams and react on them, possibly triggering their own business logic, which could produce additional events, and so forth. You saw how to combine event-driven strategies with the publish-subscribe and worker queue patterns to have clean cuts between domains and improve the scalability of your system.

RabbitMQ, with its AMQP implementation, has some tools that you used to build the new architecture: exchanges to publish event messages, queues to subscribe to them, and bindings to link them with an optional filter. Not only did you learn the core concepts about these messaging entities, but you also learned some configuration options related to message acknowledgment, message rejection, and persistence. Remember that you may need to fine-tune the RabbitMQ configuration to adjust it to your functional and nonfunctional requirements.

The coding part in this chapter remained simple thanks to the Spring Boot abstractions. You integrated RabbitMQ in your Spring Boot applications via Spring AMQP. You declared the broker entities as beans, used the `AmqpTemplate` to publish messages, and used the `@RabbitListener` annotation to consume them. The

Multiplication microservice is no longer aware of the Gamification microservice; it just publishes an event when an attempt is processed. You finally achieved loose coupling with your new event-driven software architecture.

A relevant part of this chapter is the last section, where you went through different scenarios to demonstrate that the patterns you implemented really helped you improve resilience and scalability, provided that you build your code with these nonfunctional requirements in mind.

The good news about the concepts in this chapter is that, once you grasp them, you can apply them to other systems using different technologies. An event-driven software architecture based on Scala and Kafka, for example, faces the same challenges and usually requires similar patterns: multiple subscribers for the same Kafka topic, load balancing between consumers (using consumer groups), configuring delivery guarantees like at-least-once and at-most-once, and so on. Just remember that, with different tools, you may get different pros and cons.

At this stage, we hope you have already observed that the important part of building a good software architecture is understanding the design patterns and how they relate to the functional and nonfunctional requirements. Only after you get to know these patterns can you analyze the tools and frameworks that implement them, comparing the characteristics they offer.

Sometimes, you might want to build an event-driven architecture because you think it's the best technical solution, but it might not be the best pattern for your business requirements. You should avoid these situations because the software will tend to evolve to adapt to the real business case, and that can cause many problems. I've seen microservice architectures that are plagued with synchronous calls between them, either because the requirements were not adapted to embrace eventual consistency or simply because that's not even possible according to the functional requirements. Take sufficient time to analyze the problem you want to solve before jumping into technical solutions, and be skeptical about new architectural patterns that promise to solve all possible requirements.

While we were developing our system, we encountered a few new challenges that we couldn't figure out. We need HTTP load balancing with unavailable instance detection. Besides, the UI is pointing directly to each microservice, so it's aware of the backend structure. Managing this system is getting harder in aspects such as starting it up or checking logs in multiple places. The complexity of a microservice architecture is starting to become more noticeable. The next chapter covers some patterns and tools that help you deal with this complexity.

Chapter's Achievements:

- You learned the core concepts of event-driven architecture. For that, you have a good knowledge base of how message brokers work.

- You went through the pros and cons of event-driven architectures to know when applying this pattern in your future projects makes sense.

- You learned how to implement different messaging patterns depending on your use cases.

- You applied all the learned concepts using a RabbitMQ message broker in the practical case.

- You learned how Spring Boot abstracts many functionalities of RabbitMQ, allowing you to do a lot with just some little code additions.

- You refactored a tight-coupled system and converted it into a proper event-driven architecture.

- You played with the application to understand how resilience works, how you can scale up your consumers, and how you deal with transactionality.

## CHAPTER 8

Common Patterns in Microservice Architectures

In the last two chapters, you have been transitioning from solutions that meet functional requirements to pattern implementations that do not add any business functionality. Despite this, these implementations are crucial for your system to become more scalable, resilient, and better performing.

When you finished the Gamification microservice and connected its logic to the web client, you completed the new requested feature in user story 3. However, the new functional requirements came together with other nonfunctional requirements: system capacity, availability, and organizational flexibility.

After some analysis, we decided to move to a distributed system architecture based on microservices because that approach would bring advantages to this case study.

We started as simply as possible, connecting services synchronously over HTTP and pointing the user's interface to the two microservices. Then, using the practical example, you saw how that approach would undermine the plan due to the tight coupling between microservices and the inability to scale. To fix that situation, you learned how to adopt asynchronous communication, in which the sender does not wait for a response from the receiver and eventual consistency. In eventual consistency, the data changes are gradually propagated across multiple systems and may not immediately be reflected in all copies of the data. We introduced a message broker (an intermediate software to facilitate communication between different microservices) to implement an event-driven architecture design. By decoupling components through event-driven

© Moisés Macero García and Tarun Telang 2023
M. Macero García and T. Telang, *Learn Microservices with Spring Boot 3*,
https://doi.org/10.1007/978-1-4842-9757-5_8

architecture, the system can be more flexible, scalable, and resilient. As a result, you solved the tight-coupling challenge, and now your microservices are nicely isolated. You have also addressed load balancing to some extent as the broker handles it for event consumers.

As you worked on your architecture, we discussed various patterns that could assist you in reaching your objectives. For example, we touched on the gateway pattern and the load balancer for HTTP interfaces. However, there are additional significant practices for microservice architectures that we have yet to cover. These include service discovery, health checks, configuration management, logging, tracing, end-to-end testing, and more.

This chapter covers all these patterns using the Multiplication system as an example. That will help you understand the problem before you dive into the solution. Your journey through the microservice's common patterns and tools has just started.

Gateway

You already know some problems that are solved by introducing the gateway pattern in your architecture. Currently, your React application needs to connect to multiple backend microservices to access their APIs. This approach is problematic because the frontend should perceive the backend as a single server with various APIs. This way, you don't expose your architecture, thus making it more flexible in case you want to make changes in the future.

Moreover, if you introduce multiple instances of your backend services, your UI doesn't know how to balance the load between them. Neither would it know how to redirect all requests to a different backend instance if one of the instances is not available. Even though it's technically possible to implement load balancing and resilience patterns in your web clients, this is logic that you should place on the backend side. You implement it only once, and it's valid for any client. Furthermore, you can keep the frontend's logic as simple as possible.

Also, if you add user authentication to your system, you would be required to validate the security credentials in every backend microservice, which can be cumbersome. A more sensible approach is to place this logic at the *edge* of your backend, validating API calls and forwarding simple requests to other microservices. As long as you ensure the rest of the backend services are not externally reachable, you don't need to worry about security concerns.

The first section of the chapter introduces a Gateway microservice to solve these problems. The gateway pattern centralizes the HTTP access and takes care of proxying requests to other underlying services. Usually, the gateway decides where to route a request based on some configured rules (aka, predicates). Additionally, this routing service can modify requests and responses as they pass through, with pieces of logic that are called *filters*. You'll soon put in practice rules and filters in your implementation to understand them better. See Figure 8-1 for a high-level overview of how the gateway fits into your system.

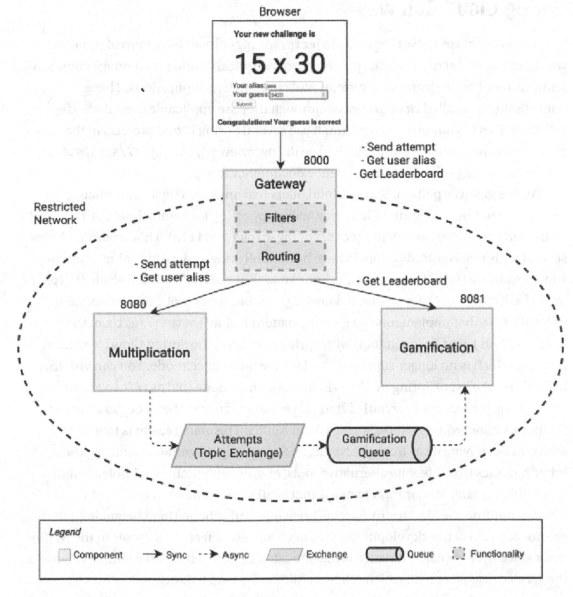

Figure 8-1. *Gateway: high-level overview*

Sometimes people refer to the gateway as an *edge service* because it's how other systems have to access your backend, routing external traffic to the corresponding internal microservices. As mentioned, introducing a gateway usually restricts access to other backend services. For the first part of this chapter, we skip this restriction since you're running all services directly on your machine. You'll change this when we introduce *containerization*.

Spring Cloud Gateway

Spring Cloud (`https://spring.io/projects/spring-cloud`) is a group of projects within the Spring ecosystem that provides tools to quickly build and manage common patterns required in distributed systems and cloud-native applications. These patterns are also called *cloud patterns*, although they are applicable even if you deploy microservices in your own servers. You'll use several Spring Cloud projects in this chapter. To check out the complete list, see the overview page (`https://spring.io/projects/spring-cloud`) in the reference documentation.

For the gateway pattern, Spring Cloud offers two options. The first alternative is to use an integration that Spring Cloud has been supporting for a long time: Spring Cloud Netflix (`https://spring.io/projects/spring-cloud-netflix`). This project includes several tools that Netflix developers have been publishing and maintaining as open-source software (OSS) for many years. You can look at the Netflix OSS website (`https://netflix.github.io/`) if you want to know more about these tools. The component in Netflix OSS that implements the gateway pattern is Zuul (`https://github.com/Netflix/zuul`), and its integration with Spring comes via the Spring Cloud Netflix Zuul module, which is no longer supported and is in maintenance mode. You can visit this link to view the list of Spring modules in maintenance mode (`https://cloud.spring.io/spring-cloud-netflix/multi/multi__modules_in_maintenance_mode.html`).

In this book, you won't use Spring Cloud Netflix. The main reason is that Spring seems to be moving away from the Netflix OSS tool integrations and replacing them with other modules that integrate alternative tools, or even with their own implementations. A possible explanation for this change is that Netflix put some of its projects in maintenance mode, like Hystrix (circuit-breaking) and Ribbon (load balancing), so they are no longer in active development. This decision also affects other tools in the Netflix stack since they implement patterns that are often used together. An example is Eureka, the service discovery tool, which relies on Ribbon for load balancing.

We'll go for a newer alternative to implement the gateway pattern: the Spring Cloud Gateway (`https://spring.io/projects/spring-cloud-gateway`). In this case, this replacement for Zuul is a stand-alone Spring project, so it doesn't depend on any external tool.

Knowing the Patterns, You Can Exchange Tools   Keep in mind that what's important to learn from this book are the microservice architecture patterns and the reasons why they're introduced from a practical perspective. You could use any other alternative in the market. Some of these alternatives include:

- Nginx (`https://www.nginx.com/`), a powerful and lightweight web server, reverse proxy, and load balancer. Its high performance and low resource usage makes it an excellent choice as a reverse proxy in front of microservices for load balancing, SSL termination, caching and serving static content.

- HAProxy (`https://www.haproxy.org/`) is an open-source load balancer and proxy server that provides high availability for TCP- and HTTP-based applications. It also improves the performance and reliability of applications by distributing network traffic across many servers.

- Kong Gateway (`https://konghq.com/`) is a lightweight, cloud-native, fast, and flexible distributed API gateway. It is built on the NGINX platform, and you can extend it through modules and plugins to deliver advanced features like advanced security, traffic management, observability, and administration. It is available in both open-source and enterprise versions to cater to the different needs of small to large organizations.

The Spring Cloud Gateway project defines some core concepts (also shown in Figure 8-2).

- *Predicate*: A condition to be evaluated to decide where to route a request. Cloud Gateway provides a bunch of condition builders based on the request path, request headers, time, remote host, and so on. You can even combine them as expressions. They're also known as *route predicates* since they always apply to a route.

- *Route*: It's the URI where the request will be proxied to if it matches the assigned predicate. For example, it could address an external request to an internal microservice endpoint, as you'll see later in practice.

- *Filter*: An optional processor that can be either attached to a route (route filters) or applied globally (global filters) to all the requests. Filters allow modifying requests (incoming filters) and responses (outgoing filters). There are a lot of built-in filters in Spring Cloud Gateway, so you can, for example, add or remove headers in the request, limit the number of requests from a given host, or transform a response from the proxied service before returning it to the requester.

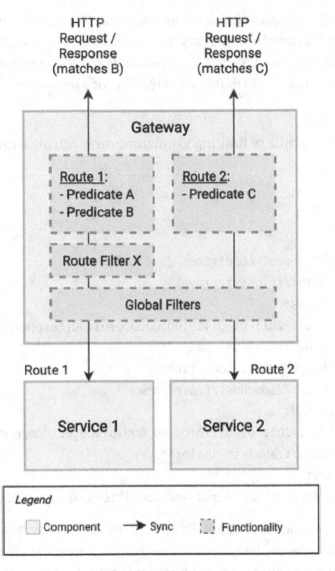

Figure 8-2. *Gateway: routes, predicates, and filters*

To define this configuration, you use Spring Boot's application properties. However, this time you'll use the YAML format because it's more readable for defining routes. The Cloud Gateway documentation defines a specific notation for predicates, routes, and filters. Additionally, you have two options when defining predicates and filters: *shortcut* and *fully expanded* configuration. They both work the same; the only difference is that you can use one-line expressions and avoid extra YAML with the shortcut version. If you want to see how they compare, check out the "Shortcut Notation" section (`https://docs.spring.io/spring-cloud-gateway/docs/current/reference/html/#shortcut-configuration`) in the docs. Listing 8-1 is an example block of configuration that uses shortcut notation to define two routes. Keep reading for a detailed explanation of how they work.

Listing 8-1. An Example of Routing Configuration in Spring Cloud Gateway

```
spring:
  cloud:
    gateway:
      routes:
        - id: old-travel-conditions
          uri: http://oldhost/travel
          predicates:
            - Before=2021-01-01T10:00:00.000+01:00[Europe/Madrid]
            - Path=/travel-in-spain/**
        - id: change-travel-conditions
          uri: http://somehost/travel-new
          predicates:
            - After=2021-01-01T10:00:00.000+01:00[Europe/Madrid]
            - Path=/travel-in-spain/**
          filters:
            - AddResponseHeader=X-New-Conditions-Apply, 2021-Jan
```

Imagine that the gateway is externally accessible at `http://my.travel.gateway/`. This example configuration defines two routes that share a path route predicate (included in the gateway); see `https://docs.spring.io/spring-cloud-gateway/docs/current/reference/html/#the-path-route-predicate-factory`. Any request that starts with `http://my.travel.gateway/travel-in-spain/` is captured by that predicate definition. The additional condition in each route, defined by a `Before` (`https://docs.spring.io/spring-cloud-gateway/docs/current/reference/html/#the-before-route-predicate-factory`) and an `After` route (`https://docs.spring.io/spring-cloud-gateway/docs/current/reference/html/#the-after-route-predicate-factory`) predicate, respectively, determines where to proxy the request.

- If the request happens before January 1, 2021, at 10 a.m. in Spain, it'll be proxied to `http://oldhost/travel-conditions/`. For example, the request `http://my.travel.gateway/travel-in-spain/tapas` gets proxied to `http://oldhost/travel/tapas`.

- Any request that happens after that time is captured by the `change-travel-conditions` route since it's using the counterpart predicate, `After`. In this case, the same request shown previously would be proxied to `http://somehost/travel-new/tapas`. Additionally, the extra `filter` will add a response header, `X-New-Conditions-Apply`, with a value of `2021-Jan`.

Keep in mind that `http://oldhost` and `http://somehost` in this example don't need to be accessible from the outside; they're only visible to the gateway and other internal services in the backend.

The built-in predicates and filters allow you to fulfill a wide variety of requirements you may have for your gateway. In this application, you'll use mainly path route predicates to proxy external requests to the corresponding microservice, based on the API they're calling.

If you want to extend your knowledge about the Spring Cloud Gateway capabilities, check out the reference docs (`https://docs.spring.io/spring-cloud-gateway/docs/current/reference/html/#gateway-starter`).

The Gateway Microservice

Source Code   The source code in this chapter has been split into four parts. This way, you can better understand how the system evolves in smaller steps. The source code for this first part, including the Gateway implementation, are in the `chapter08a` project.

As you can imagine, Spring Boot provides a starter package for Spring Cloud Gateway. Only by adding this starter dependency to an empty Spring Boot application, can you get a Gateway microservice that is ready to use. Actually, the Gateway project is built on top of Spring Boot, so it can work only within a Spring Boot application.

For that reason, the autoconfiguration logic is located in this case in the core Spring Cloud Gateway artifact, and not in the Spring Boot's autoconfigure package. The class name is GatewayAutoConfiguration (see https://github.com/spring-cloud/ spring-cloud-gateway/blob/main/spring-cloud-gateway-server/src/main/java/ org/springframework/cloud/gateway/config/GatewayAutoConfiguration.java), and, among other tasks, it reads the application.yml configuration and builds the corresponding routing filters, predicates, and so on.

You'll build this new microservice as usual, via Spring Initializr's website (see https://start.spring.io/). Select the Gateway dependency and name the artifact gateway, as shown in Figure 8-3.

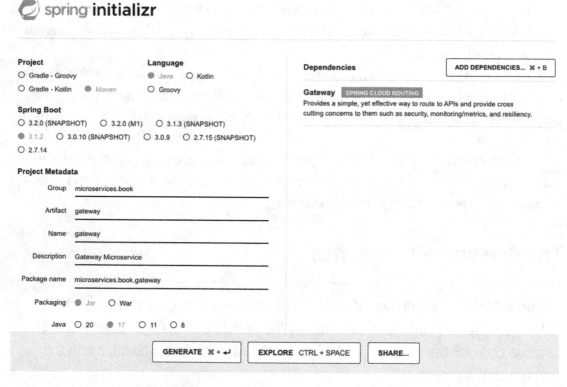

Figure 8-3. *Creating the Gateway microservice*

After downloading the ZIP file, copy its contents inside your main workspace folder, at the same level as the Multiplication and Gamification microservices. Load the project as an extra module in your workspace and take a moment to explore the contents of the generated pom.xml file. When compared to the other projects, you'll see there is a new dependencyManagement node and a new property for the Spring Cloud version to use (2022.0.3). See Listing 8-2 for the main changes in the file. You need this additional Maven configuration since the Spring Cloud artifacts are not defined directly in the Spring Boot's parent project.

Listing 8-2. Spring Cloud Gateway Dependencies in Maven

```xml
<?xml version="1.0" encoding="UTF-8"?>
<project>
    <!-- ... -->
    <name>gateway</name>
    <properties>
        <spring-cloud.version>2022.0.3</spring-cloud.version>
        <!-- ... -->
    </properties>
    <dependencies>
        <dependency>
            <groupId>org.springframework.cloud</groupId>
            <artifactId>spring-cloud-starter-gateway</artifactId>
        </dependency>
        <!-- ... -->
    </dependencies>
    <dependencyManagement>
        <dependencies>
            <dependency>
                <groupId>org.springframework.cloud</groupId>
                <artifactId>spring-cloud-dependencies</artifactId>
                <version>${spring-cloud.version}</version>
                <type>pom</type>
                <scope>import</scope>
            </dependency>
        </dependencies>
    </dependencyManagement>
    <!-- ... -->
</project>
```

The next step is to change the extension of the application.properties file to application.yml and add some configuration to proxy all the endpoints that belong to the Multiplication microservice to that application, and it's the same for Gamification's endpoints. You also changed the server port of this new service to 8000 to avoid port conflicts when deploying locally. Additionally, you'll append some CORS configuration for the UI to be allowed to make requests from its origin. Spring Cloud Gateway has a configuration-based style (https://docs.spring.io/spring-cloud-gateway/docs/current/reference/html/#cors-configuration) to accomplish this using the globalcors properties. See all these changes in Listing 8-3.

Listing 8-3. Gateway Configuration: First Approach

```
server:
  port: 8000
spring:
  cloud:
    gateway:
      routes:
        - id: multiplication
          uri: http://localhost:8080/
          predicates:
            - Path=/challenges/**,/attempts,/attempts/**,/users/**
        - id: gamification
          uri: http://localhost:8081/
          predicates:
            - Path=/leaders
      globalcors:
        cors-configurations:
          '[/**]':
            allowedOrigins: "http://localhost:3000"
            allowedHeaders:
              - "*"
            allowedMethods:
              - "GET"
              - "POST"
```

```
    - "OPTIONS"
default-filters:
    - DedupeResponseHeader=Access-Control-Allow-Origin,
      RETAIN_UNIQUE
```

The routes in that file will make the Gateway act as follows:

- Any request to or under `http://localhost:8000/attempts` will be proxied to the Multiplication microservice, deployed locally at `http://localhost:8080/`. The same will happen to other API contexts located in the same microservice, like `challenges` and `users`.

- Requests to `http://localhost:8000/leaders` will be translated to requests to the Gamification microservice, which uses the same host (`localhost`) but the port 8081.

- The `DedupeResponseHeader` default filter is used to remove duplicate response `Access-Control-Allow-Origin` headers. The `RETAIN_UNIQUE` filter parameter ensures that only one occurrence of the `Access-Control-Allow-Origin` response header is in the gateway response. Avoiding header duplication issues and providing consistent CORS-related headers is essential for client applications to be able to consume the services using the gateway.

Alternatively, it would be possible to write a simpler configuration that wouldn't require an explicit list of endpoints routed to each microservice. You could do this by using another feature of the gateway that allows capturing path segments. If you get an API call such as `http://localhost:8000/multiplication/attempts`, you could extract `multiplication` as a value and use it to map to the corresponding service's host and port. However, this approach is valid only when each microservice contains only one API domain. In any other case, you'd be exposing your internal architecture to the client. In this case, you need require the client to call `http://localhost:8000/multiplication/users`, whereas you prefer them to point to `http://localhost:8000/users` and hide the fact that the Users domain still lives in the multiplication's deployable unit.

Changes in Other Projects

With the introduction of the Gateway microservice, you can keep all the configuration intended for external requests in the same service. This means you no longer need to add CORS configuration to the Multiplication and Gamification microservices. You can keep this configuration in the gateway since the other two services are placed behind this new proxy service. As a result, you can remove both WebConfiguration files from the existing project folders. Listing 8-4 shows the contents of the file in the Gamification microservice. Remember to delete not only this one but the equivalent class in the Multiplication microservice.

Listing 8-4. The WebConfiguration Class That You Can Remove

```
package microservices.book.gamification.configuration;

import org.springframework.context.annotation.Configuration;
import org.springframework.web.servlet.config.annotation.CorsRegistry;
import org.springframework.web.servlet.config.annotation.WebMvcConfigurer;

@Configuration
public class WebConfiguration implements WebMvcConfigurer {
    /**
      * Enables Cross-Origin Resource Sharing (CORS)
      * More info: https://docs.spring.io/spring-framework/reference/web/
      webmvc-cors.html
      */
    @Override
    public void addCorsMappings(final CorsRegistry registry) {
        registry.addMapping("/**").allowedOrigins("http://localhost:3000");
    }
}
```

You also need to change the React application to point to the same host/port for both services. See Listings 8-5 and 8-6. You could also refactor the GameApiClient and ChallengesApiClient classes as per your preferences for the UI structure: one single service to call all endpoints or a service per API context (challenges, users, etc.). You don't need two different server URLs anymore since the UI now treats the backend as a single host with multiple APIs.

Listing 8-5. Changing the Multiplication API URL to Point to the Gateway

```
class ChallengesApiClient {
    static SERVER_URL = 'http://localhost:8000';
    static GET_CHALLENGE = '/challenges/random';
    static POST_RESULT = '/attempts';
    // ...
}
```

Listing 8-6. Changing the Gamification API URL to Point to the Gateway

```
class GameApiClient {
    static SERVER_URL = 'http://localhost:8000';
    static GET_LEADERBOARD = '/leaders';
    // ...
}
```

Running the Gateway Microservice

To run your entire application, you have to add an extra step to the list. Remember that all Spring Boot apps can be executed from your IDE or from the command line, using the Maven wrapper.

1. Run the RabbitMQ server.

2. Start the Multiplication microservice.

3. Start the Gamification microservice.

4. Start the new Gateway module.

5. Run the frontend app with npm start from the challenges-frontend folder.

Within this chapter, this list will keep growing. It's important to highlight that you don't need to follow the order of the previous steps since you could even run all of these processes at the same time. During the start, the system might be unstable, but it'll eventually become ready. Spring Boot will retry to connect to RabbitMQ until it works.

When you access the UI, you won't notice any changes. The leaderboard gets loaded, and you can send attempts as usual. One way to verify that the requests are being proxied is to look at the Network tab in the browser's developer tools and select any request to the backend to see how the URL begins now with `http://localhost:8000`. A second option is to add some trace logging configuration to the gateway, so you see what's happening. See Listing 8-7 for the configuration you can add to the `application.yml` file in the Gateway project to enable these logs.

Listing 8-7. Adding Trace-Level Logs to the Gateway

```
# ... route config
logging:
  level:
    org.springframework.cloud.gateway.handler.predicate: trace
```

If you restart the gateway with this new configuration, you'll see logs per request that the gateway handles. These logs are the result of going through all defined routes to see whether there are any that match the request pattern. The patterns use the /** wildcard to match any subpath. The log entry is confirming that the route pattern /leaders is successfully matching the request path /leaders. See Listing 8-8.

Listing 8-8. Gateway Logs with Pattern-Matching Messages

```
TRACE 12964 --- [ctor-http-nio-3] o.s.c.g.h.p.PathRoutePredicateFactory
: Pattern "[/challenges/**, /attempts, /attempts/**, /users/**]" does not
match against value "/leaders"
TRACE 12964 --- [ctor-http-nio-3] o.s.c.g.h.p.PathRoutePredicateFactory
: Pattern "/leaders" matches against value "/leaders"
TRACE 12964 --- [ctor-http-nio-2] o.s.c.g.h.p.PathRoutePredicateFactory
: Pattern "/users/**" matches against value "/users/302,202,402"
```

Now, let's remove this logging configuration again to avoid a too verbose output.

Next Steps

You already have a few advantages with this new setup.

- The frontend remains unaware of the backend structure.

- The common configuration for external requests remains in the same place. In your case, that's the CORS setup, but there could also be other common concerns such as user authentication, metrics, and so on.

Next, we introduce load balancing to your gateway, so it can distribute the traffic across all available instances of each service. With that pattern, you'll add scalability and redundancy to your system. However, to make load balancing work properly, you need some prerequisites.

- The gateway needs to know the available instances for a given service. The initial configuration points directly to a specific port because you assumed that there is only one instance. What would that look like with multiple replicas? You shouldn't include a hard-coded list in your routing configuration since the number of instances should be dynamic: you want to bring new ones up and down transparently.

- You need to implement the concept of healthiness of a backend component. Only then will you know when an instance is not ready to handle traffic and switch to any other healthy instance.

To fulfill the first prerequisite, you need to introduce the service discovery pattern, with a common registry that the different distributed components can access to know the available services and where to find them.

For the second prerequisite, you'll use Spring Boot Actuator. Your microservices will expose an endpoint that indicates whether they're healthy or not, so other components will know. This is what you'll do next since it's also a requirement for service discovery.

Health

A system running on a production environment is never safe from errors. Network connections may fail, or a microservice instance may crash due to an out-of-memory problem caused by a bug in the code. You're determined to build a resilient system, so you want to be prepared against these errors with mechanisms like *redundancy* (multiple replicas of the same microservice) to minimize the impact of these incidents.

So, how do you know when a microservice is not working? If it's exposing an interface (like a REST API or RabbitMQ), you could interact with a sample probe and see if it reacts to it. But then, you should be careful when selecting that probe since you want to cover all possible scenarios that would make your microservice transition to an unhealthy state (not functional). Instead of leaking the logic to determine whether a service is working or not to the caller, it's much better to provide a standard, dumb probe interface that just indicates whether the service is healthy. It's up to the service's logic to decide when to transition to an unhealthy state, based on the availability of the interfaces it uses, its own availability, and the criticality of the error. If the service can't even provide a response, the callers can also assume that it's unhealthy. See Figure 8-4 for a high-level, conceptual view of this health interface.

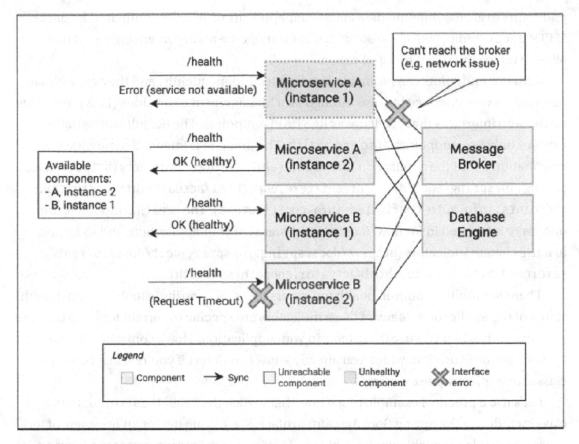

Figure 8-4. Health: high-level overview

This simple interface convention to determine the healthiness of services is required by many tools and frameworks (and not only for microservices). For example, load balancers can temporarily stop diverting traffic to an instance that doesn't respond to the health probe or responds with a non-ready state. Service discovery tools may remove an instance from the registry if it's unhealthy. Container platforms like Kubernetes can decide to restart a service if it's not healthy for a configured period (we explain what a container platform is later in this chapter).

Spring Boot Actuator

Same as with other aspects of this application, Spring Boot provides an out-of-the-box solution to make your microservices report their health status: Spring Boot Actuator. Actually, that's not the only feature that Actuator contains; it can also expose other endpoints to access different data about your application, like the configured loggers, HTTP traces, audit events, and so on. It can even open a management endpoint that allows you to shut down the application.

Actuator endpoints can be enabled or disabled independently, and they're available not only via web interface but also through Java Management eXtensions (JMX). We focus on the web interfaces that you'll use as REST API endpoints. The default configuration exposes only two endpoints: `info` and `health`. The first one is intended to provide general information about the application that you can enrich using contributors (`https://docs.spring.io/spring-boot/docs/current/reference/html/actuator.html#actuator.endpoints.info.auto-configured-info-contributors`). The `health` endpoint is the one we're interested in for now. It outputs the status of your application, and to resolve it, it uses health indicators (`https://docs.spring.io/spring-boot/docs/current/reference/html/actuator.html#actuator.endpoints.health`).

There are multiple built-in health indicators that can contribute to the overall health status of the application. Many of these indicators are specific to certain tools, so they are available only when you use these tools in your application. That's controlled by Spring Boot's autoconfiguration, which you already know can detect if you're using certain classes and inject some extra logic.

Let's use a practical example to see how that works: the `RabbitHealthIndicator` class included in the Spring Boot Actuator artifact. See Listing 8-9 for an overview of its source code (also available online at `https://github.com/spring-projects/spring-boot/blob/main/spring-boot-project/spring-boot-actuator/src/main/java/org/springframework/boot/actuate/amqp/RabbitHealthIndicator.java`). The health check implementation uses a `RabbitTemplate` object, which is Spring's way to interact with the RabbitMQ server. If this code can access the RabbitMQ server's version, the health check passes (it doesn't throw an exception).

Listing 8-9. The RabbitHealthIndicator Included in Spring Boot Actuator

```
public class RabbitHealthIndicator extends AbstractHealthIndicator {
    private final RabbitTemplate rabbitTemplate;
    public RabbitHealthIndicator(RabbitTemplate rabbitTemplate) {
        super("Rabbit health check failed");
        Assert.notNull(rabbitTemplate, "RabbitTemplate must not be null");
        this.rabbitTemplate = rabbitTemplate;
    }
```

```java
@Override
protected void doHealthCheck(Health.Builder builder) throws Exception {
    builder.up().withDetail("version", getVersion());
}
private String getVersion() {
    return this.rabbitTemplate
            .execute((channel) -> channel.getConnection()
                    .getServerProperties().get("version").toString());
}
}
```

This indicator is automatically injected in the context if you use RabbitMQ. It
contributes to the overall health status. The RabbitHealthContributorAutoConfiguration
class, included in the artifact spring-boot-actuator-autoconfigure (part of Spring
Boot Actuator dependency), takes care of that. See Listing 8-10 (also available at https://
github.com/spring-projects/spring-boot/blob/main/spring-boot-project/
spring-boot-actuator-autoconfigure/src/main/java/org/springframework/boot/
actuate/autoconfigure/amqp/RabbitHealthContributorAutoConfiguration.java).
This configuration is conditional on the existence of a RabbitTemplate bean, which
means you're using the RabbitMQ module. It creates a HealthContributor bean, in this
case, a RabbitHealthIndicator that will be detected and aggregated by the overall health
autoconfiguration.

Listing 8-10. How Spring Boot Autoconfigures the RabbitHealthContributor

```java
@Configuration(proxyBeanMethods = false)
@ConditionalOnClass(RabbitTemplate.class)
@ConditionalOnBean(RabbitTemplate.class)
@ConditionalOnEnabledHealthIndicator("rabbit")
@AutoConfigureAfter(RabbitAutoConfiguration.class)
public class RabbitHealthContributorAutoConfiguration
        extends CompositeHealthContributorConfiguration<RabbitHealthIndicat
        or, RabbitTemplate> {
    @Bean
    @ConditionalOnMissingBean(name = { "rabbitHealthIndicator",
    "rabbitHealthContributor" })
```

```
public HealthContributor rabbitHealthContributor(Map<String,
RabbitTemplate> rabbitTemplates) {
    return createContributor(rabbitTemplates);
  }
}
```

You'll see soon how this works in practice since you'll add Spring Boot Actuator to your microservices in the next section.

Keep in mind that you can configure multiple settings of the Actuator's endpoints, and you can create your own health indicators as well. For a complete list of features, check out the official Spring Boot Actuator documentation (`https://docs.spring.io/ spring-boot/docs/current/reference/html/actuator.html`).

Including Actuator in Your Microservices

Source Code   The source code for the introduction of the health endpoints, service discovery, and load balancing is located in the `chapter08b` repository.

Adding the health endpoint to your applications is as easy as adding a dependency in the `pom.xml` file to your projects: `spring-boot-starter-actuator`. See Listing 8-11. You'll add this new artifact to all your Spring Boot applications: the Multiplication, Gamification, and Gateway microservices.

Listing 8-11. Adding Spring Boot Actuator to your Microservices

```
<dependency>
    <groupId>org.springframework.boot</groupId>
    <artifactId>spring-boot-starter-actuator</artifactId>
</dependency>
```

The default configuration exposes the `health` and `info` web endpoints on the `/actuator` context. That's enough at this point, but this could be adjusted via properties if needed. Rebuild and restart the backend applications to verify this new feature. You can use the command line, or your browser, to poll each service for its health status, just by switching the port number. Note that you're not exposing the `/health` endpoints via the gateway because it's not a feature you want to expose to the outside, but just internal to your system. See Listing 8-12 for the request and response of the Multiplication microservice.

Listing 8-12. Testing the /health Endpoint the First Time

```
$ http :8080/actuator/health

HTTP/1.1 200
Connection: keep-alive
Content-Type: application/vnd.spring-boot.actuator.v3+json
Date: Wed, 26 Jul 2023 17:34:35 GMT
Keep-Alive: timeout=60
Transfer-Encoding: chunked

{
    "status": "UP"
}
```

If your system is running properly, you'll get the UP value and an HTTP status code 200. What you'll do next is stop the RabbitMQ server and try this same request again. You already saw that the Actuator project contains a health indicator to check the RabbitMQ server, so this one should fail, causing the aggregated health status to switch to DOWN. This is indeed what you get if you make the request while the RabbitMQ server is stopped. See Listing 8-13.

Listing 8-13. The Status of the App Switches to DOWN When RabbitMQ Is Unreachable

```
HTTP/1.1 503
Connection: close
Content-Type: application/vnd.spring-boot.actuator.v3+json
Date: Wed, 26 Jul 2023 17:36:03 GMT
Transfer-Encoding: chunked

{
    "status": "DOWN"
}
```

Note that the HTTP status code returned also changed to 503, Service Unavailable. Therefore, the caller doesn't even need to parse the response body; it can just check whether the response code is 200 to determine that the application is healthy. You can also see the logs of the failed attempt from RabbitHealthIndicator to retrieve the server's version in the Multiplication application's output. This is because you stopped the RabbitMQ server. See Listing 8-14.

Listing 8-14. Rabbit Health Check Failing in the Multiplication Microservice

```
2023-07-26T23:06:03.285+05:30  INFO 19644 --- [nio-8080-exec-3] o.s.a.r.c.C
achingConnectionFactory       : Attempting to connect to: [localhost:5672]
2023-07-26T23:06:03.292+05:30  WARN 19644 --- [nio-8080-exec-3]
o.s.b.a.amqp.RabbitHealthIndicator       : Rabbit health check failed
[...]
org.springframework.amqp.AmqpConnectException: java.net.ConnectException:
Connection refused at org.springframework.amqp.rabbit.support.
RabbitExceptionTranslator.convertRabbitAccessException(RabbitExceptionTrans
lator.java:61) ~[spring-rabbit-3.0.4.jar:3.0.4]
        at org.springframework.amqp.rabbit.connection.
        AbstractConnectionFactory.createBareConnection(AbstractConnectionFact
        ory.java:594) ~[spring-rabbit-3.0.4.jar:3.0.4]
        at org.springframework.boot.actuate.endpoint.web.servlet.Abstra
        ctWebMvcEndpointHandlerMapping$ServletWebOperationAdapter.handl
        e(AbstractWebMvcEndpointHandlerMapping.java:321) ~[spring-boot-
        actuator-3.1.0.jar:3.1.0]
        at org.springframework.boot.actuate.endpoint.web.servlet.AbstractWebM
        vcEndpointHandlerMapping$OperationHandler.handle(AbstractWebMvcEndpoi
        ntHandlerMapping.java:428) ~[spring-boot-actuator-3.1.0.jar:3.1.0]
        at java.base/jdk.internal.reflect.NativeMethodAccessorImpl.
        invoke0(Native Method) ~[na:na]
```

The Spring Boot application remains alive, and it can recover from that error. If you start the RabbitMQ server and check for the health status again, it'll switch to UP. The application keeps trying to establish a connection to the server until it succeeds. This is exactly the behavior you want for a robust system: if the microservice has issues, it should flag it for other components to know; in the meantime, it should try to recover from the error and switch to a healthy state again when possible.

Service Discovery and Load Balancing

Now that you have the ability to know whether services are available, you can integrate service discovery and load balancing in your system.

The service discovery pattern consists of two main concepts.

- *The service registry*: A central place with a list of available services, the address where they're located, and some extra metadata like their name. It may contain entries for different services, but also multiple instances of the same service. In the last case, clients accessing the registry can obtain a list of available instances by querying a *service alias*. For example, various instances of the Multiplication microservice can register with the same alias, `multiplication`. Then, when querying that value, all instances are returned. That's the case of the example shown in Figure 8-5.

- *The registrar*: The logic in charge of registering the service instance at the registry. It can be an external running process observing the state of your microservice, or it can be embedded in the service itself as a library, like it'll be this case.

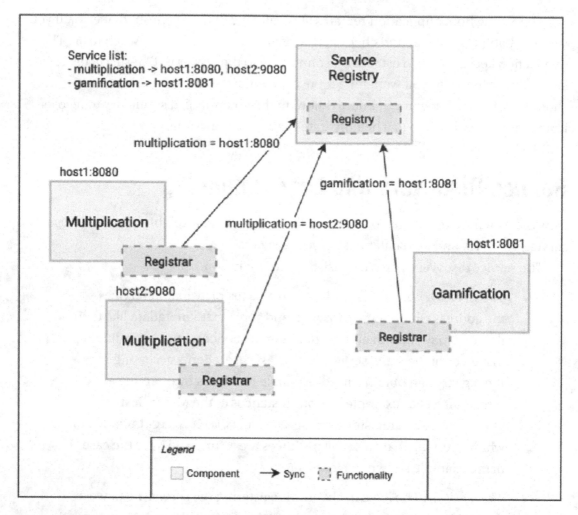

Figure 8-5. *Service discovery: pattern overview*

In Figure 8-5, you see an example of service registration with three services. The host1, a server's DNS address, has one instance of Multiplication at port 8080 and one instance of Gamification at port 8081. The host2, a different machine, has a second instance of Multiplication, located at port 9080. All of these instances know where they're located and send their corresponding URIs to the service registry using the registrar. Then, a Registry client can simply ask for the location of a service using its name (e.g., multiplication), and the registry returns the list of instances and their locations (e.g., host1:8080, host2:9080). You'll see this in practice soon.

The load balancing pattern is closely related to service discovery. If more than one service uses the same name upon registration, that implies there are multiple replicas available. You want to balance the traffic between them so you can increase the capacity of the system and make it more resilient in case of errors thanks to the added redundancy.

Other services may query a given service name from the registry, retrieve a list, and then decide which instance to call. This technique is known as *client-side discovery*, and it implies that clients are aware of the service registry and perform load balancing themselves. Note that, by *client*, we mean an application, microservice, browser, and so on, that wants to perform an HTTP call to another service. See Figure 8-6.

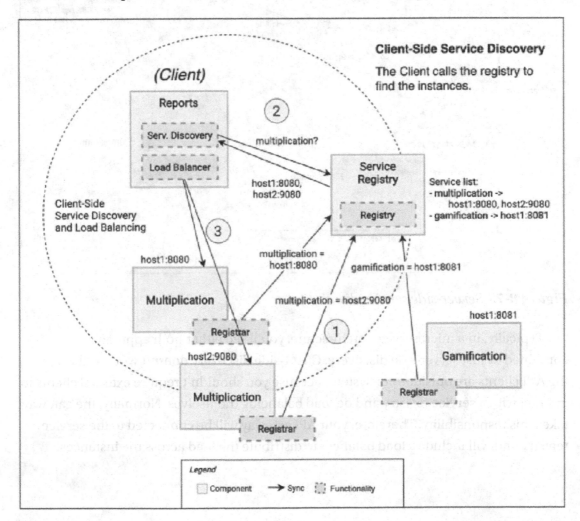

Figure 8-6.   Client-side service discovery

On the other side, *server-side discovery* abstracts all this logic from the clients by providing a unique address, known in advance, where callers can find a given service. When they make the request, it's intercepted by a load balancer, which is aware of the registry. This balancer will proxy the request to one of the replicas. See Figure 8-7.

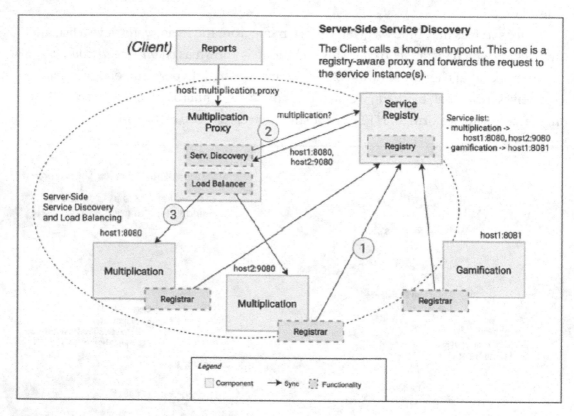

Figure 8-7. *Server-side service discovery*

Typically, in a microservices architecture, you'll see either both approaches combined or just server-side discovery. Client-side discovery doesn't work well when the API clients are outside your system, because you shouldn't require external clients to interact with a service registry and do load balancing themselves. Normally, the gateway takes this responsibility. Therefore, your API gateway will be connected to the service registry and will include a load balancer to distribute the load across the instances.

For any other service-to-service communication in your backend, you could either connect all of them to the registry for client-side discovery or abstract each cluster of services (all its instances) as a unique address with a load balancer. The latter is the technique chosen in some platforms like Kubernetes, where each service is assigned a unique address no matter how many replicas there are and in which node they're located (we come back to this later in this chapter).

Your microservices are no longer calling each other, but if that would be needed, it'd be straightforward to implement client-side discovery. Spring Boot has integrations to connect to the service registry and implement a load balancer (similar to what you'll do in the gateway).

As mentioned already, any non-internal HTTP communication to your backend will use a server-side discovery approach. That means your gateway will not only route traffic but also take care of load balancing. See Figure 8-8, which also includes the solution to use when you need interservice communication. This diagram also introduces the name of the tool you'll use to implement service discovery, Consul, and the Spring Cloud projects you'll add to your dependencies to integrate this tool and include a simple load balancer. You'll learn about them soon.

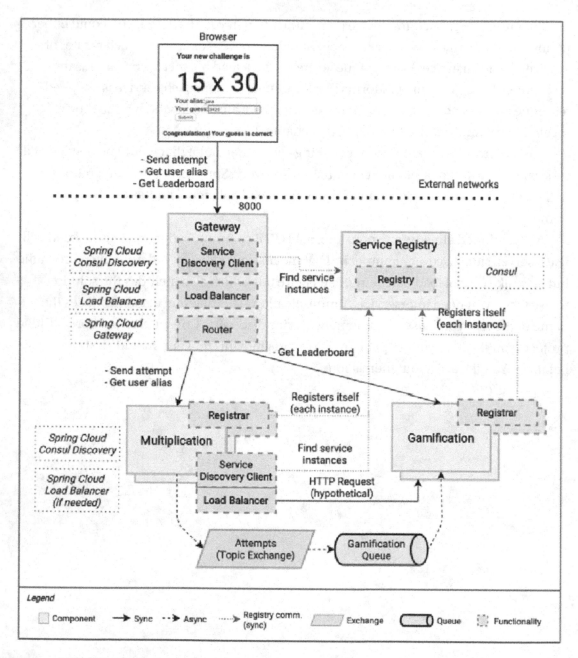

Figure 8-8. *Gateway and service discovery integrations*

Consul

Many tools implement the service discovery pattern: Consul, Eureka, Zookeeper, and so on. There are also complete platforms that include this pattern as one of their features, as we describe later.

In the Spring ecosystem, Netflix's Eureka has been the most popular choice for a long time. However, for the reasons stated previously (components in maintenance mode, new tools developed by Spring developers), that preference is no longer a sound option. This book uses Consul (`https://developer.hashicorp.com/consul`), a tool that provides service discovery among other features and has also good integration via a Spring Cloud module. Besides, you'll take advantage of one of the other Consul features later in this chapter to implement another pattern in microservice architectures, centralized configuration.

First, install the Consul Tools, which are available for multiple platforms at the Downloads page (`https://developer.hashicorp.com/consul/downloads`). Once you have installed them, you can run the Consul Agent in development mode with the command shown in Listing 8-15.

Listing 8-15. Starting the Consul Agent in Development Mode

```
$ consul agent -node=learnmicro -dev
==> Starting Consul agent...
              Version: '1.16.0'
           Build Date: '2023-06-26 20:07:11 +0000 UTC'
              Node ID: 'c6270c9c-8b3a-4a9d-4a05-6f8138bc5a5d'
            Node name: 'learnmicro'
           Datacenter: 'dc1' (Segment: '<all>')
               Server: true (Bootstrap: false)
          Client Addr: [127.0.0.1] (HTTP: 8500, HTTPS: -1, gRPC: 8502,
                       gRPC-TLS: 8503, DNS: 8600)
         Cluster Addr: 127.0.0.1 (LAN: 8301, WAN: 8302)
    Gossip Encryption: false
     Auto-Encrypt-TLS: false
...
```

The logs should display some information about the server and some startup actions. Run the agent in *development mode* since you're using it locally, but a proper production setup of Consul would consist of a cluster with multiple data centers. These data centers may run one or more agents, where only one of them per server would act as a server agent. Agents use a protocol to communicate between them to sync information and elect a leader via consensus. All this setup ensures high availability. If a data center becomes unreachable, agents will notice it and elect a new leader. If you want to know more about deploying Consul in production, check out the Deployment Guide (`https://developer.hashicorp.com/consul/tutorials/production-deploy/deployment-guide`). we stick to the development mode in this book, with a stand-alone agent.

As you see in the output, Consul runs an HTTP server on port 8500. It offers a RESTful API that you can use for service registration and discovery, among other features. Besides, it provides a UI that you can access if you navigate from a browser to `http://localhost:8500`. See Figure 8-9.

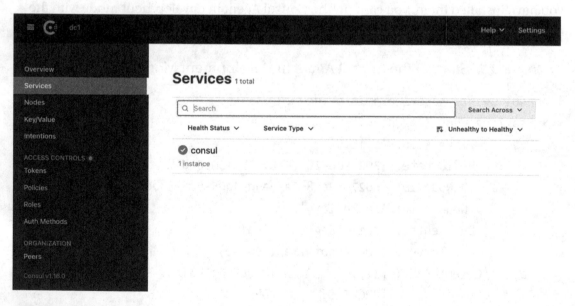

Figure 8-9. *Consul UI*

The Services section displays a list of registered services. Since you didn't do anything yet, the only available service is the Consul server. The other tabs show the available Consul nodes, the key-value functionality you'll use later in this chapter, and some additional Consul features such as ACL and intentions that you won't learn about in this book.

You can also access the list of available services via the REST API. For example, using HTTPie, you can ask for a list of available services, which will output an empty response body for now. See Listing 8-16.

Listing 8-16. Requesting the List of Services from Consul

```
$ http -b :8500/v1/agent/services
{}
```

The Service API allows you to list services, query their information, know if they're healthy, register them, and deregister them. You won't use this API directly because the Spring Cloud Consul module does this for you, as we cover soon.

Consul includes functionality to verify the state of all services: the health checks feature. It offers multiple options that you can use to determine healthiness: HTTP, TCP, Scripts, and so on. As you can imagine, the plan is to make Consul contact your microservices via the HTTP interface, more specifically on the `/actuator/health` endpoints. The health check location is configured at service registration time, and Consul triggers them on a periodic interval basis that can also be customized. If a service fails to respond or it does so with a non-OK status (other than 2XX), Consul will flag that service as unhealthy. You'll see a practical example soon. Read the Checks page (`https://developer.hashicorp.com/consul/api-docs/agent/check`) on the Consul documentation if you want to know more about how to configure them.

Spring Cloud Consul

You don't need to use the Consul API to register services, define health checks, or access the registry to find a service address. All these functionalities are abstracted by the Spring Cloud Consul (`https://spring.io/projects/spring-cloud-consul`) project, so all you need is to include the corresponding starter in your Spring Boot applications and configure some settings if you choose not to use the default values.

The version of Spring Cloud Consul you'll use here still comes with Netflix's Ribbon as an included dependency to implement the load balancer pattern. This tool is in maintenance mode, and the Spring documentation discourages its usage (see `https://spring.getdocs. org/en-US/spring-cloud-docs/spring-cloud-netflix/spring-cloud-eureka-server/ disabling-ribbon-with-eureka-server-and-client-starters.html`). We explain the alternative you'll use in the next section. For now, to keep your project clean, you're going to use Maven to exclude the transitive dependency on the Ribbon's starter. See Listing 8-17.

Listing 8-17. Adding the Spring Cloud Consul Discovery Dependency in Maven

```
<dependency>
    <groupId>org.springframework.cloud</groupId>
    <artifactId>spring-cloud-starter-consul-discovery</artifactId>
    <exclusions>
        <exclusion>
            <groupId>org.springframework.cloud</groupId>
            <artifactId>spring-cloud-starter-netflix-ribbon</artifactId>
        </exclusion>
    </exclusions>
</dependency>
```

You'll see how to add this dependency to the Gateway project a bit later. For the other two microservices, you're adding a Spring Cloud dependency for the first time. Therefore, you need to add the dependencyManagement node to your pom.xml files and the Spring Cloud version. See Listing 8-18 for the required additions.

Listing 8-18. Adding Consul Discovery to Multiplication and Gamification

```
<project>
    <!-- ... -->
    <properties>
        <!-- ... -->
        <spring-cloud.version>2022.0.3</spring-cloud.version>
    </properties>
    <dependencies>
        <!-- ... -->
        <dependency>
            <groupId>org.springframework.cloud</groupId>
            <artifactId>spring-cloud-starter-consul-discovery</artifactId>
            <exclusions>
                <exclusion>
                    <groupId>org.springframework.cloud</groupId>
                    <artifactId>spring-cloud-starter-netflix-ribbon
                    </artifactId>
                </exclusion>
```

```
            </exclusions>
        </dependency>
    </dependencies>
    <dependencyManagement>
        <dependencies>
            <dependency>
                <groupId>org.springframework.cloud</groupId>
                <artifactId>spring-cloud-dependencies</artifactId>
                <version>${spring-cloud.version}</version>
                <type>pom</type>
                <scope>import</scope>
            </dependency>
        </dependencies>
    </dependencyManagement>
    <!-- ... -->
</project>
```

The included Spring Boot autoconfiguration defaults for Consul are fine for this case: the server is located at `http://localhost:8500`. See the source code (`https://github.com/spring-cloud/spring-cloud-consul/blob/main/spring-cloud-consul-core/src/main/java/org/springframework/cloud/consul/ConsulProperties.java`) of `ConsulProperties` if you want to see these default values. If you need to change them, you can use these and other properties available under the `spring.cloud.consul` prefix. For a complete list of settings that you can override, check out Spring Cloud Consul's reference docs (`https://cloud.spring.io/spring-cloud-consul/reference/html/`).

However, there is a new configuration property you need in your applications: the application name, specified by the `spring.application.name` property. You haven't needed it so far, but Spring Cloud Consul uses it to register the service with that value. This is the line you have to add to the `application.properties` file inside the Multiplication project:

```
spring.application.name=multiplication
```

Make sure to add this line to the Gamification microservice's configuration too, this time with the value `gamification`. In the Gateway project, you use YAML properties, but the change is similar.

```
spring:
  application:
    name: gateway
```

Now, start the Multiplication and Gamification microservices to see how they register themselves with their corresponding health checks. Remember to start the RabbitMQ server and the Consul agent as well. You still need to make changes to the Gateway service, so you don't need to start it yet. In the application logs, you should see a new line like the one shown in Listing 8-19 (note that it's only one line, but a very verbose one).

Listing 8-19. Gamification's Log Line Showing the Consul Registration Details

```
INFO 14396 --- [              main] o.s.c.c.s.ConsulServiceRegistry           :
Registering service with consul: NewService{id='gamification-8081',
name='gamification', tags=[], address='172.20.10.2', meta={secure=false},
port=8081, enableTagOverride=null, check=Check{script='null',
dockerContainerID='null', shell='null', interval='10s', ttl='null',
http='http://172.20.10.2:8081/actuator/health', method='null', header={},
tcp='null', timeout='null', deregisterCriticalServiceAfter='null',
tlsSkipVerify=null, status='null', grpc='null', grpcUseTLS=null},
checks=null}
```

This line shows the service registration via Spring Cloud Consul when the application starts. You can see the request's contents: a unique ID composed of the service name and port, the service name that may group multiple instances, the local address, and a configured health check over HTTP to the address of the service's health endpoint exposed by Spring Boot Actuator. The interval in which Consul will verify this check is set to ten seconds by default.

You can run the following command to start the Consul monitor with a log level set to debug.

```
$ consul monitor -log-level=debug
```

The `consul monitor` command is used to continuously monitor the state of services registered with Consul. The `-log-level` flag allows you to set the level of logging that you want to see in the output. In this case, it will show all log messages, including those at the debug level.

See Listing 8-20 to understand how Consul processes service registration requests and triggers the health checks.

Listing 8-20. Consul Agent Logs

```
[DEBUG] agent.http: Request finished: method=PUT url=/v1/agent/service/
register?token=<hidden> from=127.0.0.1:52954 latency="970.708µs"
[DEBUG] agent: Node info in sync
[DEBUG] agent.http: Request finished: method=GET url="/v1/catalog/services?
wait=2s&index=213&token=<hidden>" from=127.0.0.1:52543 latency=2.011289625s
[DEBUG] agent: Service in sync: service=multiplication
[DEBUG] agent: Service in sync: service=gamification-8081
[DEBUG] agent: Check in sync: check=service:multiplication
[DEBUG] agent: Check in sync: check=service:gamification-8081
```

Once you start both microservices with this new configuration, you can access the Consul's UI to see the updated status. See Figure 8-10.

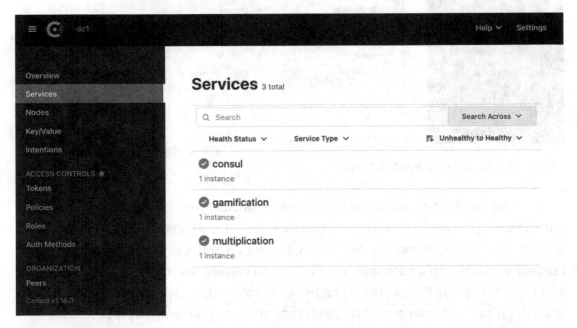

Figure 8-10. *Services listed in Consul*

Now navigate to Services, click Multiplication, and click the only Multiplication row displayed there. You'll see the service's health check. You can verify that Consul is getting an OK status (200) from the Spring Boot application. See Figure 8-11.

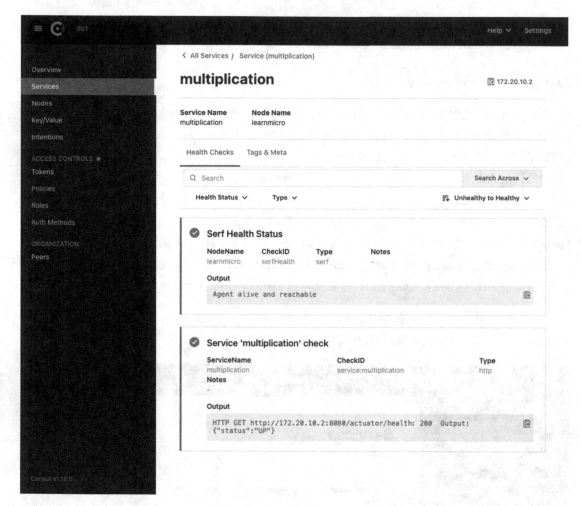

Figure 8-11. *Service health check*

You can also start a second instance of one of the microservices to see how this is managed by the registry. You can do that from your IDE if you override the port or directly from the command line. See Listing 8-21 for an example of how to start a second instance of the Multiplication microservice. As you can see, you can override the server port using the Spring Boot's Maven plugin (see `https://docs.spring.io/spring-boot/docs/current/maven-plugin/reference/htmlsingle/#run.examples.using-application-arguments` for more details).

Listing 8-21. Running a Second Instance of the Multiplication Microservice from the Command Line

```
multiplication $ ./mvnw spring-boot:run -Dspring-boot.run.arguments="--
server.port=9080"
[... logs ...]
```

In the Consul registry, there will still be a single `multiplication` service. If you click this service, you'll navigate to the Instances tab. See Figure 8-12. There, you can see both instances, each of them with their corresponding health check. Note that the port is not used in the ID by Spring Boot when it's the default value: 8080.

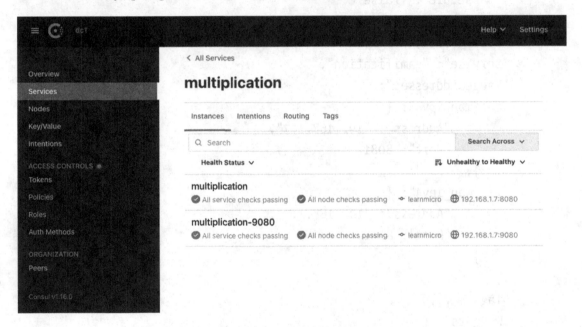

Figure 8-12. *Multiple instances in the Consul's registry*

An API request to get the list of services from Consul retrieves these two services, including information about both instances of the Multiplication application. See Listing 8-22 for a shortened version of the response.

Listing 8-22. Retrieving Registered Services Using the Consul API

```
$ http -b :8500/v1/agent/services
{
    "gamification-8081": {
        "Address": "192.168.1.7",
        "Datacenter": "dc1",
        "EnableTagOverride": false,
        "ID": "gamification-8081",
        "Meta": {
            "secure": "false"
        },
        "Port": 8081,
        "Service": "gamification",
        "TaggedAddresses": {
            "lan_ipv4": {
                "Address": "192.168.1.7",
                "Port": 8081
            },
            "wan_ipv4": {
                "Address": "192.168.1.7",
                "Port": 8081
            }
        },
        "Tags": [],
        "Weights": {
            "Passing": 1,
            "Warning": 1
        }
    },
    "multiplication": {
        "Address": "192.168.1.7",
        "Datacenter": "dc1",
        "EnableTagOverride": false,
        "ID": "multiplication",
        "Meta": {
```

```
            "secure": "false"
        },
        "Port": 8080,
        "Service": "multiplication",
        "TaggedAddresses": {
            "lan_ipv4": {
                "Address": "192.168.1.7",
                "Port": 8080
            },
            "wan_ipv4": {
                "Address": "192.168.1.7",
                "Port": 8080
            }
        },
        "Tags": [],
        "Weights": {
            "Passing": 1,
            "Warning": 1
        }
    },
    "multiplication-9080": {
        "Address": "192.168.1.7",
        "Datacenter": "dc1",
        "EnableTagOverride": false,
        "ID": "multiplication-9080",
        "Meta": {
            "secure": "false"
        },
        "Port": 9080,
        "Service": "multiplication",
        "TaggedAddresses": {
            "lan_ipv4": {
                "Address": "192.168.1.7",
                "Port": 9080
            },
            "wan_ipv4": {
```

```
                "Address": "192.168.1.7",
                "Port": 9080
            }
        },
        "Tags": [],
        "Weights": {
            "Passing": 1,
            "Warning": 1
        }
    }
}
```

You can surely picture now how you would work with Consul as a client service if you didn't have the Spring abstraction. First, all services would need to know the HTTP host and port to reach the registry. Then, if the service wanted to interact with the Gamification API, it would use Consul's Service API to get the list of available instances. The API also has an endpoint to retrieve information about the current health status for a given service identifier. Following a client-side discovery approach, the service would apply load balancing (e.g., round robin) and pick one healthy instance from the list. Then, knowing the address and the port to target the request, the client service could perform the request. You don't need to implement this logic since Spring Cloud Consul does that for you, including load balancing, as we cover in the next section.

Given that Gateway is the only service in your system that is calling others, that's where you'll put into practice the Consul's service discovery logic. However, before doing that, we need to introduce the pattern you're still missing: the load balancer.

Spring Cloud Load Balancer

You'll implement a client-side discovery approach, where the backend services query the registry and decide which instance to call if there is more than one available. This last part is logic you could build yourself, but it's even easier to rely on tools that do that for you. The Spring Cloud load balancer project (https://github.com/spring-cloud/spring-cloud-commons/tree/main/spring-cloud-loadbalancer) is a component of Spring Cloud Commons that integrates with the service discovery integrations (both Consul and Eureka) to provide a simple load balancer implementation. By default, it autoconfigures a round-robin load balancer that goes through all instances iteratively.

As mentioned earlier, Netflix's Ribbon used to be the preferred choice to implement the load balancer pattern. Since it's in maintenance mode, let's discard that option and choose the Spring's load balancer implementation. Both Ribbon and the Spring Cloud load balancer are included as dependencies in the Spring Cloud Consul starter, but you can switch between the two using configuration flags or explicitly excluding one of the dependencies (like you did when adding the Consul starter).

To make load-balanced calls between two applications, you can simply use the @ LoadBalanced annotation when creating a RestTemplate object. Then, you use the service name as the hostname in your URLs when performing requests to that service. The Spring Cloud Consul and load balancer components will do the rest, querying the registry and selecting the next instance in order.

You used to have a call from the Multiplication service to the Gamification service before you moved to an event-driven approach, so let's use that one as an example. Listing 8-23 shows how you could have integrated service discovery and load balancing in the client, the Multiplication microservice. This was also illustrated in Figure 8-8. As you can see, you only need to declare a RestTemplate bean configured with the @ LoadBalanced annotation and use the http://gamification/attempts URL. Note that you don't need to specify the port number, because it'll be included in the resolved instance URL after contacting the registry.

Listing 8-23. Example of How to Use a RestTemplate with Load Balancing Capabilities

```
@Configuration
public class RestConfiguration {
    @LoadBalanced
    @Bean
    RestTemplate restTemplate() {
        return new RestTemplate();
    }
}
@Slf4j
@Service
public class GamificationServiceClient {
    private final RestTemplate restTemplate;
```

```java
    public GamificationServiceClient(final RestTemplate restTemplate) {
        this.restTemplate = restTemplate;
    }
    public boolean sendAttempt(final ChallengeAttempt attempt) {
        try {
            ChallengeSolvedDTO dto = new ChallengeSolvedDTO(attempt.
            getId(),
                    attempt.isCorrect(), attempt.getFactorA(),
                    attempt.getFactorB(), attempt.getUser().getId(),
                    attempt.getUser().getAlias());
            ResponseEntity<String> r = restTemplate.postForEntity(
                    "http://gamification/attempts", dto,
                    String.class);
            log.info("Gamification service response: {}",
            r.getStatusCode());
            return r.getStatusCode().is2xxSuccessful();
        } catch (Exception e) {
            log.error("There was a problem sending the attempt.", e);
            return false;
        }
    }
}
```

You won't follow this path since you already got rid of HTTP calls between your microservices, but this is a good approach when you need to have interservice HTTP interactions. With service discovery and load balancing, you reduce the risk of failure since you increase the chances that there is at least one instance available to handle these synchronous requests.

The plan here is to integrate service discovery and load balancing in the gateway. See Figure 8-13.

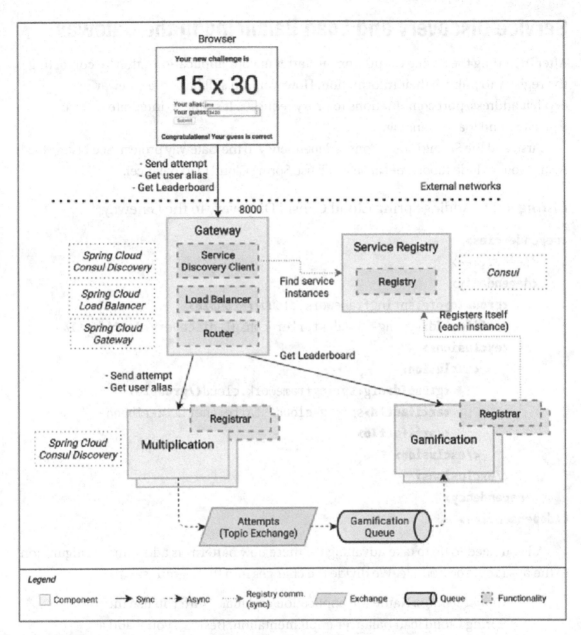

Figure 8-13. *Gateway, service discovery, and load balancing in your system*

Service Discovery and Load Balancing in the Gateway

After including the Spring Cloud Consul starter in your applications, they're contacting the registry to publish their information. However, you still have the gateway using explicit address/port combinations to proxy requests. It's time to integrate service discovery and load balancing.

First, add the Spring Cloud Consul dependency to the Gateway project. See Listing 8-24. Again, you exclude Ribbon because you'll use Spring Cloud load balancer.

Listing 8-24. Adding Spring Cloud Consul Discovery to the Gateway

```
<dependencies>
    <!-- ... -->
    <dependency>
        <groupId>org.springframework.cloud</groupId>
        <artifactId>spring-cloud-starter-consul-discovery</artifactId>
        <exclusions>
            <exclusion>
                <groupId>org.springframework.cloud</groupId>
                <artifactId>spring-cloud-starter-netflix-ribbon
                </artifactId>
            </exclusion>
        </exclusions>
    </dependency>
</dependencies>
```

All you need to do to take advantage of these new patterns is add some configuration to the application.yml file. We divide the changes into three groups.

- *Global settings*: Name the application and make sure you use the Spring Cloud load balancer implementation. Besides, you'll add a configuration parameter to instruct the service discovery client to retrieve only the healthy services.

- *Routing configuration*: Instead of using explicit hosts and ports, switch to service names with a URL pattern that also enables load balancing.

- *Resilience*: In case the gateway fails to proxy a request to a service, you want it to retry a few times. We elaborate on this topic in a bit.

See Listing 8-25 for the complete source code of your new Gateway configuration (application.yml) including these changes.

Listing 8-25. Gateway Configuration Including Load Balancing

```
server:
  port: 8000
spring:
  application:
    name: gateway
  cloud:
    loadbalancer:
      ribbon:
        # Not needed since we excluded the dependency, but
        # still good to add it here for better readability
        enabled: false
    consul:
      enabled: true
      discovery:
        # Get only services that are passing the health check
        query-passing: true
    gateway:
      routes:
        - id: multiplication
          uri: lb://multiplication/
          predicates:
            - Path=/challenges/**,/attempts,/attempts/**,/users/**
        - id: gamification
          uri: lb://gamification/
          predicates:
            - Path=/leaders
      globalcors:
        cors-configurations:
          '[/**]':
```

```
            allowedOrigins: "http://localhost:3000"
            allowedHeaders:
              - "*"
            allowedMethods:
              - "GET"
              - "POST"
              - "OPTIONS"
      default-filters:
        - name: Retry
          args:
            retries: 3
            methods: GET,POST
```

With the `query-passing` parameter set to `true`, the Spring implementation will use the Consul API with a filter to retrieve only those services that have a passing health check. You only want to proxy requests to healthy instances. A `false` value could make sense in cases where the service doesn't poll very often for the updated service list. In that case, it's good to get the complete list because you don't know their latest status and they have mechanisms to deal with unhealthy instances (for example retries, as you'll learn soon).

The most relevant changes are those applied to the URLs. As you can see, you use URLs like `lb://multiplication/`. Since you added the Consul client, the application will use the Service API to resolve the service name, `multiplication`, to the available instances. The `lb://` prefix tells Spring that it should use the load balancer.

In addition to the basic configuration, the gateway filter applies to all the requests because it's under the `default-filters` node: the Retry `GatewayFilter` (see `https://docs.spring.io/spring-cloud-gateway/docs/current/reference/html/#the-retry-gatewayfilter-factory` for details). This filter intercepts error responses and transparently retries the request again. When combined with a load balancer, this means the request will be proxied to the next instance, so you get a nice resilience pattern (retry) easily. You configure this filter to make three retries maximum for the HTTP methods you're using, which is more than enough to cover most failure situations. If all the retries fail, the gateway returns an error response to the client (service unavailable) because it can't proxy the request.

You might be wondering why it's necessary to include retries in the service discovery client, because that you configured it to get only healthy instances. In theory, if they're all healthy, all calls should succeed. To understand this, we have to review how Consul (and typically any other service discovery tool) works. Each service registers itself with a configured health check to be polled every ten seconds (the default value, but you can change it). The registry doesn't know in real time when services are not ready to handle the traffic. It could be the case that Consul successfully checks the health of a given instance and that one goes down immediately after. The registry will list this instance as healthy for a few seconds (almost ten with your configuration) until it notices it's not available during the next check. Since you want to minimize request errors during that interval too, you can take advantage of the retry pattern to cover these situations. Once the registry is updated, the Gateway won't get the unhealthy instance in the service list, so the retries won't be necessary anymore. Note that lowering the time between checks can reduce the number of errors, but it increases the network traffic.

Circuit Breakers   There might be cases where you don't want to keep trying future requests to a given service after you know it's failing. By doing that, you can save time wasted in response timeouts and alleviate potential congestion of the target service. This is especially useful for external service calls when there are no other resilience mechanisms in place like the service registry with health checks.

For these scenarios, you can use a circuit breaker. The circuit is *closed* when everything works fine. After a configurable number of request failures, the circuit becomes *open*. Then, the requests are not even tried, and the circuit breaker implementation returns a predefined response. Now and then, the circuit may switch to *half-open* to check again if the target service is working. In that case, the circuit will transition to *close*. If it's still failing, it goes back to the *open* state. Check out `https://martinfowler.com/bliki/CircuitBreaker.html` for more information about this pattern.

After applying the new configuration, the Gateway microservice connects to Consul to find the available instances of other microservices and their network locations. Then, it balances the load based on a simple round-robin algorithm included in Spring Cloud load balancer. see Figure 8-8 again for a complete overview.

Given that you added the Consul starter, the Gateway service is also registering itself in Consul. That is not strictly necessary since other services won't call the gateway, but it's still useful to check its status. Alternatively, you could set the configuration parameter `spring.cloud.consul.discovery.register` to `false` to keep using the service discovery client features but disable the registration of the Gateway service.

In this setup, all the external HTTP traffic (not between microservices) goes through the Gateway microservice via `localhost:8000`. In a production environment, you would typically expose this HTTP interface on port 80 (or 443 if you use HTTPS) and use a DNS address (e.g., `bookgame.tpd.io`) to point to the IP where your server lives. Nevertheless, there would be a single entry point for public access, and that makes this service a critical part of your system. It must be as highly available as possible. If the Gateway service goes down, your entire system goes down.

To reduce the risk, you could introduce *DNS load balancing* (a hostname that points to multiple IP addresses) to add redundancy to the gateway. However, it relies on the client (e.g., a browser) to manage the list of IP addresses and handle failover when one of the hosts doesn't respond (see `https://www.nginx.com/resources/glossary/dns-load-balancing/` for an explanation). You could see this as an extra layer on top of the gateway, which adds client-side discovery (DNS resolution to a list of IP addresses), load balancing (choose an IP address from the list), and fault tolerance (try another IP after a timeout or error). This is not a typical approach.

Cloud providers such as Amazon, Microsoft, and Google offer the routing and load balancing patterns as managed services with high availability guarantees, so that's also an alternative to making sure the gateway remains operational at all times. Kubernetes, on the other hand, allows you to create a load balancer on top of your own gateway, so you can add redundancy to that layer too. You'll read more about platform implementations at the end of this chapter.

Playing with Service Discovery and Load Balancing

Let's put into practice the service discovery and load balancing features.

Before running your applications, you'll add a log line to `UserController` (Multiplication) and `LeaderBoardController` (Gamification) to quickly see in the logs the interactions with their APIs. See Listings 8-26 and 8-27.

Listing 8-26. Adding a Log Line to UserController

```
@Slf4j
@RequiredArgsConstructor
@RestController
@RequestMapping("/users")
public class UserController {
    private final UserRepository userRepository;
    @GetMapping("/{idList}")
    public List<User> getUsersByIdList(@PathVariable final List<Long>
    idList) {
        log.info("Resolving aliases for users {}", idList);
        return userRepository.findAllByIdIn(idList);
    }
}
```

Listing 8-27. Adding a Log Line to LeaderBoardController

```
@Slf4j
@RestController
@RequestMapping("/leaders")
@RequiredArgsConstructor
class LeaderBoardController {
    private final LeaderBoardService leaderBoardService;
    @GetMapping
    public List<LeaderBoardRow> getLeaderBoard() {
        log.info("Retrieving leaderboard");
        return leaderBoardService.getCurrentLeaderBoard();
    }
}
```

Now run your complete system. The required steps are the same as before, plus the new command to run the service registry:

1. Run the RabbitMQ server.

2. Run the Consul agent in development mode.

3. Start the Multiplication microservice.

4. Start the Gamification microservice.

5. Start the new Gateway microservice.

6. Run the frontend app.

Once you run the minimal setup, you add one extra instance of each of your services running business logic: Multiplication and Gamification. Remember that you need to override the `server.port` property. From a terminal, you could use the commands shown in Listing 8-28 in two separate tabs or windows (note that the folder where you run each command is different).

Listing 8-28. Running Two Additional Instances of Multiplication and Gamification

```
multiplication $ ./mvnw spring-boot:run -Dspring-boot.run.arguments="--
server.port=9080"
[... logs ...]
gamification $ ./mvnw spring-boot:run -Dspring-boot.run.arguments="--
server.port=9081"
[... logs ...]
```

All the instances will publish their details in the registry (Consul). Besides, all of them can act as registry clients to retrieve the details of the different instances of a given service name and where they are located. In your system, this is done only from the gateway. See an overview of the services in the Consul UI (the Nodes/Services section) after booting up the two extra instances in Figure 8-14.

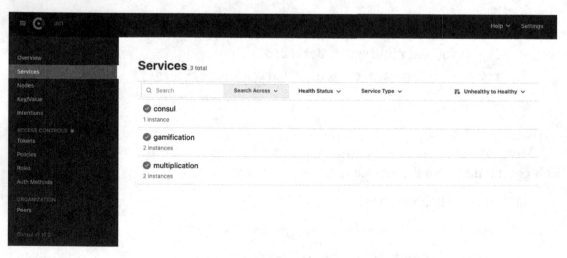

Figure 8-14. *Consul: multiple instances*

Verifying that the gateway's load balancer works is simple: check the logs of both Gamification service instances. With the newly added log lines, you can quickly see how both are getting alternating requests from the UI, related to leaderboard updates. If you refresh the browser's page a few times to force new challenge requests, you'll see similar behavior. Listings 8-29, 8-30, 8-31, and 8-32 show extracts for the same time window of logs for both Multiplication instances and both Gamification instances. As you can see, requests alternate between the available instances every five seconds.

Listing 8-29. Logs for Multiplication, First Instance (Port 8080)

```
2023-07-27T14:44:11.477+05:30   INFO 12391 --- [nio-8080-exec-6]
m.b.multiplication.user.UserController   : Resolving aliases for users
[125, 49, 72, 60, 101, 1, 96, 107, 3, 45, 6, 9, 14, 123]
2023-07-27T14:44:11.489+05:30   INFO 12391 --- [nio-8080-exec-7]
m.b.multiplication.user.UserController   : Resolving aliases for users
[125, 49, 72, 60, 101, 1, 96, 107, 3, 45, 6, 9, 14, 123]
2023-07-27T14:44:11.610+05:30   INFO 12391 --- [nio-8080-exec-9]
m.b.multiplication.user.UserController   : Resolving aliases for users
[125, 49, 72, 60, 101, 1, 96, 107, 3, 45, 6, 9, 14, 123]
```

Listing 8-30. Logs for Multiplication, Second Instance (Port 9080)

```
2023-07-27T14:44:11.497+05:30   INFO 49793 --- [nio-9080-exec-7]
m.b.m.challenge.ChallengeController      : Generating a random challenge:
Challenge(factorA=58, factorB=96)
2023-07-27T14:44:11.559+05:30   INFO 49793 --- [nio-9080-exec-8]
m.b.multiplication.user.UserController   : Resolving aliases for users
[125, 49, 72, 60, 101, 1, 96, 107, 3, 45, 6, 9, 14, 123]
2023-07-27T14:47:11.590+05:30   INFO 49793   INFO 49793 --- [io-9080-exec-10]
m.b.multiplication.user.UserController   : Resolving aliases for users
[125, 49, 72, 60, 101, 1, 96, 107, 3, 45, 6, 9, 14, 123]
```

Listing 8-31. Logs for Gamification, First Instance (Port 8081)

```
2023-07-27T14:29:58.317+05:30   INFO 49557 --- [nio-8081-exec-6]
m.b.g.game.LeaderBoardController      : Retrieving leaderboard
2023-07-27T14:29:58.437+05:30   INFO 49557 --- [nio-8081-exec-8]
m.b.g.game.LeaderBoardController      : Retrieving leaderboard
2023-07-27T14:29:58.527+05:30   INFO 49557 --- [io-8081-exec-10]
m.b.g.game.LeaderBoardController      : Retrieving leaderboard
```

Listing 8-32. Logs for Gamification, Second Instance (Port 9081)

```
2023-07-27T14:42:57.766+05:30   INFO 3485 --- [nio-9081-exec-4]
m.b.g.game.LeaderBoardController      : Retrieving leaderboard
2023-07-27T14:42:57.780+05:30   INFO 3485 --- [nio-9081-exec-6]
m.b.g.game.LeaderBoardController      : Retrieving leaderboard
2023-07-27T14:42:57.995+05:30   INFO 3485 --- [nio-9081-exec-8]
m.b.g.game.LeaderBoardController      : Retrieving leaderboard
```

That's a great achievement: You scaled up your system, and everything works as expected. The HTTP traffic is now balanced across all instances equally, in a similar way to how your RabbitMQ setup is distributing messages across consumers. You just smoothly doubled the capacity of your system!

Actually, you could start as many instances as you want of both microservices, and the load would be transparently distributed across all of them. Besides, with the gateway, you made your API clients unaware of your internal services, and you could easily implement cross-cutting concerns such as user authentication or monitoring.

You should also check whether you're achieving the other nonfunctional requirements you aimed for: resilience, high availability, and fault tolerance. Let's start creating some chaos.

To see what happens when services become unexpectedly unavailable, you can stop them via your IDE or with a Ctrl-C signal in the terminal. However, that doesn't cover all potential incidents you could have in real life. When you do that, the Spring Boot application stops gracefully, so it has the opportunity to deregister itself from Consul. You want to simulate a *major incident* like a network issue or a service abruptly terminated. The best way to mimic that is to kill the Java process for a given instance. To know which process to kill, examine the logs. The default Spring Boot's Logback configuration prints the process ID after the log level (e.g., INFO) in every log line. As an example, this line indicates you're running the Gamification microservice with a process ID of 97817:

```
2023-07-27T14:44:51.002+05:30 INFO 3485 --- [main]
m.b.m.GamificationApplication      : Started GamificationApplication in
5.371 seconds (JVM running for 11.054)
```

In a Linux or Mac system, you can kill the process with the kill command, passing the -9 argument to force an immediate termination.

```
$ kill -9 3485
```

If you're running Windows, you can use the taskkill command with the /F flag to force its termination.

```
> taskkill /PID 3485 /F
```

Now that you know how to create disruption, kill one of the Gamification microservice's instance processes. Make sure you have the UI opened in a browser so it keeps making requests to the backend. What you'll see is how, after you kill one of the instances, the other one receives all requests and responds to them successfully. Users don't even notice this. The leaderboard, which calls the API in the Gamification service, remains working. Users can also send new challenges; all attempts will end up in the only instance available. What happens here is that the retry filter in the gateway executes a second request transparently, which gets routed to the healthy instance thanks to the load balancer. See Figure 8-15.

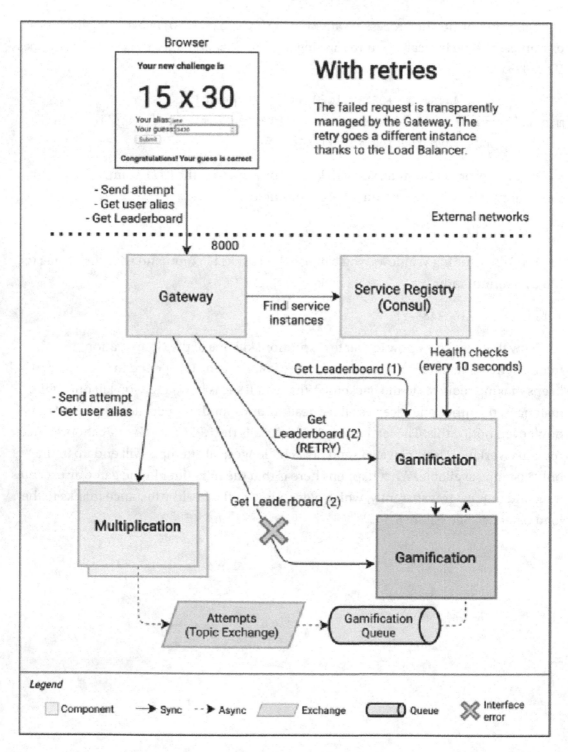

Figure 8-15. *Resilience: retry pattern*

You also want to verify how the patterns you introduced collaborate to achieve this successful result. To do that, temporarily remove the retry filter configuration in the gateway. See Listing 8-33.

Listing 8-33. Commenting a Block of Configuration in the Gateway

```
# We can comment this block of the configuration
#  default-filters:
#    - name: Retry
#      args:
#        retries: 3
#        methods: GET,POST
```

Then, rebuild and restart the Gateway service (to apply the new configuration) and repeat a similar scenario. Make sure you boot up a second instance of Gamification again and give some time for the Gateway service to start routing traffic to it. Then, kill one of its instances while you look at the UI. What you'll see this time is that every other request fails to complete, causing an alternating error while displaying the leaderboard. This happens because Consul needs some time (the configured health check interval) to detect that the service is down. In the meantime, the gateway still gets both instances as healthy and proxies some requests to a dead server. See Figure 8-16. The retry mechanism you just removed handled this error transparently and made a second request to the next instance in the list, the one still working.

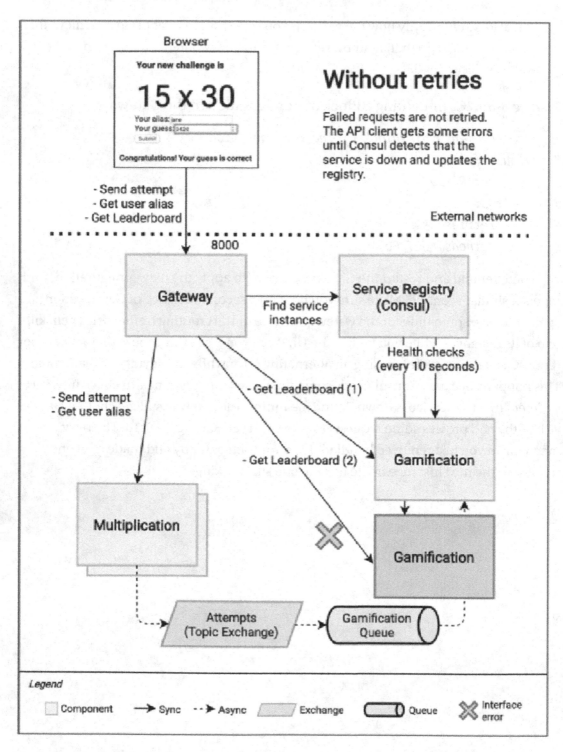

Figure 8-16. *Resilience: no retry pattern*

It Works on My Machine   Note that if you accidentally kill the process right before the health check, Consul will notice the problem immediately. In that case, you may not see the error in the UI. You can try the same scenario again, or you can configure a longer health check interval in Spring Cloud Consul (via the application properties), so you have a higher chance of reproducing this error scenario.

The Consul registry UI also reflects the failing health checks if you navigate to Services. See Figure 8-17.

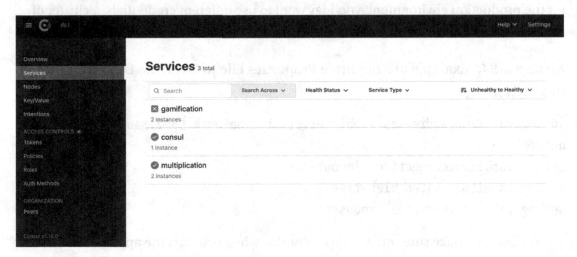

Figure 8-17. *Consul UI: health check fails after killing the service*

You completed an important milestone in your learning path: you implemented scalability in a microservice architecture. Besides, you achieved proper fault tolerance via a load balancer that uses a service discovery registry, which is aware of the health of the different components in your system. We hope that the practical approach has helped you understand all these key concepts.

Configuration per Environment

As introduced in Chapter 2, one of the main advantages of Spring Boot is its ability to configure profiles. A *profile* is a set of configuration properties that you can enable depending on your needs. For example, you could switch between connecting to a local RabbitMQ server while testing locally and the real RabbitMQ server running on production when you deploy it to that environment.

To introduce a new `rabbitprod` profile, create a file named `application-rabbitprod.properties`. Spring Boot uses the `application-{profile}` naming convention (for both `properties` and YAML formats) to define profiles in separate files. See Listing 8-34 for some example properties you could include. If you use this profile for the production environment, you may want to use different credentials, a cluster of nodes to connect to, a secure interface, and so on.

Listing 8-34. Example of a Separate Properties File to Override Default Values in Production

```
spring.rabbitmq.addresses=rabbitserver1.tpd.network:5672,rabbitserver2.tpd.
network:5672
spring.rabbitmq.connection-timeout=20s
spring.rabbitmq.ssl.enabled=true
spring.rabbitmq.username=produser1
```

You have to make sure you enable this profile when you start the application in the target environment. To do that, you use the `spring.profiles.active` property. Spring Boot aggregates the base configuration (in `application.properties`) with the values in this file. In this case, all extra properties will be added to the resulting configuration. You can use a Spring Boot's Maven plugin command to enable this new profile for the multiplication microservice:

```
multiplication $ ./mvnw spring-boot:run -Dspring-boot.run.arguments="--
spring.profiles.active=rabbitprod"
```

As you can imagine, all your microservices could have a lot of common configuration values per environment. Not only are the connection details for RabbitMQ probably the same, but so are some extra values you added, like the exchange name (amqp.exchange. attempts). The same applies to the common configuration for databases or in general to any other Spring Boot configuration that you want to apply to all your microservices.

You could keep these values in separate files per microservice, per environment, and per tool. For example, these four files could include different configurations for RabbitMQ and the H2 database in the staging and production environments.

- application-rabbitprod.properties

- application-databaseprod.properties

- application-rabbitstaging.properties

- application-databasestaging.properties

Then, you could copy them across microservices wherever they're needed. By grouping the configuration into separate profiles, you can reuse these values easily.

However, keeping all these copies still involves a lot of maintenance. If you want to change one of the values in these common configuration blocks, you have to replace the corresponding file in each project's folder.

A better approach is to put this configuration in a common place in your system and make the applications sync its contents before they start. Then, you keep a centralized configuration per environment, so you need to adjust the values only once. See Figure 8-18. The good news is that this is a well-known pattern, known as *externalized* (or centralized) *configuration*, so there are out-of-the-box solutions to build a centralized configuration server.

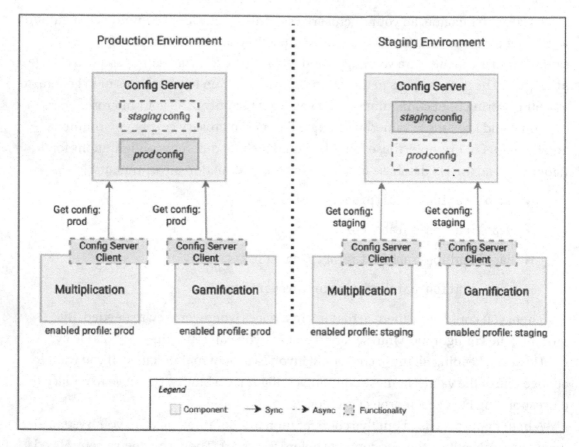

Figure 8-18. *Centralized configuration: overview*

The first solution that comes out from a simple web search when looking for a configuration server pattern for Spring is the Spring Cloud Config Server project. This is a native implementation included in the Spring Cloud family, which allows you to keep a set of configuration files distributed in folders and exposed via a REST API. On the client side, the projects using this dependency access the config server and request the corresponding configuration resources, depending on their active profiles. The only drawback of this solution is that you need to create another microservice to act as the configuration server and expose the centralized files.

An alternative is to use Consul KV, a feature included in the default Consul package that you didn't explore yet. Consul KV is a simple, distributed key-value store that can store configuration data, metadata, and other small pieces of information to be shared across a cluster. Spring Cloud also has an integration with this tool to implement a centralized configuration server. You use this approach to reuse components and keep your system as simple as possible, with Consul combining service discovery, health checks, and centralized configuration.

Configuration in Consul

Consul KV is a key-value store installed with the Consul agent. Like with the service discovery feature, you can access this functionality via a REST API and a user interface. When you set up Consul as a cluster, this feature also benefits from replication, so there is less risk of data loss or downtime due to services being unable to get their configuration.

This simple functionality can be also accessed from the browser since it's included in the Consul agent you already installed. With the agent running, navigate to `http://localhost:8500/ui/dc1/kv` (the Key/Value tab). Now, click Create. You'll see the editor to create a new key-value pair, as shown in Figure 8-19.

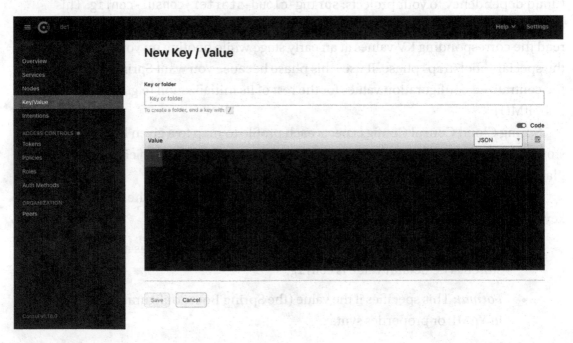

Figure 8-19. *Consul: creating a key-value pair*

You can use the toggle to switch between the code and the plain editor. The code editor has support for syntax coloring in a few notations, including YAML. Note that, as shown in Figure 8-19 under the Text field, you can also create folders if you add a forward slash character to the end of the key name. You'll put this into practice soon.

The Consul KV REST API also allows you to create key-value pairs and folders via HTTP calls and retrieve them using their key names. Check out `https://developer` `.hashicorp.com/consul/api-docs/kv` if you're curious about how it works. Like with the service discovery feature, you won't need to interact with this API directly since you'll use a Spring abstraction that communicates with Consul KV: Spring Cloud Consul Config.

Spring Cloud Consul Config

The Spring Cloud project that implements centralized configuration with Consul KV is Spring Cloud Consul Configuration. To use this module, you need to add a new Spring Cloud dependency to your projects: `spring-cloud-starter-consul-config`. This artifact includes autoconfiguration classes that will try to find the Consul agent and read the corresponding KV values at an early stage while booting up your application, the special "bootstrap" phase. It uses this phase because you want Spring Boot to apply the centralized configuration values for the rest of its initialization (e.g., to connect to RabbitMQ).

Spring Cloud Consul Config expects each profile to map to a given key in the KV store. Its value should be a set of Spring Boot configuration values, in either YAML or plain format (`.properties`).

You can configure a few settings that help your application find the corresponding keys in the server. These are the most relevant ones:

- *Prefix*: This is the root folder in Consul KV where all profiles are stored. The default value is `config`.

- *Format*: This specifies if the value (the Spring Boot configuration) is in YAML or properties syntax.

- *Default context*: This is the name of the folder used by all applications as common properties.

- *Profile separator*: Keys may combine multiple profiles. In that case, you can specify the character you want to use as a separator (e.g., with a comma `prod,extra-logging`).

- *Data key*: This is the name of the key that holds the properties or YAML content.

All the configuration values related to the setup of the config server must be placed in a separate file for each of your applications, called `bootstrap.yml` or `bootstrap.properties` (depending on the format you choose). See Figure 8-20.

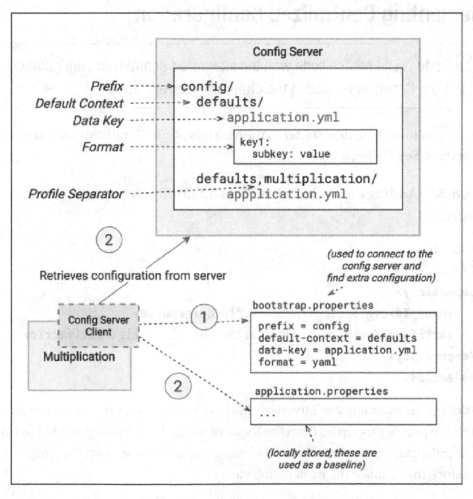

Figure 8-20. *Config server properties: explanation*

Keep in mind that, as shown in Figure 8-20, there is a difference between the application configuration to connect to the config server (in the bootstrap file) and the application configuration that results from merging the local properties (e.g., application.properties) with those downloaded from the config server. Since the first is a metaconfiguration, it can't be downloaded from the server, so you have to copy these values across your projects in the corresponding bootstrap configuration files.

Given that all these concepts are hard to understand without an example, let's use the system to explain how Consul Config works.

Implementing Centralized Configuration

Source Code   The source code with the integrated centralized configuration solution from Consul is located in the chapter08c repository.

First, you need to add the new starter to the Multiplication, Gamification, and Gateway microservices. See Listing 8-35.

Listing 8-35. Adding the Spring Cloud Consul Config Dependency to Your Microservices

```
<dependencies>
    <!-- ... -->
    <dependency>
        <groupId>org.springframework.cloud</groupId>
        <artifactId>spring-cloud-starter-consul-config</artifactId>
    </dependency>
</dependencies>
```

By doing that, your apps will try to connect to Consul during the bootstrap phase and fetch the profile properties from the KV store using the defaults provided in Consul KV autoconfiguration. However, instead of using the defaults, we override some of these settings since that'll make the explanation clearer.

The Multiplication and Gamification projects use the `properties` format, so let's be consistent and create a separate file at the same level, named `bootstrap.properties`. In both applications, you'll set up the same settings. See Listing 8-36.

Listing 8-36. The New bootstrap.properties File in Multiplication and Gamification

```
spring.cloud.consul.config.prefixes=config
spring.cloud.consul.config.format=yaml
spring.cloud.consul.config.default-context=defaults
spring.cloud.consul.config.data-key=application.yml
```

The `bootstrap.properties` file is loaded before the `application.properties` file. This means that any properties present in the `bootstrap.properties` file will take precedence over those present in the `application.properties` file. The reason for this is that the `bootstrap.properties` file is used to configure the essential components of the application, such as the config server and client. These components need to be properly configured before the application can start running.

Note   We chose YAML as the format for the remote configuration, but the local file is in the `.properties` format. That's not a problem at all. Spring Cloud Consul Config can merge the values contained in the remote `application.yml` key with those stored locally in a different format.

Then, you create the equivalent settings in a `bootstrap.yml` file in the Gateway project, where you employed YAML for the application configuration. See Listing 8-37.

Listing 8-37. The New bootstrap.yml File in the Gateway Project

```
spring:
  cloud:
    consul:
      config:
        data-key: application.yml
        prefix: config
        format: yaml
        default-context: defaults
```

With these settings, your goal is to store all configuration in a root folder named config in Consul KV. Inside, you'll have a defaults folder, which may contain a key named application.yml with the configuration that applies to all your microservices. You can have extra folders per application, or per combination of application and profiles that you want to use, and each of them may contain the application.yml key with the properties that should be added or overridden. To avoid mixing up formats in the configuration server, we stick to the YAML syntax. Review Figure 8-20 again to understand the overall structure of the configuration. What you've done until now is add the bootstrap files to Multiplication, Gamification, and Gateway, so they can connect to the config server and find the externalized configuration (if any). To enable this behavior, you added the Spring Cloud Consul Config starter dependency to all these projects too.

To use a more representative example, you could create the hierarchy shown in Listing 8-38 as folders and keys in Consul KV.

Listing 8-38. An Example Configuration Structure in the Configuration Server

```
+- config
|  +- defaults
|      \- application.yml
|  +- defaults,production
|      \- application.yml
|  +- defaults,rabbitmq-production
|      \- application.yml
|  +- defaults,database-production
|      \- application.yml
|  +- multiplication,production
|      \- application.yml
|  +- gamification,production
|      \- application.yml
```

Then, if you run the Multiplication application with a list of active profiles equal to production,rabbitmq-production,database-production, the processing order would be the following (from lower to higher precedence):

1. The baseline values are included in the local application.properties of the project that is accessing the configuration server, in this example Multiplication.

2. Then, Spring Boot merges and overrides the remote values included in the `application.yml` key inside the `defaults` folder, because it applies to all the services.

3. The next step is to merge the default values for all active profiles. That means all files that match the `defaults,{profile}` pattern: `defaults,production`, `defaults,rabbitmq-production`, `defaults,database-production`. Note that, if there are multiple profiles specified, the last one's values win.

4. After that, it tries to find more specific settings for the corresponding application name and active profiles, following the pattern `{application},{profile}`. In this example, the key `multiplication,production` matches the pattern, so its configuration values will be merged. The precedence order is the same as before: the last profile in the enumeration wins.

See Figure 8-21 for a visual representation that will help you understand how all the configuration files are applied.

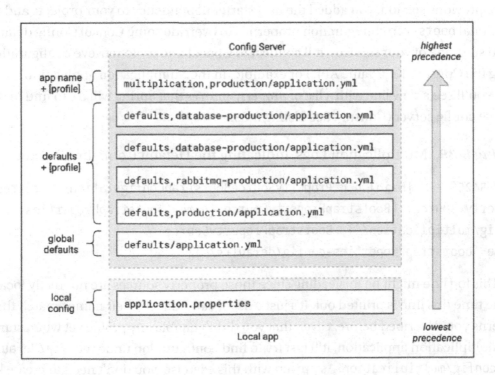

Figure 8-21. *Configuration stack example*

A practical approach to structure configuration values could be as follows:

- Use `defaults` when you want to add global configuration to all the applications for all the environments such as when customizing JSON serialization.

- Use `defaults,{profile}` with a profile name representing a `{tool}`-`{environment}` pair to set up common values for a given tool per environment. For example, in this case, RabbitMQ connection values could be included to `rabbitmq-production`.

- Use `{application},{profile}` with a profile name equal to `{environment}` to set up specific settings for an application in a given environment. For example, you could reduce logging of the Multiplication microservice on production using properties inside `multiplication,production`.

Centralized Configuration in Practice

In the previous section, you added the new starter dependency to your projects and the additional `bootstrap` configuration properties to override some Consul Config defaults. If you start one of your services, it'll connect to Consul and try to retrieve configuration using the Consul's Key/Value API. For example, in the Multiplication application's logs, you'll see a new line with a list of *property sources* that Spring will try to find in the remote config server (Consul). See Listing 8-39.

Listing 8-39. Multiplication Logs, Indicating the Default Configuration Sources

```
INFO 54256 --- [main] b.c.PropertySourceBootstrapConfiguration : Located
property source: [BootstrapPropertySource {name='bootstrapProperties-
config/multiplication/'}, BootstrapPropertySource
{name='bootstrapProperties-config/defaults/'}]
```

This log line might be misleading since those property sources are not really located by the time this line is printed out. It's just a list of candidates. Their names match the patterns you described before. Given that you didn't enable any profile yet when starting the Multiplication application, it'll just try to find configuration under `config/defaults` and `config/multiplication`. As proven with this exercise, you don't need to create keys in Consul that match all possible candidates. Keys that don't exist will be just ignored.

Let's start creating some configuration in Consul. From the UI, on the Key/Value tab, click Create and enter `config/` to create the root folder with the same name that you configured in your settings. Since you added the / character in the end, Consul knows it must create a folder. See Figure 8-22.

Figure 8-22. *Consul: creating the config root folder*

Navigate to the `config` folder by clicking the newly created item and create a subfolder called `defaults`. See Figure 8-23.

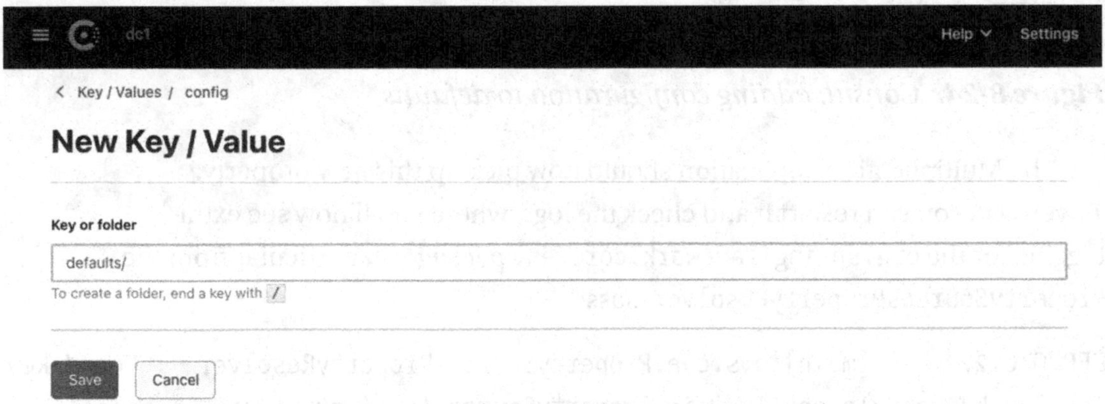

Figure 8-23. *Consul: creating the defaults folder*

Once more, navigate to the newly created folder by clicking it. You'll see the contents of `config/defaults`, which is empty for now. Within this folder, you have to create a key named `application.yml` and add the values you want to apply to all applications by default. Note that we use a key name that looks like a filename to better distinguish folders from configuration contents. Let's add some logging configuration to enable the DEBUG level for a Spring package whose classes output some useful environment information. See Figure 8-24.

Figure 8-24.   *Consul: adding configuration to defaults*

The Multiplication application should now pick up this new property. To verify it, you can restart it and check the logs, where you'll now see extra logging for the org.springframework.core.env package, in particular from the PropertySourcesPropertyResolver class:

```
DEBUG 61279 --- [main] o.s.c.e.PropertySourcesPropertyResolver  : Found key
'spring.h2.console.enabled' in PropertySource 'configurationProperties'
with value of type String
```

This proves that the service reached the centralized configuration server (Consul) and applied the settings included in the existing expected keys, in this case config/defaults.

To make it more interesting, let's enable some profiles for the Multiplication application. From the command line, you can execute the following:

```
multiplication $ ./mvnw spring-boot:run -Dspring-boot.run.arguments="--
spring.profiles.active=production,rabbitmq-production"
```

With that command, you're running the application with the production and rabbitmq-production profiles. The logs show the resulting candidate keys to look for. See Listing 8-40.

Listing 8-40. Multiplication Logs, Indicating All Candidate Property Sources After Enabling Extra Profiles

```
INFO 52274 --- [main] b.c.PropertySourceBootstrapConfiguration : Located
property source: [BootstrapPropertySource {name='bootstrapProperties-
config/multiplication,rabbitmq-production/'}, BootstrapPropertySource
{name='bootstrapProperties-config/multiplication,production/'},
BootstrapPropertySource {name='bootstrapProperties-config/
multiplication/'}, BootstrapPropertySource {name='bootstrapProperties-
config/defaults,rabbitmq-production/'}, BootstrapPropertySource
{name='bootstrapProperties-config/defaults,production/'},
BootstrapPropertySource {name='bootstrapProperties-config/defaults/'}]
```

Let's extract the property source names as a list for a better visualization. The list follows the same order as in the logs, from highest to lowest precedence.

1. `config/multiplication,rabbitmq-production/`

2. `config/multiplication,production/`

3. `config/multiplication/`

4. `config/defaults,rabbitmq-production/`

5. `config/defaults,production/`

6. `config/defaults/`

As described in the previous section, Spring looks for keys that result from combining defaults with each profile, and then it looks for the combination of the application name with each profile. So far, you only added a key config/defaults, so that's the only one the service picks up.

In real life, you probably don't want to have the logs you added to all the applications on the production environment. To achieve this, you can configure the production profile to revert what you did earlier. Since this configuration has higher precedence, it'll override the previous value. Go to Consul UI and create a key in the config folder called defaults,production. Inside, you have to create a key called application.yml, and its value should be the YAML configuration to set the log level of the package back to INFO. See Figure 8-25.

Figure 8-25. *Consul: adding configuration to defaults,production*

When you restart the application using the same last command (which enables the production profile), you'll see how the debug logging for that package is gone.

Remember that, same as you did with this simple logging example, you could add YAML values to tune any other configuration parameters in your Spring Boot applications to adapt them to the production environment. Also, note how you can play with the scope of the configuration using any of the six possible combinations listed earlier, which you got by adding two active profiles. For example, you could add values that apply only to RabbitMQ on production inside a key named defaults,rabbitmq-production. The most specific combinations are multiplication,rabbitmq-production and multiplication,production. Check out Figure 8-21 again for some visual help if you need it.

To demonstrate that configuration is not limited to logging, let's imagine that you want to run the Multiplication microservice on a different port (e.g., 10080) when deployed to production. To get this working, you only need to add an `application.yml` key inside the `multiplication,production` key in Consul and change the `server.port` property. See Figure 8-26.

The next time you start the Multiplication app with the production profile active, you'll see that it's running on this newly specified port:

```
INFO 29019 --- [main] o.s.b.w.embedded.tomcat.TomcatWebServer  : Tomcat
```

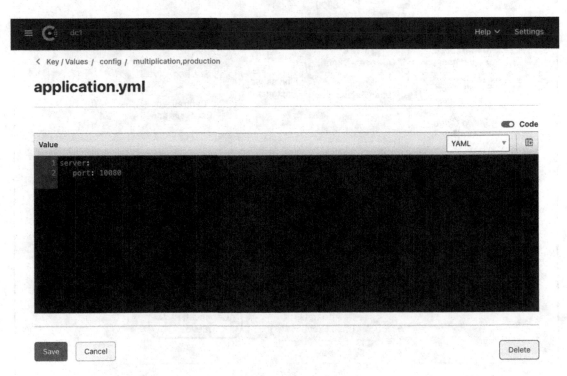

Figure 8-26. *Consul: adding configuration to multiplication,production*

```
started on port(s): 10080 (http) with context path ''
```

With this exercise, you have completed the overview of the centralized configuration pattern. You now know how to minimize the maintenance of common configuration and how to adapt applications to the environment they're running. See Figure 8-27 for an updated architecture view of your system, including the new configuration server.

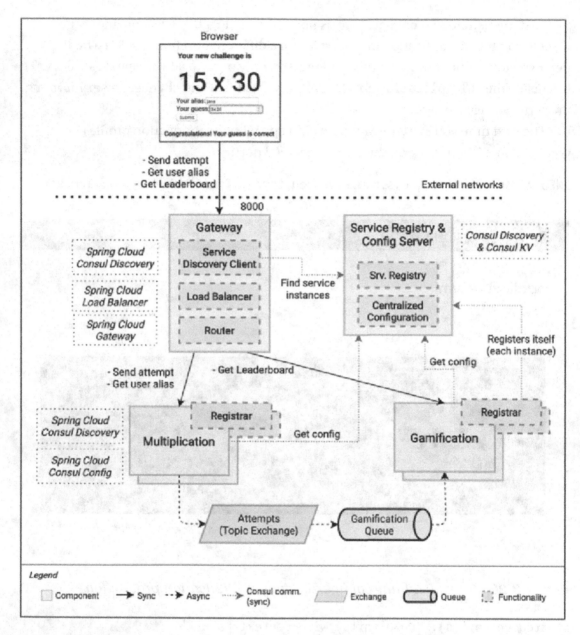

Figure 8-27. *High-level overview: configuration server*

Note that the applications now have a dependency with the configuration server at starting time. Luckily, you can configure Consul to be highly available in production, as we mentioned when covering the service discovery pattern (check out https://developer.hashicorp.com/consul/tutorials/production-deploy/deployment-guide). Additionally, Spring Cloud Consul counts with a retry mechanism by default, so your applications will keep retrying the connection to Consul when it's not available. This dependency is only at starting time; if Consul goes down while your applications are running, they keep working with the configuration loaded initially.

Note: Consul Configuration and Tests   By default, the integration tests in your projects will use the same application configuration. That means your controller tests and the default @SpringBootTest created by the Initializr will fail if Consul is not running because they keep waiting for the configuration server to be available. You can disable Consul Config for tests easily; check out https:// github.com/Book-Microservices-v2/chapter08c if you're curious.

Centralized Logs

You already have multiple components in your system that produce logs (Multiplication, Gamification, Gateway, Consul, and RabbitMQ), and some of them might be running multiple instances. That's a lot of log outputs running independently, which makes it hard to get an overall view of the system activity. If a user reports an error, it would be hard to find out which component or instance failed. Arranging multiple log windows on a single screen would help for a while, but that's not a viable solution when your microservice instances grow in number.

To properly maintain a distributed system like your microservice architecture, you need a central place where you can access all the aggregated logs and search across them.

Log Aggregation Pattern

Basically, the idea is to send all the log outputs from your applications to another component in your system, which will consume them and put them all together. Besides, you want to persist these logs for some time, so this component should have data storage. Ideally, you should be able to navigate through these logs, search, and filter out messages per microservice, instance, class, and so on. To do this, many of these tools offer a user interface that connects to the aggregated logs storage. See Figure 8-28.

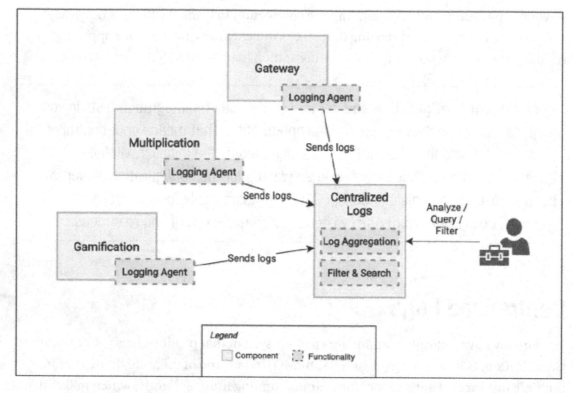

Figure 8-28. *Log aggregation: overview*

A common best practice when implementing the centralized logging approach is to keep the application logic unaware of this pattern. The services should just output messages using a common interface (e.g., a `Logger` in Java). The logging agent that channels these logs to the central aggregator works independently, capturing the output that the application produces. This page on Log Aggregation Microservices Architecture Pattern (`https://microservices.io/patterns/observability/application-logging.html`) has a good overview on this topic.

There are multiple implementations of this pattern available in the market, both free and paid solutions. Among the most popular ones is the ELK stack, an alias for a combination of products from Elastic (`https://www.elastic.co/`): Elasticsearch (the storage system with powerful text search features), Logstash (the agent to channel logs to Elasticsearch from multiple sources), and Kibana (the UI tool to manage and query logs).

Even though setting up an ELK stack is becoming easier over time, it's still not a simple task. For that reason, you won't use an ELK implementation in this book since it could easily extend to cover a full chapter. In any case, we recommend you check the ELK docs (https://www.elastic.co/what-is/elk-stack) after reading this book, so you can learn how to set up a production-ready logging system.

A Simple Solution for Log Centralization

Source Code   The rest of the source code o this chapter is in the repository `chapter08d`. It includes the changes for adding centralized logs, distributed tracing, and containerization.

You'll set up a new microservice to aggregate logs from all your Spring Boot applications. To keep it simple, it won't have a data layer to persist logs; it'll just receive log lines from other services and print them together to the standard output. This basic solution will serve to demonstrate this pattern and the next one, distributed tracing.

To channel the log outputs, you'll use a tool you already have in your system and is perfect for that purpose: RabbitMQ. To capture each logged line in the applications and send them as RabbitMQ messages, you'll benefit from Logback (`https://logback` `.qos.ch/`), the logger implementation you've been using within Spring Boot. Logback is a logging framework for Java that implements SL4J (Simple Logging Facade for Java). Given that this tool is driven by an external configuration file, you don't need to modify the code in your applications.

In Logback, the piece of logic that writes a log line to the specific destination is called an *appender*. This logging library includes some built-in appenders to print messages to the console (`ConsoleAppender`) or files (`FileAppender` and `RollingFileAppender`). You didn't need to configure them because Spring Boot includes some default Logback configuration within its dependencies and also sets up the printed message patterns.

The good news is that Spring AMQP provides a Logback AMQP logging appender that does exactly what you need: it takes each log line and produces a message to a given exchange in RabbitMQ, with a format and some extra options that you can customize.

First, let's prepare the Logback configuration you need to add to your applications. Spring Boot allows you to extend the defaults by creating a file named `logback-spring.xml` in the application resources folder (`src/main/resources`), which will be picked up automatically upon application initialization. See Listing 8-41. In this file, you import the existing default values and create and set a new appender for all messages that have level INFO or higher. The AMQP appender documentation (`https://docs.spring.io/spring-amqp/docs/current/reference/html/#logging`) lists all parameters and their meanings; let's look at the ones you need.

- `applicationId`: Set it to the application name so you can distinguish the source when you aggregate logs.

- `host`: This is the host where RabbitMQ is running. Since it can be different per environment, you'll connect this value to the `spring.rabbitmq.host` Spring property. Spring allows you to do this via the `springProperty` tag. You give this Logback property a name, `rabbitMQHost`, and you use the `${rabbitMQHost:-localhost}` syntax to either use the property value if it's set or use the default `localhost` (defaults are set with the `:-` separator).

- `routingKeyPattern`: This is the routing key per message, which you set to a concatenation of the `applicationId` and `level` (notated with `%p`) for more flexibility if you want to filter on the consumer side.

- `exchangeName`: Specify the name of the exchange in RabbitMQ to publish messages. It'll be a topic exchange by default, so you can call it `logs.topic`.

- `declareExchange`: Set it to `true` to create the exchange if it's not there yet.

- `durable`: Also set this to `true` so the exchange survives server restarts.

- `deliveryMode`: Make it `PERSISTENT` so log messages are stored until they're consumed by the aggregator.

- `generateId`: Set it to `true` so each message will have a unique identifier.

- `charset`: It's a good practice to set it to `UTF-8` to make sure all parties use the same encoding.

Listing 8-41 shows the full contents of the `logback-spring.xml` file in the Gamification project. Note how you're adding a `layout` with a custom `pattern` to your new appender. This way, you can encode your messages including not only the message (`%msg`) but also some extra information like the time (`%d{HH:mm:ss.SSS}`), the thread name (`[%t]`), and the logger class (`%logger{36}`). If you're curious about the pattern notation, check out the Logback's reference docs (`https://logback.qos.ch/manual/layouts.html#conversionWord`). The last part of the file configures the root logger (the default one) to use both the `CONSOLE` appender, defined in one of the included files, and the newly defined `AMQP` appender.

Listing 8-41. New src/main/resources/logback-spring.xml File in the Gamification Project

```
<configuration>
    <include resource="org/springframework/boot/logging/logback/
    defaults.xml" />
    <include resource="org/springframework/boot/logging/logback/console-
    appender.xml" />
    <springProperty scope="context" name="rabbitMQHost" source="spring.
    rabbitmq.host"/>
    <appender name="AMQP"
             class="org.springframework.amqp.rabbit.logback.AmqpAppender">
        <layout>
            <pattern>%d{HH:mm:ss.SSS} [%t] %logger{36} - %msg</pattern>
        </layout>
        <applicationId>gamification</applicationId>
        <host>${rabbitMQHost:-localhost}</host>
        <routingKeyPattern>%property{applicationId}.%p</routingKeyPattern>
        <exchangeName>logs.topic</exchangeName>
        <declareExchange>true</declareExchange>
        <durable>true</durable>
        <deliveryMode>PERSISTENT</deliveryMode>
        <generateId>true</generateId>
        <charset>UTF-8</charset>
    </appender>
```

```
<root level="INFO">
    <appender-ref ref="CONSOLE" />
    <appender-ref ref="AMQP" />
</root>
</configuration>
```

You have to make sure you add this file to the three Spring Boot projects you have: Multiplication, Gamification, and Gateway. In each one of them, you must change the applicationId value accordingly.

In addition to this basic setup of log producers, you can adjust the log level for the class that the appender uses to connect to RabbitMQ as WARN. This is an optional step, but it avoids hundreds of logs when the RabbitMQ server is not available (e.g., while starting up your system). Since the appender is configured during the bootstrap phase, you need to add this configuration setting to the corresponding bootstrap.properties and boostrap.yml files, depending on the project. See Listings 8-42 and 8-43.

Listing 8-42. Reducing RabbitMQ Logging Level in Multiplication and Gamification

```
logging.level.org.springframework.amqp.rabbit.connection.
CachingConnectionFactory = WARN
```

Listing 8-43. Reducing RabbitMQ Logging Level in the Gateway

```
logging:
  level:
    org.springframework.amqp.rabbit.connection.
    CachingConnectionFactory: WARN
```

The next time you start your applications, all logs will be output not only to the console but also as messages produced to the logs.topic exchange in RabbitMQ. You can verify that by accessing the RabbitMQ Web UI at localhost:15672. See Figure 8-29.

Figure 8-29.   RabbitMQ UI: logs exchange

Consuming Logs and Printing Them

Now that you have all logs together published to an exchange, you'll build the consumer side: a new microservice that consumes all these messages and outputs them together.

First, navigate to the Spring Initializr site start.spring.io (https://start.spring.io/) and create a logs project using the same setup as you chose for other applications: Maven and JDK 17. In the list of dependencies, add Spring for RabbitMQ, Spring Web, Validation, Spring Boot Actuator, Lombok, and Consul Configuration. Note that you don't need to make this service discoverable, so don't add Consul Discovery. See Figure 8-30.

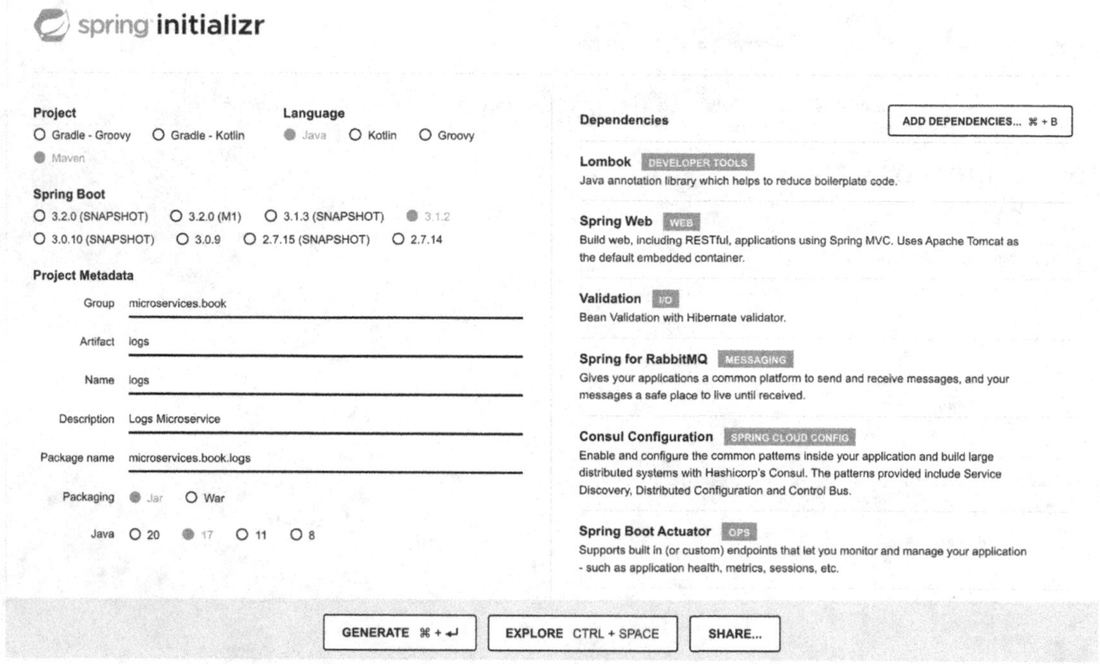

Figure 8-30. *Creating the Logs microservice*

Once you import this project into your workspace, you can add some configuration to make it possible to connect to the configuration server. You're not going to add any specific configuration for now, but it's good to do this to make it consistent with the rest of the microservices. In the `main/src/resources` folder, copy the contents of the `bootstrap.properties` file you included in other projects. Set the application name and a dedicated port in the `application.properties` file as well. See Listing 8-44.

Listing 8-44. Adding Content to the application.properties File in the New Logs Application

```
spring.application.name=logs
server.port=8580
```

You need a Spring Boot configuration class to declare the exchange, the queue where you want to consume the messages from, and the binding object to attach the queue to the topic exchange with a binding key pattern to consume all of them containing the special character (#). See Listing 8-45. Remember that since you added the logging level to the routing keys, you can also adjust this value to get only errors, for example. Anyway, in this case, subscribe to all messages (#).

Listing 8-45. AMQPConfiguration Class in the Logs Application

```java
package microservices.book.logs;
import org.springframework.amqp.core.*;
import org.springframework.context.annotation.Bean;
import org.springframework.context.annotation.Configuration;
@Configuration
public class AMQPConfiguration {
    @Bean
    public TopicExchange logsExchange() {
        return ExchangeBuilder.topicExchange("logs.topic")
                .durable(true)
                .build();
    }
    @Bean
    public Queue logsQueue() {
        return QueueBuilder.durable("logs.queue").build();
    }
    @Bean
    public Binding logsBinding(final Queue logsQueue,
                               final TopicExchange logsExchange) {
        return BindingBuilder.bind(logsQueue)
                .to(logsExchange).with("#");
    }
}
```

The next step is to create a simple service with the @RabbitListener that maps
the logging level of the received messages, passed as a RabbitMQ message header, to a
logging level in the Logs microservice, using the corresponding log.info(),
log.error(), or log.warn(). Note that you use the @Header annotation here to extract
AMQP headers as method arguments. You also use a logging Marker to add the
application name (appId) to the log line without needing to concatenate it as part of the
message. This is a flexible way in the SLF4J standard to add contextual values to logs. See
Listing 8-46.

Listing 8-46. The Consumer Class That Receives All Log Messages via RabbitMQ

```
package microservices.book.logs;

import org.springframework.amqp.rabbit.annotation.RabbitListener;
import org.springframework.messaging.handler.annotation.Header;
import org.springframework.stereotype.Service;

import org.slf4j.Marker;
import org.slf4j.MarkerFactory;

import lombok.extern.slf4j.Slf4j;
@Slf4j
@Service
public class LogsConsumer {
    @RabbitListener(queues = "logs.queue")
    public void log(final String msg,
                    @Header("level") String level,
                    @Header("amqp_appId") String appId) {
        Marker marker = MarkerFactory.getMarker(appId);
        switch (level) {
            case "INFO" -> log.info(marker, msg);
            case "ERROR" -> log.error(marker, msg);
            case "WARN" -> log.warn(marker, msg);
        }
    }
}
```

Finally, customize the log output produced by this new microservice. Since it'll aggregate multiple logs from different services, the most relevant property is the application name. You must override the Spring Boot defaults this time and define a simple format in a logback-spring.xml file for the CONSOLE appender that outputs the marker, the level, and the message. See Listing 8-47.

Listing 8-47. The Logback Configuration for the Logs Application

```
<configuration>
    <appender name="CONSOLE" class="ch.qos.logback.core.ConsoleAppender">
        <layout class="ch.qos.logback.classic.PatternLayout">
            <Pattern>
                [%-15marker] %highlight(%-5level) %msg%n
            </Pattern>
        </layout>
    </appender>
    <root level="INFO">
        <appender-ref ref="CONSOLE" />
    </root>
</configuration>
```

That's all the code you need in this new project. Now you can build the sources and start this new microservice with the rest of the components in your system.

1. Run the RabbitMQ server.

2. Run the Consul agent in development mode.

3. Start the Multiplication microservice.

4. Start the Gamification microservice.

5. Start the Gateway microservice.

6. Start the Logs microservice.

7. Run the frontend app.

Once you start this new microservice, it'll consume all log messages produced by the other applications. To see that in practice, you can solve a challenge. You'll see the log lines shown in Listing 8-48 in the console of the Logs microservice.

Listing 8-48. Centralized Logs in the New Logs Application

```
[multiplication ] INFO  15:14:20.203 [http-nio-8080-exec-1]
m.b.m.c.ChallengeAttemptController - Received new attempt from test1
[gamification   ] INFO  15:14:20.357 [org.springframework.amqp.rabbit.
RabbitListenerEndpointContainer#0-1] m.b.g.game.GameEventHandler -
Challenge Solved Event received: 122
[gamification   ] INFO  15:14:20.390 [org.springframework.amqp.rabbit.
RabbitListenerEndpointContainer#0-1] m.b.g.game.GameServiceImpl - User
test1 scored 10 points for attempt id 122
```

This simple log aggregator didn't take you much time, and now you can search for logs in the same source and see a near-real-time output stream from all your services together. Figure 8-31 shows an updated version of the high-level architecture diagram including this new component.

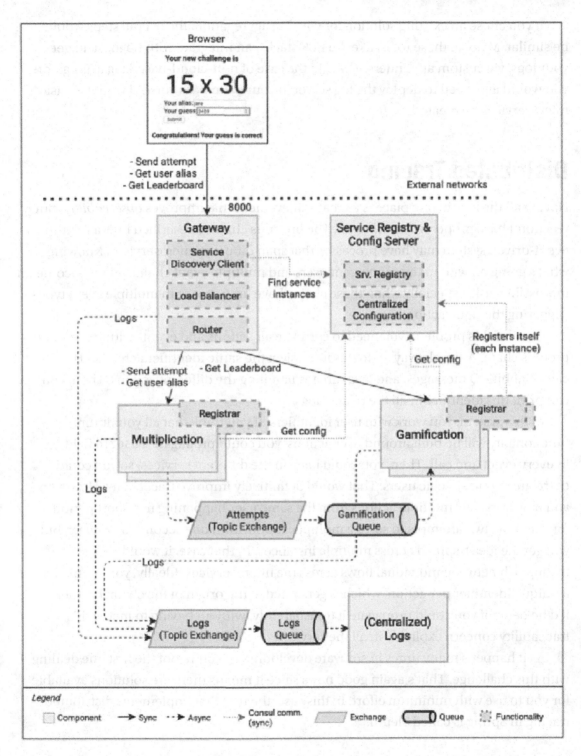

Figure 8-31. *High-level overview: centralized logs*

If you chose an existing solution for your log aggregation, the overall steps would be similar. Many of these tools, like the ELK stack, can integrate with Logback to get your logs, via custom appenders. Then, in the case of non-cloud-based log aggregators, you would also need to deploy the log server in your system, as you did with the basic microservice you created.

Distributed Tracing

Having all the logs in one place is a great achievement that improves *observability*, but you don't have proper *traceability* yet. The previous chapter described how a mature event-driven system may have processes that span different microservices. Knowing what's going on with many concurrent users and multiple event chains might become an impossible task, especially when these chains have branches with multiple event types triggering the same action.

To solve this problem, you need to correlate all actions and events within the same process chain. A simple way to do this is to inject the same identifier across all HTTP calls, RabbitMQ messages, and Java threads handling the different actions. Then, you can print this identifier in all the related logs.

In this system, you work with user identifiers. If you think that all your future functionality will be built around user actions, you could propagate a `userId` field in every event and call. Then, you could log it in the different services, so you could correlate logs to specific users. That would definitely improve traceability. However, you may also have multiple actions from the same user happening in a short period, for example, two attempts to solve a multiplication within one second (a fast user, but you get the idea), spread across multiple instances. In that case, it would be hard to distinguish between individual flows across the microservices. Ideally, you should have a unique identifier per action, which is generated at the origin of the chain. Furthermore, it'd be better if you could propagate it transparently, without having to model this traceability concern explicitly in all the services.

As it happens many times in software development, you're not the first one dealing with this challenge. That's again good news since it means there are solutions available for you to use with minimum effort. In this case, the tool that implements distributed tracing in Spring is called Sleuth.

Spring Cloud Sleuth

Sleuth (https://spring.io/projects/spring-cloud-sleuth) is part of the Spring Cloud family, and it uses the Brave library (https://github.com/openzipkin/brave) to implement distributed tracing. It builds traces across different components by correlating units of work called *spans*. For example, in your system, one span is checking the attempt in the Multiplication microservice, and a different one is adding scores and badges based on the RabbitMQ event. Each span has a different unique identifier, but both spans are part of the same trace, so they have the same trace identifier. Besides, each span links to its parent, except the root one because it's the original action. See Figure 8-32.

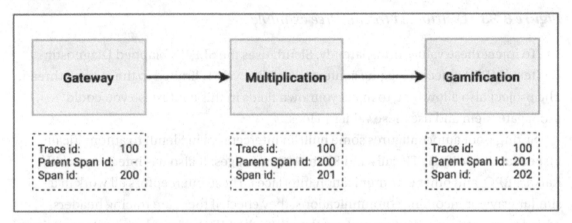

Figure 8-32. *Distributed tracing: simple example*

In more evolved systems, there might be complex trace structures where multiple spans have the same parent. See Figure 8-33.

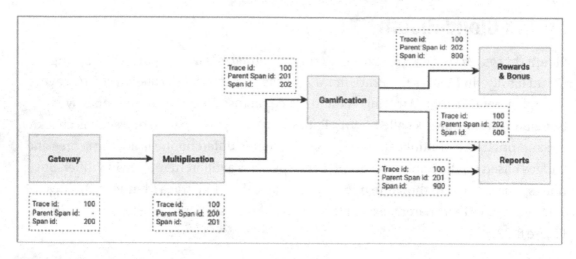

Figure 8-33. *Distributed tracing: tree example*

To inject these values transparently, Sleuth uses the SLF4J's Mapped Diagnostic Context (MDC) object, a logging context whose lifecycle is limited to the current thread. The project also allows you to inject your own fields in this context, so you could propagate them and use these values in logs.

Spring Boot autoconfigures some built-in interceptors in Sleuth to automatically inspect and modify HTTP calls and RabbitMQ messages. It also has integration with Kafka, gRPC, and other communication interfaces. These interceptors all work in a similar way: for incoming communications, they check if there are tracing headers added to the calls or messages and put them into the MDC; when doing calls as a client or publishing data, these interceptors take these fields from the MDC and add headers to the requests or messages.

Sleuth is sometimes combined with Zipkin, a tool that uses trace sampling to measure the time spent in each span and therefore in the complete chain. These samples can be sent to a Zipkin server, which exposes a UI that you can use to see the trace hierarchy and the time it takes for each service to do its part. You don't use Zipkin in this book since that doesn't add much value on top of a centralized logging system with trace and span identifiers, where you can also determine the time spent in each service if you check the logged timestamps. Anyway, you can easily integrate Zipkin in your example project by following the instructions in the reference docs (`https://docs.spring` `.io/spring-cloud-sleuth/docs/current/reference/html/project-features` `.html#features-zipkin`).

Implementing Distributed Tracing

As mentioned, Spring Cloud Sleuth provides interceptors for REST APIs and RabbitMQ messages, and Spring Boot autoconfigures them for you. It's not hard to have distributed tracing in your system.

First, let's add the corresponding Spring Cloud starter to the Gateway, Multiplication, Gamification, and Logs microservices. See Listing 8-49 for the dependency you have to add to the pom.xml files.

Listing 8-49. Adding Spring Cloud Sleuth to All Your Spring Boot Projects

```
<dependency>
    <groupId>org.springframework.cloud</groupId>
    <artifactId>spring-cloud-starter-sleuth</artifactId>
</dependency>
```

Only by adding this dependency will Sleuth inject the trace and span identifiers to every supported communication channel and to the MDC object. The default Spring Boot logging patterns are also automatically adapted to print the trace and span values in the logs.

To make your logs more verbose and see the trace identifiers in action, add a log line to `ChallengeAttemptController` to print a message each time a user sends an attempt. See the change in Listing 8-50.

Listing 8-50. Adding a Log Line to ChallengeAttemptController

```
@PostMapping
ResponseEntity<ChallengeAttempt> postResult(
        @RequestBody @Valid ChallengeAttemptDTO challengeAttemptDTO) {
    log.info("Received new attempt from {}", challengeAttemptDTO.
    getUserAlias());
    return ResponseEntity.ok(challengeService.verifyAttempt(challengeAtt
    emptDTO));
}
```

You want to have the trace and parent identifiers in your centralized logs as well. To do that, manually add the X-B3-TraceId and X-B3-SpanId properties from the MDC context (injected by Sleuth using Brave) to your pattern in the logback-spring. xml file in the Logs project. These headers are part of the OpenZipkin's B3 Propagation

405

specification (see https://github.com/openzipkin/b3-propagation for more details), and they are included in the MDC by the Sleuth's interceptors. You need to do this manually for your Logs microservice since you're not using the Spring Boot defaults in this logging configuration file. See Listing 8-51.

Listing 8-51. Adding Trace Fields to Each Log Line Printed by the Logs Application

```
<configuration>
    <appender name="CONSOLE" class="ch.qos.logback.core.ConsoleAppender">
        <layout class="ch.qos.logback.classic.PatternLayout">
            <Pattern>
                [%-15marker] [%X{X-B3-TraceId:-},%X{X-B3-SpanId:-}]
                %highlight(%-5level) %msg%n
            </Pattern>
        </layout>
    </appender>
    <root level="INFO">
        <appender-ref ref="CONSOLE" />
    </root>
</configuration>
```

Once you restart all backend services, Sleuth will do its part. You can use the terminal to send a correct attempt directly to the backend.

```
$ http POST :8000/attempts factorA=15 factorB=20
userAlias=test-user-tracing guess=300
```

Then, check the output of the Logs service. You'll see the two fields showing the common trace identifier across the Multiplication and Gamification microservices, fa114ad129920dc7. Each line also has its own span ID. See Listing 8-52.

Listing 8-52. Centralized Logs with Trace Identifiers

```
[multiplication ] [fa114ad129920dc7,4cdc6ab33116ce2d] INFO  10:16:01.813
[http-nio-8080-exec-8] m.b.m.c.ChallengeAttemptController - Received new
attempt from test-user-tracing
```

```
[multiplication ] [fa114ad129920dc7,f70ea1f6a1ff6cac] INFO  10:16:01.814
[http-nio-8080-exec-8] m.b.m.challenge.ChallengeServiceImpl - Creating new
user with alias test-user-tracing
[gamification   ] [fa114ad129920dc7,861cbac20a1f3b2c] INFO  10:16:01.818
[org.springframework.amqp.rabbit.RabbitListenerEndpointContainer#0-1]
m.b.g.game.GameEventHandler - Challenge Solved Event received: 126
[gamification   ] [fa114ad129920dc7,78ae53a82e49b770] INFO  10:16:01.819
[org.springframework.amqp.rabbit.RabbitListenerEndpointContainer#0-1]
m.b.g.game.GameServiceImpl - User test-user-tracing scored 10 points for
attempt id 126
```

As you can see, with very little effort, you get a powerful feature that allows you to discern separate processes in your distributed system. As you can imagine, this works even better when you output all logs with their traces and spans to a more sophisticated centralized logs tooling like ELK, where you could use these identifiers to perform filtered text searches.

Containerization

Until now, you have been locally executing all your Java microservices, the React frontend, RabbitMQ, and Consul. To make that work, you needed to install the JDK to compile the sources and run the JAR packages, Node.js to build and run the UI, the RabbitMQ server (Erlang included), and Consul's agent. As the architecture evolves, you might need to introduce other tools and services, and they surely have their own installation processes that may differ depending on the operating system and its version.

As an overall goal, you want to be able to run your backend system in multiple environments, no matter what OS version they're running. Ideally, it'd be great to benefit from a "build once, deploy anywhere" strategy, and avoid repeating all the configuration and installation steps in every environment you want to deploy your system. Besides, the deployment process should be as straightforward as possible.

In the past, a common approach to package complete systems to run them anywhere was to create a virtual machine (VM). There are a few solutions to create and run VMs, and they're called *hypervisors*. An advantage of hypervisors is that a physical machine can run multiple VMs at the same time, and they all share the hardware resources. Every VM requires its own operating system, which is then connected via the hypervisor to the host's CPU, RAM, hard disks, and so on.

In this case, you could create a VM starting with a Linux distribution and set up and install all the tools and services that are needed to run your system: Consul, RabbitMQ, a Java Runtime, the JAR applications, and so on. Once you know that the virtual machine works, you can transfer it to any other computer running the hypervisor. Since the package contains everything it needs, it should work the same in a different host. See Figure 8-34.

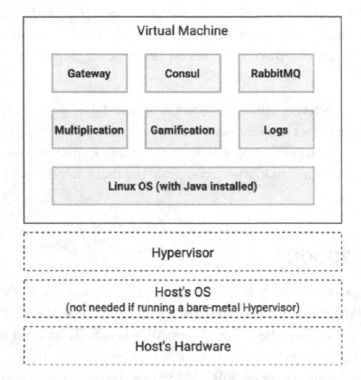

Figure 8-34.   *Virtual machine deployment: single*

However, putting everything together in the same VM is not very flexible. If you want to scale up your system, you have to go inside the virtual machine, add new instances, make sure you allocate more CPU, memory, and so on. You need to know how everything works, so the deployment process is not that easy anymore.

A more dynamic approach is to have separate virtual machines per service and tooling. Then, you add some network configuration to make sure they can connect to each other. Since you use service discovery and dynamic scaling, you could add more instances of virtual machines running microservices (e.g., `Multiplication-VM`), and they will be used transparently. These new instances just need to register themselves in Consul using their address (within the VM network). See Figure 8-35. That's better than the single VM, but it's a huge waste of resources given that each virtual machine requires its own operating system. Also, it would bring a lot of challenges in terms of VM orchestration: monitoring them, creating new instances, configuring networks, storage, and so on.

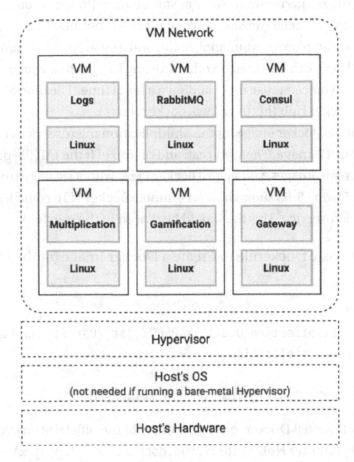

Figure 8-35. *Virtual machine deployment: multiple*

With the evolution of containerization technologies in the early 2010s, VMs have fallen into disuse, and containers have emerged as the most popular way of application virtualization. Containers are much smaller because they don't need the operating system; they run on top of a host's Linux operating system.

On the other hand, the introduction of containerization platforms like Docker has facilitated cloud and on-premise deployments drastically, with easy-to-use tools to package applications, run them as containers, and share them in a common registry. Let's explore this platform's features in more detail.

Docker

It would be impossible to cover in this book all the concepts of the Docker platform, but we try to give an overview that is good enough for you to understand how it facilitates the deployment of a distributed system. The Get Started page (`https://docs.docker.com/get-started/`) on the official website is a good place to continue learning from here.

In Docker, you can package your application and any supporting component it may need as images. These can be based on other existing images that you can pull from a Docker registry, so you can reuse them and save a lot of time. The official public registry of images is the Docker Hub (`https://hub.docker.com/`).

As an example, a Docker image for the Multiplication microservice could be based on the existing JDK 17 image. Then, you can add on top of it the JAR file packaged by Spring Boot. To create images, you need a `Dockerfile`, with a set of instructions for the Docker CLI tool. Listing 8-53 shows how an example `Dockerfile` could look for the Multiplication microservice. This file should be placed in the root folder of the project.

Listing 8-53. A Basic Dockerfile to Create a Docker Image for the Multiplication Microservice

```
FROM openjdk:17
COPY ./target/multiplication-0.0.1-SNAPSHOT.jar /usr/src/multiplication/
WORKDIR /usr/src/multiplication
EXPOSE 8080
CMD ["java", "-jar", "multiplication-0.0.1-SNAPSHOT.jar"]
```

These instructions tell Docker to use version 17 of the official `openjdk` image in the public registry (Docker Hub, `https://hub.docker.com/_/openjdk`) as a base (`FROM`). Then, it copies the distributable `.jar` file from the current project to the `/usr/src/multiplication/` folder in the image (`COPY`). The third instruction, `WORKDIR`, changes the working directory of the image to this newly created folder. The `EXPOSE` command informs Docker that this image exposes a port, 8080, where you serve the REST API. Finally, you define the command to execute when running this image with `CMD`. That's just the classic Java command to run a `.jar` file, split into three parts to comply with the expected syntax. There are many other instructions that you can use in a `Dockerfile`, as you can see in the reference docs (`https://docs.docker.com/engine/reference/builder/`).

To build images, you have to download and install the Docker CLI tool, which comes with the standard Docker installation package. Follow the instructions on the Docker website (`https://docs.docker.com/get-docker/`) to get the proper package for your OS. Once downloaded and started, the Docker daemon should be running as a background service. Then, you can build and deploy images using Docker commands from a terminal. For example, the command shown in Listing 8-54 builds the `multiplication` image based on the `Dockerfile` you created earlier. Note that, as a prerequisite, you have to make sure you build and package the app in a `.jar` file, for example by running `./mvnw clean package` from the project's root folder.

Listing 8-54. Building a Docker Image Manually

```
multiplication$ docker build -t multiplication:1.0.0 .
Sending build context to Docker daemon  59.31MB
Step 1/5 : FROM openjdk:17
 ---> 4fba8120f640
Step 2/5 : COPY ./target/multiplication-0.0.1-SNAPSHOT.jar /usr/src/
multiplication/
 ---> 2e48612d3e40
Step 3/5 : WORKDIR /usr/src/multiplication
 ---> Running in c58cde6bda82
Removing intermediate container c58cde6bda82
 ---> 8d5457683f2c
Step 4/5 : EXPOSE 8080
 ---> Running in 7696319884c7
Removing intermediate container 7696319884c7
 ---> abc3a60b73b2
Step 5/5 : CMD ["java", "-jar", "multiplication-0.0.1-SNAPSHOT.jar"]
 ---> Running in 176cd53fe750
Removing intermediate container 176cd53fe750
 ---> a42cc81bab51
Successfully built a42cc81bab51
Successfully tagged multiplication:1.0.0
```

As you see in the output, Docker processes every line in the file and creates an image named `multiplication:1.0.0`. This image is available only locally, but you could *push* it to a remote location if you want others to use it, as we explain later.

411

Once you have built a Docker image, you can run it as a container, which is a running instance of an image. As an example, this command would run a Docker container in your machine:

```
$ docker run -it -p 18080:8080 multiplication:1.0.0
```

The run command in Docker pulls the image if it's not available locally and executes it on the Docker platform as a container. The -it flags are used to attach to the container's terminal, so you can see the output from your command line and also stop the container with a Ctrl+C signal. The -p option exposes the internal port 8080 so it's accessible from the host in port 18080. These are just a few options that you can use when running containers; you can see all of them by typing docker run --help from the command line.

When you start this container, it'll run on top of the Docker platform. If you're running a Linux OS, the containers will use the host's native virtualization capabilities. When running on Windows or Mac, the Docker platform sets up a Linux virtualization layer in between, which may use the native support from these operating systems if they're available.

Unfortunately, your container doesn't work properly. It can't connect to RabbitMQ or Consul, even if you have them up and running in Docker's *host machine* (your computer). Listing 8-55 shows an extract of these errors from the container logs. Remember that, by default, Spring Boot tries to find the RabbitMQ host on localhost, same as for Consul. In a container, localhost refers to the own container, and there is nothing else there but the Spring Boot app. Moreover, containers are isolated units running on a Docker platform network, so they should not connect to services running on the host anyway.

Listing 8-55. The Multiplication Container Can't Reach Consul at Localhost

```
2020-08-29 10:03:44.565 ERROR [,,,] 1 --- [
main] o.s.c.c.c.ConsulPropertySourceLocator    : Fail fast is set and there
was an error reading configuration from consul.
2020-08-29 10:03:45.572 ERROR [,,,] 1 --- [
main] o.s.c.c.c.ConsulPropertySourceLocator    : Fail fast is set and there
was an error reading configuration from consul.
2020-08-29 10:03:46.675 ERROR [,,,] 1 --- [
main] o.s.c.c.c.ConsulPropertySourceLocator    : Fail fast is set and there
was an error reading configuration from consul.
[...]
```

To properly set up your backend system to run in Docker, you have to deploy RabbitMQ and Consul as containers and connect all these different instances between them using Docker networking. See Figure 8-36.

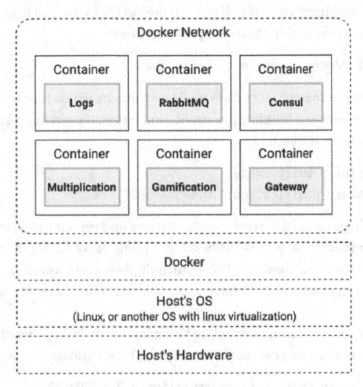

Figure 8-36. *The backend in Docker containers*

Before learning how to accomplish that, let's explore how Spring Boot can help you build Docker images, so you don't need to prepare the Dockerfile yourself.

Spring Boot and Buildpacks

Since version 2.3.0, Spring Boot's Maven and Gradle plugins have the option to build Open Container Initiative (OCI) images using Cloud Native Buildpacks (https:// buildpacks.io/), a project that aims to help package your applications so you can deploy them to any cloud provider. You can run the resulting images in Docker and in other container platforms.

A nice feature of the Buildpacks plugin is that it prepares a plan based on your project's Maven configuration, and then it packages a Docker image that is ready to be deployed. Besides, it structures the image in *layers* in a way so they can be reused by future versions of your application and even by other microservice images built with this same tool (e.g., layers with all the Spring Boot core libraries). That contributes to faster testing and deployment.

You can see Buildpacks in action if you run the `build-image` goal from the command line, for example from the Gamification's project folder:

```
gamification $ ./mvnw spring-boot:build-image
```

You should see some extra logs from the Maven plugin, which is now downloading some required images and building the application image. If everything goes well, you should see this line by the end:

```
[INFO] Successfully built image
'docker.io/library/gamification:0.0.1-SNAPSHOT'
```

The Docker tag is set to the Maven artifact's name and version you specified in the `pom.xml` file: `gamification:0.0.1-SNAPSHOT`. The prefix `docker.io/library/` is the default for all public Docker images. There are multiple options you could customize for this plugin, you can check out the reference docs (`https://buildpacks.io/docs/`) for all the details.

The same as you ran a container before for an image you built yourself, you could do that now for this new image generated by the Spring Boot's Maven plugin:

```
$ docker run -it -p 18081:8081 gamification:0.0.1-SNAPSHOT
```

Unsurprisingly, the container will also output the same errors. Remember that the application can't connect to RabbitMQ and Consul, and it requires both services to start properly. You'll fix that soon.

For your own projects, you should consider the pros and cons of using Cloud Native Buildpacks versus maintaining your own Docker files. If you plan to use these standard OCI images to deploy to a public cloud that supports them, it might be a good idea since you can save a lot of time. Buildpacks also takes care of organizing your images in reusable layers, so you can avoid doing that yourself. Besides, you can customize the base builder image used by the plugin, so you have some flexibility to customize the process. However, if you want to be fully in control of what you're building and the tools and files you want to include in your images, it might be better to define the `Dockerfile` instructions yourself. As you saw before, it's not hard for a basic setup.

Running Your System in Docker

Now you'll build or find a Docker image for each component in your system, so you can deploy it as a group of containers.

- *Multiplication, Gamification, Gateway, and Logs microservices*: You'll use the Spring Boot Maven plugin with Buildpacks to generate these Docker images.

- *RabbitMQ*: You can run a container using the official RabbitMQ image version that contains the management plugin (UI): `rabbitmq:3.11.20-management` (see Docker Hub).

- *Consul*: There is an official Docker image too. You'll use the `consul:1.15.4` tag from Docker Hub (`https://hub.docker.com/r/hashicorp/consul`). Additionally, you'll run a second container to load some configuration as key-value pairs for centralized configuration. More details are given in its specific section.

- *Frontend*: If you want to deploy the complete system in Docker, you'll also need a web server to host the generated HTML/JavaScript files from the React build. You can use a lightweight static server like Nginx, with its official Docker image `nginx:1.19` (see Docker Hub, `https://hub.docker.com/_/nginx`). In this case, you'll build your own image with `nginx` as the base since you need to copy the generated files too.

Therefore, this plan requires building six different Docker images and using two public ones. See Figure 8-37.

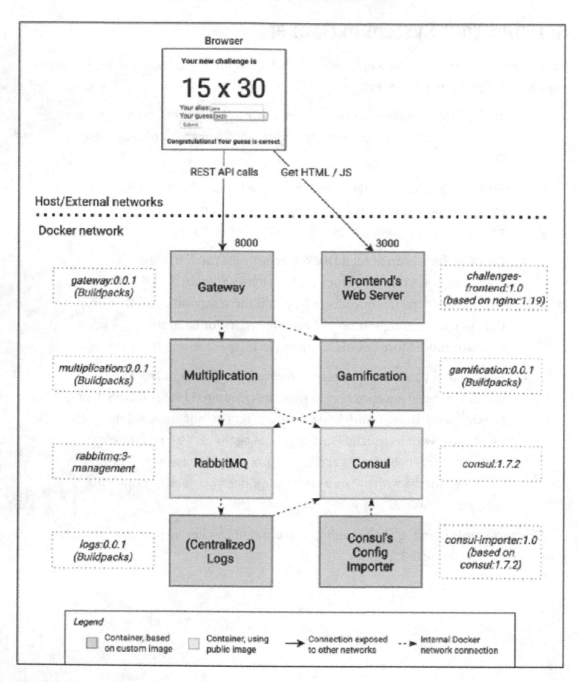

Figure 8-37. *High-level overview: containerized system*

Dockerizing Microservices

First, let's build all the images for the Spring Boot applications. From each of the project folders, you need to run this command:

```
$ ./mvnw spring-boot:build-image
```

Note that Docker has to be running locally, same as Consul and RabbitMQ, for the tests to pass. Once you generate all images, you can verify they're all available in Docker by running the docker images command. See Listing 8-56.

Listing 8-56. Listing Docker Images Generated with Cloud Native Buildpacks

```
$ docker images
REPOSITORY         TAG              IMAGE ID       CREATED        SIZE
logs               0.0.1-SNAPSHOT   2fae1d82cd5d   40 years ago   311MB
gamification       0.0.1-SNAPSHOT   5552940b9bfd   40 years ago   333MB
multiplication     0.0.1-SNAPSHOT   05a4d852fa2d   40 years ago   333MB
gateway            0.0.1-SNAPSHOT   d50be5ba137a   40 years ago   313MB
```

As you can see, the images are generated with an old date. This is a feature from Buildpacks to make builds reproducible: every time you build this image, they get the same creation date, and they're also located at the end of the list.

Dockerizing the UI

The next step is to create a Dockerfile in the challenges-frontend folder, the root directory of your React application. The only two instructions you need are the base image (Nginx) and a COPY command to put all HTML/JavaScript files inside the image. Copy them in the folder that the Nginx web server uses by default to serve contents. See Listing 8-57.

Listing 8-57. A Simple Dockerfile to Create an Image for the Frontend's Web Server

```
FROM nginx:1.25.1
COPY build /usr/share/nginx/html/
```

Before creating the Docker image, make sure you generate the latest artifacts for the frontend. To compile the React project, you have to execute the following:

```
challenges-frontend $ npm run build
```

Once the `build` folder has been generated, you can create your Docker image. You'll assign a name and a tag with the `-t` flag, and you use `.` to indicate that the `Dockerfile` is located in the current folder.

```
challenges-frontend $ docker build -t challenges-frontend:1.0 .
```

Dockerizing the Configuration Importer

Now, you will prepare a Docker image to load some predefined centralized configuration. You'll have a Consul container running the server, which can use the official image directly. The plan is to run an extra container to execute the Consul CLI to load some KV data: a `docker` profile. This way, you can use this preloaded profile configuration when running your microservices in Docker, since they require a different RabbitMQ host parameter, as an example.

To get the configuration you want to load in a file format, you can create it in your local Consul server and export it via the CLI command. You use the UI to create the `config` root, and a subfolder named `defaults,docker`. Inside, you create a key named `application.yml` with the configuration shown in Listing 8-58. This configuration does the following:

- Sets the host for RabbitMQ to `rabbitmq`, which overrides the `default, localhost`. Later, you'll make sure the message broker's container is available at that address.

- Overrides the instance identifier assigned to the running service to be used at the service registry. The default Spring Consul configuration concatenates the application name with the port number, but that approach will no longer be valid with containers. When you run multiple instances of the same service in Docker (as containers), they all use the same internal port, so they would end up with the same identifier. To solve this issue, you can use as a suffix a random integer. Spring Boot has support for that via the special `random` property notation (see the documentation at `https://docs.spring.io/spring-boot/docs/current/reference/htmlsingle/#features.external-config.random-values` for more detail).

Listing 8-58. The YAML Configuration to Connect Your Apps in Docker
Containers to RabbitMQ

```
spring:
  rabbitmq:
    host: rabbitmq
  cloud:
    consul:
      discovery:
        instance-id: ${spring.application.name}-${random.int(1000)}
```

Figure 8-38 shows this content added via the Consul UI.

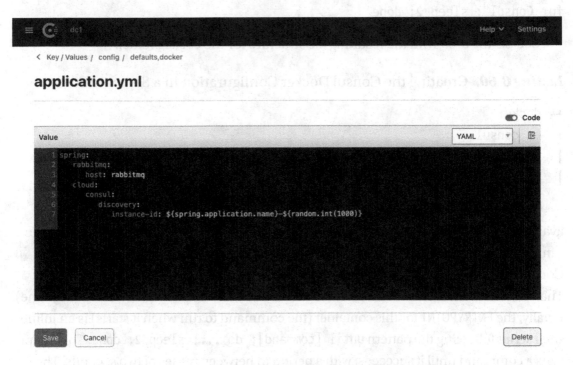

Figure 8-38. *Consul UI: prepare configuration for export*

The next step is to use a different terminal to export the configuration to a file. To do
that, execute the following:

```
$ consul kv export config/ > consul-kv-docker.json
```

Now, create a new folder named docker in the root of the workspace to place all your Docker configuration. Inside, create a subfolder called consul. The JSON file generated with the previous command should be copied there. Then, add a new Dockerfile with the instructions in Listing 8-59.

Listing 8-59. Dockerfile Contents for the Consul Configuration Loader

```
FROM consul:1.15.4
COPY ./consul-kv-docker.json /usr/src/consul/
WORKDIR /usr/src/consul
ENV CONSUL_HTTP_ADDR=consul:8500
ENTRYPOINT until consul kv import @consul-kv-docker.json; do echo "Waiting
for Consul"; sleep 2; done
```

See Listing 8-60 with the resulting file structure for the docker folder.

Listing 8-60. Creating the Consul Docker Configuration in a Separate Folder

```
+- docker
|   +- consul
|       \- consul-kv-docker.json
|       \- Dockerfile
```

The Dockerfile steps in Listing 8-59 use Consul as the base image, so the CLI tool is available. The JSON file is copied inside the image, and the working directory is set to the same location as the file. Then, the ENV instruction sets a new environment variable for Consul CLI to use a remote host to reach the server, in this case located at consul:8500. That'll be the Consul server container (you'll see soon how the host gets the consul name). Finally, the ENTRYPOINT for this container (the command to run when it starts) is an inline shell script following the pattern until [command]; do ...; sleep 2; done. This script runs a command until it succeeds, with a period in between retries of two seconds. The main command is consul kv import @consul-kv-docker.json, which imports the contents of the file to the KV storage. You need to execute this in a loop because the Consul server might not have started yet when this Consul Configuration Importer runs.

To have the importer image available in the registry, you have to build it and give it a name.

```
docker/consul$ docker build -t consul-importer:1.0 .
```

We explain soon how to run this importer in Docker to load the configuration into Consul.

Docker Compose

Once you have built all the images, you need to run your system as a set of containers, so it's time to learn how you can start all these containers together and communicate them.

You could use individual Docker commands to start all the required containers and set up the network for them to connect to each other. However, if you want to tell other people how to start your system, you need to pass them a script or documentation with all these commands and instructions. Luckily, there is a better way in Docker to group container configuration and deployment instructions: Docker Compose.

With Compose, you use a YAML file to define applications that are based on multiple containers. Then, you use the `docker-compose` command to run all services. Docker Compose is installed by default with the Windows, Mac, and Linux versions of Docker Desktop.

As a first example, see Listing 8-61 for the YAML definition of the RabbitMQ and Consul services you need to run as containers in your system. This YAML definition has to be added to a new `docker-compose.yml` file that you can create inside the existing docker folder. This book uses version 3 of the Compose syntax; the full reference is available at `https://docs.docker.com/compose/compose-file/`. Keep reading for the high-level details on how this syntax works.

Listing 8-61. A First Version of the docker-compose.yml File with RabbitMQ and Consul

```
version: "3"
services:
  consul-dev:
    image: consul:1.15.4
    container_name: consul
    # The UDP port 8600 is used by Consul nodes to talk to each other, so
    # it's good to add it here even though we're using a single-node setup.
    ports:
      - '8500:8500'
      - '8600:8600/udp'
```

```
    command: 'agent -dev -node=learnmicro -client=0.0.0.0 -log-level=INFO'
    networks:
      - microservices
  rabbitmq-dev:
    image: rabbitmq:3.11.20-management
    container_name: rabbitmq
    ports:
      - '5672:5672'
      - '15672:15672'
    networks:
      - microservices
networks:
  microservices:
    driver: bridge
```

Within the `services` section, you define two of them: `consul-dev` and `rabbitmq-dev`. You can use any name for your services, so you're adding the `-dev` suffix to these two to indicate that you're running them both in development mode (stand-alone nodes without a cluster). These two services use Docker images that you didn't create, but they are available in the Docker Hub as public images. They'll be pulled the first time you run the containers. If you don't specify the `command` to start the container, the default one from the image will be used. The default command can be specified in the `Dockerfile` used to build the image. That's what happens with the RabbitMQ service, which starts the server by default. For the Consul image, you define your own command, which is similar to the one we've been using so far. The differences are that it also includes a flag to reduce the log level, and the `client` parameter, which is required for the agent to work in the Docker network. These instructions are available on the Docker image's documentation (`https://hub.docker.com/r/hashicorp/consul`).

Both services define a `container_name` parameter. This is useful because it sets the DNS name of the container, so other containers can find it by this alias. In this case, that means the applications can connect to the RabbitMQ server using the address `rabbitmq:5672` instead of the default one, `localhost:5672` (which now points to the same container, as you saw in previous sections). The `ports` parameter in every service allows you to expose ports to the host system in the format `host-port:container-port`. The standard ports that both servers use are included here, so you can still access them from your desktop (e.g., to use their UI tools on ports 8500 and 15672, respectively).

Note that you're mapping to the same ports in the host, which means you can't have the RabbitMQ and Consul server processes running locally (as we've been doing until now) at the same time because that would cause a port conflict.

In this file, you also define a network of type `bridges` called `microservices`. This driver type is the default one, used to connect stand-alone containers. Then, you use the parameter `networks` in each service definition to set the `microservices` network as the one they have access to. In practice, this means these services can connect to each other because they belong to the same network. The Docker network is isolated from the host network, so you can't access any service except the ones you exposed explicitly with the `ports` parameter. This is great since it's one of the good practices we were missing when we introduced the Gateway pattern.

You can use this new `docker-compose.yml` file to run both Consul and RabbitMQ Docker containers. You just need to execute the `docker-compose` command from a terminal:

```
docker $ docker-compose up
```

Docker Compose takes `docker-compose.yml` automatically without specifying the name because that's the default filename that it expects. The output for all containers is *attached* to the current terminal and containers. If you wanted to run them in the background as *daemon* processes, you would just need to add the `-d` flag to the command. In this case, you'll see all the logs together in the terminal output, for both the `consul` and `rabbitmq` containers. See Listing 8-62.

Listing 8-62. Docker Compose Logs, Showing the Initialization of Both Containers

```
Creating network "docker_microservices" with driver "bridge"
Creating consul   ... done
Creating rabbitmq ... done
Attaching to consul, rabbitmq
consul         | ==> Starting Consul agent...
consul         |            Version: 'v1.15.4'
consul         |            Node ID: 'a69c4c04-d1e7-6bdc-5903-
                              c63934f01f6e'
consul         |          Node name: 'learnmicro'
consul         |         Datacenter: 'dc1' (Segment: '<all>')
consul         |             Server: true (Bootstrap: false)
```

```
consul           |            Client Addr: [0.0.0.0] (HTTP: 8500, HTTPS: -1,
                               gRPC: 8502, DNS: 8600)
consul           |           Cluster Addr: 127.0.0.1 (LAN: 8301, WAN: 8302)
consul           |             Encrypt: Gossip: false, TLS-Outgoing: false,
                               TLS-Incoming: false, Auto-Encrypt-TLS: false
consul           |
consul           | ==> Log data will now stream in as it occurs:
[...]
rabbitmq         | 2023-07-29 05:36:28.785 [info] <0.8.0> Feature flags:
                   list of feature flags found:
rabbitmq         | 2023-07-29 05:36:28.785 [info] <0.8.0> Feature flags:
                   [ ] drop_unroutable_metric
rabbitmq         | 2023-07-29 05:36:28.785 [info] <0.8.0> Feature flags:
                   [ ] empty_basic_get_metric
rabbitmq         | 2023-07-29 05:36:28.785 [info] <0.8.0> Feature flags:
                   [ ] implicit_default_bindings
rabbitmq         | 2023-07-29 05:36:28.785 [info] <0.8.0> Feature flags:
                   [ ] quorum_queue
rabbitmq         | 2023-07-29 05:36:28.786 [info] <0.8.0> Feature flags:
                   [ ] virtual_host_metadata
rabbitmq         | 2023-07-29 05:36:28.786 [info] <0.8.0> Feature flags:
                   feature flag states written to disk: yes
rabbitmq         | 2023-07-29 05:36:28.830 [info] <0.268.0> ra: meta data
                   store initialised. 0 record(s) recovered
rabbitmq         | 2023-07-29 05:36:28.831 [info] <0.273.0> WAL:
                   recovering []
rabbitmq         | 2023-07-29 05:36:28.833 [info] <0.277.0>
rabbitmq         |  Starting RabbitMQ 3.8.2 on Erlang 22.2.8
[...]
```

The output shows that we have successfully started the Consul and RabbitMQ
Docker containers.

You can also verify that you can access the Consul UI from your browser at
localhost:8500. This time, the website is served from the container. It works exactly
the same because you exposed the port to the same host's port, and it's being redirected
by Docker.

To stop these containers, you can press Ctrl+C, but that could make Docker keep some state in between executions. To properly shut them down and remove any potential data they created in Docker *volumes* (the units that containers define to store data), run the command in Listing 8-63 from a different terminal.

Listing 8-63. Stopping Docker Containers and Removing Volumes with Docker Compose

```
docker $ docker-compose down -v
Stopping consul    ... done
Stopping rabbitmq ... done
Removing consul    ... done
Removing rabbitmq ... done
Removing network docker_default
WARNING: Network docker_default not found.
Removing network docker_microservices
```

The next step is to add the image you created for loading configuration into Consul KV, the `consul-importer`, to the Docker Compose file. See Listing 8-64.

Listing 8-64. Adding the Consul Importer Image to the docker-compose.yml File

```
version: "3"
services:
  consul-importer:
    image: consul-importer:1.0
    depends_on:
      - consul-dev
    networks:
      - microservices
  consul-dev:
    # ... same as before
  rabbitmq-dev:
    # ... same as before
networks:
  microservices:
    driver: bridge
```

This time, the image `consul-importer:1.0` is not a public one; it's not available in the Docker Hub. However, it's available in the local Docker registry because you built it earlier, so Docker can find it by its name and tag you defined earlier.

You can establish dependencies in the compose file with the `depends_on` parameter. Here, you use it to make this container start after the `consul-dev` container, which runs the Consul server. That doesn't guarantee that the server is ready by the time the `consul-importer` runs. The reason is that Docker knows only when the container has started but doesn't know when the Consul server has booted up and is ready to accept requests. That's why you added a script to the importer image, which retries the import until it succeeds (see Listing 8-59).

When you run `docker-compose` up again with this new configuration, you'll see the output from this new container too. Eventually, you should see the lines that load the configuration, and then Docker will inform you that this container exited successfully (with code 0). See Listing 8-65.

Listing 8-65. Running docker-compose the Second Time to See the Importer's Logs

```
docker $ docker-compose up
[...]
consul-importer_1  | Imported: config/
consul-importer_1  | Imported: config/defaults,docker/
consul-importer_1  | Imported: config/defaults,docker/application.yml
docker_consul-importer_1 exited with code 0
[...]
```

The new container runs as a function, not as a continuously running service. This is because you replaced the default command in the `consul` image, which is defined in the internal `Dockerfile` to run the server as a process, with a command that simply loads configuration and then finishes (it's not an indefinitely running process). Docker knows that the container has nothing more to do because the command exited, so there is no need to keep the container alive.

You can also determine the running containers for a `docker-compose` configuration. To get this list, execute `docker-compose` ps from a different terminal. See Listing 8-66.

Listing 8-66. Running docker-compose ps to See the Status of the Containers

```
docker $ docker-compose ps
Name                        Command          State    Ports
-------------------------------------------------------------------
consul                      docker-e[...]    Up       8300/tcp, [...]
docker_consul-importer_1    /bin/sh [...]    Exit 0
rabbitmq                    docker-e[...]    Up       15671/tcp, [...]
```

The output (trimmed for better readability) also details the command used by the container, its state, and the exposed ports.

If you navigate with your browser to the Consul UI at http://localhost:8500/ui, you'll see how the configuration has been properly loaded, and you have a config entry with the nested defaults,docker subfolder and the corresponding application.yml key. See Figure 8-39. The importer works perfectly.

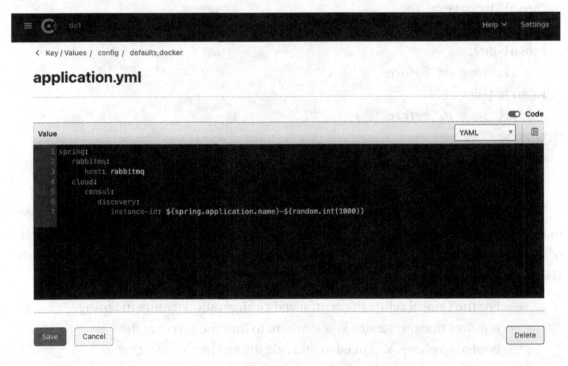

Figure 8-39. *Docker configuration inside the Consul container*

Let's continue with the frontend definition in Docker Compose. This one is easy; you just need to add the image you built based on Nginx and expose port 3000 with a redirection to the internal one, which is 80 by default in the base image (as per `https://hub.docker.com/_/nginx`). See Listing 8-67. You can change the exposed port but then remember to adjust the CORS configuration in the Gateway accordingly (or refactor it so it can be configured via external properties).

Listing 8-67. Adding the Web Server to the docker-compose.yml File

```
version: "3"
services:
  frontend:
    image: challenges-frontend:1.0
    ports:
      - '3000:80'
  consul-importer:
    # ... same as before
  consul-dev:
    # ... same as before
  rabbitmq-dev:
    # ... same as before
networks:
  microservices:
    driver: bridge
```

To make the complete system work, you need to add the Spring Boot microservices to the Docker Compose file. Configure them to use the same network you created. Each of these containers needs to reach the `consul` and `rabbitmq` containers to work properly. You can use two different strategies for that.

- For the Consul setup, the centralized configuration feature in Spring requires that the service knows where to find the server at the bootstrap phase. You need to override the `spring.cloud.consul.host` property used in the local `bootstrap.yml` file and point it to the Consul container. You'll do this via environment variables. In Spring Boot, if you set an environment variable that matches an existing property or that follows a certain naming convention (like `SPRING_CLOUD_CONSUL_HOST`), its value overrides the local configuration. For more details, see `https://docs.spring.io/spring-boot/docs/current/reference/html/features.html#features.external-config.typesafe-configuration-properties.relaxed-binding.environment-variables` in the Spring Boot docs.

- For RabbitMQ configuration, you'll use the `Docker` profile. Given that the microservices will connect to Consul and the configuration server has a preloaded entry for `defaults,docker`, all of them will use the properties in there. Remember that you changed the RabbitMQ host in that profile to `rabbitmq`, the DNS name of the container. To activate the `docker` profile in each microservice, use the Spring Boot property to enable profiles, passed via an environment variable: `SPRING_PROFILES_ACTIVE=docker`.

Consider these extra considerations for the configuration of the Spring Boot containers in Compose:

- You don't want to expose the backend services directly to the host except for the Gateway service, on `localhost:8000`. Therefore, you don't add the `ports` section to Multiplication, Gamification, and Logs.

- Additionally, you'll use the `depends_on` parameter for the backend containers to wait until the `consul-importer` runs, so the Consul configuration for the `docker` profile will be available by the time the Spring Boot apps start.

- You should also include `rabbitmq` as a dependency for these services, but remember that this doesn't guarantee that the RabbitMQ server will be ready before your applications boot up. Docker only verifies that the container has started. Luckily, Spring Boot retries to connect by default to the server as a resilience technique, so eventually, the system will become stable.

See Listing 8-68 for the complete Docker Compose configuration required to start your system.

Listing 8-68. docker-compose.yml File with Everything Needed to Run the Complete System

```
version: "3"
services:
  frontend:
    image: challenges-frontend:1.0
    ports:
      - '3000:80'
  multiplication:
    image: multiplication:0.0.1-SNAPSHOT
    environment:
      - SPRING_PROFILES_ACTIVE=docker
      - SPRING_CLOUD_CONSUL_HOST=consul
    depends_on:
      - rabbitmq-dev
      - consul-importer
    networks:
      - microservices
  gamification:
    image: gamification:0.0.1-SNAPSHOT
    environment:
      - SPRING_PROFILES_ACTIVE=docker
      - SPRING_CLOUD_CONSUL_HOST=consul
    depends_on:
      - rabbitmq-dev
      - consul-importer
    networks:
      - microservices
  gateway:
    image: gateway:0.0.1-SNAPSHOT
    ports:
      - '8000:8000'
    environment:
      - SPRING_PROFILES_ACTIVE=docker
      - SPRING_CLOUD_CONSUL_HOST=consul
```

```
    depends_on:
      - rabbitmq-dev
      - consul-importer
    networks:
      - microservices
logs:
  image: logs:0.0.1-SNAPSHOT
  environment:
    - SPRING_PROFILES_ACTIVE=docker
    - SPRING_CLOUD_CONSUL_HOST=consul
  depends_on:
    - rabbitmq-dev
    - consul-importer
  networks:
    - microservices
consul-importer:
  image: consul-importer:1.0
  depends_on:
    - consul-dev
  networks:
    - microservices
consul-dev:
  image: consul:1.7.2
  container_name: consul
  ports:
    - '8500:8500'
    - '8600:8600/udp'
  command: 'agent -dev -node=learnmicro -client=0.0.0.0 -log-level=INFO'
  networks:
    - microservices
rabbitmq-dev:
  image: rabbitmq:3-management
  container_name: rabbitmq
  ports:
    - '5672:5672'
    - '15672:15672'
```

```
    networks:
        - microservices
networks:
    microservices:
        driver: bridge
```

It's time to test your complete system running as Docker containers. As before, run the docker-compose up command. You'll see many logs in the output, produced by multiple services that are starting simultaneously, or right after the ones defined as dependencies.

The first thing you might notice is that some backend services throw exceptions when trying to connect to RabbitMQ. This is an expected situation. As mentioned, RabbitMQ may take longer to start than the microservice applications. This should fix by itself after the rabbitmq container becomes ready.

You could also experience errors caused by not having enough memory or CPU in your system to run all the containers together. This is not exceptional since each microservice container can take up to 1GB of RAM. If you can't run all these containers, we hope the book explanations still help you understand how everything works together.

To determine the status of the system, you can use the aggregated logs provided by Docker (the attached output) or the output from the logs container. To try the second option, use another Docker command from a different terminal, docker-compose logs [container_name]. See Listing 8-69. Note that your service name is logs, which explains the word's repetition.

Listing 8-69. Checking the Logs of the Logs Container

```
docker $ docker-compose logs logs
[...]
logs_1              | [gamification   ] [aadd7c03a8b161da,34c00bc3e3197ff2]
INFO  07:24:52.386 [main] o.s.d.r.c.DeferredRepositoryInitializationListener
- Triggering deferred initialization of Spring Data repositories?
logs_1              | [multiplication ] [33284735df2b2be1,bc998f237af7bebb]
INFO  07:24:52.396 [main] o.s.d.r.c.DeferredRepositoryInitializationListener
- Triggering deferred initialization of Spring Data repositories?
logs_1              | [multiplication ] [b87fc916703f6b56,fd729db4060c1c74]
INFO  07:24:52.723 [main] o.s.d.r.c.DeferredRepositoryInitializationListener
- Spring Data repositories initialized!
```

```
logs_1              | [multiplication ] [97f86da754679510,9fa61b768e2
6aeb5] INFO  07:24:52.760 [main] m.b.m.MultiplicationApplication - Started
MultiplicationApplication in 44.974 seconds (JVM running for 47.993)
logs_1              | [gamification   ] [5ec42be452ce0e04,03dfa6fc3656b7fe]
INFO  07:24:53.017 [main] o.s.d.r.c.DeferredRepositoryInitializationListener
- Spring Data repositories initialized!
logs_1              | [gamification   ] [f90c5542963e7eea,a9f52df128ac5
c7d] INFO  07:24:53.053 [main] m.b.g.GamificationApplication - Started
GamificationApplication in 45.368 seconds (JVM running for 48.286)
logs_1              | [gateway        ] [59c9f14c24b84b32,36219539a1a0d01b]
WARN  07:24:53.762 [boundedElastic-1] o.s.c.l.core.RoundRobinLoadBalancer -
No servers available for service: gamification
```

Additionally, you can also monitor the service statuses by checking the Consul UI's service list, available at localhost:8500. There, you'll see if the health checks are passing, which means the services are already serving and connected to RabbitMQ. See Figure 8-40.

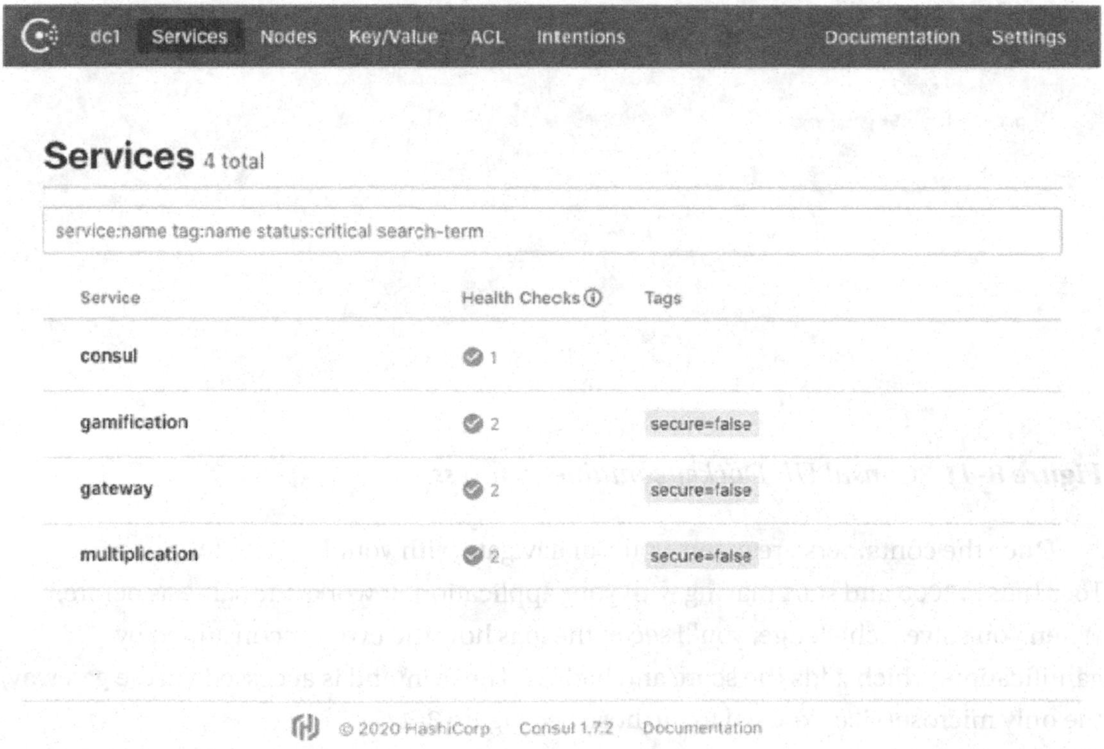

Figure 8-40. *Consul UI: checking containers health*

If you click one of the services (e.g., `gamification`), you'll see how the host address is now the container's address in the docker network. See Figure 8-41. This is an alternative to the container name for services to connect to each other. Actually, this dynamic host address registration in Consul allows you to have multiple instances of a given service. If you used a `container_name` parameter, you couldn't start more than one instance since their addresses would conflict.

The applications use in this case the Docker's host address because Spring Cloud detects when an application is running on a Docker container. Then, the Consul Discovery libraries use this value at registration time.

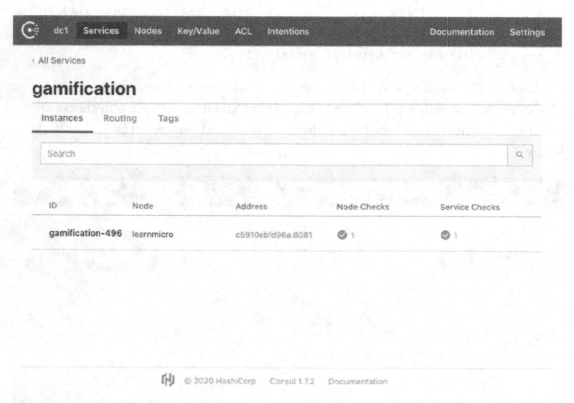

Figure 8-41. *Consul UI: Docker container address*

Once the containers are green, you can navigate with your browser to `localhost:3000` and start playing with your application. It works the same as before. When you solve a challenge, you'll see in the logs how the event is consumed by gamification, which adds the score and badges. The frontend is accessed via the gateway, the only microservice exposed to the host. See Figure 8-42.

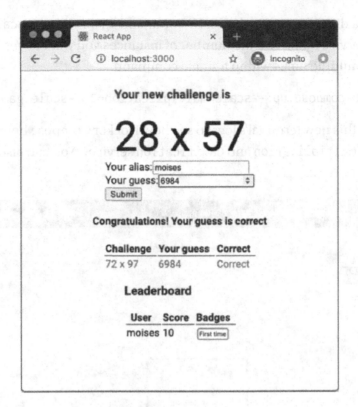

Figure 8-42. *Application running on Docker*

We didn't add any persistence, so all the data will be gone when you bring the containers down. If you want to extend your knowledge of Docker and Docker Compose, consider adding *volumes* to store the DB files (see https://docs.docker.com/compose/compose-file/#volume-configuration-reference). Also, don't forget to remove the -v flag when executing docker-compose down, so the volumes are kept between executions.

Scaling Up the System with Docker

With Docker Compose, you can also scale services up and down with a single command. First, boot up the system as it was before. If you brought it down already, execute the following:

```
docker$ docker-compose up
```

Then, from a different terminal, run the command again with the `scale` parameter, indicating the service name and the number of instances you want to get. You can use the parameter multiple times within a single command.

```
docker$ docker-compose up --scale multiplication=2 --scale gamification=2
```

Now, check this new terminal's logs to see how Docker Compose boots up an extra instance for the `Multiplication` and `Gamification` services. You can also verify this in Consul. See Figure 8-43.

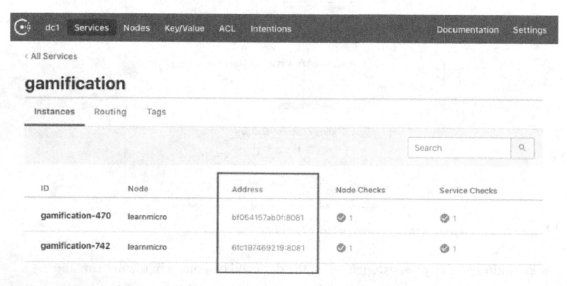

Figure 8-43. *Consul UI: two containers for Gamification*

Thanks to Consul Discovery, your gateway pattern, the Spring Cloud load balancer, and RabbitMQ consumer's load balancing, you'll get your system to properly balance the load across multiple instances. You can verify that either by solving a few challenges from the UI or by directly executing some HTTP calls to the Gateway service. If you go for the terminal option, you can run this HTTPie command multiple times:

```
$ http POST :8000/attempts factorA=15 factorB=20
userAlias=test-docker-containers guess=300
```

In the logs, you'll see how `multiplication_1` and `multiplication_2` both handle requests from the API. The same happens for `gamification_1` and `gamification_2`, which also take different messages from the broker's queue. See Listing 8-70.

Listing 8-70. Scalability in Action with Docker Containers

```
multiplication_1    | 2020-07-30 09:48:34.559  INFO [,85acf6d095516f55,956486d18
6a612dd,true] 1 --- [nio-8080-exec-8] m.b.m.c.ChallengeAttemptController
: Received new attempt from test-docker-containers
logs_1              | [multiplication ] [85acf6d095516f55,31829523bbc1d6ea]
INFO  09:48:34.559 [http-nio-8080-exec-8] m.b.m.c.ChallengeAttemptController
- Received new attempt from test-docker-containers
gamification_1      | 2020-07-30 09:48:34.570  INFO [,85acf6d095516f55,
44508dd6f09c83ba,true] 1 --- [ntContainer#0-1] m.b.gamification.game.
GameEventHandler    : Challenge Solved Event received: 7
gamification_1      | 2020-07-30 09:48:34.572  INFO [,85acf6d095516f55,
44508dd6f09c83ba,true] 1 --- [ntContainer#0-1] m.b.gamification.game.
GameServiceImpl     : User test-docker-containers scored 10 points for
attempt id 7
logs_1              | [gamification   ] [85acf6d095516f55,8bdd9b6
febc1eda8] INFO  09:48:34.570 [org.springframework.amqp.rabbit.
RabbitListenerEndpointContainer#0-1] m.b.g.game.GameEventHandler - Challenge
Solved Event received: 7
logs_1              | [gamification   ] [85acf6d095516f55,247a9
30d09b3b7e5] INFO  09:48:34.572 [org.springframework.amqp.rabbit.
RabbitListenerEndpointContainer#0-1] m.b.g.game.GameServiceImpl - User test-
docker-containers scored 10 points for attempt id 7
multiplication_2    | 2020-07-30 09:48:35.332  INFO [,fa0177a130683114,f2c2809dd
9a6bc44,true] 1 --- [nio-8080-exec-1] m.b.m.c.ChallengeAttemptController
: Received new attempt from test-docker-containers
logs_1              | [multiplication ] [fa0177a130683114,f5b7991f5b1518a6]
INFO  09:48:35.332 [http-nio-8080-exec-1] m.b.m.c.ChallengeAttemptController
- Received new attempt from test-docker-containers
gamification_2      | 2020-07-30 09:48:35.344  INFO [,fa0177a130683114,298af219a
0741f96,true] 1 --- [ntContainer#0-1] m.b.gamification.game.GameEventHandler
: Challenge Solved Event received: 7
gamification_2      | 2020-07-30 09:48:35.358  INFO [,fa0177a130683114,
298af219a0741f96,true] 1 --- [ntContainer#0-1] m.b.gamification.game.
GameServiceImpl     : User test-docker-containers scored 10 points for
attempt id 7
```

```
logs_1              | [gamification  ] [fa0177a130683114,2b9ce6c
ab6366dfb] INFO  09:48:35.344 [org.springframework.amqp.rabbit.
RabbitListenerEndpointContainer#0-1] m.b.g.game.GameEventHandler -
Challenge Solved Event received: 7
logs_1              | [gamification  ] [fa0177a130683114,536fbc803
5a2e3a2] INFO  09:48:35.358 [org.springframework.amqp.rabbit.
RabbitListenerEndpointContainer#0-1] m.b.g.game.GameServiceImpl - User
test-docker-containers scored 10 points for attempt id 7
```

Sharing Docker Images

All the images you built so far are stored in your local machine. That doesn't achieve the "build once, deploy everywhere" strategy we aimed for. However, you're very close.

You already know Docker Hub, the public registry from which you downloaded the official images for RabbitMQ and Consul, and the base images for your microservices. Therefore, if you upload your own images there, they will be available to everybody. If you're fine with that, you can create a free account at hub.docker.com and start uploading (*pushing* in Docker terms) your custom images. In case you want to restrict access to your images, they also offer plans for setting up private repositories, hosted in their cloud.

Actually, the Docker Hub is not the only option you have to store Docker images. You can also deploy your own registry following the instructions on the "Deploy a Registry Server" page (https://docs.docker.com/registry/deploying/) or choose one of the online solutions offered by the different cloud vendors, such as Amazon's ECR or Google Cloud's Container Registry.

In a Docker registry, you can keep multiple versions of your images using tags. For example, your Spring Boot images got the version number from the pom.xml file, so they got the default version created by the Initializer (e.g., multiplication:0.0.1-SNAPSHOT). You can keep your versioning strategy in Maven, but you could also set tags manually using the docker tag command. You can also use multiple tags to refer to the same Docker image. A common practice is to add the tag latest to your Docker images to point to the most recent version of an image in the registry. See the list of available tags (https://hub.docker.com/r/hashicorp/consul/tags) for the Consul image as an example of Docker image versioning.

To connect your Docker's command-line tool to a registry, the docker login command. If you want to connect to a private host, you must add the host address. Otherwise, if you're connecting to the Hub, you can use the plain command. See Listing 8-71.

Listing 8-71. Logging In to Docker Hub

```
$ docker login
Login with your Docker ID to push and pull images from Docker Hub. If you
don't have a Docker ID, head over to https://hub.docker.com to create one.
Username: [your username]
Password: [your password]
Login Succeeded
```

Once you're logged in, you can push images to the registry. Keep in mind that, to make it work, you have to tag them with your username as a prefix, since that's the Docker Hub's naming convention. Let's change the name of one of your images following the expected pattern. Additionally, you'll modify the version identifier to 0.0.1. In this example, the registered username is learnmicro.

```
$ docker tag multiplication:0.0.1-SNAPSHOT learnmicro/multiplication:0.0.1
```

You can push this image to the registry using the docker push command. See Listing 8-72 for an example.

Listing 8-72. Pushing an Image to the Public Registry, the Docker Hub

```
$ docker push learnmicro/multiplication:0.0.1
  The push refers to repository [docker.io/learnmicro/multiplication]
  abf6a2c86136: Pushed
  9474e9c2336c: Pushing
[==================================>                       ]  37.97MB/58.48MB
  9474e9c2336c: Pushing
[========>                                                 ]  10.44MB/58.48MB
  5cd38b221a5e: Pushed
  d12f80e4be7c: Pushed
  c789281314b6: Pushed
  2611af6e99a7: Pushing
[=====================================================>]  7.23MB
  02a647e64beb: Pushed
  1ca774f177fc: Pushed
  9474e9c2336c: Pushing
[=================================>                        ]  39.05MB/58.48MB
```

```
  8713409436f4: Pushing
[===>                                                    ]  10.55MB/154.9MB
  8713409436f4: Pushing
[===>                                                    ]  11.67MB/154.9MB
  7fbc81c9d125: Waiting
  8713409436f4: Pushing
[====>                                                   ]  12.78MB/154.9MB
  9474e9c2336c: Pushed
  6c918f7851dc: Pushed
  8682f9a74649: Pushed
  d3a6da143c91: Pushed
  83f4287e1f04: Pushed
  7ef368776582: Pushed
0.0.1: digest: sha256:ef9bbed14b5e349f1ab05cffff92e60a8a99e01c412341a3232
fcd93aeeccfdc size: 4716
```

From this moment on, anybody with access to the registry can pull your image and use it as a container. If you use the hub's public registry like in your example, the image becomes publicly available. If you're curious, you can verify that this image is really online by visiting its Docker Hub's link (https://hub.docker.com/r/learnmicro/multiplication). See Figure 8-44.

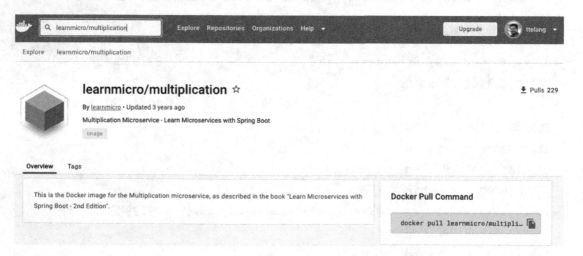

Figure 8-44. *Multiplication's Docker image in the Docker Hub*

Actually, all the Docker images that we described earlier are already available in the public registry under the author account with the prefix `learnmicro/`. All these first versions are tagged as `0.0.1`. That makes it possible for any Docker user to get a version of the complete system up and running without building anything. They just need to use a version of the same `docker-compose.yml` file you used in Listing 8-68, with image name replacements to point to existing images in the public registry. See Listing 8-73 for the required changes.

Listing 8-73. Changing the docker-compose.yml File to Use Publicly Available Images

```
version: "3"
services:
  frontend:
    image: learnmicro/challenges-frontend:0.0.1
    # ...
  multiplication:
    image: learnmicro/multiplication:0.0.1
    # ...
  gamification:
    image: learnmicro/gamification:0.0.1
    # ...
  gateway:
    image: learnmicro/gateway:0.0.1
    # ...
  logs:
    image: learnmicro/logs:0.0.1
    # ...
  consul-importer:
    image: learnmicro/consul-importer:0.0.1
    # ...
  consul-dev:
    # same as before
  rabbitmq-dev:
    # same as before
networks:
  # ...
```

You achieved your goal for this section. Deploying your application became easy, given that the only prerequisite is having Docker support. That opens up a lot of possibilities since most of the platforms to manage and orchestrate distributed systems support Docker container deployments. In the next section, you learn some basics about platforms.

Platforms and Cloud-Native Microservices

Throughout this chapter, we've been covering a few patterns that are the foundations of a proper microservice architecture: routing, service discovery, load balancing, health reporting, centralized logging, centralized configuration, distributed tracing, and containerization.

If you take a moment to analyze the components in your system, you'll realize how complex it's becoming to support three main functional parts: the Web UI and the Multiplication and Gamification backend domains. Even though you employed popular implementations for many of these patterns, you still had to configure them, or even deploy some extra components, to make the system work.

Besides, we didn't cover the *clustering strategies*. If you deploy all your applications in a single machine, there is a high risk that something will go wrong. Ideally, you want to replicate components and spread them across multiple physical servers. Luckily for you, there are tools to manage and orchestrate the different components across a cluster of servers, either in your own hardware or in the cloud. The most popular alternatives work at the container level or the application level, and we'll describe them separately.

Container Platforms

First, let's focus on container platforms like Kubernetes (`https://kubernetes.io/`), Apache Mesos (`https://mesos.apache.org/`), and Docker Swarm (`https://docs.docker.com/engine/swarm/`). In these platforms, you deploy containers either directly or by using wrapping structures with extra configuration intended for the specific tool. As an example, a deployment unit in Kubernetes is a *pod*, and its definition (to keep it simple, a *deployment*) may define a list of Docker containers to deploy (usually only one) and some extra parameters to set the allocated resources, connect the pod to a network, or add external configuration and storage.

These platforms usually integrate patterns that should be already familiar to you. Again, let's use Kubernetes as an example since it's one of the most popular options. This list gives a high-level perspective of some of its features:

- *Container orchestration* across multiple nodes forming a cluster. When you deploy a unit of work in Kubernetes (pod), the platform decides where to instantiate it. If the complete node dies or you bring it down gracefully, Kubernetes finds another place to put this unit of work, based on your configuration for concurrent instances.

- *Routing*: Kubernetes uses *ingress controllers* that allow you to route traffic to the deployed services.

- *Load balancing*: All pod instances in Kubernetes are usually configured to use the same DNS address. Then, there is a component called *kube-proxy* that takes care of balancing the load across the pods. Other services just need to call a common DNS alias, (e.g., `multiplication.myk8scluster.io`). This is a server-side discovery and load balancing strategy, applied per server component.

- *Self-healing*: Kubernetes uses HTTP probes to determine whether the services are alive and ready. If they aren't, you can configure it to get rid of those *zombie* instances and start new ones to satisfy your redundancy configuration.

- *Networking*: Similarly to Docker Compose, Kubernetes uses exposed ports and provides different network topologies you can configure.

- *Centralized configuration*: The container platform offers solutions like *ConfigMaps*, so you can separate the configuration layer from the application and therefore change that per environment.

On top of that, Kubernetes has other built-in functionalities on aspects such as security, cluster administration, and distributed storage management.

Therefore, you could deploy your system in Kubernetes and benefit from all these features. Moreover, you could get rid of some patterns you built and leave these responsibilities to Kubernetes.

People who know how to configure and manage a Kubernetes cluster would probably never recommend you deploy bare containers like you did with Docker Compose; instead, they would start directly with a Kubernetes setup. However, the extra complexity that a container orchestration platform introduces should never be underestimated. If you know the tooling very well, surely you can have your system up and running quickly. Otherwise, you'll have to dive into a lot of documentation with custom YAML syntax definitions.

In any case, we recommend you learn how one of these container platforms works and try to deploy your system there to get into the practical aspects. They're popular in many organizations since they abstract all the infrastructure layers from the applications. Developers can focus on the process from coding to building a container, and the infrastructure team can focus on managing the Kubernetes clusters in different environments.

Application Platforms

This section covers a different type of platform: application runtime platforms. These offer an even higher level of abstraction. Basically, you can write your code, build a `.jar` file, and then push it directly to an environment, making it ready for use. The application platform takes care of everything else: containerizing the app (if needed), running it on a cluster node, providing load balancing and routing, securing the access, and so on. These platforms can even aggregate logs and provide other tools such as message brokers and databases-as-a-service.

On this level, you can find solutions like Heroku or CloudFoundry. There are alternatives for you to manage these platforms in your own servers, but the most popular options are the cloud-provided solutions. The reason is that you can put your product or service alive in just a few minutes, without taking care of many of the pattern implementations or infrastructure aspects.

Cloud Providers

To complete the landscape of platforms and tools, we have to mention cloud solutions such as AWS (https://aws.amazon.com), Google (https://cloud.google.com/), Azure (https://azure.microsoft.com/), OpenShift (https://www.redhat.com/en/ technologies/cloud-computing/openshift), and so on. Many of these also offer implementations for the patterns covered in this chapter: gateway, service discovery, centralized logs, containerization, and so on.

Furthermore, they usually provide a managed Kubernetes service too. That means that, if you prefer to work at a container platform level, you can do that without needing to set up this platform manually. Of course, that means you'll have to pay for this service, on top of the cloud resources you use (machine instances, storage, etc.).

See Figure 8-45 for a first example of how you could deploy a system like this in a cloud provider. In this first case, you choose to pay only for some low-level services such as storage and virtual machines, but you set up your own installations of Kubernetes, the databases, and the Docker registry. This means you avoid paying for extra managed services, but you have to maintain all these tools yourself.

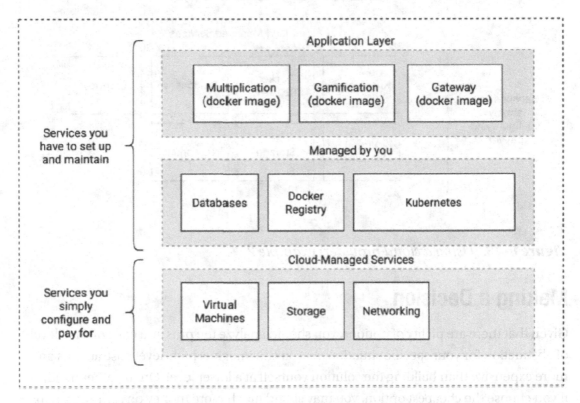

Figure 8-45. *Using a cloud provider: example 1*

See Figure 8-46 for an alternative setup. In this second case, you could use some additional managed services from the cloud provider: Kubernetes, a gateway, a Docker registry, and so on. As an example, in AWS, you can use a gateway-as-a-service solution called Amazon API Gateway to route traffic directly to your containers, or you could also choose an Amazon Elastic Kubernetes Service with its own routing implementation. In any of these cases, you avoid having to implement these patterns and maintain these tools, at the expense of paying more for these cloud-managed services. Nevertheless, take into account that, in the long run, you might save money with this approach because you need people to maintain all the tools if you decide to go that way.

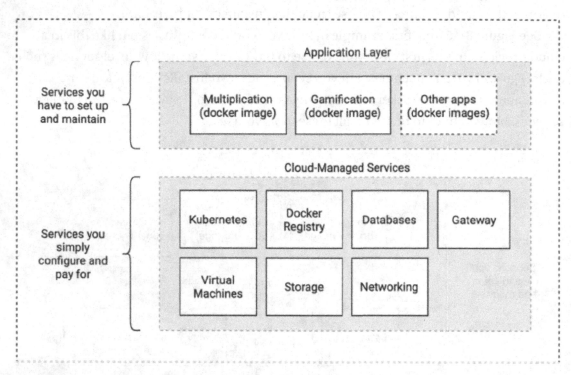

Figure 8-46. *Using a cloud provider: example 2*

Making a Decision

Given that there are plenty of options, you should analyze the pros and cons of each level of abstraction for your specific situation. As you can imagine, high-level abstractions are more expensive than building the solution yourself at a lower level. On the other hand, if you choose the cheapest option, you may spend much more money on setting that up, maintaining, and evolving it. Besides, if you're planning to deploy your system to the cloud, you should compare the costs of each vendor since there might be substantial differences.

Usually, a good idea is to start a project using high-level solutions, which translates to managed services and/or application platforms. They might be more expensive and less customizable, but you can try your product or service much faster. Then, if the project goes well, you can decide to take ownership of those services if it's worth it in terms of costs.

446

Cloud-Native Microservices

No matter what option you choose to deploy your microservices, you should respect some good practices to make sure they'll work properly in the cloud (well, ideally, in any environment): data-layer isolation, stateless logic, scalability, resilience, simple logging, and so on. You've been taking care of all these aspects while you were learning new topics in this book.

Many of these patterns you followed are usually included in the different definitions of cloud-native microservices. Therefore, you could put that label on your applications.

However, the term *cloud-native* is too ambitious, and sometimes confusing in our opinion. It's being used to pack a bunch of buzzwords and techniques across multiple aspects of software development: microservices, event-driven, continuous deployment, infrastructure-as-code, automation, containers, cloud solutions, and so on.

The problem with cloud-native as a broad-scope classification of applications is that it can lead people to think they need all the included patterns and methodologies to achieve the aimed target. Microservices? Sure, it's the new standard. Event-driven? Why not? Infrastructure as code? Go for it. It looks like only if you can check all the boxes, can you say you create cloud-native applications. All these patterns and techniques offer benefits, but do you need all of them for your service or product? Maybe not. You can build a well-structured monolith, make a container out of it, and deploy it to the cloud in minutes. On top of that, you can automate all the processes to build the monolith and take it to production. Is that a *cloud-native nonolith*? You won't find that definition anywhere, but that doesn't mean it's not a proper solution for your specific case.

Conclusions

This chapter guided you through an amazing journey of patterns and tools for microservices. In each section, you analyzed the issues you were facing with the current implementation. Then, you learned about well-known patterns that can solve these challenges while they also help make your system scalable, resilient, and easier to analyze and deploy, among other features.

For most of these patterns, we chose solutions that can be easily integrated with Spring Boot, given that it was the choice for the practical case. Its autoconfiguration features helped you, for instance, quickly set up the connection with Consul as a service discovery registry and centralized configuration server. Nevertheless, these patterns apply to many different programming languages and frameworks to build microservices, so you can reuse all the learned concepts.

The microservice architecture became mature, and everything started working together: the gateway routes traffic transparently to multiple instances of your microservices, which can be dynamically allocated depending on your requirements. All the log outputs are channeled to a central place, where you can also see the full trace of every single process.

We also introduced containerization with Docker, which helped prepare the services to be deployed easily to multiple environments. You also learned how container platforms such as Kubernetes, and cloud-based services, can help achieve the nonfunctional requirements we aimed for: scalability, resilience, and so on.

At this point, you might be asking yourself why we spent almost a full chapter (a long one) covering all these common microservice patterns if there are easier ways to achieve the same results with container and application platforms or with managed services in the cloud. The reason is simple: you need to know how the patterns work to fully understand the solutions you're applying. If you start directly with complete platforms or cloud solutions, you get only a high-level, vendor-specific view.

With this chapter, you have finalized the implementation of your microservice architecture that you started in Chapter 6. Back then, we decided to stop including extra logic in the small monolith and create a new microservice for the Gamification domain. These three chapters helped you understand the reasons to move to microservices, how to isolate and communicate them properly, and the patterns you should consider if you want to be successful with your project.

Chapter's Achievements:

- You learned how to use a gateway to route traffic to your microservices and provide load balancing between their instances.

- You scaled up a microservice architecture using service discovery, the HTTP load balancer, and RabbitMQ queues.

- You made the system resilient by checking the health of each instance to find out when they don't work. Also, you introduced retries to avoid losing requests.

- You saw how to override configuration per environment with an external configuration server.

- You implemented centralized logs with distributed traces across microservices, so you can follow a process from end to end easily.

- You integrated all these patterns in your microservice architecture with the projects from the Spring Cloud family: Spring Cloud Gateway, Spring Cloud Load Balancer, Spring Cloud Consul (Discovery & Configuration), and Spring Cloud Sleuth.

- You learned how to create Docker images for your applications using Spring Boot 3.1.2 and Cloud Native Buildpacks.

- You saw how Docker and Compose can help deploy your microservice architecture anywhere. You also saw how easy it is to spin up new instances using Docker.

- You compared the approach followed in the book with other alternatives such as container platforms and application platforms, which already include some of the patterns you need for a distributed architecture.

- You learned why we introduced the new patterns and tools in every step you made in this chapter.

Index

A

addCorsMapping method, 107

Advanced Message Queuing
  Protocol (AMQP), 17, 257–260,
  266, 269, 283–285, 302, 392

Amazon API Gateway, 445

AMQP protocol, 259
  binding, 260
  concepts, 264
  definition, 260
  messages survive, 260
  RabbitMQ, 259, 264, 285
  Spring Boot Projects, 269

AmqpTemplate, 269, 273–275, 281, 302

andExpect() method, 78

andReturn().method, 78

ApiClient Class, 95, 217

Appender, 391–394, 398

App.js file, 104, 105, 156

Application platforms, 444, 446, 448

application.properties file, 40, 125, 130,
  131, 154, 324, 380, 396

application-rabbitprod.properties,
  372, 373

Application services, 55

Application tier, 48, 86

application.yml file, 358, 383, 386

Aspect-Oriented Programming (AOP),
  11, 12

AssertJ, 7, 17, 25, 27–28, 30, 78

Asynchronous communication, 2, 8,
  232, 313

Autoconfiguration, 17, 42, 47, 71, 81,
  123–128, 152, 266, 280, 332,
  376, 447

Automatic acknowledgment, 263

@Autowired, 16, 77

B

Bean's declaration method, 280

Behavior-driven development (BDD), 22,
  24, 25, 27, 58, 86

Binding errors, 85

Bootstrapping, 16

bootstrap.properties file, 377, 379,
  394, 396

bootstrap.yml file, 377, 379, 428

Bounded contexts, 2, 51, 170, 172, 177

Business domain model
  challenge, 50
  ChallengeAttempt Class, 54
  challenge classes, 53
  DDD, 52
  domain classes, 52, 53
  microservices, 52
  vs. objects, 51
  user, 50
  user classes, 53

Business layer, 48, 86

Business logic
  random challenges, 55, 56, 58, 59
  requirements, 55
  verify attempts, 59, 61, 63

ByteBuddyInterceptor class, 151

451

C

N

Printed in the United States
by Baker & Taylor Publisher Services